Abraham James Fretz

Brief History of Jacob Wismer

and a complete genealogical family register with biographies of his descendants

from the earliest available records to the present time with portraits and other

illustrations

Abraham James Fretz

Brief History of Jacob Wismer
and a complete genealogical family register with biographies of his descendants from the
earliest available records to the present time with portraits and other illustrations

ISBN/EAN: 9783337402570

Printed in Europe, USA, Canada, Australia, Japan

Cover: Foto ©ninafisch / pixelio.de

More available books at **www.hansebooks.com**

A BRIEF HISTORY

OF

JACOB WISMER

AND A COMPLETE

GENEALOGICAL FAMILY REGISTER

WITH

BIOGRAPHIES OF HIS DESCENDANTS FROM
THE EARLIEST AVAILABLE RECORDS
TO THE PRESENT TIME.

WITH PORTRAITS AND OTHER ILLUSTRATIONS.

BY

REV. A. J. FRETZ,

OF MILTON, N. J

With an introduction by ELI WISMER, of Plumstead, Pa.

DEDICATION.

We Dedicate this Book—

To the Memory of our Worthy
Ancestors, Jacob Wismer and
Nanny, his wife.

PREFACE.

A number of the Wismer connection in Bucks Co., Pa., Canada, and elsewhere, desiring a history of the Wismer family compiled for publication in book form, requested us to undertake the work, and as a mark of favor and kindness towards those friends, we kindly consented.

As is usually the case, in the compiling of family genealogies, the work is not as complete as it should be, owing to the failure of some of the connections to respond to our communications to furnish us with their family records, and other information they possessed.

We feel indebted to many of the friends for their kindness in furnishing information for this genealogy. Prominent among those who have interested themselves in the work, and given us valuable aid, by furnishing us much information are: Eli Wismer, Plumstead, Pa.; Aaron Wismer, Jordan Sta., Ont.; Reuben W. Kratz, Pomona, Kans; H. W. Gross, Doylestown, Pa.; Samuel Nash, Doylestown, Pa.; Tillman W. Moyer, Campden, Ont., and others.

Milton, N. J., 1893.   THE AUTHOR.

INTRODUCTION.

Deeds of great men live long after them. Monuments rear their lofty heads to perpetuate their memory or commemorate some remarkable events in which they moved as leading factors. Historical volumes hand down to future generations the details of their achievements as monarchs before whom nations trembled and vanished; as warriors whose word of command spread death and desolation through the world; as statesmen whose political abilities proclaimed liberty to millions of the human race, and as religious reformers who suffered persecution and martyrdom that the light of Gospel doctrine might shine over the whole earth and dispel the darkness of superstition,—the idle fancies, rigor or excessive exactness in religious opinions and practices.

In introducing this volume to the descendants of our pioneer American ancestor, we do not claim for him any famous deeds as a man of renown, but a noble courage and a virtuous and exemplary character, embodied in a person, who never rose above a humble position in life, which, if strongly formed in the people of a nation, does more towards promoting its prosperity and welfare than the courage and character of many men of fame.

Any one somewhat acquainted with the early history of our country well knows, that the principal motive that led many people from different parts of Europe to come to America, was to escape from the various religious persecutions which they had to endure in their native countries. That our ancestor, Jacob Wismer, who settled in Bucks Co., Pa., about one hundred and seventy years ago, was one of those who abandoned the land of their births, and faced the dangers and hardships which confronted the early settlers in the New World, we have reason to believe; not from a positive knowledge of facts prior to his arrival in America, but from subsequent events in connection with the organization of the Mennonite Congregation at Deep Run, of which he was one of the leading originators.

It is not only a pious but an instructive task, to collect and preserve the memorial of our ancestor who, in making himself a home in the wilderness, also complied with the Divine command to the ancestor of the human family, and laid the foundation of a family, in number, of thousands, whose members are now spread far and wide over the United States and Canada. People who fail to appreciate and cherish the virtues and exemplary deeds of their ancestors, however humble their position or insignificant their acts, are not likely to transmit anything worthy of remembrance or imitation to their descendants.

Let us pause and reflect. Let us draw a comparison of the period of our ancestor in the "fatherland," and the land of his adoption. Persecutions and intolerance in the Old World. Savages and forests in the New.

How the hearts of our fathers must have beat with mingled joy and sadness when they bade adieu to their native land and set sail for the New World. Behind them the homes of their births and rulers intolerant and oppressive. Before them the vast ocean and a land of liberty of conscience. What a contrast they must have felt after having been established in their new homes on American soil; no more bound down by the whims and caprices of tyrannical kings and rulers. These were the preliminaries that our family encountered. Few of us have tasted hardships like unto his. All of us may enjoy the gifts, the benefits and the advantages which promote our temporal prosperity and welfare, or secure our immortal felicity. Surely such blessings should awaken the gratitude of all who partake thereof.

Representatives of the family fill many important and prominent positions in the walk of life. They may be found, not only among the tillers of the soil and mechanics, but also among teachers of our public schools, and ministers of the Gospel; among the medical and legal professions, among editors and publishers of religious and secular papers, and among professors of advanced institutions of learning.

Turning over the leaves of this volume may be a melancholy task to some of us. There are names in it that revive no remembrance of those that bore them; and there are others which bring before us very distinctly the forms and faces with which we were once familiar. Many of the names have long ago been chiseled on the grave-stones of their owners, to remind us of friends whose book of life was closed long ago. There are also names that belong to those who are still living and some of whom are very dear to us. It is rather a humiliating reflection that this thing of rags and sheepskin will outlast many generations of us. In the course of time its leaves will become discolored with age, and *all* will decay. But of the human volume it is only the binding that decays. The contents are immortal, and if found worthy will re-appear with rare embellishments where the mildew of time can never mar them.

ELI WISMER.

Plumsteadville, Pa., Jan. 1893.

LIST OF EXPLANATIONS AND ABBREVIATIONS.

In the preparation of this work it will be observed that all descendants are recorded in the regular order of birth, from the oldest to the youngest, each generation being marked consecutively from first to last. The Roman numerals placed before each name indicates the generation to which they belong, as:—

    I. Jacob Wismer (First generation).
    II. Jacob Wismer (Second generation).
    III. Rev. Abraham Wismer (Third generation).
    IV. Barbara Wismer (Fourth generation).

Beginning with the first (I) ancestor, Jacob Wismer, all his children are named in the order of birth as near as possible. Then follows his oldest son, Jacob Wismer (II. Generation), and his children (III. Generation) next. Rev. Abraham, being the oldest, is followed down to the last of his descendants; then the second in order of birth of the III. Generation, and so on until the end of the entire branch of Jacob Wismer of the II. Generation is reached. Then the second child of Jacob Wismer of the I. Generation, viz.: Elizabeth (Wismer) Angeny (II. Generation), is carried down in like manner to the last of her descendants, and so on throughout the entire connection.

Where marriages occur between members of the connection, the husband carries the record. In all such cases a numbered reference is placed after name and marriage of the wife, as, for example: (See Index of References No. 1). In the Index of References will be found No. 1. Catharine Gross, Page —. On the page given, in the body of the book, the family records will be found.

In the General Index will be found the names of all the descendants of eighteen years and over, also the pages on which their family records are given in the body of the book.

To find family records see Index of Branches, where names of all that had issue of the first, second, third and fourth generations are given.

Abbreviations: Mrd. signifies Married; bn. born; Dec'd. Deceased; S. Single; Montg. Co. Montgomery Co.; Twp. Township; ch. church; Menn. Mennonite; Ev. Ass'n. Evangelical Association; Presby. Presbyterian; Luth. Lutheran; Ger. Bap. German Baptist; Ger. Ref. German Reformed; Meth. Ep. Methodist Episcopal; Cong. Congregationalist.

THE WISMER FAMILY HISTORY.

1. Jacob Wismer, ancestor of the numerous family of that name in Bucks and Montgomery Counties Pa., and other portions of the United States and Canada, was born in Germany about 1684, and died in Bedminster Township, Bucks Co., Pa., Feb. 4, 1787 in his one hundred and third year.

The precise time when he emigrated to America is not known, but may have been as early, or before 1710.

The place of landing is also an unsettled fact. It is admitted by most of his descendants that he landed on one of the Carolina States.

By some it is thought that the site of Charleston in South Carolina had been the place of landing, and that he had taken up land in that section. Others state that he landed in North Carolina* which is thought to be the most probable, and he may have been one of the number of a hundred German families, who, driven from their homes on the Rhine by persecution, and in 1709, settled along the Roanoke and head waters of the Neuse river, in N. C. At the outbreak of the Indian war, led by the Tuscaroras, the savages, on the night of October 2, 1711, fell with such fury upon this German settlement that one hun-

---

* W. W. H. Davis' History of Bucks Co., states that he emigrated to North Carolina, where he lived ten years, etc.

dred and thirty of them perished. That he had been among the unfortunate emigrants in this German settlement is not in the least improbable, although there is no positive proof that such was the case. A tradition of the family says, that a sister accompanied him to America, that after they settled, the Indians fell upon them and killed the former, the latter held out some tobacco before the savages, which caused their savage nature to yield to such an extent that he was enabled to make his escape. It is said that after he made his escape he walked and ran ninety miles in one day. He traveled north as far as Byberry in Philadelphia County, Pa., from whence he later, moved to Bucks County.

The motive that impelled the Wismer ancestor to these shores is not known, but undoubtedly was on account of religious persecution which raged in the father-land, and which was the chief cause of the emigration in those early days of so many of the pioneer fathers to the New World where no cruel persecution was waged against the devout worshipers of God. Here was a refuge for the oppressed people of God, of other nations, and hither they came by the thousands where they might worship God under the bright sun of religious freedom, untrammeled and unoppressed.

As to his nationality, it has been insisted upon by some that he was an Englishman, but of this there is no proof in fact. On the contrary, evidence point more directly and conclusively to German nationality.

The fact of his having been a member of a distinctively German church is strong evidence in favor of Germany having been the father-land.

The deed of William Allen to the denomination of Mennonites for fifty acres of land at Deep Run, was drawn in favor of six persons, who are named in the deed as being members of said denomination and who are supposed to have been the principal or leading originators of the Deep Run congregation. Among the six was Jacob Wismer, who, we have every reason to believe was the ancestor, or Jacob the first, and which shows that he was a Mennonite, and worshiped with German people, and from which we infer that he himself was a German.

Also the fact that there are now in the United States, Wismers who were born in Germany and Switzerland, and that there are to this day Wismers still residing in those countries is strong evidence against the Bucks County ancestor's having been an Englishman.

An aged lady still living in Bucks Co., a great-granddaughter of Mark Wismer, son of Jacob the first, relates that she heard the oldest of her ancestors say that Jacob Wismer came from Germany.

She also says that among her great-grandfather Mark Wismer's books, was an old German Bible, strongly bound, with brass plates and clasps, that had belonged to Jacob Wismer, and contained a record of his family.

After Mark's death the Bible came into the possession of an aunt to the lady referred to, and later was owned by herself, and was finally destroyed by fire during the burning of her house.

Jacob Wismer was the first white man to settle upon the tract he purchased in Bucks County.

Tradition says that the party who brought him from Byberry unloaded family and effects under a big tree in the woods, and on leaving him gave the following tart advice, "Now Wismer work or die."

In what year he settled in Bucks County is not positively known, but is supposed to have been in 1726, in which year the first sum of money was paid by the Leeches. According to the contract of Penn and Alcok, the rent on the tract did not become due until the tract had become occupied, hence there is evidence of considerable weight showing the time of settlement to have been as stated.

The tract on which Jacob Wismer settled in Bucks County, previous to his purchasing it, was comprised of 375 acres, and which William Penn Proprietor and Governor of the Province of Pennsylvania, granted and conveyed by indenture on the 16th of July 1691, unto one Jeffrey Alcok of Ordslyford, County of Chester, Kingdom of England.

Alcok was held by the same indenture under a yearly rent of one shilling for every one hundred acres, to become due and payable as soon as occupied. On the 6th of February 1723 Alcok granted and conveyed the same tract to Peter Dicks of Upper Providence Chester Co., Pa., under the same rent as Alcok. On May 22, 1725, Dicks granted and conveyed the same tract to John Leech of Philadelphia, and his brother Isaac Leech of Cheltenham Twp., Philadelphia Co. Up to this time the tract had been unoccupied and indefinitely located (in the Province of Pennsylvania towards the Susquehanna river). By order of Jacob Taylor surveyor general under date of January 28, 1726, the aforesaid tract was located, surveyed and laid out unto Leech and brother by Thomas Watson, County surveyor on the 3d of February 1726, and for which they probably paid £60 lawful money of

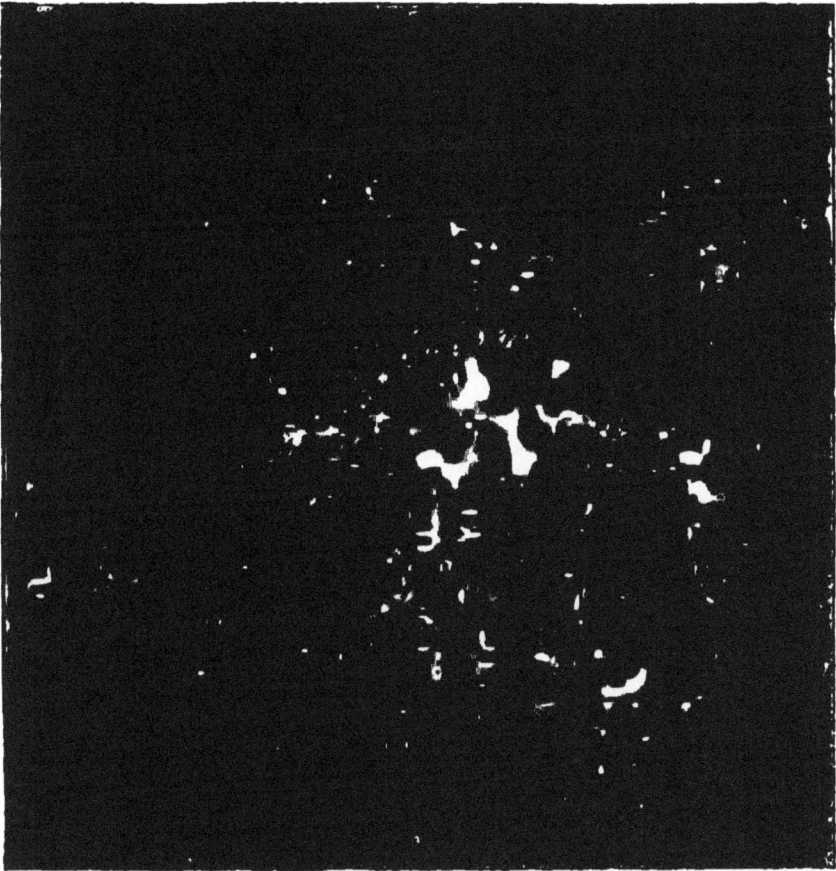

Signatures of Jacob and Nanny Wismer

America, and which was the first sum paid for the entire tract.

On Apr. 29, 1727 John Leech granted and conveyed his share of the tract unto his brother Isaac, who in his will, bearing date Oct. 14, 1744 authorized and empowered his wife Rebecca, and brother Thomas Leech to convey to Jacob Wismer, and other persons in the will named, the 375 acres.

On May 17, 1749, Rebecca Leech and Thomas Leech gave title to Jacob Wismer of Bedminster Township, Bucks County, Pennsylvania for 210 acres being the south western portion of the 375 acre tract, and for which he paid £100 lawful money.

On the 12th of April 1773, Jacob Wismer sold the tract to his son Henry of Hilltown for £500 which was to be paid in installments after his (Jacob's) death to his nine children. About the same time he made a will in which he stated the time when the share of each should become due after his death. The amount of £54 12 s. 6 pence was the sum that fell to each of the nine heirs; viz., Jacob, Mark, Abraham, Daniel, John, Christian, Mary, Elizabeth and Nanny.

Henry the purchaser of the Homestead received no share of the £500.

Jacob Wismer's son Henry, and son-in-law Henry Kephart, were appointed executors of his estate.

The old Homestead is divided into six tracts and occupied as follows,— Abraham Wismer, a great great-grandson of Jacob Wismer, and great-grandson of Henry Wismer of the second generation, owns the old homestead with 72 acres; Samuel Wismer, brother to Abraham Wismer mentioned above, owns and resides upon a tract of 49½ acres on the S. W. and 6 or 8 acres S. E. of the homestead belong to David K. Landis; William D. High, is the owner of 90 acres on the N. E.; Jacob M. Rush, owns 5 acres which is surrounded on three sides by the High tract, and Jacob D. Swartz owns 11 acres S.W. of High's tract.

Towards the close of his life his occupation was that of wheelwright, and which he may have carried on in connection with farming for many years.

He is said to have had three wives, and was married to his third wife after coming north about 1720, and with whom he lived 67 years, she being 84 years old at the time of his death. Her Christian name was "Nanny," and she was the mother of all his children. Her maiden name is unknown, but it is known that the children and grandchildren received legacies from one Jacob Sowder, and it is presumed that she was the daughter of Jacob Sowder.

*A pear tree raised from a seed which had been planted by Nanny is still standing on the homestead a living monument to the memory of the distinguished couple. Thirty five years ago it was the most magnificent tree known in that vicinity. In wonder and astonishment, it is said, many a mortal stood gazing at its stately form and admiring its magnitude, a strange contrast to its primitive state. Age and storms have overcome its strength, and greatly reduced and diminished its former usefulness and noble appearance.

It is not known that Jacob Wismer ever held any official position in the county or township, but he was a petitioner for the new Township of Bedminster, as the "Jacob Weismore," signed to the petition for the township in 1741 was no doubt meant for Jacob Wismer.

*Extract from sketch of Wismer family, by Eli Wismer, of Plumstead, Pa.

At the time of his death he had one hundred and seventy children and grandchildren.

Although living to the great age of 103 years, he retained his mind until within about two months, and could walk out and dress and undress himself within about two weeks of his death.

The remains of himself and wife were no doubt laid to rest in the grave-yard of the Old Mennonite church at Deep Run, the scene of their zeal for God's cause, and where for many years they worshiped the God of their fathers, and left to their numerous posterity an undying example, to "go and do likewise." And so shall they remain until that day when the great angel shall descend from heaven with a shout, and swear with a solemn oath, that "time was, time is and time shall be no more," when God shall again quicken the bones, and bid the sleepers come forth. Then may it be their great joy to see their numerous posterity safely sheltered in the fold of the great Shepherd, and together join in the triumphant shout of the redeemed.

The children of Jacob and Nanny Wismer, as near in the order of birth as could be placed were:— Jacob, Mary, Elizabeth, Joseph, Henry, Mark, Daniel, John, Christian, Nanny, Abraham.

DESCENDANTS OF JACOB WISMER, SON OF JACOB WISMER.

II. Jacob Wismer,* bn. in Bucks Co., Pa., about 1721. Mrd. Margaret —. The dates of death of himself and wife are not known. He received his portion of his father's estate in 1783. Lived in Plumstead Twp. at what is known as the burnt mill, where he followed the occupation of miller. Children: Abraham, Isaac, Anna, Mary, Elizabeth, Jacob, Mary, Barbara, Hannah, Margaret.

III. Rev. Abraham Wismer, bn. in Bucks Co., Aug. 21, 1746. Mrd.—. He was familiarly known as Abraham Wisner, the "long-beard." It is related that as he and his nephew, Martin Overholt, were coming near where a number of people were gathered, some one among the crowd seeing his long snowy white beard, inquired, "What is that coming there?" and another replied, "Why, that is preacher Wisner; he has swallowed a white horse and that is its tail hanging out of his mouth." Martin Overholt, who heard the remark, became very angry, and was about taking off his coat to resent the insult when his grandfather laid his hand on his shoulder, holding him back, saying, "Du musst nicht fechten." Abraham Wismer was ordained to the ministry of the Mennonite church at Deep Run, where he served as one of the ministers. Children: Barbara, Margaret, Elizabeth, Hannah, Magdalena.

Jacob Wismer's old family Bible, printed in Nurnberg, Germany, in 1736, containing his family records, is now in the possession of his great-grandson, Jacob L. Shaddinger, of Hilltown, Pa.

IV. Barbara Wismer, bn. April 9, 1778; died Aug. 21, 1854. Mrd. Rev. Christian Gross, Apr. 26, 1803. He was born Dec. 24, 1776; died July 22, 1865. Farmer and minister. Menn. Children: Abraham, Jacob, Mary, John, Christian, Isaac.

V. Abraham Gross, born Feb. 12, 1805; died June, 1853. S.

V. Jacob Gross, bn. Jan. 29, 1807. Mrd. Mary Overholt in 1830. She died—. P. O., Fountainville, Pa. Farmer, weaver and school-teacher. Menn. Children: Margaret, Christian, Isaac.

VI. Margaret Gross, bn.—; died—. S.

VI. Christian A. Gross, born July 8, 1835. Mrd. Anna M. Moyer, Feb. 7, 1866. P. O., Landisville, N. J. Farmer and teacher. Ev. Ass'n. Children: **(VII.)** Lizzie R. Gross, bn. Sept. 22, 1872. **(VII.)** Mary Jane Gross, bn. Dec. 9, 1874. **(VII.)** Jacob W. Gross, bn. June 26, 1879. **(VII.)** David B. Gross, bn. Mar. 2, 1883.

VI. Isaac M. Gross, bn. Oct. 28, 1837. Mrd. Jane A. Carroll, Dec. 31, 1868. P. O., Kirksville, Mo. Teacher. Presby. One child: **(VII.)** Mary Carroll Gross, bn. Feb. 9, 1870.

V. Mary Gross, born Nov. 4, 1810. Mrd. Abraham Leatherman—. P. O., Seville, O. No issue.

V. Rev. John Gross, bn, Dec. 3, 1814. Mrd. Catharine Wismer,—. P. O., Plumsteadville, Pa. Farmer and minister. He was ordained to the ministry of the Menn. ch. at Deep Run in 1852, where he is still engaged in the active work of the ministry. Children: Abraham, Mary.

VI. —, bn.—; died.

VI. Abraham C. Gross, bn. Jan. 13, 1844. Mrd. Sarah, daughter of Rev. Samuel Godshall, Oct. 1, 1865. P. O., Plumsteadville, Pa. Farmer. Menn. Children: **(VII.)** William S. Gross, bn. Oct. 10, 1866. Farmer. S. **(VII.)** Catharine Gross, bn. Dec. 8, 1867. Mrd. Abraham W. Shaddinger. (See Index of References No. 1.) **(VII.)** Mahlon Gross, bn. Sept. 1, 1873. Teacher. S. **(VII.)** Jacob Gross, bn. Nov. 9, 1879.

VI. Mary Gross, bn. July 18, 1848. Mrd. Samuel Gayman. (See Index of References No. 2.)

V. Christian Gross, bn. July 10, 1817; died Jan. 25, 1838. S.

V. Isaac Gross, bn. July 18, 1821. Mrd. Deborah Wismer, Jan 15, 1852. Farmer. Menn. Children: David, Samuel, Sarah, Mary, Barbara, Tobias, John, Ephraim.—Mrd. second wife, Annie Smith (widow Dirks) of Russia,—. Children: Isaac, Alfred.

VI. David Gross, bn. Oct. 16, 1852; died same day.

VI. Samuel Gross, bn. Jan. 3, 1854. Mrd. Emma L. Hunsberger,—. P. O., Plumsteadville, Pa. Taught school from 1875 to 1887. Since then farmer. Menn. No issue.

VI. Sarah Gross, bn. May 22, 1855. Mrd. Harvey Gayman. (See Index of References No. 3.)

VI. Mary W. Gross, born May 28, 1857. Mrd. John H. Myers, Dec. 20, 1877. P. O., New Britain. Menn. Children: **(VII.)** Isaac G. Myers, bn. Oct. 20, 1878. **(VII.)** Debbie May Myers, bn. Sept. 24, 1881. **(VII.)** Elsie Myers, bn. Oct. 30, 1883. **(VII.)** Joseph Walton Myers, bn. Feb. 9, 1888; died Nov. 25, 1888.

VI. Barbara Gross, bn. Aug. 26, 1859; died Aug. 31, 1862.

VI. Tobias Gross, bn. June 13, 1862; died June 25, 1862.

VI. John Gross, bn. Oct. 21, 1863; died Jan. 3, 1864.

VI. Ephraim Gross, bn. June 10, 1865. S.

VI. Isaac Gross, bn.—.

VI. Alfred Gross, bn.—.

IV. Margaret Wismer, bn.—. Mrd. Abraham Overholt.—. Children: Jacob, Abraham, Isaac, Henry.

V. Jacob Overholt, bn.—; died—. Mrd. Barbara Gross,—. One child: **(VI.)** Maria Overholt, bn.—. Mrd. David K. Landis.—. P. O., Plumsteadville, Pa. No issue.

V. Abraham Overholt, bn.—. Mrd. Magdalena Gross. . Children: Joseph, Mary, Rebecca, Henry, Susanna, Isaac, Abraham.

VI. Joseph G. Overholt, bn.—. Mrd. Elizabeth Leatherman.—. P. O., Bedminster, Pa. Children: **(VII.)** Barbara Overholt. **(VII.)** — Overholt.

VI. Mary Overholt, bn. Sept. 1, 1833. Mrd. William Markley, Apr. 25, 1857. He was bn. Feb. 10, 1830;

died June 12, 1870. Blacksmith. Menn. Children:
(VII.) Lanah Markley, bn. Feb. 26, 1858. (VII.) Rebecca Markley, bn. Oct. 31, 1859; died Aug. 27, 1882.
Mrd. — Weatherwax.—. (VII.) Jacob Markley, bn.
Mar. 30, 1861. (VII.) Joseph Markley, bn. Jan. 23,
1863; died Sept. 22, 1865. (VII.) Susanna Markley,
bn. Dec. 5, 1864. (VII.) Isaac Markley, bn. Aug. 18,
1867. (VII.) Elizabeth Markley, bn. Apr. 8, 1870.
Mary mrd. second husband, Rev. Daniel Royer, Jan.
18, 1877. P. O., Clay City, Ind. Farmer. Menn's.

VI. Rebecca Overholt, bn. Aug. 18, 1836. Mrd.
Samuel Histand, Dec. 17, 1864. P. O., Doylestown,
Pa. Farmer. Menn. Children: (VII.) Susanna Histand, born Oct. 21, 1865; died next day. (VII.)
Anna L. Histand, born Mar. 8, 1867. (VII.) Abraham O. Histand, bn. Feb. 10, 1869. Mrd. Emma B.
Wismer, Oct. 3, 1891. P. O., Gardenville, Pa. (VII.)
Samuel S. Histand, bn. Apr. 9, 1871. (VII.) Lydia L.
Histand, bn. Dec. 2, 1873. (VII.) Lizzie S. Histand,
bn. Dec. 10, 1876. (VII.) Maggie O. Histand, born
Sept. 11, 1879.

VI. Henry Overholt, bn.—. Mrd.— Moyer.

VI. Susanna Overholt, bn.—. S.

VI. Isaac Overholt, bn.—. Mrd. Elizabeth Procter,
—. P. O., Plumsteadville, Pa. Children: Mary,
Hannah, Annie, John.—Isaac mrd. second wife, Mary
(Hunsberger) Detweiler.
VII. Mary Overholt, born Dec. 21, 1868. Mrd.
Enos B. Wismer. (See Index of References No. 4.)
VII. Hannah Overholt, bn.—. Mrd. William Gross.
P. O., Plumsteadville, Pa. One child: (VIII.) — .
VII. Annie Overholt, bn.—. S.
VII. John Overholt, bn.—; died—.

VI. Abraham G. Overholt, born—. Mrd. Mary,
daughter of Abraham Wismer, Sen., Feb. 13, 1875.
P. O., Doylestown, Pa. Carpenter. Menn. Children:
(VII.) Katie Overholt, bn. Apr. 21, 1876. (VII.) Maggie Overholt, bn. Nov. 11, 1879. (VII.) Emma Overholt, bn. July 15, 1881. (VII.) Mary Overholt, born
June 21, 1884. (VII.) Carrie Overholt, bn. Aug. 16,
1887.

V. Isaac Overholt, bn.--. Mrd. Susan Miller,—. Reside in Ohio. No issue.

V. Henry Overholt, bn. in Bucks Co., Pa., Jan. 25, 1817. Mrd. Elizabeth Marley, Nov. 11, 1847. P. O., Blake, O. Blacksmith. Menn. Children: Margaret, Salome, Susan, Maria, Jacob, Isaac, Joseph, Abraham, John, Samuel, Henry, Elizabeth.

VI. Margaret Overholt, bn. in Medina Co., O., Sept. 29, 1848. Mrd. Lewis Loahr, May 3, 1867. P. O., Acme, O. Farmer. Luth. Children: **(VII.)** Amanda Loahr, bn. July 5, 1869. **(VII.)** Kietta Loahr, born Nov. 14, 1870. Mrd. Charles Rinehart, Dec. 25, 1890. P. O., Blake, O. Farmer. **(VII.)** Ellen Loahr, bn. Aug. 30, 1872. **(VII.)** Emry Loahr, bn. Sept. 11, 1874. **(VII.)** Charles Loahr, bn. June 30, 1876.

VI. Salome Overholt, bn. Oct. 13, 1849; died May 30, 1860.

VI. Susan M. Overholt, born Feb. 3, 1851. Mrd. Noah N. Yoder, Apr. 1, 1875. He was bn. Jan. 11, 1850. P. O., Acme, O. Farmer. He was elected commissioner of Medina Co. in 1888 and re-elected in 1891. Meth. Children: **(VII.)** Isaac Ivan Yoder, bn. Dec. 30, 1875. **(VII.)** Harvey Yoder, bn. Nov. 6, 1877. **(VII.)** Enos Yoder, bn. Apr. 17, 1880. **(VII.)** Mary Elizabeth Yoder, bn. Jan. 2, 1882. **(VII.)** Henry Harrison Yoder, bn. Oct. 28, 1888.

VI. Maria Overholt, born Sept. 29, 1852. Mrd. Levi H. Kindy, Sept. 7, 1873. He was born Nov. 1, 1844. P. O., Medina, O. Harness-maker. Children: **(VII.)** Myrtle Leora Kindy, bn. Aug. 6, 1874; died Apr. 9, 1875. **(VII.)** Henry Clayton Kindy, bn. June 24, 1876. **(VII.)** Infant daughter, born and died Feb. 19, 1882. **(VII.)** Floidy Kindy, bn. May 12, 1885; died Sept. 28, 1885. **(VII.)** Wardie B. Kindy, born July 17, 1890.

VI. Jacob M. Overholt, bn. July 25, 1854. Mrd. Emaline Shelly, May 10, 1881. She was bn. Nov. 5, 1861. P. O., Blake, O. Carpenter and farmer. Children: **(VII.)** Frankie Overholt, bn. Sept. 7, 1882. **(VII.)** Elty May Overholt, bn. July 13, 1885. **(VII.)** Rollie Overholt, bn. May 22, 1887. **(VII.)** Bessie Overholt, bn. July 3, 1888.

VI. Isaac M. Overholt, bn. Jan. 11. 1856; Mrd. Jessie A. Darsey, June 20, 1878. P. O., Seville, Ohio. Machinist. Children: **(VII.)** George Overholt, born Feb. 4, 1879. **(VII.)** John R. Overholt, bn. Aug. 4, 1880. **(VII.)** Fred M. Overholt, bn. Sept. 7, 1882. **(VII.)** Isaac C. Overholt, bn. Sept. 16, 1884.

VI. Joseph Overholt, bn. June 10, 1858; died Oct. 7, 1858.

VI. Abraham Overholt, bn. June 10, 1858; died Aug. 15, 1858. Twin to Joseph.

VI. John M. Overholt, bn. Sept. 11, 1859. Carpenter. S.

VI. Samuel M. Overholt, bn. Jan. 5, 1861. P. O., Eleria, O. Runner for Confectionery Co. S.

VI. Henry M. Overholt, bn. Oct. 3, 1864. P. O., Gecago, Ill. Carpenter. S.

VI. Elizabeth M. Overholt, bn. May 27, 1866. Mrd. Charles D. Reed, Apr. 25, 1891. P. O., Medina, O. Iron moulder.

IV. Elizabeth Wismer, bn. —; died—. Mrd. Joseph Overholt,—. Children: Sarah, Elizabeth, Mary, Martin, Joseph, Margaret.

V. Sarah Overholt, bn. in Bucks Co., Pa., in 1800; died 1886. Mrd. John Leatherman in 1819. Farmer. Menn. Children: Elizabeth, Martin, Jacob, Margaret, Joseph, Mary, Sarah, John.

VI. Elizabeth Leatherman, bn. Sept. 28, 1822; died June 21, 1864. Mrd. William Overholt, Nov. 18, 1841. Farmer. Menn. Children: Amos, Martin, John, Aaron, Abraham, William, Jonas, Levi, Sarah, Jacob, Leah, Mary, Elizabeth, Rufus.

VII. Amos Overholt, bn. Jan. 6, 1843. Mrd. Elizabeth Moyer,—. P. O., Clarion, Mich. Farmer. United Brethren. Children: **(VIII.)** Alice Overholt, bn. 1870. Mrd. U. G. Keiser,—. **(VIII.)** John U. Overholt, bn. 1873. **(VIII.)** Fannie Overholt, bn. 1876. **(VIII.)** Edna E. Overholt, bn. 1879. **(VIII.)** Clarence L. Overholt, bn. 1883. **(VIII.)** Claude Overholt, bn. 1888.

VII. Martin Overholt, bn. Feb. 23, 1844. Mrd. Catharine Nusbaum, Jan. 9, 1870. P. O., Bliss, Mich. Farmer and carpenter. Menn. Brethren in Christ. Children: **(VIII.)** Lester Overholt, bn. May

20, 1872. (VIII.) Orpha Overholt, bn. July 20, 1875. (VIII.) Cora Overholt, bn. May 1, 1879. (VIII.) Florence Overho.t; (VIII.) Lawrence Overholt (twins), bn. Mar. 7, 1881. (VIII.) Oscar Overholt, bn. March 10, 1888.

VII. John Overholt, bn. Aug. 22, 1845. Mrd. Lydia Ann Brown, Feb. 22, 1880. P. O., Goshen, Ind. Carpenter. Children: (VIII.) Ellen May Overholt, bn. Dec. 27, 1880. (VIII.) John Wm. Overholt, bn. Apr. 6, 1882. (VIII.) Bertha B. Overholt, bn. Feb. 10, 1884. (VIII.) Rufus F. Overholt, bn. Dec. 18, 1885.

VII. Aaron Overholt, bn. Dec. 5, 1846; died Feb. 16, 1865.

VII. Abraham Overholt, bn. Jan. 27, 1848. Mrd. Linda N. Miller, Sept. 6, 1888. P. O., Grand Rapids, Mich. Christian ch. One child: (VIII.) Zoe Elnora Overholt, bn. Feb. 2, 1890.

VII. William Overholt, Jr., bn. Mar. 20, 1849; died May 21, 1878. Mrd. Sarah Wismer, Apr. 3, 1870. Farmer. Menn. Children: (VIII.) Clara Overholt, bn. Jan. 23, 1871; died Dec. 14, 1884. (VIII.) Mary Elizabeth Overholt, bn. Nov. 19, 1872. (VIII.) Elmer Francis Overholt, bn. Mar. 10, 1875; died June 10, 1888.

VII. Jonas Overholt, bn. in Ohio Aug. 12, 1850. Mrd. Catharine Nusbaum in 1873. P. O., Dutton, Mich. Farmer and minister. Ger. Bap. Children: (VIII.) Alpha Virt Overholt, bn. in 1874. (VIII.) Arthur Francis Overholt, bn. in 1876. (VIII.) Rosa Ann Overholt, bn. in 1878. (VIII.) John William Overholt, bn. in 1880. (VIII.) Charles Monroe Overholt, bn. in 1882. (VIII.) Walter Clyde Overholt, born in 1885. (VIII.) Lloyd LeRoy Overholt, bn. in 1891.

VII. Levi Overholt, bn. Jan. 18, 1852; died Aug. 31, 1852.

VII. Sarah Overholt, bn. May 2, 1853; died Apr. 23, 1861.

VII. Jacob Overholt, bn. July 4, 1854. Mrd. Ettie I. Hammond in 1879. P. O., Conklin, Mich. Farmer. Children: (VIII.) M. Clare Overholt, bn. Apr. 24, 1881; died Nov. 22, 1881. (VIII.) W. Clyde Overholt,

bn. Feb. 13, 1883. (VIII.) Harold L. Overholt, born
Dec. 27, 1887.

VII. Leah Overholt, bn. Nov. 9, 1856; died April 9,
1885.

VII. Mary Ann Overholt, bn. May 7, 1858; died Dec.
12, 1888.

VII. Elizabeth Overholt, bn. Mar. 16, 1860; died
Mar. 22, 1882.

VII. Rufus Overholt, bn. Jan. 25, 1863. Mrd. Ida
Hammond, Dec. 12, 1888. P. O., Dutton, Mich.
Dairy farmer. One child: (VIII.) Blanch E. Overholt,
bn. Aug. 19, 1891.

VI. Rev. Martin Leatherman, born Dec. 9, 1823.
Mrd. Susanna Meyers, Feb. 8, 1848. P. O., Wads-
worth, Ohio. Retired farmer and minister. He was
ordained to the ministry of the Mennonite church in
Medina Co., Ohio, Oct. 2, 1880, and preaches in the
Guilford and Wadsworth churches. Children: Alfred,
Elias, Melinda, Levi, Sarah, Elmer, Mary.

VII. Alfred Leatherman, bn. Apr. 25, 1849. P. O.,
Belle Plain, Kans. Salesman in dry goods store. S.

VII. Elias M. Leatherman, bn. Nov. 5, 1850. Mrd.
Ella L. Pelton, Nov. 6, 1873. P. O., Cuyahoga Falls,
Ohio. Miller. Attends Meth. ch. Children: (VIII.)
Perry B. Leatherman, bn. Oct. 24, 1875; died Feb.
23, 1886. (VIII.) Eva O. Leatherman, bn. July 22,
1878. (VIII.) Jerry M. Leatherman, born April 29,
1881. (VIII.) E. Roy Leatherman; bn. Dec. 25, 1885.
(VIII.) Harley P. Leatherman, bn. Oct. 5, 1888.

VII. Melinda Leatherman, bn. in Medina Co., Ohio,
July 31, 1853. Mrd. Luther Keagle, Jan. 1, 1878.
P. O., Pomoma, Mich. Farmer. Free Meth. Chil-
dren: (VIII.) Alfred Keagle, bn. Oct. 20, 1878. (VIII.)
Susanna Grace Keagle, bn. Sept. 19, 1882. (VIII.) In-
fant, bn. June 16; died June 19, 1884. (VIII.) Floyd
Millard Keagle, bn. Oct. 4, 1891.

VII. Levi Leatherman, bn. Dec. 7, 1855. Mrd. Carrie E. Pelton, Nov. 18, 1880. P. O., Wadsworth, O.
Farmer. Children: (VIII.) Kleber M. Leatherman,
bn. Nov. 24, 1881. (VIII.) Wallace P. Leatherman,
bn. May 17, 1884.

VII. Sarah Leatherman, bn. Nov. 18, 1861; died July 20, 1891. Mrd. Richard Stephens, Apr. 10, 1890.
VII. Elmer Leatherman, bn. July 6, 1865. Mrd. Sue Weisz, July 18, 1891. P. O., Wadsworth, O.
VII. Mary Leatherman, bn. Nov. 11, 1867. S.
VI. Jacob Leatherman, bn. Aug. 12, 1825. Mrd. Elizabeth Landis, Sept. 21, 1853. P. O., Goshen, Ind. Farmer. Menn. Children: Alvin, Levi, Susanna, Samuel, Martin, Daniel, William.
VII. Alvin Leatherman, bn. May 22, 1855. Mrd. Maggie Sink,—. P. O., Goshen, Ind. Children: (**VIII.**) Irvin Ulysses Leatherman, bn. June 15, 1882. (**VIII.**) Charles Edwin Leatherman, bn. May 3, 1886. (**VIII.**) Florence Edith Leatherman, bn. Apr. 6, 1888. (**VIII.**) Gracie Ellen Leatherman, bn. June 3, 1891.
VII. Levi Leatherman, bn. June 4, 1857. Mrd. Mary Kreider,—. P. O., Goshen, Ind. Children: (**VIII.**) David Elmer Leatherman, bn. Dec. 26, 1878. (**VIII.**) Ella; (**VIII.**) Alice Leatherman (twins), bn. Nov. 24, 1879. (**VIII.**) Mandie E. Leatherman, bn. Apr. 9, 1882. (**VIII.**) Jacob Irvin Leatherman, bn. Feb. 1, 1884. (**VIII.**) John Arthur Leatherman, bn. Sept. 12, 1885. (**VIII.**) Salome Leatherman, bn. Oct. 14, 1886; died Mar. 12, 1892. (**VIII.**) William Leatherman, bn. Jan. 29, 1888; died Mar. 18, 1888. (**VIII.**) Orpha A. Leatherman, bn. Apr. 12, 1889. (**VIII.**) Mervin A. Leatherman, bn. Aug. 12, 1890. (**VIII.**) Anna Mary Leatherman, bn. Oct. 16, 1891.
VII. Susanna Leatherman, bn. Jan. 26, 1859. Mrd. Henry Hygema, Feb. 4, 1883. P. O., Wakarusa, Ind. Farmer. Menn. Br. in Christ. No issue.
VII. Samuel L. Leatherman, bn. Jan. 30, 1862. P. O., Goshen, Ind. Mrd. Emma Ganger, of Girard, Ill., Dec. 28, 1892.
VII. Martin Leatherman, bn. Feb. 14, 1864. Mrd. Maggie M. Leatherman, Dec. 25, 1888. P. O., River Styx, O. Employed in store at River Styx, O. One child: (**VIII.**) Beulah E. Leatherman, bn. Apr. 7, 1892.
VII. Daniel Leatherman, bn. Mar. 11, 1868. Resides in Elkhart, Ind. S.
VII. William Leatherman, bn. Jan. 24, 1871.

VI. Margaret Leatherman, bn. in Bucks Co., Pa., Jan. 29, 1827. Mrd. Wm. Moser, in 1846. He was bn. Jan. 1, 1824. P. O., Nappanee, Ind. Farmer. Christian ch. Children: Minerva, Sybilla, Sarah, Rufus, Myron, Orpha, Gladius.

VII. Minerva Moser, bn. Jan. 14, 1848; died Sept. 12, 1878. S.

VII. Sybilla Moser, bn. Mar. 29, 1849. Mrd. Wm. Albright, in 1866. P. O., Goshen, Ind.

VII. Sarah Moser, bn. Feb. 3, 1851. Mrd. Fielding Price, Apr. 18, 1870. P. O., Nappanee, Ind. Farmer. Children: **(VIII.)** De Etta Price, bn. Nov. 22, 1873. **(VIII.)** Eunice Price, bn. Dec. 22, 1876.

VII. Rufus Mosher, bn. in Elkhart Co., Ind., Nov. 20, 1853. Mrd. Bertha Anderson, Apr. 4, 1884. P. O., Grand Rapids, Nebr. Farmer. Christian ch. Children: **(VIII.)** Daltie Mabel Mosher, bn. May 10, 1885. **(VIII.)** Reba Joy Mosher, bn. Mar. 13, 1887.

VII. Myron Moser, bn. at Goshen, Ind., July 10, 1859. Mrd. Alice Walker, in 1880. P. O., Millwood, Ind. Farmer. Christian ch.; wife, Seventh Day Adventist. Children: **(VIII.)** Carrie A. Moser. **(VIII.)** George Rufus Moser. **(VIII.)** Irwin C. I. Moser. **(VIII.)** Lottie Joy Moser. **(VIII.)** Walker E. Moser.

VII. Orpha Moser, bn. Aug. 20, 1863. Mrd. Chauncey Miller, Nov. 29, 1889. P. O., Nappanee, Ind. Barber. Christian ch. No issue.

VII. Gladius Mosher, born June 1, 1871; died Feb. 18, 1873.

VI. Joseph Leatherman, bn. in Bucks Co., Pa., Dec. 26, 1830. Mrd. Elizabeth Moyer, June 20, 1850. P. O., Grand Rapids, Nebr. Farmer. Meth. Children: Abraham, Rosanna, Franklin, Martin, Sarah, Elizabeth, Lorinda, Mary, Joseph, Nellie, Jessie, Orpha.

VII. Abraham Leatherman, bn. Mar. 20, 1850. Mrd. Christiann Pegley, Oct. 18, 1879. P. O., Plainview, Minn. Farmer. Meth's. Children: **(VIII.)** Nellie Harriet Leatherman, bn. July 5, 1881. **(VIII.)** Nettie Elizabeth Leatherman, bn. Apr. 27, 1883. **(VIII.)** Clarence Martin Leatherman, bn. Dec. 4, 1885.

VII. Rosanna Leatherman, bn. in Elkhart Co., Ind., Sept. 3, 1851. Mrd. George W. Swift, May 29, 1873. P. O., Garden City, Minn. Farmer. Meth's. Children: **(VIII.)** Cora E. Swift, bn. Apr. 7, 1874. **(VIII.)** H. Ione Swift, bn. Nov. 21, 1882.

VII. Franklin Leatherman, bn. Apr. 17. 1856. Mrd. Isabella Swift, in 1882. P. O., Grand Rapids, Nebr. Farmer. Meth. Children: **(VIII.)** Charles Frank Leatherman, bn. Nov. 17, 1882. **(VIII.)** Alfred Joseph Leatherman, bn. July 11, 1884. **(VIII.)** Mary Genevieve Leatherman, bn. Jan. 10, 1886. **(VIII.)** Ada Mary Leatherman, bn. Feb. 9, 1888. **(VIII.)** Burney Le Roy Leatherman, bn. Jan. 24, 1890.

VII. Martin Leatherman, bn. Dec. 29, 1858. Mrd. Cora Kendal, Oct. 25, 1883. P. O., Garden City, Minn. Farmer and school-teacher. Seventh Day Adventists. Children: **(VIII.)** Charles Fay Leatherman, bn. Nov. 21, 1884. **(VIII.)** Sona Elizabeth Leatherman, bn. Jan. 19, 1887. **(VIII.)** Spurr K. Leatherman, bn. Feb. 11, 1889.

VII. Sarah Leatherman, bn. Aug. 23, 1862. Mrd. Wm. E. Leonard, July 25, 1887. P. O., Grand Rapids, Nebr. Farmer. Meth. Children: **(VIII.)** Leo Lawrence Leatherman, bn. Nov. 22, 1888. **(VIII.)** Sylva Laurinda Leatherman, bn. Nov. 16, 1891.

VII. Elizabeth Leatherman, bn. Feb. 1, 1864. Mrd. Samuel Molten Marston, Apr. 11, 1884. P. O., Garden City, Minn. Farmer. Meth. Children: **(VIII.)** Ethel F. Marston, bn. Dec. 30, 1886. **(VIII.)** Hannah Elizabeth Marston, bn. Oct. 21, 1890.

VII. Lorinda Jane Leatherman, bn. at Plainview, Minn., Apr. 10, 1866. Mrd. Ervin M. Cram, Apr. 19, 1885. P. O., Butte City, Nebr. Blacksmith and farmer. Children: **(VIII.)** Addie Beulah Cram, bn. Jan. 22, 1886. **(VIII.)** Ralph William Cram, bn. June 22, 1887. **(VIII.)** Mary Elizabeth Cram, bn. Nov. 23, 1888. **(VIII.)** Roy Elmer Cram, bn. Sept. 26, 1890.

VII. Mary Leatherman, born at Plainview, Minn., July 22, 1869. Mrd. Ransom W. Springer, July 25, 1887. P. O., Grand Rapids, Nebr. Farmer. Meth. One child: **(VIII.)** Nellie May Springer, bn. Oct. 15, 1890.

VII. Joseph Leatherman, bn. Feb. 1, 1871. P. O., Plainview, Minn. S.

VII. Nellie Leatherman, bn. July 27, 1873. S.

VII. Jessie Leatherman, bn. Aug. 8, 1876.

VII. Orpha Leatherman, bn. Oct. 24, 1880.

VI. Mary Leatherman, bn. —; died in 1852, aged 14 years.

VI. Sarah Leatherman, bn. --; died in 1856, aged 17 years.

V. Elizabeth Overholt, bn.—; died—. S.

V. Mary Overholt, bn. in 1804; died in 1889. Mrd. Abraham Beam. He died—. No issue. Mary mrd. second husband, Abraham Wismer. (See Index of References No. 5.)

V. Martin Overholt, bn. —; died —. Mrd. Elizabeth Dinstman, July 1, 1820. Carpenter and cabinet maker. Menn. Children: Sarah, Abraham, Elizabeth Judith, Anthony, Joseph, Simeon, Eli, Jacob.

VI. Sarah Overholt, bn. Feb. 10, 1822; died May 6, 1884. Mrd. D. S. Waterman, Dec. 25, 1845. P. O., Wadsworth, Ohio. Farmer and carpenter. Children: Abraham, Infant, Infant, Noah, Albert, Harvey, Elizabeth, Caroline, Louisa, Sarah.

VII. Abraham Waterman, bn. July 22, 1846; died Aug. 28, 1846.

VII. Infant son still born May 21, 1847.

VII. Infant daughter, bn. Aug. 13, 1848; died next day.

VII. Noah Waterman, bn. Dec. 10, 1849. Mrd. Fyetta Miller, June 8, 1871. Carpenter at Massillon, Ohio. Presby. Children: (**VIII.**) William B. Waterman, bn. Sept. 23, 1872; died Apr. 20, 1874. (**VIII.**) Sarah J. Waterman, bn. Feb. 28, 1875. (**VIII.**) Milton H. Waterman, bn. Jan. 23, 1881. (**VIII.**) Arthur G. Waterman, bn. Feb. 2, 1883; died July 10, 1883.

VI. Albert Waterman, bn. Mar. 4, 1853; died July 18, 1872.

VII. Harvey Waterman, bn. Sept. 13, 1854. Mrd. Lucy Y. Foster, Jan. 8, 1873. Carpenter at Massillon, Ohio. Ger. Ref. Children: (**VIII.**) Alfred E. Waterman, born Nov. 6, 1873. (**VIII.**) Harley A. Waterman, born Oct. 24, 1875. (**VIII.**) Emma M.

Waterman, bn. Mar. 19, 1878; died June 1, 1879.
(VIII.) Jessie E. Waterman, born Sept. 26, 1881.
(VIII.) Myrtle B. Waterman, bn. Sept. 30, 1883; died
May 19, 1887. (VIII.) Arthur L. Waterman, born
Nov. 27, 1886.
VII. Elizabeth Waterman, bn. Sept. 16, 1856. Mrd.
Rev. J. S. Kendall, Sept. 16, 1880. Minister of the
U. B. Ch. One child: (VIII.) Alta Lucretia Kendall,
bn. Jan. 18, 1882: died Jan 7, 1887.
VII. Caroline Waterman, bn. Oct. 15, 1859. Mrd.
Jackson S. Burgner, Oct. 19, 1876. Farmer. Ger.
Ref. Children: (VIII.) Clarence L. Burgner, bn. May
11, 1878. (VIII.) Clemens J. Burgner, bn. July 15,
1879; died Sept. 1, 1881. (VIII.) Clyde S. Burgner,
bn. Dec. 4, 1882. (VIII.) Floyd S. Burgner, bn. Jan.
29, 1885.
VII. Louisa Waterman, bn. Oct. 19, 1861.
VII. Sarah Waterman, bn. Oct. 1, 1864; died infant.
VI. Abraham Overholt, born Nov. 19, 1826. Mrd.
Catharine Ault, Feb. 24, 1853. She died Apr. 29,
1879. Children: Mary, Cynthia, Elizabeth.- Abraham
mrd. second wife Amelia M. Fuller, Aug. 7, 1882.
Blacksmith, now farmer in Medina Co., Ohio. Free
Meth.
VII. Mary Jane Overholt, bn. Feb. 1, 1854. Mrd.
James Keagle, Oct. 7, 1875. Wesleyan Meth. Chil-
dren: (VIII.) Arthur C. Keagle, bn. Aug. 13, 1876.
(VIII.) John A. Keagle, bn. Aug. 17, 1877. (VIII.)
Walter C. Keagle, bn. Apr. 13, 1879. (VIII.) Carrie
E. Keagle, born Nov. 7, 1880. (VIII.) George L.
Keagle, bn. Aug. 31, 1887.
VII. Cynthia E. Overholt, born Dec. 25, 1857. Mrd.
Stephen C. Crooks, Sept. 11, 1879. Sawyer. Free
Meth. Children: (VIII.) Mary A. Crooks, bn. July 5,
1881. (VIII.) Frances C. Crooks, bn. Nov. 23, 1887.
(VIII.) Stephen A. Crooks, bn. Aug. 23, 1889.
VII. Elizabeth A. Overholt, bn. Nov. 23, 1864.
VI. Elizabeth Overholt, born Nov. 12, 1828. Mrd.
Rev. Ephraim Hunsberger, Mar. 13, 1862. Farmer
and bishop of New Mennonite ch., Wadsworth, Ohio.
Children: (VII.) Matilda Hunsberger, born Mar. 26,
1863; died Oct. 21, 1863. (VII.) Franklin Hunsberger,

PEAR TREE.

Jacob Wismer Homestead, Bedminster, Bucks Co., Pa. (See page 6)

bn. Mar. 31, 1864. P. O., Wadsworth, Ohio. Clerk.
Menn. (VII.) Augusta Hunsberger, born Apr. 22,
1867.

VI. Judith Overholt, born Sept. 22, 1831. Mrd.
Abraham Fry, Oct. 27, 1867. Farmer in Barry Co.,
Mich. Menn. Children: (VII.) Charles Fry, bn. Jan.
3, 1871; died May 26, 1873. (VII.) Anna E. Fry, bn.
Nov. 14, 1875.

VI. Anthony Overholt, bn. in Ohio, Mar. 4, 1834.
Mrd. Hannah Nash, in 1857. P. O., Wadsworth, O.
Farmer. Menn. Children: (VII.) Elmina Overholt,
bn. May 16, 1858; died Mar. 1859. (VII.) Twin boys,
bn. and died Dec. 26, 1859. (VII.) Ida Overholt, bn.
June 21, 1863. (VII.) Minerva Overholt, bn. Jan. 1,
1865. (VII.) Reuben Overholt, born Apr. 4, 1868.
(VII.) Alverna Overholt, bn. Mar. 2, 1872.

VI. Joseph Overholt, bn. Nov. 30, 1836; died in 1838.

VI. Simeon Overholt, born Oct. 25, 1838. Mrd.
Almira F. Miller, Mar. 27, 1862. She died in Oct.
1875. P. O., Nashville, Mich. Meth. Children:
(VII.) Lucy Ellen Overholt, bn. in Elkhart Co., Ind.,
Mar. 13, 1864. Mrd. Jacob H. Heckathorne, June
27, 1888. Cashier in M. C. Freight office at Marshall,
Mich. Meth. (VII.) John Wesley Overholt, born
Sept. 28, 1865. Meth. S. (VII.) Francis Asbury
Overholt, born Aug. 27, 1870. S. (VII.) Elizabeth
Overholt, bn. in 1873; died aged 1 year.

VI. Eli Overholt, bn. Jan. 23, 1841. Mrd. Catharine Baughman, Oct. 6, 1869. She died Nov. 23, 1877.
Children: (VII.) Olive Belle Overholt, born Aug. 19,
1870. (VII.) Albert Overholt, bn. Sept. 6, 1872.
Eli mrd. second wife Mary E. Millar (widow) Sept.
11, 1881. Children: (VII.) Arthur B. Overholt, bn.
Mar. 11, 1883; died Aug. 26, 1883. (VII.) Flossy M.
Overholt, bn. May 2, 1889. Mr. Overholt enlisted
in Co. H., 29th Reg't. O. V. V. I., Oct. 23, 1861,
fought in battles of Winchester, Port Republic and
Chancellorsville, Va. He was captured by the enemy
at Port Republic, and imprisoned at Belle Isle about
3 months. He was wounded at Chancellorsville and
was discharged Dec. 3, 1863. Has served as post-

3

master at Wadsworth, Ohio. under the administrations of Grant, Hayes, Garfield and Harrison.

VI. Jacob L. Overholt, born Mar. 23, 1844. Mrd. Ellen Showalter, in 1868. P. O., Wadsworth, Ohio. Foreman in planing mill. Children: **(VII.)** Mary Overholt. **(VII.)** Emma Overholt.

V. Joseph Overholt, bn. —; died —. Mrd. Anna Dinstman, Nov. 8, 1827. Shoemaker and farmer. Dunkards. Children: Jonas, Margaret, Fannie, Benjamin, Henry.

VI. Jonas Overholt, bn. in Medina Co., Ohio. Oct. 2, 1828; died Mar. 9, 1889. Mrd. Sarah Ann Means, in 1850. She died —. Moved to Iowa in 1854. Carpenter and farmer. Christians. Children: Benjamin, Nettie, Henry, Ira, Joseph, Eli.

VII. Benjamin F. Overholt, bn. in Medina Co., O. Dec. 3, 1851. Mrd. Mary A. Morgan, Mar 12, 1877. Stock breeder in Iowa. Children: **(VIII.)** Grace Gertrude Overholt, bn. Apr. 30, 1878. **(VIII.)** Eldora Myrtle Overholt, bn. July 4, 1880. **(VIII.)** Olive Pearl Overholt, bn. June 12, 1887.

VII. Antoinetta Overholt, bn. in Medina Co., Ohio, Dec. 11, 1853. Mrd. Bryan McClure, Mar. 10, 1874. Farmer in Dallas Co., Iowa. Presby. Children: **(VIII.)** Sarah Maud McClure, bn. July 19, 1877. **(VIII.)** Harry McClure, bn. Mar. 22, 1879. **(VIII.)** Elsie Prudence McClure, bn. Aug. 25, 1883.

VII. Henry Overholt, bn. in 1855; died in 1859.

VII. Ira M. Overholt, bn. May 5, 1857; died July 14, 1882.

VII. Joseph Owen Overholt, bn. in Jones Co., Iowa, July 19, 1860. Mrd. Ursula Goodchild, Sept. 7, 1883. Teacher and R. R. tax contractor. Children: **(VIII.)** Jonas Ira and Anna Imy Overholt, bn. Sept. 13, 1884. **(VIII.)** George Sigel Overholt, bn. Mar. 25, 1890.

VII. Eli Sigel Overholt, bn. May 5, 1862. Mrd. Phœbe Mitchell, Jan. 1, 1885. Farmer in Iowa. Children: **(VIII.)** Joseph Owen Overholt, bn. Feb. 8, 1887. **(VIII.)** George Overholt, bn. Jan. 26, 1888.

VI. Margaret Overholt, bn. July 16, 1830; died Nov. 1, 1865. Mrd. Wm. H. Ruby, Oct. 17, 1852. Farmer.

Christians. Died in the service of the U. S. at St.
Louis in 1864. Children: Etta, George, Horatio.

VII. Etta Ruby. bn. in Ohio, Dec. 29, 1853. Mrd.
L. W. Hubbard, July 10, 1875. Druggist at Mon-
mouth, Iowa. Meth. Children: (VIII.) Jerome C.
Hubbard. (VIII.) Pearl M. Hubbard. (VIII.) Ira Carl
Hubbard.

VII. George W. Ruby, bn. in Iowa, Jan. 12, 1857.
Mrd. Linnie Johnson, Aug. 27, 1876. Farmer in
Guthrie Co., Iowa. Christians. Children: (VIII.) Irene
Agnes Ruby. (VIII.) Cynthia Caroline Ruby. (VIII.)
Owen M. Ruby.

VII. Horatio N. Ruby, bn. in Iowa, Mar. 26, 1859.
Farmer in Guthrie Co., Iowa. S.

VI. Fannie Overholt, bn. Nov. 2, 1833. Mrd. Joseph
Hudson in 1850. Photographer at Tama City, Iowa.
Disciples. Children: (VII.) Edgar A. Hudson, bn. in
Ohio, Jan. 9, 1852. Mrd. M. F. George, Mar. 6,
1878. Photographer. No issue. (VII.) Almond B.
Hudson, bn. in 1859; died, aged 3 years.

VI. Benjamin F. Overholt, bn. Nov. 18, 1841; died
Sept. 16, 1843.

VI. Henry Overholt, bn. Jan. 11, 1846. Mrd.—.
Children: (VII.) Fannie. (VII.) David. (VII.) Jennie.
(VII.) Sadie.

V. Margaret Overholt, bn. Jan. 2, 1807; died Sept.
16, 1872. Mrd. Jacob F. Leatherman, Mar. 25, 1827.
P. O., River Styx, Ohio. Retired farmer. Menn.
Children: Henry, Joseph, Sarah, Elizabeth, Mary,
Samuel, Catharine, Anna, Fannie, John, Margaret,
Jacob, Manasseh.

VI. Henry Leatherman, bn. in Bucks Co., Pa., Feb.
10, 1828. Mrd. Elizabeth, daughter of Martin Overholt, Sept. 26, 1848. Carpenter, farmer. Ordained
minister of the Church of God about 1879. Children:
Sybilla, Martin, Maria, Maggie, Jacob, Minnie, Lizzie, Anna.

VII. Sybilla Leatherman, bn. in Ohio, July 1, 1860.
Mrd. Philip C. Ahl, Jan. 18, 1880. Carpenter. Ch.
of God. No issue.

VII. Martin Leatherman, bn. Mar. 18, 1863. Mrd.
Barbara East, Nov. 1, 1888. Clerk and teacher. One

child: (VIII.) Clayton H. Leatherman, bn. Oct. 29, 1889.
VII. Maria Leatherman, bn. Jan. 6, 1865.
VII. Maggie M. Leatherman, bn. Jan. 10, 1866.
Mrd. Martin Leatherman. (See Index of References No. 27.)
VII. Jacob H. Leatherman, bn. Feb. 15, 1869.
VII. Minnie Leatherman, bn. Oct. 27, 1870.
VII. Lizzie Leatherman, bn. Sept. 21, 1872.
VII. Anna Leatherman, bn. Mar. 7, 1876.
VI. Joseph Leatherman (twin), bn. Feb. 10, 1828; died Mar. 26, 1848.
VI. Sarah Leatherman, bn. Oct. 22, 1829. Mrd. Tobias Kreider, Mar. 18, 1875. Carpenter, farmer. Menn. No issue.
VI. Elizabeth Leatherman, bn. Aug. 25, 1831. Mrd. Henry Kehr, Nov. 30, 1856. Farmer in Ind. Menn. Children: Margaret, Mary, Martin, John, Laura, David.
VII. Margaret Kehr, bn. Aug. 25, 1857. Mrd. Chancey Claus, Apr. 25, 1877. Farmer in Ind. Menn. Children: (VIII.) Rosa Claus. (VIII.) Clayton Claus. (VIII.) Maud Claus.
VII. Mary Magdalena Kehr, bn. Jan. 9, 1859. Mrd. Granville Landis, Sept. 28, 1884. Menn. Bre. in Christ. Children: (VIII.) Anna Landis. (VIII.) Henry Landis.
VII. Martin Kehr, bn. May 6,1860. Mrd. Martha Eyer, Dec. 27, 1884. Farmer in Ind. Menn. Bre. in Christ. One child: (VIII.) Nellie Elizabeth Kehr.
VII. John Kehr, bn. Aug. 14, 1864. Mrd. Louisa Bechtel, July 26, 1885. Farmer in Ind. Menn. Bre. in Christ. Children: (VIII.) Roscoe B. Kehr. (VIII.) Roy F. Kehr.
VII. Laura Kehr, bn. Mar. 11, 1862; died next day.
VII. David F. Kehr, bn. Sept. 25, 1870.
VI. Mary Leatherman, bn. in Ohio, Oct. 20, 1832. Mrd. Abraham Means, Feb. 2, 1851. Farmer in Kansas. Mrs. M. Menn. Mr. M. River Brethren. Children: Malinda, David, Franklin, Anna.
VII. Malinda Means, bn. in 1852; died in 1853.

VII. David Means, bn. May 2, 1854. Mrd. Malinda Berkey, Dec. 27, 1877. In stone business in Kansas. Meth. Children: **(VIII.)** Malinda M. Means. **(VIII.)** Orville B. Means. **(VIII.)** Frank I. Means, bn. in 1883; died in 1886. **(VIII.)** Wilbur R. Means, bn. in 1886; died in 1887. **(VIII.)** Mary B. Means.

VII. Franklin Means, bn. Apr. 5, 1857. Mrd. Ellen Garberich, Jan. 22, 1880. Farmer in Kansas. U. B. ch. Children: **(VIII.)** Willie H. Means, bn. 1880; died 1882. **(VIII.)** Infant, born and died in 1883. **(VIII.)** Bertha J. Means. **(VIII.)** Boyd J. Means.

VII. Anna Means, bn. Dec. 22, 1859. Mrd. J. S. Garberich, Mar. 6, 1879. Farmer in Kansas. Children: **(VIII.)** John W. Garberich. **(VIII.)** David F. Garberich. **(VIII.)** Mary Maud Garberich.

VI. Samuel Leatherman, bn. Oct. 20, 1834. Mrd. Maria Bishel, Apr. 26, 1862. Farmer in Ohio. Ch. of God. Children: **(VII.)** Eli Leatherman, bn. Nov. 16, 1864. Farmer. **(VII.)** Ida Leatherman, bn. June 29, 1869. **(VII.)** Franklin Leatherman, bn. Feb. 17, 1873.

VI. Catharine Leatherman, bn. June 5, 1836. Mrd. Abraham Capp, Jan. 10, 1857. Commercial professor and writer. Ch. of God. Children: James, Mary, Lizzie, Sarah, Franklin, Allen.

VII. James Capp, bn. Nov. 24, 1857. Mrd.—.

VII. Mary Capp, bn. Oct. 31, 1858. Ch. of God.

VII. Lizzie Capp, bn. Mar. 18, 1860. Mrd. Abel Dintaman, Dec. 11, 1879. Farmer in Mo. Children: **(VIII.)** Ira Dintaman. **(VIII.)** Ivan C. Dintaman, bn. 1883; died 1883. **(VIII.)** Lydia E. Dintaman. **(VIII.)** Earl A. Dintaman, bn. 1888; died 1889.

VII. Sarah Capp, bn. Aug. 25, 1861. Mrd. Alpha Holderman, Mar. 4, 1883. Farmer in Mo. Ch. of God. Children: **(VIII.)** James H. Holdeman. **(VIII.)** Sarah E. Holdeman. **(VIII.)** Alpha A. Holdeman. **(VIII.)** John Holdeman.

VII. Franklin Capp, bn. Feb. 10, 1866. Farmer in Cal.

VII. Allen B. Capp; bn. Dec. 25, 1870. Mrd. Zora McCoy,—. Farmer in Medina Co., O.

VI. Anna Leatherman. bn. Feb. 7, 1838. Mrd. Abraham J. Moyer, Dec. 28, 1861. Farmer in Elkhart Co., Ind. Mr. M. Menn. Bre. in Christ, Mrs. M. River Bre. ch. Children: Fannie, Salome, Minerva, John, James, Manasseh, Anna.

VII. Fannie Moyer, bn. Nov. 10, 1863. Teacher. Menn. Bre. in Christ.

VII. Salome Moyer, bn. Mar. 25, 1865. Mrd. David Buzzard, Mar. 10, 1887. Canvasser. Resides in Elkhart, Ind. One child: (**VIII.**) Edith M. Buzzard.

VII. Minerva Moyer, bn. Aug. 31, 1866.

VII. John W. Moyer, bn. Aug. 19, 1868.

VII. James F. Moyer, bn. Jan. 23, 1871; died Mar. 24, 1871.

VII. Manasseh Moyer, bn. Oct. 11, 1874.

VII. Anna Moyer, bn. Mar. 10, 1880.

VI. David Leatherman, bn. in Medina Co., O., in 1839. P. O., Gormley, Ont. Teacher, at present nurse. S.

VI. Fannie Leatherman, bn. Apr. 7, 1841. Mrd. John O. Smith, Jan. 7, 1871. Reside in Branch Co., Mich. Children: (**VII.**) Manasseh Smith. (**VII.**) Jacob Smith. (**VII.**) Margaret Smith. (**VII.**) Mary Smith. (**VII.**) Samuel Smith. (**VII.**) William Smith. (**VII.**) Sarah Smith.

VI. John Leatherman, bn. Dec. 11, 1842; died June 19, 1865. Mrd. Anna Leatherman,—. Carpenter. Menn. No issue.

VI. Margaret Leatherman, bn. Sept. 2, 1844. S.

VI. Jacob O. Leatherman, bn. Mar. 19, 1846. Mrd. Christina Hounstein. Jan. 10, 1875. Farmer. Ch. of God. Children: (**VII.**) Catharine Leatherman. (**VII.**) Joel Leatherman. (**VII.**) Martha Leatherman. (**VII.**) Alpha Leatherman. (**VII.**) Franklin Leatherman, died Aug. 9, 1883. (**VII.**) Mary Leatherman. (**VII.**) Noah Leatherman.

VI. Manasseh Leatherman, bn. Aug. 14, 1848. Mrd. Katie E. Long, June 13, 1861. P. O., River Styx, Ohio. Farmer. Mrs. L. mem. Ref. ch.

IV. Hannah Wismer, bn.—; died—. Mrd. Henry Landis,—. Children: Abraham, Jacob, Henry, Joseph, Sarah, Susan, Hannah, Daniel, Elizabeth.

V. Abraham Landis, bn.—; died young.
V. Jacob Landis, bn. Oct. 9, 1801; died Mar. 3, 1867. Mrd. Catharine Wismer, Nov. 7, 1826. Children: Mary, Henry, Hannah, Eliza.—Jacob mrd. second wife, Mary, widow of Samuel Bleam, Oct. 21, 1852. Children: Abraham, Amanda.
VI. Mary Landis, bn. in Bucks Co., Oct. 12. 1827. Mrd. William S. Wismer. (See Index of References No. 6.)
VI. Henry Landis, bn. Jan. 19, 1833; died aged 11 days.
VI. Hannah Landis, bn. Apr. 28, 1834; died in 1856.
VI. Eliza W. Landis, bn. in Bucks Co., Apr. 10, 1835. P. O., 2260 Fair Hill St., Phila., Pa. S.
VI. Abraham H. Landis, bn. Feb. 27, 1854; died Feb. 13, 1879. Mrd. Kate Rheinhart.—. One child: **(VII.)** Frank Pierce Landis.
VI. Amanda Landis, bn. Mar. 8, 1856. Mrd. Frank P. Dungan, July 1, 1877. Res. Phila. Children: **(VII.)** Warren H. Dungan, bn. Apr. 18. 1879; died Apr. 28, 1880. **(VII.)** Laura May Dungan. bn. Apr. 7, 1882. **(VII.)** Mary Lizzie Dungan, bn. May 5, 1884.
V. Henry Landis, bn.—. Mrd.—.
V. Joseph Landis, bn.—. Disappeared.
V. Sarah Landis, bn.—. Mrd. — Landis.
V. Susan Landis, bn.—. S.
V. Hannah Landis, bn. in Bucks Co., Sept. 6, 1810; died in Medina Co., Ohio, Mar. 25, 1849. Mrd. Abraham Leatherman,— (his first wife). He was bn. Aug. 14, 1808; died Sept. 12, 1871. Soon after marriage they moved to Medina Co., Ohio, bought a 160-acre tract of woodland upon which they settled in the wilderness and engaged in farming. Menn. Children: Jacob, Elizabeth, Henry, Mary, Daniel, Hannah, Annie, Susanna, Abraham.
VI. Jacob L. Leatherman, bn. in Medina Co., Ohio, Mar. 7, 1834. Mrd. Elizabeth, daughter of John Swartz, Jan. 27, 1867. P. O. Pipersville, Pa. His boyhood was spent at home with his parents, aiding in clearing the land and running the saw mill. At the age of 21 he learned the carpenter's trade which he followed until he married. In 1854 he was drafted

in the army, but procured a substitute. He afterwards came to Bucks Co., Pa., and in 1872 purchased the farm of Israel D. Fox, near Pipersville, where he still resides. Menn. Children: (VII.) Annie S. Leatherman, bn. Dec. 24, 1867; died Aug. 23, 1869. (VII.) Abraham S. Leatherman, bn. Oct. 28, 1870. P. O., Pipersville, Pa School-teacher. (VII.) John S Leatherman, bn. Dec. 12, 1872. (VII.) Daniel S. Leatherman, bn. Sept. 8, 1874. (VII.) Jacob S. Leatherman, bn. Apr. 14, 1877. (VII.) Lizzie S. Leatherman, bn. Feb. 20, 1881.

VI. Elizabeth L. Leatherman, bn. Mar. 15, 1835; died Nov. 11, 1854.

VI. Henry L. Leatherman, bn. in Medina Co., Ohio, Jan. 31, 1837. Mrd. Angelina Bentler, Jan. 8, 1867. She died in 1884. P. O., Freeport, Mich. Farmer. Attends Menn. ch. Children: Abraham, Herman, Mary, Ida, John, Orvin.

VII. Abraham Leatherman, bn. May 12, 1868. S.

VII. Herman Leatherman, bn. Oct. 24, 1869.

VII. Mary Leatherman, bn. Apr. 27, 1872. Mrd. John Shively, Oct. 2, 1889. P. O., Freeport, Mich. Engineer. Cong's. One child: (VIII.) Hazel Shively, bn. Feb. 29, 1890.

VII. Ida Leatherman, bn. Oct. 10, 1874.

VII. John Leatherman, bn. Oct. 15, 1878.

VII. Orvin Leatherman, bn. May 24, 1884.

VI. Mary L. Leatherman, bn. Aug. 6, 1838; died Nov. 5, 1852.

VI. Daniel Leatherman, bn. in Medina Co., O., Jan. 21, 1840. Mrd. Esther Zimmerman, May 8, 1873. P. O., Seville, O. Farmer. Children: (VII.) Mary Leatherman, bn. July 17, 1875. (VII.) Emma Leatherman, bn. Mar. 17, 1879.

VI. Hannah Leatherman, bn. Mar. 19, 1841. Mrd. Jacob B. Overholt, Apr. 21, 1867. P. O., Seville, O. Ch. of God. Children: (VII.) Daniel Overholt, bn. Sept. 10, 1870. (VII.) Mary Overholt, bn. Oct. 23, 1872.

VI. Annie L. Leatherman, bn. July 5, 1842; died May 13, 1882. Mrd. John Leatherman,—. He died 5 months after marriage from a bruise received by

the kick of a horse.--Annie mrd. second husband,
Peter D. Steiner, Jan. 8, 1870. Farmer in Mich.
Mrs. S., Menn. Children: (VII.) Leah Steiner, bn.
Nov. 4, 1870. (VII.) Menno Steiner, bn. Jan. 8, 1872.
(VII.) Samuel Steiner, bn. Apr. 5. 1873. (VII.) John
Steiner, bn. Apr. 29. 1874. (VII.) Enos Steiner, bn.
Oct. 23. 1875. (VII.) Peter Steiner, bn. Jan. 14, 1877;
died Feb. 27, 1877. (VII.) Mary Steiner, bn. Feb. 3,
1878. (VII.) Noah Steiner, bn. Dec. 31, 1879. (VII.)
Anna Steiner, bn. May 8. 1882.

VI. Susanna L. Leatherman, bn. in Medina Co., O.,
Mar. 9, 1844. Mrd. Tobias S. Eby. May 1. 1870. P. O.,
Pandora, O. The first winter after marriage Mr. Eby
taught school. Apr. 4, 1871, they moved to Wayne
Co., Ohio, where he and his brother had purchased a
farm, on which they lived 16 years, after which they
purchased a farm in Richland Twp., Allen Co., O.,
and moved thereon in 1887. Menn's. Children: (VII.)
Henry W. Eby, bn. Mar. 28, 1872. Menn. (VII.)
Clara D. Eby, bn. May 9, 1873. Menn. (VII.) Harvey L. Eby, bn. Oct. 4, 1874. (VII.) M. Amanda Eby,
bn. Jan. 10, 1876. Menn. (VII.) Emma L. Eby, bn.
Dec. 22, 1876. (VII.) Samuel L. Eby, bn. Apr. 23,
1878. (VII.) Ada L. Eby, bn. May 31, 1881.

VI. Abraham L. Leatherman, bn. Mar. 19, 1849;
died Mar. 30, 1849.

V. Daniel Landis, bn. in Bucks Co., Pa., June 10,
1815; died in Ohio, June 28, 1852. Mrd. Mary Landis,—. She was born in Lancaster Co., O., July 20,
1810; died July 6, 1846. Oil miller. Menn. Children: Barbara, Joseph, Enos.

VI. Barbara Landis, bn.—; died small.

VI. Joseph Landis, bn. Apr. 30, 1843. Mrd. Chris-
tiana Freed, Jan. 2, 1870. P. O., Wakarusa, Ind.
Blacksmith, farmer. Menn. One child: (VII.) Rhoda
Priscilla Landis, bn. Jan. 8, 1876.

VI. Enos Landes, bn. Nov. 9, 1844. Mrd. Sarah Ann
Rosenberger, Aug. 30, 1876. P. O., Reserve, Kans.
Plasterer and farmer. Ger. Bap. Children: (VII.)
William Henry Landes, bn. June 25, 1878. (VII.) El-
len Jane Landes, bn. Dec. 20, 1880. (VII.) Mary Edna
Landes, bn. May 7, 1884.

V. Elizabeth Landis, bn. Mar. 14, 1818; died Mar. 22, 1888.

IV. Magdalena Wismer, bn.—; died—. S.

III. Isaac Wismer, bn. June 3, 1748; died—.

III. Anna Wismer, bn. Apr. 6, 1750; died—.

III. Mary Wismer, bn. Aug. 17, 1752; died young.

III. Elizabeth Wismer, bn. Sept. 1, 1753; died Sept. 9, 1837. Mrd. Joseph Nash,—. He was bn. Sept. 30, 1753; died May 31, 1830. Farmer and weaver. Lived in Tinicum Twp. Members of the Menn. ch. of which he was a deacon for many years. Children: Mary, Abraham, Jacob, Henry, Elizabeth.

IV. Mary Nash, bn. May 5, 1776; died Mar. 8, 1833. Mrd. Henry Overholt,—. Farmer, turner, spinning-wheel maker, and distiller. Menn. Children: Magdalena, Elizabeth, Anna, Mary.

V. Magdalena Overholt, bn. Mar.—, 1796; died Apr. —, 1862. Mrd. Christian Meyers,—. Farmer and German school-teacher. Menn. Children: Mary, Salome, Eliza, Elias, Susanna, Sarah, Emeline, Alfred.

VI. Mary Meyers, bn. Mar. 7, 1818. Mrd. Jacob Kratz, Nov. 28, 1838. He was bn. June 3, 1814. P. O., Dublin, Pa. Farmer. Menn. Children: Salome, Henry, Anna, Isaiah.

VII. Salome Kratz, bn. in Bucks Co., July 30, 1839. Mrd. Rev. John F. Funk. (See Index of References No. 7.)

VII. Henry M. Kratz, bn. in Bucks Co., July 23, 1845. Mrd. Sophia L. Shaddinger, Jan. 4, 1868. P. O., Dublin, Pa. Farmer. Menn. One child: **(VIII.)** Mary Emma Kratz, bn. Sept. 23, 1868.

VII. Anna Kratz, bn. July 22, 1850. S.

VII. Isaiah Kratz, bn. May 7, 1856; died Aug. 31, 1856.

VI. Salome Meyers, bn. Dec. 26, 1819. Mrd. Alpheus Myers, Jan. 13, 1842. He was bn. July 10, 1818; died Mar. 1, 1878. P. O., Western Star, Ohio.

Millwright and farmer. Menn. Children: Mary,
William, Lavina, Joseva, Harvey, Owen.

VII. Mary Magdalena Myers, bn. Nov. 5, 1843.
Mrd. Isaac Tinsman, Mar. 31, 1861. P. O., Akron,
Ohio. Day watchman at Rubber works. U. B. ch.
Children: Salome, Cora, Ina, Lavina, Joseva, Edgar,
John, Harvey.

VIII. Salome C. Tinsman, bn. 1861. Mrd. J. W.
Roth. P. O., Lexor, O.

VIII. Cora Adel Tinsman, bn. July 30, 1863. Mrd.
William J. McLister, July 12, 1885. P. O., North
Pine St., Akron, O. Rubber works. U. B. ch. One
child: (**IX.**) Clemy McLister, bn. Apr. 10, 1887.

VIII. Ina Aurelia Tinsman, bn. July 1, 1866. Mrd.
David Metting, July 8, 1884. P. O., 206 Bowery St.,
Akron, O. Rubber works. U. B. ch. Children: (**IX.**)
Edgar Metting, bn. Sept. 29, 1886. (**IX.**) Earl Met-
ting, bn. Oct. 6, 1888. (**IX.**) Josie Metting, bn. Aug.
25, 1891; died Feb. 2, 1892.

VIII. Lavina Ketura Tinsman, bn. Apr. 11, 1868.

VIII. Joseva Ann Tinsman, bn. May 30, 1871.

VIII. Edgar Alpheus Tinsman, bn. Apr. 12, 1875.

VIII. John C. Tinsman, bn. Oct. 10, 1877; died Oct.
17, 1881.

VIII. Harvey Benjamin Tinsman, bn. Mar. 15, 1885.

VII. William Henry Myers, bn. Mar. 21, 1846. Mrd.
Emaline Johnson. P. O., Akron, O.

VII. Lavina Keturah Myers, bn. Oct. 25, 1848. Mrd.
Solomon Kraver, Oct. 25, 1866. P. O., Windfall, O.
Farmer. Luth. Children: (**VIII.**) Edwin Ellsworth
Kraver, bn. Feb. 15, 1869; died Dec. 10, 1885. (**VIII.**)
Harvey Franklin Kraver, bn. July 3, 1874. (**VIII.**)
Elsie Irene Kraver, bn. Aug. 13, 1882.

VII. Joseva Ann Myers, bn. Apr. 25, 1851. Mrd.
Septimus Seiberling, in 1868. He died July 8, 1873.
Machinist. Children: (**VIII.**) Allen S. Seiberling, bn.
Nov. 19, 1868. (**VIII.**) James Francis Seiberling, bn.
Sept. 20, 1870. (**VIII.**) Elsie May Seiberling, bn. Dec.
18, 1872.—Joseva mrd. second husband, Jacob J.
Slanker, June 9, 1883. P. O., Wooster, O. Sewing
machine agent. Luth. One child: (**VIII.**) Anna Mabel
Slanker, bn. June 29, 1889.

VII. Harvey Anson Meyers, bn. Dec. 29, 1853.
Mrd. Alice B. Miller, in 1876. P. O., Western Star,
Ohio. Farmer. Children: (VIII.) Franklin A. Myers.
bn. Mar. 8, 1877. (VIII.) Freddie H. Myers, bn. Sept.
29, 1878. (VIII.) Sadie M. Myers, bn. June 18, 1881.
(VIII.) Mattie S. Myers, bn. Aug. 23, 1884. (VIII.)
Hattie L. Myers, bn. Sept. 6. 1887. (VIII.) Elsie C.
Myers, bn. Jan. 21. 1889. (VIII.) Vernie J. Myers,
bn. Dec. 20, 1890.
VII. Owen Franklin Myers, bn. May 7, 1857. Mrd.
Alice Helmich, Mar. 20, 1889. P. O., Akron, Ohio.
Clerk. Ger. Ref. Children: (VIII.) Eddie Alpheus
Myers, bn. June 26. 1880. (VIII.) Bertha May Myers.
bn. Oct. 26, 1881. (VIII.) George William Myers, bn.
June 26, 1887.
VI. Eliza Meyers. bn. Nov. 3. 1822; died May 25,
1869. Mrd. Tobias Kreider, Jan. 8. 1846. P. O.,
Wadsworth, O. Carpenter. Menn. Children: Sarah,
Susanna, Mary, Emeline, Levi, Lucinda, Amanda,
Pricilla.
VII. Sarah Ann Kreider, bn. May 23. 1848; died
June, 1876. Mrd. George Beery. P. O., Bronson,
Mich.
VII. Susanna Kreider, bn. Sept. 28, 1850. Mrd.
Willis E. Van Alstine,—. P. O., Shipshewana, Ind.
Photographer. Children: (VIII.) Charles Guy Van
Alstine, bn. Nov. 2, 1873. (VIII.) Nettie Maud Van
Alstine, bn. Jan. 8, 1875. (VIII.) Cora Bell Van Al-
stine, bn. Feb. 17. 1877. (VIII.) Willis Edwin Van
Alstine, bn. Feb. 7, 1879. (VIII.) Claud Edgar Van
Alstine, bn. Feb. 10, 1881. (VIII.) Lucinda May Van
Alstine. bn. Feb. 22, 1883. (VIII.) Lee Coe Van Al-
stine, bn. Sept. 5, 1885. (VIII.) Philip Laley Van Al-
stine, bn. Oct. 15, 1887. (VIII.) Mary Frances Van
Alstine, bn. Mar. 3, 1889. (VIII.) Fred Frank Van
Alstine, bn. Feb. 9, 1890.
VII. Mary Magdalena Kreider, bn. Jan. 26, 1853;
died Apr. 17, 1865.
VII. Emaline Kreider, bn. Sept. 2, 1855; died Feb.
10, 1857.
VII. Levi Kreider, bn. Nov. 13, 1857. Mrd. Rebecca
Keller, June 4, 1881. P. O., Nappanee, Ind. Cabi-

net maker. One child: (VIII.) Lydia L. Kreider, bn.
June 27, 1882.

VII. Lucinda Kreider, bn. July 15. 1860. Mrd.
Dexter E. Wilder, Oct. 10, 1886. P. O.. Orland,
Ind. Farmer. Children: (VIII.) Bessie Wilder, bn.
Dec. 6, 1888. (VIII.) Jesse Wilder, bn. Apr. 19, 1890.
(VIII.) Charles Henry Wilder, bn. June 2, 1891.

VII. Amanda Kreider, bn. in Ind. June 8. 1863.
Mrd. Christian Greenenwald. He was bn. in Germany, Sept. 21, 1859. Res.. Chicago, Ill. Carpenter. Luth. Children: (VIII.) Bertha Greenenwald, bn.
Aug. 26, 1879. (VIII.) Rudolph Greenenwald. bn.
Feb. 20, 1881. (VIII.) Sarah Greenenwald, bn. Mar.
30, 1883. (VIII.) Freddie Greenenwald, bn. Apr. 27.
1885. (VIII.) Albert Greenenwald, bn. May 11, 1887.
(VIII.) Christena Greenenwald, bn. Nov. 8, 1889.

VII. Pricilla Kreider, bn. June 5, 1866. Mrd. Eugene Moore, Nov. 24. 1887. P. O.. Elida, O. Farmer.
Menn. Children: (VIII.) Laban Miles Moore, bn. Dec.
7, 1888; died Dec. 16, 1888. (VIII.) Levi Tobias
Moore, bn. Nov. 1, 1889.

VI. Sarah Meyers, bn. in Bucks Co., Pa., Sept. 19,
1836. Mrd. Daniel Friedt, Jan. 1. 1857. P. O.,
Blake, O. Farmer. Menn. Children: Lavina, Emeline, Elias, Noah, Malinda, David, Samuel, Daniel,
Salome.

VII. Lavina Friedt, bn. Sept. 14, 1858. Mrd. Henry
Houseworth, Nov. 21. 1878. P. O., Poe, Ohio. Laborer. Children: (VIII.) Norman Houseworth, bn.
Dec. 5, 1879. (VIII.) Freddie Houseworth, bn. Feb.
18, 1881; died Aug. 18, 1881. (VIII.) Sadie Houseworth, bn. Nov. 21, 1882. (VIII.) William Houseworth, bn. Jan. 19, 1890.

VII. Emeline Friedt, bn. Sept. 16, 1861.

VII. Elias Friedt, bn. Sept. 14, 1863. Mrd. Lizzie
Lesher, Feb. 14, 1891. P. O., Acme, O. Carpenter.

VII. Noah Friedt, bn. May 7, 1866.

VII. Malinda Friedt, bn. Sept. 3, 1869. Mrd. Charles
Henshue, Feb. 14, 1891. P. O., River Styx. Ohio.
Farmer. Luth.

VII. David Friedt, bn. Dec. 15, 1872.

VII. Samuel Friedt, bn. Nov. 10, 1874.

VII. Daniel Friedt, bn. July 28, 1877; died Feb. 21, 1880.

VII. Salome Friedt, bn. May 23, 1882.

VI. Emeline Meyers, bn. in Medina Co., Ohio, Aug. 14, 1839. Mrd. David Nold, Oct. 13, 1861. P. O., Elkhart, Ind. Carpenter in Lake Shore R. R. shops. Menn. No issue.

VI. Elias Meyers, bn.—. S.

VI. Susanna Meyers, bn.—. Mrd. Rev. Martin Leatherman. (See Index of References No. 8.)

VI. Alfred Meyers, bn—; died S.

V. Elizabeth Overholt, bn.—. Mrd. Daniel Gross, —. He was bn. Mar. 24, 1784; died Mar. 15, 1875. One child: Salome.

VI. Salome Gross, bn.—. Mrd. Rev. Isaac Rickert, —. P. O., Fountainville, Pa. Minister of the Menn. ch. Children: Lizzie, Isaiah.

VII. Lizzie Rickert, bn.—. Mrd. Harvey Myers, Jan. 20, 1883. P. O., Gardenville, Pa. Farmer. Menn. Children: (**VIII.**) Bertha Myers, bn. Dec. 22, 1883. (**VIII.**) Isaac Myers, bn. June 16, 1886.

VII. Isaiah Rickert, bn.—. Mrd. Emma Mack.

V. Anna Overholt, bn. June 14, 1805; died Apr. 13, 1864. Mrd. Christian Gross, May 18, 1828. He died Sept. 21, 1832. Tinsmith. Menn. Children: Mary, Magdalena, Henry. —Anna mrd. second husband, Abraham Shaddinger, Mar. 12, 1835. He died May 2, 1877. Farmer. Menn. Children: Lewis, Sarah, Huldah, Harvey, Isaac, William, Wesley.

VI. Mary Gross, bn. June 14, 1829; died Mar. 27, 1886. Mrd. Abraham Bergey,—. He died,—. No issue.

VI. Magdalena Gross, bn. Dec. 24, 1830. Mrd. Henry Fly, Nov. 7, 1850. He died Oct. 9, 1888. Farmer. Menn. Children: Samuel, Mary, Anna.

VII. Samuel G. Fly, bn. Jan. 5, 1852. Mrd. Sarah Gross,—. P. O., Fountainville, Pa. Children: (**VIII.**) Laura Fly. (**VIII.**) Henry Fly. (**VIII.**) Joseph Fly. (**VIII.**) Edith Fly.

VII. Mary Fly, bn. Feb. 9, 1853; died Feb. 17, 1875. Mrd. Abraham M. Moyer,—. Children: (**VIII.**) Janetta Moyer. (**VIII.**) Mary Moyer.

VII. Anna Fly, bn. May 17, 1858. Mrd. Abraham M. Moyer,—. P. O., Chalfont, Pa. Children: **(VIII.)** Maggie Moyer. **(VIII.)** Henry Moyer. **(VIII.)** Theodore Moyer. **(VIII.)** Alma Moyer.

VI. Henry Gross, bn. May 5, 1832. Mrd. Mary Funk, Dec. 2, 1854. P. O., Doylestown, Pa. Harness-maker. Presby. Children: **(VII.)** Milton H. Gross, bn. –; died Mar. 16, 1859. **(VII.)** Samuel H. Gross, bn.—; died Sept. 4, 1877. **(VII.)** M. Ida Gross, bn.—. **(VII.)** Anna M. Gross, bn.—. Mrd. Isaiah Godshall, Jan. 13, 1885. Mrs. G., Presby. **(VII.)** A. Lincoln Gross, bn.—; died Mar. 25, 1863. **(VII.)** Emma L. Gross, bn. Mar. 5, 1864. Mrd. Jacob Bissey, Mar. 5, 1887. Farmer. Presby. No issue. **(VII.)** Ella E. Gross, bn.—. **(VII.)** J. Asher Gross, bn.—.

VI. Lewis Shaddinger, bn. in Bucks Co., Pa., Mar. 2, 1836. Mrd. Charlotte McKay,—. P. O., LeMars, Iowa. Farmer. Presby. One child: **(VII.)** Anna Belle Shaddinger, bn. Jan. 1883.

VI. Sarah Ann Shaddinger, bn. June 12, 1838; died Oct. 11, 1868. S.

VI. Huldah J. Shaddinger, bn. Sept. 26, 1840. Mrd. John F. Landis, Aug. 29, 1872. P. O., Dublin, Pa. Both Mr. and Mrs. Landis in early life taught school, and have also been officially connected with Sunday-school work. Farmer. Menn. Children: **(VII.)** Ada May Landis, bn. Jan. 31, 1874. **(VII.)** Fannie E. Landis, bn. Oct. 23, 1875. **(VII.)** Wilmer Landis, bn. June 30, 1878; died Jan. 14, 1886. **(VII.)** George W. Landis, bn. Feb. 22, 1881. **(VII.)** Eugene S. Landis, bn. Aug. 30, 1886.

VI. Harvey G. Shaddinger, bn. Jan. 7, 1843. Mrd. Elizabeth Ann Fretz, Mar. 18, 1866. P. O., Dublin, Pa. He enlisted in Co. A, 104 Penna. Vol., Sept. 6, 1861, for three years, and served in the following engagements: Lee's Mills, Williamsburg, Chickahominy, Seven Pines, Fair Oaks, Bottom Bridge, White Oak Swamp, Carter's Hill, James' Island, Siege of Fort Wagner, and Siege of Charleston. He was appointed Corporal, April 1, 1863. He was discharged on expiration of enlistment Sept. 30, 1864, and re-enlisted as Sergeant in Co. I., 213 Pa. Vol., Feb. 16, 1865, for one year, or during the war, and was discharged at the close of the war Nov. 18, 1865. Menn. Children: (VII.) A. Wesley Shaddinger, bn. Aug. 5, 1866. Mrd. Catharine Gross, Apr. 9, 1892. P. O., Fountainville, Pa. Teacher. Menn. (VII.) Elmer F. Shaddinger, bn. Apr. 12, 1869; died Aug. 24, 1869. (VII.) Anna Charlotta Shaddinger, bn. Sept. 6, 1870. Menn. (VII.) Jonas Moyer Shaddinger, bn. Apr. 21, 1873. (VII.) M. Magdalena Shaddinger, bn. Oct. 4, 1875. (VII.) Dora May Shaddinger, bn. May 3, 1878.

VI. Isaac Shaddinger, bn. Apr. 24, 1845; died Oct. 30, 1860.

VI. William J. Shaddinger, bn. Mar. 24, 1847; died Oct. 8, 1860.

VI. Wesley Clymer Shaddinger, bn. in Bucks Co., June 3, 1850. Mrd. Kate H. Moyer, Oct. 14, 1871. She died Apr. 15, 1874. No issue.—Wesley mrd. second wife, Maggie R. Mininger, Oct. 16, 1875. Harness-maker. Luth. Children: (VII.) Annie Minerva Shaddinger, bn. Nov. 14, 1876; died Apr. 11, 1879. (VII.) Elmer M. Shaddinger, bn. Feb. 1, 1878. (VII.) Edwin M. Shaddinger, bn. Mar. 17, 1880; died Jan. 11, 1881. (VII.) Lizzie May Shaddinger, bn. June 13, 1881. (VII.) Mary Alice Shaddinger, bn. Mar. 31, 1884. (VII.) Charles M. Shaddinger, bn. Feb. 25, 1889. (VII.) Ella Nora Shaddinger, bn. Aug. 16, 1891.

V. Mary Overholt, bn. Dec. 25, 1807. Mrd. Jacob Gross. (See Index of References No. 9.)

IV. Abraham Nash, bn. July 1, 1778; died July 22, 1823. Mrd. Mary Gross, —. Children: Elizabeth, Mary, Joseph, Rebecca, Abraham, Jacob, Anna.

V. Elizabeth Nash, bn. Feb. 18, 1805; died May 25, 1880. Mrd. Jacob Fry. (See Index of References No. 10.) Elizabeth mrd. second husband John Hipple. Ev. Ass'n ch.

V. Mary Nash, bn. in Bucks Co., Pa., Mar. 2, 1808; died Nov. 8, 1885. Mrd. Abraham B. Moyer, about 1830. He was born in Lincoln Co., Ont., Jan. 19, 1809; died Apr. 21. 1865. Farmer. Menn. until about 1850, when they joined the Ev. Ass'n ch.

Children: Anna, Tobias, Samuel, Abraham, Mary, Jacob, Levi, Sophia, Jesse.

VI. Anna Moyer, bn. Jan. 9, 1831. Mrd. John Wismer. (See Index of References No. 11.) Anna mrd. second husband William W. Moyer. (See Index of References No. 12.)

VI. Tobias Moyer, bn. —. S.

VI. Rev. Samuel G. Moyer, bn. —. Mrd. —. P. O., Cedar Falls, Iowa.

VI. Abraham N. Moyer, born in Haldimand Co., Ont., Aug. 10, 1837. Mrd. Nannie Entrekin, Sept. 7, 1870. P. O., Kansas City, Kan. The first 19 years of his life were spent on his father's farm in Canada. Hard work, limited school privileges, but with some extra study enabled him to pass his examinations, and began teaching at the age of 20. For 18 years he continued teaching with slight interruption. His fields of labor having been in Canada, Illinois, Missouri, and Kansas. In 1859 '60 a few terms in Clark Seminary, Aurora, Ill., aided him in making a start in the classics. He prized his mother-tongue, and taught classes in German in the Public Schools of Independence, Mo., in 1868-'70 and in Wyandotte, Kan., from 1872 to 1875. In 1879 he engaged in editorial work on the *Wyandotte Gazette*, later called the *Kansas City Gazette*, until 1887 when he sold his half interest in the paper, and engaged in banking, being (1892) Vice President of the Wyandotte National Bank, and Treasurer of the Kansas City Savings Bank. Presby. Children: (**VII.**) Metta Sophia Moyer, bn. May 9, 1873. (**VII.**) Clyde Entrekin Moyer, bn. Mar. 18, 1879.

VI. Mary Moyer, bn —. Mrd. Tobias Schantz, Aug. 6, 1863. P. O., Berlin, Ont. Book agent. U. Bre. in Christ. Children: (**VII.**) Orpha Moyer Schantz, bn. May 27, 1864. (**VII.**) Lydia Mary Etta Schantz, bn. Oct. 9, 1866. (**VII.**) Sophia Emma Schantz, bn. May 4, 1869. (**VII.**) Austin Tobias Schantz, bn. Oct. 5, 1871. (**VII.**) Arthur Benjamin Schantz, bn. Nov. 22, 1876. (**VII.**) Florence Annie Catharine Schantz, bn. Dec. 28, 1879. (**VII.**) Herbert Cecil Palmer Schantz, bn. May 3, 1883.

4

VI. Jacob N Moyer, bn. Oct. 23, 1842. Mrd. Mary Jane Miller, Apr. 20, 1886. P. O., Harrisburg, Pa. Accountant. Meth. Children: **(VII.)** Willard White Moyer, bn. Apr. 12, 1887. **(VII.)** Frances Moyer, bn. July 19, 1889. **(VII.)** Richard Moyer, bn. Sept. 9, 1891.

VI. Levi N. Moyer, bn. June 19, 1845. Mrd. Mary E. Raymond, June 20, 1871. P. O., Chicago, Ill. Dry goods merchant. Meth. Children: **(VII.)** Charles Raymond Moyer, bn. June 20, 1872; died Nov. 25, 1878. **(VII.)** Harry Rollin Moyer, bn. Jan. 6, 1875. **(VII.)** Eva Maud Moyer, bn. June 24, 1876; died Dec. 11, 1878. **(VII.)** Mary Emma Moyer, bn. Nov. 1, 1877. **(VII.)** Edward Warren Moyer, bn. Mar. 15, 1880. **(VII.)** Jennie Moyer, bn. Feb. 4, 1885.

VI. Sophia Moyer, bn. —; died Nov. 20, 1870. Mrd. John H. Book, —, **(VII.)** Infant daughter died unnamed.

VI. Jesse G. Moyer, bn. Feb. 28, 1850. Mrd. Anna E. Tomlins, Oct. 15, 1874. P. O., Kansas City, Kan. Real Estate Agt., Notary Public. Ev. Ass'n ch. Children: **(VII.)** Lillian Moyer, bn. Feb. 26, 1876. **(VII.)** Manirve Moyer, bn. July 7, 1877. **(VII.)** Herbert Moyer, bn. Oct. 12, 1879. **(VII.)** Mabel Moyer, bn. Feb. 3, 1881. **(VII.)** Edna Moyer, bn. Feb. 25, 1885. **(VII.)** Etta Edith Moyer, bn. Feb. 5, 1887. **(VII.)** Bertha Moyer, bn. June 24, 1890.

V. Rev. Joseph Nash, bn. in Bucks Co., Pa., about 1812. Mrd. Mary Shelly, Sept. 8, 1833. P. O., Campden, Ont. Mr. Nash emigrated to Canada in 1828, and 1836 settled in South Cayuga, Ont., where he cleared up and worked a farm, and in the fall and winter worked at his trade that of weaving. He was ordained a minister of the Mennonite church about 1841. Some years later he united with the Evangelical Association church, of which he is still a member, and has been for many years a local preacher. Children: Elizabeth, Mary, Rebecca, Abraham, Sophia, Jacob. Samuel, Anna, Saloma.

VI. Elizabeth Nash, bn. in Clinton Twp., Ont., Aug. 14, 1834. Mrd. Amos Albright, June 17, 1849. P. O., Faulkton, S. Dak. Carpenter. Meth's. Children: Angeline, Jemima, Mary, John, Rebecca, Joseph.

VII. Angeline Albright, bn. in 1851. Mrd. Henry Livens, —. P. O., Seaforth, Ont. Merchant. Meth's. Children: **(VIII.)** Dell Livens. **(VIII.)** May Livens. **(VIII.)** Harry Livens.

VII. Jemima Albright, bn. 1852; died 1882. Mrd. — Herrick, —. P. O., Ostrander, Ont. Farmer. Meth's. Children: **(VIII.)** Olive Gertrude Herick. **(VIII.)** Muriel Margerette Elizabeth Herick.

VII. Mary Albright, bn. in 1854. P. O., Faulkton, S. Dak. S.

VII. John Henry Albright, bn. in 1856. Mrd. — McCloud, of London, Ont., —. She died —. P. O., Sioux City, Iowa. Contractor and builder. One child: **(VIII.)** Maybell Albright.

VII. Rebecca Albright, bn. in 1858. Mrd. James Norton, —. Electrician. No issue.

VII. Joseph Albright, bn. 1860. Mrd.—. P. O., Detroit, Mich. Conductor on street car. One child: **(VIII.)** Joseph Albright.

VI. Mary Nash, bn. Dec. 3, 1836. Mrd. Daniel Albright, Jan. 2, 1855. P. O., Campden, Ont. Boot and shoe merchant. Ev. Ass'n ch. Children: Mary Joseph, John, Jacob.

VII. Mary Margaret Albright, born Nov. 24, 1855. Mrd. Lewis A. Moyer in 1874. P. O., Hamilton, Ont. Book-keeper. Meth. Children: **(VIII.)** Clayton H. Moyer, bn. in 1874. **(VIII.)** Gertrude H. Moyer, born 1880. **(VIII.)** Thomas S. Moyer, born 1885. **(VIII.)** Mary Winnifred Moyer, bn. 1889.

VII. Joseph Watson Albright, bn. Oct. 2, 1857; died Oct. 16, 1857.

VII. John Arthur Albright, bn. Feb. 3, 1859; died in Winnipeg, Manitoba, Sept. 11, 1887.

VII. Jacob High Albright, bn. Oct. 16, 1861. Mrd. Priscilla Culp, Aug. 1884. P. O., Grimsby, Ont. Painter and paper hanger.

VI. Rebecca Nash, bn. in Haldimond Co., Ont., Jan. 15, 1839; died Sept. 24, 1862. She attended the common schools of her section until her 18th year. But desiring to pursue a more complete course, preparatory thereto she attended a Grammar school, but on account of ill health she was compelled to discontinue her school attendance.

When about 17 years of age she began teaching school, and continued, except when attending school, until within about three months of her death. When in her 18th year she was converted and soon after united with the Ev. Ass'n church, and though often in darkness, with conflicts, doubts, and fears, yet bright hope as often intervened to cheer and light her path until the end came, and the crown won.

Among her writings were many pieces of her own composition, mostly of a religious character, that speak well of her poetical talents. We make room for one written for an intimate friend and schoolmate.

RESPONSE.

You smooth the tangles from my hair
With gentle touch and tend'rest care,
And count the years ere you shall mark
Bright silvery threads among the dark,—
Smiling the while to hear me say,
"You'll think of this again some day!
"Some day!"

I do not scorn the power of time,
Nor count on years of *fadeless* prime;
But no white gleams will ever shine
Among these heavy locks of mine.
Ah, laugh as gaily as you may,
You'll think of this again some day,
Some day!

Some day I shall not feel as now,
Your soft hands move about my brow;
I shall not slight your light commands,
And draw the long braids through my hands;
I shall be silent and obey,—
And you—you will not laugh *that day*,
That day!

I know how long your loving hands
Will linger with these glossy bands,
When you shall weave my latest crown
Of these thick braidings long and brown;
But you shall see no touch of gray
Adown their shining lengths that day,
      That day!

And while your tears are falling hot
Upon the lips which answer not,
You'll take from these one treasured tress,
And leave the rest to silentness,
Remembering that I used to say,
" *You'll think of this again some day*,
      "Some day!"

VI. Abraham Nash, bn. Mar. 28, 1841. Mrd. Sarah A. Logan, in 1876. P. O., Perry Station, Ont. Meth. One child: **(VII.)** Richard Nelson Nash, born Jan. 28, 1877.

VI. Sophia Nash, bn. May 1, 1843; died Aug. 22, 1844.

VI. Jacob Nash, bn. Oct. 3, 1845. Mrd. Mary Snyder,—. P. O., St. Anns, Ont. Children: **(VII.)** Chester Allan Nash. **(VII.)** Nellie Josephine Nash. **(VII.)** Zoey Nash. **(VII.)** George Nash.

VI. Samuel S. Nash, bn. in Haldimand Co., Ont., June 5, 1848. Mrd. Sarah A. Moyer, Dec. 4, 1871. Teacher. Ev. Ass'n ch. Children: **(VII.)** Florence Beatrice Nash, bn. Feb. 28, 1876. **(VII.)** Aubrey De Witt Nash, bn. May 26, 1881. **(VII.)** Justus Hugh Nash, bn. Dec. 28, 1885. **(VII.)** Samuel Leland Nash, bn. Aug. 26, 1888.

VI. Anna Nash, bn. Jan. 12, 1851. Mrd. David F. Houser, Sept. 12, 1873. P. O., Campden, Ont. Butcher. Ev. Ass'n ch. Children: **(VII.)** Maynard Houser, bn. 1874. **(VII.)** George A. Houser, bn. 1879. **(VII.)** Judson Stanley Houser, bn. June 22, 1886; died Sept. 7, 1886. **(VII.)** Joseph Henry Houser, bn. Jan. 1, 1888.

VI. Salome Nash, bn. May 19, 1856. Mrd. Judson Anderson. P. O., Virgil, Ont.

V. Rebecca Nash, bn. Nov. 27, 1812; died Aug. 16, 1884. Mrd. David B. Moyer, Mar. 4, 1833. Farmer. In early life they were Mennonites, but during the great revival of God's work at the "Twenty" in Clinton Twp., Lincoln Co., Ont., in 1849-1851, they experienced the grace of God in the renewal of their hearts, and subsequently united with the Evangelical Association church, of which they remained faithful and active members until death. Children: Samuel, Mary, Anna, Barbara, Eli, Elizabeth, David, Simeon.

VI. Rev. Samuel N. Moyer, bn. Aug. 10, 1834. His early life was spent on the old homestead farm at the Twenty up to about the age of twenty years. During the winter months he attended the common school "in dem Schulhaus an der Krick." In Jan. 1854 he commenced teaching school, taught three months, and was paid $11.00 per month and board. The following year he also taught three months, and then decided to make teaching his life work, and at once took a course in the Normal school, and followed the profession of teaching until 1868. In the 15th year of his age he was converted, and united with the Evangelical Association church. In 1857 he commenced to exercise his talents for the Lord in the Sabbath-school work, and weekly tract distribution in Port Elgin, where he was teaching. This he followed up for years both summer and winter. He was also appointed Class-leader at the first organization of the Ev. Ass'n church at that place in 1859. During these years he was impressed, and knew that he should go forth as a herald of the cross of Christ, but his unfitness seemed so great that he dared not venture to let even his dearest friends know of his convictions. Finally, through the searching inquiry of a father in Israel, he yielded his assent, and was given work as a local preacher in 1867. At the next Annual Conference held in Blenheim Twp., under the Presidency of Bishop Joseph Long, he was licensed as probationer, and sent as Junior preacher to Upper Wolwich Circuit to assist Rev. Theo. Hand. In 1869 he was sent to Blenheim Circuit alone; Hamburg Circuit, 1871-1872; Lincoln and Gainsboro Mission, 1873-1876, and

Campden Station one year; Hespeler Mission, 1877—;
Credition Station, 1880—; Hespler Mission, 1883—.
In 1884 he was elected Presiding Elder and sent to
the Ottawa District, and also as pastor of the Golden
Lake Mission. In 1887 he was stationed on the North
District, and 1889 on the West District. He was ordained Deacon in 1870 at Credition, and Elder in
1872 at Lingelbach's church. Preaching Christ and
pointing sinners to the Lamb of God, has been and
still is the greatest joy of his life, and the Lord has
richly crowned his feeble endeavors to glorify His
name, and given him many seals to his ministry on
every pastoral charge he has served. In Sept. 1858
he was married to Martha Jane, daughter of Benjamin and Lavina Brown, of Gainsboro, Ont. She died
without issue, May 21, 1871. For second wife he mrd.
Mary Anna, widow of Conrad Seibert, and daughter
of William and Anna (Schweitzer) Lingelbach, June
4, 1872. P. O., Sebringville, Ont. Children: (VII.)
Ida Susanna Moyer, bn. Mar. 23, 1873; died Apr. 16,
1876. (VII.) Eli Simpson Moyer, bn. Feb. 28, 1876.
(VII.) Anna Margaret Moyer, bn. Aug. 2, 1878. (VII.)
Samuel Nehemiah Moyer, bn. Aug. 1, 1881. (VII.)
Mary Rosa, Ettie A. Moyer, bn. Nov. 6, 1883.

VI. Mary Moyer, bn. Sept. 30, 1836; died May 11,
1837.

VI. Anna Moyer, bn. Aug. 26, 1838. Mrd. Christian A. Gross. (See Index of References No. 13.)

VI. Barbara N. Moyer, bn. May 8, 1841; died April
11, 1885. Mrd. Gilgian Trachsel. Feb. 27, 1873. P.
O., Shakespeare, Ont. Farmer. Ger. Ev. ch. Chil-
dren: (VII.) Edwin Trachsel, bn. Feb. 28, 1874. (VII.)
Lizzie Trachsel, bn. Aug. 2, 1875. (VII.) John Gideon
Trachsel, bn. Jan. 6, 1877. (VII.) Samuel Trachsel,
bn. Oct. 30, 1878. (VII.) Sarah Rebecca Trachsel, bn.
Feb. 28, 1885.

VI. Eli N. Moyer, bn. July 14, 1843. Mrd. Sarah
Hipple, Feb. 4, 1866. P. O., Toronto, Ont. Manufacturer and dealer in school supplies. Meth. Children: Rebecca, Maggie, Martha, Harry.

VII. Rebecca Arminta Moyer, bn. Dec. 2?, 1866.
Mrd. Ezra Albright, Dec. 28, 1887. P. O., Jordan,

Ont. Meth. One child: (VIII.) Ethel Edna May Albright, bn. Dec. 15, 1890.

VII. Maggie May Moyer, bn. Sept. 25, 1869. Meth.

VII. Martha Dell Moyer, bn. Jan. 12, 1873. Meth.

VII. Harry Rollison Amdeus Moyer, bn. Jan. 17, 1878. Meth.

VI. Elizabeth N. Moyer, bn. Dec. 1, 1845. P. O., Dunnville, Ont.

VI. David N. Moyer, bn. in Lincoln Co., Ont., June 12, 1849. Mrd. Margaret Tweddle, of Quebec, Aug. 12, 1875. P. O., Naperville, Ill. Traveling salesman. Children: (**VII.**) Ernest J. T. Moyer, bn. July 31, 1876. (**VII.**) David Bertram Moyer, bn. Jan. 4, 1878. (**VII.**) Leland Percy Moyer, bn. Aug. 21, 1879. (**VII.**) Reginald Woods Moyer, bn. Jan. 29, 1882. (**VII.**) Margaret Moyer, bn. Feb. 21, 1892.

VI. Simeon N. Moyer, bn. Aug. 13, 1852. Mrd. Rhoda Moyer, July 28, 1874. P. O., Dunnville, Ont. Carriage maker. Meth. Children: (**VII.**) Sarah Luella Moyer, bn. July 7, 1875. (**VII.**) Earnest Sidney Moyer, bn. Dec. 9, 1881. (**VII.**) Florence Mabel Moyer, bn. May 6, 1883. (**VII.**) John Curtis Moyer, bn. Nov. 2, 1885.

V. Abraham Nash, bn. Nov. 27, 1812. Mrd. Frances Wismer, Oct. 10, 1843. P. O., Upper, Ont. Land surveyor, conveyancer and farmer. Ev. Ass'n ch. Children: Susanna, Mary, Daniel, Frances, Samuel.

VI. Susanna Nash, bn. May 24, 1846. Mrd. Abraham G. Wismer. (See Index of References No. 43.)

VI. Mary Nash, born Jan. 2, 1848. Mrd. Isaac Hoover, Mar. 28, 1878. P. O., Rodney, Ont. Carpenter. Meth. Children: (**VII.**) Lorne Hoover, bn. Nov. 27, 1879. (**VII.**) Fannie Hoover, bn. May 20, 1881. (**VII.**) Pelma Hoover, bn. Apr. 6, 1885.

VI. Daniel Wismer Nash, bn. Jan. 5, 1850. Mrd. Anna Wismer, Jan. 29, 1879. P. O., South Cayuga, Ont. Farmer. Ev. Ass'n ch. Children: (**VII.**) William Warren Nash, bn. Jan. 4, 1880. (**VII.**) Ardel Theodore Nash, bn. Nov. 12, 1881. (**VII.**) Lottie Mabel Nash, bn. Dec. 4, 1883. (**VII.**) Lulu Constance Nash, bn. Sept. 3, 1887.

VI. Frances Deborah Nash, bn. Feb. 27, 1852. Mrd. Jonathan Carter, Mar. 24, 1888. P. O., Rodney, Ont. Butcher. Meth. One child: **(VII.)** Abraham Nash Carter, bn. July 27, 1890.

VI. Samuel Abraham Nash, bn. May 7, 1854; died Sept. 2, 1854.

V. Jacob Nash, bn. —; died —. Mrd. —. Children: **(VI.)** Jacob. **(VI.)** William. **(VI.)** Ann. &c.

V. Anna Nash, bn. in Bucks Co., Pa., Sept. 29, 1819. Mrd. Samuel Fry. (See Index of References No. 14.)

IV. Jacob Nash, bn. Jan. 25, 1781; died Nov. 25, 1851. Mrd. Elizabeth Myers, —. Mason and farmer. Lived in Tinicum Twp. Menn. Children: Samuel, Susan, Elizabeth, Joseph, William, Henry, Tobias, Levi, Mary, Eli, Anna, Jacob.

V. Samuel Nash, bn. Jan. 10, 1810. Mrd. Barbara Wismer, Mar. 27, 1832. P. O., Doylestown, Pa. Mr. Nash followed farming for some years. He was also a well known auctioneer and general business agent. Some years ago he retired from active work, and moved to Doylestown, Pa., where he still resides. Children: Sophia, Susanna, Reuben, Levi, Samuel, Huldah, Amanda, Deborah, Marietta, Lizzie.

VI. Sophia Nash, bn. Jan. 1, 1833. Mrd. David Kepler, Jan. 1, 1855. P. O., Wismer, Pa. Farmer. Baptists. Children: Elwood, Wilson, Joanna, Harvey.

VII. S. Elwood Kepler, bn. Aug. 1, 1856. Mrd. Abbie F. Naylor, Feb. 28, 1884. P. O., Dawson, N. Dak. Merchant. Cong. Children: **(VIII.)** G. Donald Kepler, bn. Dec. 15, 1885. **(VIII.)** J. Faires Kepler, bn. Feb. 2, 1890.

VII. Wilson Kepler, bn. June 8, 1860; died July 6, 1861.

VII. Joanna Kepler, bn. Apr. 3, 1863. Mrd. W. A. Reed, —. P. O., Jamestown, N. Y. One child: **(VIII.)** Harvey Roy Reed.

VII. Harvey Kepler, bn. Feb. 8, 1869. P. O., Dawson, N. Dak. Compositor. Baptist.

VI. Susan W. Nash, bn. Apr. 26, 1834. Mrd. John R. Lear. (See Index of References No. 47.)

VI. Reuben W. Nash, bn. Jan. 6, 1836; died May 27, 1892. Mrd. Catharine Myers, in 1860. Farmer. Children: Anderson, John, Huldah, Samuel, Annie, Reed, Mary.

VII. Anderson Nash, bn. Nov. 11, 1860. Mrd. Emma Skillman, Feb. 25, 1888. P. O., Wismer, Pa. Farmer. One child, son: **(VIII.)** — Nash, bn. Sept. 15, 1892.

VII. John M. Nash, bn. Apr. 5, 1863. Mrd. Catharine C. Smith, in 1884. Farmer. Luth. One child: **(VIII.)** Sallie S. Nash, bn. Oct. 31, 1884.

VII. Huldah Nash, bn. Sept 3, 1864; died Dec. 15, 1864.

VII. Samuel N. Nash, bn. July 11, 1866. S.

VII. Annie Nash, bn. June 2, 1868; died, Sept. 28, 1868.

VII. Reed Nash, bn. July 28, 1869. S.

VII. Mary Ellen Nash, bn. Nov. 9, 1875.

VI. Levi W. Nash, bn. Mar. 26, 1838. P. O., Wismer, Pa. Owns the old Nash homestead. S.

VI. Samuel Nash, born Jan. 20, 1841; died Oct. 3, 1841.

VI. Huldah J. Nash, bn. July 28, 1842. Mrd. Theodore J. Kline, Oct. 4, 1865. He was bn. May 13, 1841; died Aug. 4, 1868. P. O., Doylestown, Pa. He served as Lieutenant of the 128 Pa. regiment. His occupation had been that of school teacher and photographer. He was elected Justice of the Peace of Whitehall Twp., Lehigh Co., Apr. 14, 1868, and at the same time superintendent and time-keeper of outside hands of Hokendauqua iron works of Lehigh County. Baptists. Children: Jeannetta, Theodore.

VII. Jeannetta N. Kline, born Jan. 10, 1867. She attended the Millersville State Normal School during the winter and spring of '83 and '84. She then passed an examination, and taught Union school, Bedminster, a term of six months. Again attended Millersville the summer session of '85. Taught the South Western school, Plumstead Twp., the terms of '85, '86, '87, '88. In the fall of 1889 she received a Professional Certificate under County Supt. W. H. Slotter, and taught Dyer's Hill school, Plumstead Twp.,

until December when she was married to U. S.
Grant Myers. (See Index of References No. 15.)
VII. Theodore J. Kline, born April 6, 1869. He at
tended the Groveland school, Plumstead Twp., until
Feb. 1885, when he became an apprentice in the
"Intelligencer Printing Office," at Doylestown, Pa.,
and served for four years. He then entered the
composing room, where he remained for a time, and
was then promoted to the printing department,
which position he still occupies. S.

VI. Amanda Nash, bn. May 11, 1844; died Feb.
28, 1871.

VI. Debbie Ann Nash, bn. May 11, 1846. Mrd.
Philip Z. Jenkins, May —, 1868. P. O., Plumstead-
ville, Pa. Wheelwright. Presby. Children: (**VII.**)
Flora N. Jenkins, bn. Jan 16, 1869. Mrd. William
E. McElderry, Mar. 5, 1891. P. O., Boonville, Ind.
(**VII.**) S. Frank Jenkins, bn. Apr. 9, 1872. (**VII.**) A.
Lizzie Jenkins, bn. May 28, 1875. (**VII.**) Lily May
Jenkins, bn. July 10, 1879.

VI. Marietta Nash, bn. Oct. 20, 1850; died Jan. 13,
1871.

VI. Elizabeth Nash, bn. in Bucks Co., Pa., Apr. 20,
1854. Mrd. George W. McIntosh, of Doylestown,
Pa., Apr. 22, 1880. Mr. McIntosh learned the
printing trade in the office of the Bucks County *Intelligencer*, where for several years he served as press-
man, and job printer, and was subsequently appointed
foreman of the establishment. In 1879 he removed
to Illinois and bought one-half interest in the *Republican*, published at Watseka, Iroquois Co. After a
short residence there he sold his interest in the *Republican*, and returned to Doylestown, Pa., and resumed work again in the *Intelligencer* office in his old
position as foreman. When the daily edition of the
Intelligencer was started in 1886, he was appointed
business manager, but for the past three years he has
served as local editor of the daily and weekly *Intelligencer*. Mr. McIntosh, Presbyterian, Mrs. McIntosh,
Baptist. One child: (**VII.**) Florence Nash McIntosh,
bn. Nov. 4, 1887.

V. Susan Nash, bn. Dec. 30, 1810. Mrd. Samuel Myers, Dec. 24, 1835. Farmer. Menn. Children: Hannah, Jacob, Tobias, Christian, Amos, Charles, Anna.
VI. Hannah Myers, bn. Jan. 10, 1836; died Sept. 3, 1838.
VI. Jacob N. Myers, bn. Feb. 19, 1838. Mrd. Anna Maria Myers, Nov. 9, 1861. P. O., Fricks, Pa. Farmer. Menn. Children: John, Samuel, Sarah, Amos, Damon, Anna, Alfred, Amanda, Christian, Susan.
VII. John Myers, bn. Oct. 28, 1862. Mrd. Susan Rosenberger, Nov. 11, 1886. P. O., Lawndale, Pa. Children: (**VIII.**) Ottomar Myers, bn. Feb. 28, 1888. (**VIII.**) Titus Myers, bn. Jan. 9, 1891.
VII. Samuel Myers, bn. Mar. 7, 1864; died Aug. 9, 1864.
VII. Sarah Myers, bn. Apr. 28, 1865; died same day.
VII. Amos Myers, born Jan. 26, 1867; died Apr. 7, 1867.
VII. Damon Myers, bn. Apr. 17, 1868.
VII. Anna Elizabeth Myers, bn. Dec. 19, 1869; died July 25, 1881.
VII. Alfred Myers, bn. Dec. 17, 1871; died Sept. 20, 1872.
VII. Amanda Myers, bn. Jan. 25, 1873.
VII. Christian Myers, bn. Aug. 24, 1874; died Jan. 14, 1875.
VII. Susan Myers, bn. Mar. 29, 1878.
VI. Tobias N. Myers, bn.—. Mrd. Rosanna Kratz, Jan. 19, 1865, P. O. 39 N. 11th St., Philadelphia, Pa. Merchant and real estate agent. Children: Ulysses, Allen, Laura, Lillie, Rosa.
VII. Ulysses S. Grant Myers, bn. Nov. 23, 1865. Mrd. Jeannetta N. Kline, Jan. 1, 1890. He attended Sandy Ridge school, Doylestown Twp., until fall of '82, when he commenced the term at Doylestown Seminary. He then entered the store of William Thompson & Son of Doylestown, as clerk for a year, then took the regular course of three years at the Doylestown Seminary, graduating in June, 1886. He then attended the School of Phonography, 1320

Chestnut St., Philadelphia, after which he started in the house furnishing business at 39 N. 11th St., Philadelphia. One child: **(VIII.)** Russel Blair Myers.

VII. S. Allen Myers, bn. Oct. 24, 1869.

VII. Laura Bertha Myers, bn. Mar. 1876; died 1878.

VII. Lillie May Myers, bn. Aug. 25, 1878.

VII. Rosa Pearl Myers, bn. July 2, 1882.

VI. Christian M. Myers, bn. Apr. 29, 1841. Mrd. Eliza B. Stover, Feb. 7, 1863. P. O., Pipersville, Pa. Miller. Children: **(VII.)** Samuel Horace Myers, bn.—, 1864. Graduated at Lafayette College in 1888, since then has been studying law, and engaged in real estate business. He received the Master's degree from Lafayette College in 1891. Graduated in the Law Dept. of U. of P. in June 1892, and is engaged in the practice of the same. **(VII.)** Hugh Ely Myers, bn.—. **(VII.)** Ira Stover Myers, bn.—.

VI. Amos Myers, bn.—. Mrd. Huldah Myers, in 1868. Farmer. Menn. Children: **(VII.)** Clara Myers, bn. 1869. **(VII.)** Henry Myers, bn. and died 1870. **(VII.)** Horace Watson Myers, bn. 1871. Edward M. Myers, bn. 1874. **(VII.)** Annetta Myers, bn. 1876. **(VII.)** Samuel Myers, bn. 1878. **(VII.)** Alice Myers, bn. 1881. **(VII)** Susanna Myers, bn. and died 1885. **(VII.)** Charles Elmer Myers bn. 1886. **(VII.)** Howard Myers, bn. 1889.

VI. Charles Myers, bn. Sept. 25, 1847. Mrd. Emma J. Zeigler, daughter of Eli L. Zeigler, Esq., May 30, 1874. Merchant and Postmaster at Orvilla, Pa. Ger. Ref. No issue.

VI. Anna Myers, bn.—. Mrd. David Kratz,—. He died,—. No issue.

V. Elizabeth Nash, bn. Aug 17, 1812; died—. Mrd. Christian Fretz, son of Deacon Abraham Fretz, (his second wife). No issue.

V. Joseph Nash, bn. Aug. 20, 1814; died June 7, 1851. S.

V. William Nash, bn. Nov. 24, 1816; died Dec. 15, 1851. S.

V. Henry Nash, bn. Nov. 22, 1818. Killed in sand pit at Jenkintown, Pa., Sept. 8, 1849.

V. Tobias Nash, bn. Apr. 6, 1821. Mrd. Rebecca L. Solliday. Res. Wormansville, Pa. Children: **(VI.)** William. **(VI.)** Mary. **(VI.)** Samuel. **(VI.)** John.

V. Levi Nash, bn. Jan. 7, 1823; died Mar. 5, 1823.

V. Mary Nash, bn. Feb. 15, 1824; died Mar. 25, 1850.

V. Eli Nash, bn. July 8, 1826; died Dec. 1, 1851. Teacher.

V. Anna Nash, bn. Aug. 5, 1829. Mrd. Samuel H. Moyer, Aug. 30, 1855. He died Jan. 22, 1884. He was ordained deacon of Mennonite church at Blooming Glen, Pa., in 1853. Children: Tobias, Levi, Susanna, Amanda.—Anna mrd. second husband, Rev. Henry B. Moyer, Oct. 22, 1885. Farmer. Menn. He was ordained to the ministry of the Mennonite church at Blooming Glen in 1843.

VI. Tobias N. Moyer, bn. Apr. 4, 1857. Mrd.—. P. O., Blooming Glen, Pa.

VI. Levi N. Moyer, bn. Apr. 23, 1864. Mrd. Annie High, Jan. 11, 1886. P. O., Blooming Glen, Pa. Farmer, Menn. Children: **(VII.)** William Moyer, bn. Apr. 13, 1888. **(VII.)** Christian Moyer, bn. June 18, 1891.

VI. Susanna Moyer, bn. Mar. 15, 1859. Mrd.— Yoder,—. P. O., Dublin, Pa.

VI. Amanda Moyer, bn. July 10, 1868. Mrd. Milton Stover,—. P. O., Dublin, Pa.

V. Jacob Nash, bn. Dec. 24, 1831; died Jan. 26, 1841.

IV. Henry Nash, bn. Sept. 30, 1783; died Oct. 18, 1861. Mrd. Margaret Overholt,—. Moved to Ohio about 1835. Children: Levi, Samuel, Henry, Julia, Hannah.

V. Levi Nash, bn.—. Mrd.—. P. O., Western Star, Ohio.

V. Samuel Nash, bn—. Mrd.—. in Michigan.

V. Henry Nash—.

V. Julia Ann Nash, bn. in Bucks Co., Pa., Mar. 9, 1832. Mrd. Charles Schall, Oct. 24, 1852. He died Nov. 28, 1863. P. O., Wadsworth, O. Menn. Children: Meredith, Hannah, Sabina.

VI. Meredith Schall, bn Aug. 17, 1853; died Nov. 9, 1853.

VI. Hannah Elizabeth Schall, bn. Oct. 2, 1854. Mrd. John P. Overholt, Jan. 31, 1878. P. O., Wadsworth, O. Farmer. Menn. Children: **(VII.)** Infant still-born, Oct. 11, 1879. **(VII.)** Julia Pearl Overholt, bn. July 30, 1881. **(VII.)** Mary Ann Overholt, bn. Apr. 15, 1883. **(VII.)** Merton Franklin Overholt, bn. Sept. 7, 1886.

VI. Sabina Catharine Schall. bn. Oct. 12, 1856. Mrd. Jacob B. Transue, Aug. 24, 1880. P. O., Ravenna, O. Kiln burner in tile factory. Mrs. T. Congregationalist. Children: **(VII.)** Edwin Franklin Transue, bn. Aug. 14, 1881. **(VII.)** Julia Margaret Transue, bn. Sept. 23, 1889.

V. Hannah Nash, bn. in 1838. Mrd. Anthony Overholt. (See Index of References No. 16.)

IV. Elizabeth Nash. bn. June 25, 1788; died Nov. 9, 1823. Mrd. Daniel Gross, June 20, 1809. Farmer and weaver. Menn. Was deacon of the Doylestown Menn. ch. for about thirty years. Children: Mary, Joseph, Eliza, Sophia.

V. Mary Gross, bn. May 20, 1812; died in infancy.

V. Joseph N. Gross, bn. Aug. 3, 1816. Mrd. Sarah Wismer, Mar. 16, 1841. P. O., Doylestown. Pa. Farmer in New Britain Twp., where he lived on the same farm for 56 years from the age of twelve. In 1884 he moved to Doylestown Twp., where he lives retired. Menn. Children: Henry, Susanna, Daniel, Levi, Isaiah.

VI. Henry W. Gross, bn. Feb. 4, 1842. Mrd. Susan E. Funk, June 17, 1875. P. O., Doylestown, Pa. Mr. Gross worked on the farm until 19 years of age, going to a country school three or four months in the winter. In 1861 he began teaching at Pipersville at a salary of $22.00 per month of 22 days, teaching every alternate Saturday. The summer of 1868 he spent in Canada and the western part of Pennsylvania. The winter of 1868-69 he taught school in Robinson Twp., Allegheny Co., Pa., and the two following years in Allegheny City. In the summer of 1873 he finished a regular Normal Course at the Millersville State Normal School, and in 1875 received the degree of Master of the Elements. After graduating he was

Principal of the Etna Borough, Allegheny Co., Pa., Public Schools five consecutive years. His health then needing a change of employment, he resigned his position, and engaged in farming in Bucks Co., and later engaged in the Creamery business. He and wife are members of the Doylestown Presbyterian ch. of which he was ordained elder in Jan. 1890. Children: (VII.) Sarah Ella. (VII.) Emma Laura. (VII.) Esther. (VII.) Walter Gross died 1890, aged 8 months.

VI. Susanna Gross, bn. June 4, 1843; died Dec. 11, 1873. Mrd. William J. Leatherman, —. Children: (VII.) Harvey K. Leatherman, died Mar. 10, 1870, aged 7 months, 17 days. (VII.) Daniel G. Leatherman, bn. —. Mrd. Ida L. Algard, in 1892. Clerk in Philadelphia, Pa. (VII.) Abraham G. Leatherman, bn. —. Clerk in Philadelphia, Pa. (VII.) Edwin G. Leatherman, bn. —. Clerk in Philadelphia, Pa.

VI. Daniel W. Gross, bn. June 3, 1846; died, aged 33 years, 8 months and 9 days. He was a graduate of the Millersville, Pa., State Normal School. When about 18 years old he commenced teaching and taught several years in the Public Schools of Harrisburg, Pa. Was principal of the schools of Sharpsburgh, Pa., and at the time of his last illness he was a member of the faculty of the Millersville, Pa., State Normal School. Presby.

VI. Levi N. Gross, bn. Oct. 24, 1854. Mrd. Anna Worthington, Apr. 5, 1881. She was born Apr. 20, 1856. P. O., Portland, Oregon. Supt. of syrup manufacturing. Meth. Children: (VII.) Mary Lucretia Gross, bn. in Chicago, Ill. (VII.) Joseph Watson Gross, bn. at Mitchel, Dakota. (VII.) Levi Worthington Gross, bn. at Wheaton, Ill.

VI. Isaiah W. Gross, bn. Jan. 10, 1861. Mrd. Mary Ann Fretz, Oct. 14, 1884. She was bn. June 8, 1864. Foreman in Samuel S. Fretz's umbrella factory in Philadelphia. Menn. One child: (VII.) Anna Elizabeth Gross, bn. Jan 11, 1887.

V. Eliza Gross, bn. Sept. 18, 1819; died, S.

V. Sophia Gross, born Sept. 20, 1821; died July 12, 1848.

R. H. Andrews, M. D.

(See page 60.)

III. Jacob Wismer, bn. Feb. 8, 1756; probably died young.

III. Mary Wismer, bn. Jan. 29, 1759.

III. Barbara Wismer, born in Bucks Co., Pa., Oct. 11, 1761; died May 17, 1801. Mrd. David High, —. He was bn. July 3, 1752; died Sept. 20, 1847, aged over 94 years. Farmer, lived in Hilltown Twp., on farm now owned by his grandson Jacob H. High. Menn. Children: Philip, Jacob, John, Annie, Barbara, Mary.

IV. Philip High, bn. Mar. 3, 1783; died Dec. 15, 1863. Mrd. Mary Hunsicker, —. She was bn. Dec. 22, 1786; died Jan. 14, 1871. Farmer. Menn. Children: Elizabeth, Annie, David, John, Jacob, Henry, Mary, Lydia.
V. Elizabeth High, bn. —; died Feb. 5, 1845. Mrd. Henry L. Kulp, Mar. 1835. Farmer. Menn. Children: Mary, Dilman, Hester.
VI. Mary Kulp, bn. Mar. 29, 1836. Mrd. Jacob Kulp, —. Farmer. Children: (VII.) Henry Kulp. (VII.) Dillman Kulp. (VII.) Amanda Kulp. (VII.) Lizzie Kulp.
VI. Dilman Kulp, bn. Aug. 12, 1839; died, infant.
VI. Hester Kulp, bn. Sept. 23, 1840; died Jan. 21, 1878. Mrd. Joseph B. Fretz, Nov. 23, 1867. P. O., Dublin, Pa. Farmer. Menn. Children: (VII.) Sarah Ann Fretz, bn. Feb. 10, 1869. (VII.) Henry K. Fretz, bn. Apr. 14, 1870. (VII.) Emma Jane Fretz, bn. Apr. 18, 1872; died Dec. 6, 1876. (VII.) Catharine K. Fretz, bn. Apr. 7, 1875. (VII.) Harvey K. Fretz, bn. Jan. 12, 1878.
V. Annie High, bn. —. Mrd. Garret Shoemaker, —. He died —. Farmer. Menn. One child:
VI. Mary Ann Shoemaker, bn. Nov. 25, 1844. Mrd. Tobias Schrauger, Nov. 10, 1864. P. O., Souderton, Pa. Farmer. Menn. Children:
VII. Garet Schrauger, bn. Sept. 27, 1866. Mrd. Tillie Barnt, Jan. 5, 1888. One child: (VIII.) Wellington Schrauger, bn. Nov. 12, 1888.

VII. Annie Schrauger, bn. June 29, 1873; died Mar. 27, 1883.

VII. Katie Schrauger, bn. Mar. 27, 1879.

VII. Ellen Schrauger, bn. Aug. 26, 1881.

V. David High, bn. —; died —, aged 20 years.

V. John H. High, bn. —. Mrd. Rebecca Fry, Nov. 8, 1846. P. O., Plumsteadville, Pa. Farmer. Menn. Children: Mahlon, Amanda, Mary, Henry.

VI. Mahlon F. High, bn. Feb. 27, 1848. Mrd. Annie Detweiler, —. Farmer. Menn. Children: **(VII.)** John High. **(VII.)** Joseph High. **(VII.)** —.

VI. Amanda High, bn. June 26, 1850. Mrd. David Myers. P. O., Bedminster, Pa. Hotel-keeper. Children: **(VII.)** Oscar High. **(VII.)** Mary Lizzie High. **(VII.)** Anna May High.

VI. Mary High, bn. June 18, 1856. S.

VI. Henry High, bn. Mar. 20, 1858. Mrd. Sue Johnson, —. Children: **(VII.)** A son, bn. —; died —. **(VII.)** A son, —.

V. Jacob H. High, bn. in 1819. Mrd. Anna Moyer, daughter of Jacob Moyer, —. P. O., Dublin, Pa. Farmer. Menn. Children: Abraham, Jacob, Henry, Elizabeth, Philip.

VI. Abraham M. High, bn. —. Mrd. — Lapp. P. O., Chalfont, Pa. Seven children.

VI. Jacob M. High, bn. —. Mrd. Lydia Meyers. P. O., Dublin, Pa. Three children.

VI. Henry M. High, bn. —. Mrd. Ida Keller, —. P. O., Dublin, Pa. Merchant-tailor. One child **(VII.)** —.

VI. Elizabeth High, bn. —. Mrd. Jacob Frank. P. O., 312, 2d St., Allentown, Pa. Laborer. Ger. Ref. ch. Children: **(VII.)** Ida Frank, bn. —. **(VII.)** — Frank, bn. —; died —.

VI. Philip High, bn. —; died —, aged 29 years, 11 months. S.

V. Henry H. High, bn. Oct. 26, 1821. Mrd. Lydia Moyer, Nov. 1, 1850. She was bn. May 13, 1831; died Oct. 19, 1856. Children: Mary, Lizzie, Samuel. —Henry mrd. second wife, Annie Yoder, Mar. 21, 1880. P. O., Blooming Glen, Pa. Farmer. Menn. Children: Sue, Henry, Annie.

VI. Mary High, bn. Feb. 2, 1852. Mrd. John D. Detweiler, —. P. O., Sellersville, Pa. Farmer. Children: (VII.) Clayton Detweiler, bn. July 29, 1878. (VII.) Lizzie Detweiler, bn. Nov. 4, 1879. (VII.) Allen Detweiler, bn. Dec. 3, 1882. (VII.) Anna Detweiler, bn. Feb. 22, 1884. (VII.) Katie Detweiler, bn. Dec. 14, 1885. (VII.) Mamie Detweiler, bn. Dec. 25, 1887. (VII.) Susie Detweiler, bn. Mar. 1, 1889.

VI. Lizzie High, bn. Oct. 27, 1854. Mrd. Jacob Derstine, —. P. O., Sellersville, Pa. Farmer. Menn. Children: (VII.) Henry Derstine, bn. —; died —. (VII.) Mamie Derstine. (VII.) Katie Derstine. (VII.) Ida Derstine.

VI. Samuel High, bn. Oct. 11, 1856; died May 11, 1858.

VI. Sue High, bn. Apr. 28, 1859. S.

VI. Henry High, bn. Dec. 18, 1862. Mrd. Mary Hunsberger, Jan. 15, 1887. She was bn. Mar. 1, 1866. P. O., Blooming Glen, Pa. Farmer, lives on the old homestead. Menn. One child: (VII.) Elmer High, bn. Jan. 17, 1888.

VI. Annie High, bn. Aug. 23, 1866. Mrd. Levi N. Moyer. (See Index of References No. 17.)

V. Mary High, bn. —; died —. Mrd. Henry L. Kulp (his second wife), Oct. 26, 1846. Children: Elizabeth, Philip, Sarah, Jacob, Isaac.

VI. Elizabeth Kulp, bn. May 19, 1848. Mrd. Jacob S. Kulp in 1869. Farmer. Children: (VII.) Catharine Kulp, bn. 1870; died Apr. 11, 1877. (VII.) Henry Kulp, bn. 1872; died Apr. 11, 1877. (VII.) Abraham Kulp, bn. 1873; died Apr. 7, 1877. (VII.) Sarah Kulp, bn. 1876; died Apr. 24, 1876. (VII.) Jacob Kulp, bn. 1878. (VII.) Annie Kulp, born 1879. (VII.) Isaac Kulp, born 1880. (VII.) Lizzie Kulp, born 1882. (VII.) Harvey Kulp, born 1884. (VII.) John Kulp, bn. 1886. (VII.) Samuel Kulp, bn. 1888.

VI. Philip Kulp, bn. Dec. 25, 1850; died, infant.

VI. Sarah Ann Kulp, bn. Aug. 13, 1853. Mrd. Eli S. Strouse, Jan. 19, 1878. Laborer. Menn. Children: (VII.) Katie K. Strouse, bn. Aug. 22, 1879. (VII.) Lizzie K. Strouse, bn. July 3, 1881. (VII.)

Mary K. Strouse, bn. Nov. 1, 1882. **(VII.) Emma**
K. Strouse, bn. May 23, 1884. **(VII.)** Harry K.
Strouse, bn. July, 23, 1885. **(VII.)** Harvey K.
Strouse, bn. Feb. 8, 1887. **(VII.)** Annie K. Strouse,
bn. July 16, 1888.
VI. Jacob H. Kulp, bn. Sept. 13, 1855. Mrd. Sarah
Ann D. Kulp, Jan. 11, 1879. Farmer. Menn.
Children: **(VII.)** Harvey K. Kulp, bn. May 28, 1881.
(VII.) David K. Kulp, bn. May 10, 1884; died Apr.
30, 1888. **(VII.)** Katie K. Kulp, bn. Apr. 4. 1887;
died Aug. 27, 1887.
VI. Isaac H. Kulp, bn. Jan. 28, 1863. Mrd. Mary
Angeny, Feb. 19, 1887. P. O., Blooming Glen, Pa.
Laborer. Menn.
V. Lydia High, bn. —; died, aged about 20 years.
IV. Jacob High, bn. —; died —. Mrd. Annie Huns-
berger. No issue.
IV. John High, bn. Sept. 20, 1795; died May 20,
1874. Mrd. Mary Keypert,—. She was bn. July 24,
1797; died Dec. 15. 1858. Mr. High, Menn. Mrs.
High, Ger. Ref. Children: David, Jacob, Hannah,—,
Annie, Catharine, Lavina, Barbara.
V. David High, bn.—. Mrd.--Yeakel—. One child:
(VI.) Mary High, bn.—. Mrd. Wilson Hendricks.
V. Jacob High, bn.—; died Aug. 29, 1863. Mrd.
Mary Meyer, Apr. 9, 1859. She was bn. Oct. 23,
1839; died May 22, 1872. Laborer. Menn's. Children:
Lizzie, Mahlon.
VI. Lizzie High, bn. May 26, 1860. Mrd. Isaac
Bishop, Dec. 16, 1882. P. O., Dublin, Pa. Farmer.
Menn's. No issue.
VI. Mahlon M. High, bn. May 13, 1863; died Dec.
1888. Mrd. Mary Krout, in 1882. Shoemaker and
carriage trimmer. Ger. Ref. Children: **(VII.)** Oscar K.
High. **(VII.)** Henry High. **(VII.)** Susan High.
V. Hannah High, bn.- . Mrd. Reuben Moyer—.
V. Annie High, bn.—. Mrd. Jesse Klein,—. He died
-. Farmer. Luth. Children: Sarah, James.—Annie,
mrd. second husband Anthony Grass,—. P. O., Hill-
town, Pa. Farmer. Ger. Ref. One child: Levi.
VI. Sarah Jane Klein, bn.- . Mrd. Levi Snyder.
Farmer. Ger. Ref. One child: **(VII.)** Francis Snyder.

VI. James Klein, bn.—. Mrd. Ella Brunner,—. P. O.,
Souderton, Pa. Farmer. Luth. Children: **(VII.)** Irvin
Klein, bn. Dec. 30, 1876. **(VII.)** Leidy Klein, bn. Aug.
8, 1880. **(VII.)** Lizzie Florence Klein, bn.—.
VI. Levi Grass, bn.—.
V. Catharine High, bn, Feb. 14, 1820. Mrd. Henry
Albright, Esq.—. He died June 24, 1874. Farmer.
Justice of the Peace and conveyancer for nearly
twenty-five years. Was highly esteemed, and re-
spected by all. Ger. Ref. Children: Lucy, Reuben,
Mahlon, Henry, Mary, Charles, Lydia, Daniel, Titus.
VI. Lucy Albright, bn.—. Mrd. Simon Klein.—. P.
O., Lansdale, Pa. Teamster. Children: Emma, etc.
VII. Emma Kline, bn. May 3, 1856. Mrd. Jacob H.
Moyer, Oct. 11, 1873. P. O., Blooming Glen, Pa.
Superintendent of Blooming Glen Creamery. Menn.
Children: **(VIII.)** Azalia Moyer, bn. July 19, 1875;
died June 17, 1882. **(VIII.)** Titus K. Moyer, bn. Apr.
11, 1877. **(VIII.)** Abraham E. Moyer, bn. Mar. 25,
1879; died June 15, 1882. **(VIII.)** Mary Estella Moyer,
bn. July 16, 1881. **(VIII.)** Alice Kline Moyer, bn.
Sept. 14, 1883. **(VIII.)** Lucy Ann Moyer, bn. Dec. 12,
1885. **(VIII.)** Charlotte Grace Moyer, bn. Apr. 24,
1889.
VI. Reuben Albright, bn.—. Mrd. Christiana Huns-
berger, Oct. 29, 1870. P. O., Dublin, Pa. Farmer.
Presby. Children: **(VII.)** Oliver H. Albright, bn. Aug.
17, 1871. **(VII.)** Maggie Albright, bn. Aug. 24, 1873.
(VII.) Reuben H. Albright, bn. Aug. 4, 1875. **(VII.)**
Sadie Albright, bn. Aug. 1, 1877. **(VII.)** Philip H.
Albright, bn. Jan. 1, 1880; died Mar. 14, 1882. **(VII.)**
Howard H. Albright, bn. Mar. 24, 1882. **(VII.)** Grover
Cleveland Albright, bn. Mar. 28, 1885. **(VII.)** Katie
Albright, bn. Feb. 24, 1888. **(VII.)** Walter Albright,
bn. Feb. 27, 1891.
VI. Mahlon Albright, bn.—. Mrd.—. P. O., Colmar,
Pa.
VI. Henry Albright, bn. Aug. 6, 1850. Mrd. Sue M.
Bishop, Oct. 2, 1875. Ticket Ag't at Lansdale, Pa.
Ger. Ref.
VI. Mary Albright, bn. Dec. 22, 1852. Mrd. Isaiah
S. Bissey, Sept. 25, 1875. P. O., 1247 Sergent St,

Phila., Pa. Clerk P. R. R. R. Lehigh Ave. Phila.
Luth. Children: (VII.) Raymond Bissey, bn. Apr. 15,
1877. (VII.) Elwood Bissey, bn. Apr. 15, 1877; died
Apr. 17, 1877. (VII.) Oscar Bissey, bn. Jan. 25, 1879;
died Mar. 18, 1882. (VII.) Arabella Bissey, bn. Nov.
26, 1881; died Apr. 22, 1889.

VI. Charles Albright, bn.—. Mrd. Camilla Moyer
—. P. O., Blooming Glen, Pa. Tailor. Children:
(VII.)Bessie Albright. (VII.) Abner Albright.

VI. Lydia Albright, bn. in Hilltown Twp. Nov. 3,
1856. Mrd. George W. Scheip, Feb. 10, 1876. P. O.,
Fricks, Pa. Farmer. Ger. Ref. Children: (VII.) Will-
iam F. Scheip, bn. May 13, 1877. (VII.) Maria Scheip,
bn. Apr. 4, 1879; died Jan. 22, 1882. (VII.) Estella
Scheip, bn. July 14, 1880. (VII.)Martha Scheip, bn.
Mar. 2, 1883. (VII.) Viola Scheip, bn. Feb. 20, 1885.
(VII.) Mary Scheip, bn. Nov. 21, 1887. (VII.) Catha-
rine Scheip, bn. June 8, 1889. (VII.) Anna Scheip, bn.
Nov. 22, 1890.

VI. Daniel Albright, bn. Jan. 10, 1859. Mrd. Elizabeth Krupp, of Lansdale, Pa., Oct. 11, 1883. His
boyhood days were spent on his father's farm in Hilltown, Pa. When 16 years of age his father died. At
that time having shown some proficiency in his studies, his teacher Miss Emily Rowland, advised him to
prepare for the profession of teaching. Having a great
desire for knowledge, and receiving encouragement
at home, he concluded on a course, and in the spring
of 1875 entered the Millersville, Pa., State Normal
School, where he remained a number of terms, after
which he received license to teach, and taught the
home school in his native township for six months.
Feeling a lack of qualifications to teach properly, and
detesting the yearly examinations for provisional cer-
tificates, he concluded to overcome these obstacles,
and returned to the Millersville Normal School and
completed a Normal course, taking the degrees of
Master of the Elements, and Elementary Didactics,
completing the course in 1880. In the fall of 1880,
he took charge of a school in Lancaster Co. and became principal of the Borough Schools of Sellersville,
Bucks Co. in the fall of 1881, where he taught two

winters, and where he, during the summer of 1882, conducted a teacher's training class, enabling several pupils to pass satisfactorily the Superintendent's teacher's examinations. In the fall of 1882 he received the appointment of Principal of schools of the borough of Lansdale, Pa. where he remained two years. Then resigned, and discontinued teaching for a time, and later took charge of the schools of North Wales for one term. then taught a school in Durham Twp., Bucks Co., two terms. He then became ambitious for the position of County Superintendent of Bucks Co., and being solicited to become a candidate, he consented, but was defeated by a small majority. In the fall of 1887, he took charge of the schools at Hatboro, Pa. for one term, then quit teaching and entered the service of the Phila. and Reading R. R. serving one year as Station Ag't at Lansdale, after which he received the position of Freight Ag't at Phila. Meth. Ep. Children: **(VII.)** Mary Albright, bn. May 22, 1886. **(VII.)** Karl Albright, bn. Apr. 13, 1892.

VI. Titus Albright, M. D. bn. in Bucks Co., Feb. 4, 1861. Mrd. Lizzie E. Eckel, in 1883. At the age of seventeen years he entered the Millersville State Normal School taking a two years course, after which he taught school three consecutive winters in his native township. In the spring of 1882, he entered the office of his preceptor Dr. Harvey Kratz for the purpose of reading medicine. In the fall of '82 he was admitted to the University of Penna. Medical Dept., where he graduated in the spring of 1885. In the fall of '85 he located at Hatfield, Montg. Co., to practice his profession, and where he still resides and enjoys a lucrative practice. Children: **(VII.)** Eva Viola Albright. bn. Apr. 1, 1884. **(VII.)** Blanche Albright, bn. Feb. 17, 1886. **(VII.)** Markley Cameron Albright, bn. Mar. 6, 1888. **(VII.)** Robert Burdette Albright, bn. Apr. 14, 1890.

V. Lavina High, bn.—. Mrd. Thomas Kooker.—.

V. Barbara High, bn. in Hilltown Twp., Bucks Co., Aug. 29, 1827. Mrd. Aaron Andrews, in spring of 1849. He was bn. in Rockhill Twp., Oct. 19, 1823;

died in Hilltown Twp., Bucks Co., May 13, 1861. Carpenter and miller. Luth. One child:

VI. Reuben High Andrews, M. D. bn. in Hilltown Twp., Bucks Co., Pa., Jan. 20, 1850. He was the only child of Aaron and Barbara Andrews. His father was for some years a "boss" carpenter, and later on purchased a small tract of land along a creek in Hilltown Twp. located about a mile west of Dublin, near the site of an old saw mill. He erected a dwelling house and a grist mill, and the family lived there until the father died.

Reuben, after the death of his father, went to live with his grandfather Andrews in Marlborough Township near Berkyeomenville, Montg. Co., but in less than two years his grandfather also died and he went to live with his mother, who about this time married again to Henry S. Krout, a farmer of Bedminster Township, Bucks Co. There Reuben worked on the farm, attending the district school during the winter months.

When about eighteen years of age, he attended the boarding school then known as the Excelsior Normal Institute situated at Carversville and prepared himself for teaching. He taught his first term of public school at what was then called the Upper Sellersville School. After this he attended one term the Keystone State Normal School at Kutztown. This he followed by another term of teaching, this time his own district school in Bedminster Township. At the same time he commenced the study of medicine under the tutorship of the family physician Dr. Moses Rice, of Hagersville. While engaged for a few months as a substitute teacher in New Britian Township, Dr. Rice was taken ill and died. He continued his studies with Dr. Rice's successor, a Dr. Klingerman, but subsequently the late Dr. J. H. Krause of Plumsteadville became his preceptor. He entered the Medical Department of the University of Pennsylvania, and graduated in the spring of 1874. On the fourteenth of April of the same year he entered upon the practice of his profession at Kulpsville, Montg. Co., where he soon gained a liberal patronage. In

the fall of 1875, he married Miss Mary M. daughter
of Nathan Beidler, of Bedminster, Bucks County. In
the spring of 1876, he moved to Lansdale on the N.
P. Railroad where he soon purchased a lot and erected
a dwelling and an office. While here engaged in the
active duties of his profession, he conceived the idea
of publishing a monthly Medical Journal; and in
March 1879 issued the first number of "The Medical
Summary." In the early part of 1881, he bought a
half interest in the "Lansdale Reporter," the local
and weekly newspaper and printing establishment,
and in the summer of the same year built a home and
office for this business on Main Street called "Reporter Building." In the spring of 1884, on account
of failing health, and rapidly increasing duties pro-
fessionally and with his Medical Journal, he sold his
practice and dwelling to Dr. Samuel Seese. About
the same time he bought a house on Twenty-third
street Philadelphia, where he removed with his publication, "The Medical Summary." Here he lived
about a year, sold his property and removed to Lansdale, buying a building lot adjoining his former home.
There he at once commenced to build one of the finest
residences in that section at that time, and also at the
same time buying the other half interest in the "Reporter" newspaper and printing business. This business he conducted himself along with the Medical
Journal for about a year when he sold the entire interest of the Lansdale Reporter Printing and Publishing business and shortly afterwards returned to
Philadelphia, on Columbia Avenue, where, since sell-
ing out his practice in Lansdale, he has devoted al-
most his entire time, doing only a select practice, to
his medical publication "The Summary."

The monthly issue of "The Summary" has not been
less than 10,000 copies for several years past. It is a
national Journal circulating in every state and terri-
tory of the United States, and some in foreign countries.

He has three daughters, the two older ones, at
the time of the publication of this book, are attending
the Twelfth Grade in the George G. Meade, Grammar

School Philadelphia. **(VII.)** Lottie Grace Andrews, bn. Feb. 24, 1877. **(VII.)** Florence Mabel Andrews, bn. Jan. 4, 1879. **(VII.)** Beatrice Lilla Andrews, bn. Dec. 12, 1885.

IV. Annie High, born,—; died —. Mrd. Samuel Moyer, (his second wife)—. Deacon in the Menn. ch., Blooming Glen. One child:

V. Barbara Moyer, bn. July 26, 1813; died Aug. 1890. Mrd. Jacob Hunsicker, Sept. 4, 1835. He was born, Oct. 28, 1809; died May 29, 1880. Farmer. Menn. Children: Annie, Lydia, Hannah, Maria, Lana, Susan, Isaac, Sophia, Barbara, Leanna.

VI. Annie Hunsicker, bn. May 1, 1837. Mrd. Abraham Baum, Apr. 20, 1856. P. O., Blooming Glen, Pa. Farmer and butcher. Menn. Children: Henry, Mary, Hannah, Laura, Annie.

VII. Henry Baum, bn. May 11, 1857. Mrd. Sarah G. Moyer,—. P. O., Blooming Glen, Pa. Farmer and butcher. Menn. Children: **(VIII.)** Alice Baum, bn. Oct. 14, 1876; died Jan. 18, 1886. **(VIII.)** Arthur Baum, bn. Oct. 28, 1880. **(VIII.)** Stella Baum, bn. July 16, 1885. **(VIII.)** Sallie Baum, bn. Jan. 12, 1888. **(VIII.)** Addie Baum. bn. Nov. 5, 1891.

VII. Mary Ellen Baum, bn. Sept. 2, 1860. Mrd. Amandus Baringer, in 1877. P. O., Benjamin, Pa. Farmer. Ger. Ref. ch. Children: **(VIII.)** Wilson Baringer, bn. Nov. 7, 1877. **(VIII.)** Emma Baringer, bn. Aug. 13, 1879. **(VIII.)** Francis Baringer, bn. May 20, 1882. **(VIII.)** Annie Baringer, bn. July 2, 1892.

VII. Hannah Baum, bn. June 6, 1862. Mrd. Christian G. Moyer,—. P. O., Blooming Glen, Pa. Farmer. Menn. Children: **(VIII.)** Minnie Moyer, bn. Feb. 25, 1884. **(VIII.)** Mamie Moyer, bn. Aug. 22, 1885. **(VIII.)** Elmer Moyer, bn. Apr. 27, 1888.

VII. Laura Baum, bn. June 4, 1871; died Mar. 1, 1878.

VII. Annie Baum, bn. July 4, 1873; died Sept. 11, 1873.

VI. Lydia Hunsicker, bn. Nov. 2, 1839; died Mar. 8, 1845.

VI. Hannah Hunsicker, born, Sept. 8, 1841. Mrd. Joseph Johnson, in 1859. He was bn. in 1834. P.

O:. Benjamin, Pa. Ev. Ass'n. Children: (VII.) Abraham Johnson, bn. Feb. 1861; died—. (VII.) Emma Johnson, bn. June 8, 1869. S.

VI. Maria Hunsicker, born, July 26, 1843. Mrd. William Baum,—. P. O., Bedminster, Pa. Farmer, and director of Souderton National Bank. Children: Hannah, Harvey, Ida,—.

VII. Hannah Baum, bn.—. Mrd. Samuel Moyer,—. P. O., Blooming Glen, Pa. One child: (VIII.) Arthur Moyer.

VII. Harvey Baum, bn.—. Mrd.—. P. O., Dublin, Pa.

VII. Ida Baum, bn.—.

VII. — Baum,—.

VI. Lana Hunsicker, bn. Sept. 5, 1844; died Apr. 1, 1845.

VI. Susanna Hunsicker, born. Sept. 29, 1846. Mrd. Ephraim Moyer. Oct. 29, 1864. P. O., Blooming Glen, Pa. Carpenter. Menn. Children: Emma, Milton, Jacob, William, Harry, Wilson, Clayton, Susan, Ida, Florence.

VII. Emma Moyer, bn. Aug. 27, 1865. Mrd. Hiram G. Moyer, Dec. 1884. P. O.. Blooming Glen, Pa. Farmer. Menn. Children: (VIII.) Cora Moyer, born, Feb. 21, 1886. (VIII.) Della Moyer, bn. Dec. 11, 1888. (VIII.) Bertha Moyer, bn. Feb. 17, 1891.

VII. Milton Moyer, bn. Nov. 10, 1866; died Feb. 11, 1868.

VII. Jacob Moyer, bn. Nov. 16, 1868; died May 8, 1877.

VII. William Moyer, bn. Sept. 25, 1871; died Oct. 16, 1871.

VII. Harry Moyer, bn. Jan. 6, 1873.

VII. Wilson Moyer, bn, Apr. 24, 1876; died May 8, 1877.

VII. Clayton Moyer, bn. Apr. 27, 1879.

VII. Susan Madora Moyer, bn. Aug. 13, 1881.

VII. Ida May Moyer, bn. Feb. 21, 1886; died Aug. 12, 1886.

VII. Florence Moyer, bn. Feb. 10, 1890.

VI. Isaac Hunsicker, bn. Dec. 26, 1849. Mrd. Sarah Cassel, in 1871. She died Sept. 24, 1878. P. O., Ben-

― 64 ―

jamin, Pa. Farmer. Menn. Children: (VII.) Henry
Hunsicker, bn. June 4, 1872. (VII.) Jacob Hunsicker,
bn. Apr. 23, 1874; died Mar. 30, 1876. (VII.) Martin
Hunsicker, born, Sept. 11, 1875. (VII.) Allen Hun-
sicker, bn. Oct. 17, 1877; died Feb. 26, 1879. Isaac
mrd. second wife Susanna Derstine,—. Children:
(VII.) Sallie Hunsicker, bn. July 3, 1880. (VII.)
Abraham Hunsicker, bn. Dec. 4, 1881. (VII.) Lizzie
Hunsicker, bn. September 2, 1883. (VII.) Harvey
Hunsicker, bn. June 10, 1885. (VII.) Annie Hunsicker,
bn. Apr. 15, 1887. (VII.) Hiram Hunsicker, bn. Sept.
22, 1888. (VII.) Elmer Hunsicker, bn. Jan. 18, 1890.
(VII.) Wilson Hunsicker, bn. May 3, 1891.

VI. Sophia E. M. Hunsicker, bn. in Bucks Co.,
July 17, 1851. Mrd. Zachary T. Waltz, Nov. 2, 1875.
P. O., Perkasie, Pa. Custom tailor. Ger. Ref. ch.
Children: (VII.) Arthur H. Waltz, bn. July 31, 1880;
died Apr. 3. 1883. (VII.) William H. Waltz, bn. Dec.
4, 1882. (VII.) Lillie H. Waltz, bn. Feb. 25, 1877;
died same day.

VI. Barbara Hunsicker, bn. Oct. 8, 1853. Mrd.
Peter Yoder.—. P. O., Blooming Glen, Pa. Farmer.
Menn. No issue.

VI. Leanna Hunsicker, bn. Aug. 1, 1855; died Sept.
24, 1855.

IV. Barbara High, bn. Aug. 11, 1798; died Oct. 24,
1883. Mrd. Samuel Moyer,* —, (son of Deacon
Samuel Moyer, by a former wife). Lived on a farm
now owned by Christian F. Moyer, near Blooming
Glen, Pa. Menn. Children: John, Annie, Maria,
David, Abraham, Hannah, Susan.

V. John Moyer, bn. Nov. 12, 1818. Mrd. Lizzie
Moyer,—. Farmer and drover. Menn. Children:
Barbara, Hiram, Amanda, Hannah, Mary, Lizzie,
Samuel, John.

VI. Barbara Moyer, bn.—. Mrd. Abraham Cassel.
P. O., Sterling, Ill. Children: (VII.) Clayton. (VII.)
Mamie. (VII.) Gertie.

* This is a rare incident for a father and son to marry
sisters.

VI. Hiram Moyer, bn.—. Mrd.—. P. O., Sterling, Ill.

VI. Amanda Moyer, bn.—. Mrd. —Roth,—. P.O., Sterling. Ill. Children: (**VII.**) Belle. (**VII.**) Lena Pearl.

VI. Mary Moyer, bn.—.

VI. Hannah Moyer, bn.—. Mrd. —Trewdeon,—. P.O., Sterling, Ill. One child: (**VII.**) Harry Trewdeon.

VI. Lizzie Moyer, bn.—. Mrd. —Wright. P. O., Sterling, Ill.

VI. Samuel Moyer, bn.—. Mrd. Irene—. P. O., Sterling, Ill. One child: (**VII.**)—.

VI. John Moyer, bn.—.

V. Anna Moyer, bn. July 29, 1820; died—. Mrd. Henry Button. He was born about 1816; died—. Justice of the Peace, etc. Children: James, Susanna, Infant, Infant, Maria, Sylvester.—Anna mrd. second husband James Bergey,—. No issue.

VI. James Button, bn.—; died—. Mrd. Hannah Slotter,—. One child: (**VII.**) James.

VI. Susanna Button, bn.—; died aged 16 yrs. S.

VI. Infant bn.—; died unnamed.

VI. Infant bn.—; died unnamed.

VI. Maria Button, bn.—. Mrd. Charles Weisel—. P. O., Benjamin, Pa. Cigar-maker. Children: (**VII.**) Infant. (**VII.**) Infant. (**VII.**) Lottie. (**VII.**) Wallace. (**VII.**) Annie. (**VII.**) Emma.

VI. Sylvester Button, bn.—. Mrd. —Cline,—, Res. Philadelphia. Children: (**VII.**) Florence. (**VII.**) Roscoe. (**VII.**) Bertrum. (**VII.**) Della.

VI. Emma, bn—. Mrd. Abraham Groff,—. P. O., Sellersville, Pa. Blacksmith. Children: (**VII.**) Howard Groff. (**VII.**) Walter Groff.

V. Maria Moyer, bn. Nov. 30, 1822. Mrd. Peter L. Snyder,—. He died—. Farmer. Luth. One child: (**VI.**) Hannah Snyder, died aged 21 yrs. Maria mrd. second husband Jacob Baughman—. He died—. No issue.

V. David Meyers, bn. Mar. 4, 1826. Mrd. Margaret Hendricks,—. Merchant. Children: (**VI.**) Frank. (**VI.**) Phares. (**VI.**) David. (**VI.**) Lincoln. (**VI.**) Simeon. (**VI.**) Lizzie. (**VI.**)—.

V. Abraham H. Myers, bn in Bucks Co., Pa.,
June 3, 1829. Mrd. Hannah Alderfer, June 13, 1850.
P. O., Sterling, Ill. Carpenter and painter. Menn's.
Children: Isabella, James, Amanda, Jemima, Maria,
Nelson, Lincoln, Irvin, William, John, Grant, Hiram,
Frank, Nettie.

VI. Isabella Myers, bn. Jan. 7, 1851; died Aug. 5,
1852.

VI. James Myers, bn. Sept. 3, 1852. S.

VI. Amanda Myers, bn. Sept. 5, 1854. Mrd. E. I.
Stedman, July 4, 1872. P. O., Unadilla, Neb.

VI. Jemima Myers, bn. Sept. 20, 1856; died Mar.
28, 1881. Mrd. William Stedman, Jan. 1876
Children: **(VII.)** Boy Stedman, bn—; died—, aged 3
years. **(VII.)** —Stedman, bn—.

VI. Maria Myers, bn. July 7, 1858; died Sept. 12,
1858.

VI. Nelson Myers, bn. July 22, 1859. Engineer. S.

VI. Lincoln Myers, bn. Aug. 31, 1861. Mrd.—.
Farmer.

VI. Irvin Myers, bn. July 20, 1863; died Jan. 29,
1881.

VI. William Myers, bn. Sept. 17, 1865. Engineer. S.

VI. John Myers, bn. June 22, 1867. Brick-mason. S.

VI. Grant Myers, bn. Mar. 28, 1869. S.

VI. Hiram Myers, bn. Aug. 11, 1871. Mrd.— —.
One son: **(VII.)** —.

VI. Frank Myers, bn. Nov. 20, 1875; died Jan. 13,
1879.

VI. Nettie Myers, bn. Dec. 8, 1878; died Nov. 26,
1881.

V. Hannah Moyer, bn. Jan. 18, 1831. Mrd. Enos
Savacool,—. P. O., Benjamin, Pa. Merchant. Luth.
Children: Susan, James, William, Levi, Frank.

VI. Susan Savacool, bn. Oct. 9, 1854; died infant.

VI. James Irvin Savacool, bn. Jan. 8, 1856; died
aged 8 years.

VI. William Savacool, bn. Feb. 18, 1858. Mrd. Ella
Stoneback. She died in 1886. Children: **(VII.)** Lizzie
Savacool. **(VII.)** Erwin Savacool.—William married
second wife Mrs. Lavina Savacool—. P. O., Perkasie,

Pa. Dealer in coal and lumber. Luth. Children:
(VII.) Hannah Savacool. (VII.) Robert Patterson
Savacool.
   VI. Levi Savacool, bn.—; died aged about 20 years.
   VI. Frank Savacool, bn. Dec. 5, 1864. Mrd. Malinda
Wigner—. Salesman in Philadelphia, Pa. No issue.
   V. Susan Moyer, bn. Oct. 11, 1834; died Mar. 26,
1858. Mrd. Thomas B. Deetz, Oct. 14, 1854. P. O.,
Sellersville, Pa. Carriage builder. Luth. Children:
(VI.) Emma Jane Deetz, bn. Mar. 3, 1856; died Sept.
25, 1857. (VI.) Jacob Irwin Deetz, bn. Mar. 11, 1858;
died July 17, 1858.
   IV. Mary High, bn. in Bucks Co. Pa. about 1790;
died in Summit Co., Ohio, in 1861. Mrd. David
Newcomer,—. He died in 1833. Carpenter. Menn.
Children: Barbara, John, Annie, David, Mary, Susan,
Eliza, Lavina, Jacob. — Mrd. second husband Jacob
Fretz, in 1839. He died in 1865. Shoemaker. Menn.
   V. Barbara Newcomer, bn.—; died—. Mrd. Mathias
Smith,- . Children: (VI.) Jacob Smith, bn.—. P. O.,
Athens, Mich. (VI.) Caroline Smith bn.—. Mrd.
Wm. H. Yonkey. P. O., Wadsworth, O. (VI.) David
Smith, bn.—; died 1876. 24 yrs. (VI.) Elizabeth Smith,
bn:— died young. (VI.) Harvey Smith, bn—. Married
Corda Wagner. P. O., Wadsworth, O.
   V. John Newcomer, bn.--; died infant.
   V. Nancy Newcomer, bn. in Bucks Co., Pa., July
8, 1816; died at Sterling, Ill. June 7, 1888. Mrd. John
Kline, in 1838. He was bn. July 17, 1814; died June
2, 1864. Farmer. Menn. Children: Henry, Mary,
Susanna, John, Emeline, Lavina, Elizabeth, Sarah.
   VI. Henry N. Kline, bn. in Montg. Co., Pa., Nov.
18, 1838. Mrd. Mary A. Cassel—, P. O., Mendon,
Mich. Farmer. Children: (VII.) Frank Kline, bn. May
5, 1867. (VII.) Charles Kline, bn. Sept. 19, 1868.
   VI. Mary Ann Kline, bn. Oct. 1, 1840. Mrd. Lewis
Vogt, Oct. 2, 1860. P. O., Sterling, Ill. Luth.
Children: Susanna, Margaret, Josephine, Agnes,
Emeline, Edith, Ida, John, Clara.
   VII. Susanna Vogt, bn. July 13, 1861. Mrd. Ross
Overly, July 13, 1882. P. O., Sterling, Ill. One
child: (VIII.) Nellie Overly, bn. May 10, 1883.

VII. Margaret A. Vogt, bn. Oct. 10, 1862. Mrd. Norton Bush, May 25, 1883. He died Mar. 5, 1889. Children: **(VIII.)** Franklin L. Bush, bn. Apr. 1, 1884. **(VIII.)** Gertrude G. Bush, bn. July 10, 1885. **(VIII.)** Mabel M. Bush, bn. Nov. 3, 1886. **(VIII.)** Henry Oliver Bush, bn. Oct. 11, 1888.—Margaret mrd. second husband John F. Johnson, June 4, 1891. P. O., Sterling, Ill. One child: **(VIII.)** Hattie Irene Johnson, bn. May 6, 1892.

VII. Josephine Vogt, bn. July 28, 1866. Mrd. Elmer Coopernell in 1885. He died May 29, 1886. One child: **(VIII.)** Eva Maud Coopernell, bn. Mar. 4, 1885; died May 19, 1886.—Josephine mrd. second husband Daniel Grant, Dec. 31, 1891. P. O., 26 N. Ashland Ave., Chicago, Ill.

VII. Agnes May Vogt, bn. Mar. 3, 1868. Mrd. William Kraft, Mar. 17, 1892. P. O., Sterling, Ill.

VII. Emeline Vogt, bn. Mar. 14, 1871. Mrd. Fred. Duffield, Jan. 16, 1892. P. O., Sterling, Ill.

VII. Edith Vogt, bn. Jan. 30, 1873; died Apr. 4, 1873.

VII. Ida May Vogt, bn. Oct. 28, 1874.

VII. John Martin Vogt, bn. Jan. 3, 1877.

VII. Clara Vogt, bn. July 9, 1879.

VI. Susanna Kline, bn. in Montg. Co., Pa., Sept. 3, 1842. Mrd. Benjamin A. Schultz, Nov. 15, 1864. He died May 19, 1874. P. O., Sterling, Ill. Cong. Children: **(VII.)** Samuel Henry Schultz, bn. Apr. 8, 1865; died Mar. 31, 1882. **(VII.)** James K. Schultz, bn. Feb. 18, 1869. **(VII.)** Edwin K. Schultz, bn. Jan. 15, 1872.

VI. John N. Kline, bn. July 15, 1845; died Apr. 21, 1887.

VI. Emeline Kline, bn. Mar. 22, 1848. Mrd. Edward H. Wildasin, May 17, 1867. P. O., Sterling, Ill. Children: **(VII.)** Anna Larame Wildasin, born Feb. 13, 1868. **(VII.)** Joshua Wildasin, born Nov. 1, 1872.

VI. Lavina Kline, bn. Dec. 19, 1850. Mrd. Abraham B. Hunsberger, Apr. 7, 1869. P. O., Sterling, Ill. Baptists. Children: **(VII.)** Alvin R. Hunsberger,

Jacob Kratz Homestead, Hilltown Bucks Co., Pa (See page 30.)

bn. July 14, 1871. Electrician. (VII.) Bertha G.
Hunsberger, bn. July 7, 1876. Baptist. (VII.) Mabel
A. Hunsberger, bn. Mar. 7, 1885.
VI. Elizabeth Kline, bn. May 10, 1857. Mrd. Frank
Compton, Aug. 18, 1874. P. O., Sterling, Ill. Chil-
dren: (VII.) Anna Belle Compton, bn. Dec. 22, 1874.
Mrd. Ephraim B. Shumaker, Sept. 28, 1892. P. O.,
Sterling, Ill. Baptists. (VII.) Clarence Eugene
Compton, born June 14, 1877. (VII.) Claud Elmer
Compton, born June 14, 1877; died Aug. 29, 1877.
(VII.) Olive Maud Compton, bn. Mar. 26, 1879. (VII.)
Eva Blanch Compton, bn. Aug. 2, 1881.
VI. Sarah Ann Kline, bn. Mar. 9, 1859. Mrd. An-
drew J. Pexton, Apr. 11, 1881. P. O., Sterling, Ill.
One child: (VII.) Edwin H. Pexton, bn. Dec. 16, 1882.
V. David Newcomer, bn. —; died. Mrd. —. Dea-
con in Menn. ch. Children: (VI.) Annie Newcomer,
bn. —. Res. 123 Pigeon St., Elkhart, Ind. (VI,).
Mathias Newcomer, bn. —. P. O., Wakarusa, Ind.
(VI.) Barbara Newcomer, bn. —. Mrd. — Ginrich.
Res. 720 Main St., Goshen, Ind.—David mrd. second
wife Esther Wismer, in 1860. No issue.
V. Mary Newcomer, born in Bucks Co., Pa.,
Apr. 21, 1820. Mrd. Charles Cassel, Oct. 8, 1840.
He was bn. May 4, 1812; died Jan. 12, 1888. Was
blind 3 or 4 years. P. O., Doylestown, O. Farmer.
Baptists. Children: Ann, David, Mary, Lovina, Joel,
Sarah, George, Elizabeth, Susanna, Jacob, Charles.
VI. Ann Cassel, born Apr. 3, 1842. Mrd. Louis
Roland —. P. O., Port Providence, Pa. R. R. en-
gineer. Baptists. Children: (VII.) Clarence, (VII.)
Elhanan, (VII.) Benny, (VII.) Albanus, (VII.) Lewis.
Of these children Elhanan and Benny met with a
very sad death. Clarence the eldest had gone to Port
Providence for the mail, and when returning was met
about ¼ mile from home by his brothers. By the
roadside was a sand hole, into which all jumped
except little Louis. Suddenly the overhanging bank
gave way and buried the three eldest and the fourth
all but his head. Albanus told Louis to give the
alarm, and help soon came. Albanus was rescued
uninjured. Clarence was next reached, and was sup-

6

posed to be dead, but was resuscitated in a little
while. As soon as possible Elhanan and Benny were
reached, but both were dead, though only covered
with eighteen inches of sand. The funeral of the two
boys was largely attended. The ministers present
were Rev's. C. I. Tompson, Jacob Meyers, Jacob
Gottwals and C. C. Walker. The sight was a sorrow-
ful one, and many a strong man broke in tears as
they gazed upon the little forms so suddenly cut
off upon the threshold of life.

VI. David Cassel, bn. Aug. 1, 1843. Mrd. Lucy
Cramer, —. P. O., Clinton, Iowa. Children: (VII.)
Huldah May Cassel, bn. —; died —. (VII.) Walter
Cassel. (VII.) Charles Harvey Cassel. (VII.) Clara
Bell Cassel.

VI. Mary A. Cassel, bn. Feb. 28, 1845. Mrd. Henry
N. Kline. (See Index of References No. 18.)

VI. Lovina Cassel, bn. Nov. 27, 1846. Mrd. William
Kindig, —. He died in 1872. P. O., 174 East 4th
St., Canton, Ohio. Baptist. Children: (VII.) Jesse
DeCorsa Kindig. (VII.) Clyde Allen Kindig.

VI. Joel Cassel, born Mar. 27, 1850; died Feb. 11,
1853.

VI. Sarah Jane Cassel, bn. Jan. 20, 1852. Mrd.
Charles G. Folsom, July 15, 1891. P. O., 178 Elder
St., South Bend, Ind. Tinner.

VI. George Cassel, bn. Jan. 7, 1859. P. O., Tacoma,
Wash. Farmer. S.

VI. Elizabeth Cassel, bn. Sept. 18, 1855. Mrd.
David Beal, —. P. O., Doylestown, O. Contractor
and builder. Children: (VII.) Mary Beal. (VII.) Florence Adella Beal. (VII.) Willis Roy Beal.

VI. Susanna Cassel, bn. Aug, 14, 1857. Mrd. Charles
Betz, —. P. O., Medina, O. Farmer. Children:
(VII.) Ellen Betz. (VII.) Aden Betz. (VII.) Jennie
Elta Betz (dec'd). (VII.) Russel Betz. (VII.) Benny
Betz. (VII.) Mary Alfia Betz.

VI. Jacob Cassel, bn. Sept. 26, 1859. Mrd. Anna
Kuhn, Oct. 22, 1892. P. O., Tacoma, Wash. Land-
lord. Agnostic.

VI. Charles Cassel, bn. in Medina Co., O., Jan. 17,
1863. Mrd. Lucy Snyder, Jan. 17, 1885. P. O.,

Youngstown, O. Manufacturer of patterns. Children:
(VII.) George Ellis Cassel, bn. Feb. 28, 1886. (VII.)
Frank Nelson Cassel, bn. June 26, 1887. (VII.)
Charles Everett Cassel, bn. Oct. 20, 1891.

V. Susan Newcomer, bn. —. Mrd. Mathias Smith,
—. He died 1892. No issue.

V. Eliza Newcomer, born July 23, 1824. Mrd.
Hiram R. Fenimore, Oct. 10, 1860. He died Apr.
14, 1891. P. O., Akron, O. Farmer. Baptists
Children: Milton, Ella, Hiram, Adelbert.

VI. Milton M. Fenimore, bn. Aug. 9, 1861. Machinist.

VI. Ella N. Fenimore, bn. Feb. 18, 1864. Saleslady.

VI. Hiram A. Fenimore, bn. Feb. 26, 1866. Machinist. Baptist.

VI. Adelbert L. Fenimore, bn. Feb. 9, 1868. Mrd.
Nora Hunt, Dec. 24, 1890. P. O., Akron, O. Ma-
chinist. Baptist. One child: (VII.) Helen Maria
Fenimore, bn. Nov. 10, 1891.

V. Lavina M. Newcomer, born in Bucks Co., Pa.,
Oct 2, 1826. Mrd. George Decker, Sept. 30, 1852.
P. O., Johnson's Corners, O. Shoemaker. Lutheran.
No issue.

V. Jacob Newcomer, bn. —. Mrd. Catharine Daub,
—. P. O., Wakarusa, Ind. Children: (VI.) Samuel.
(VI.) Harvey.

III. Hannah Wismer, born in Bucks Co., Pa.,
Feb. 17, 1764; died —. Mrd. John Schattinger, *
son of †Hans George Schattinger, —. Farmer.
Menn. Children: Margaret, Abraham, Anna, John,
Mary, Henry, Joseph, Jacob.

---

*It is said that Schattinger was the original mode of
spelling the name, but it is now spelled Shattinger and Shaddinger, by the descendants.

†Hans George Shaddinger, according to the tradition
of the family was a native of Wittenburgh, Germany. Emigrated to America in the ship Patience from Rotterdam, last
from Cowes. Arrived Sept. 17, 1753. Taught school at
Deep Run. Had rent free for taking care of the Mennonite
meeting-house. Children: Abraham, John, Andrew, Elizabeth, (mrd. Tinsman) and other daughters.

IV. Margaret Schattinger, born —. Mrd. Jacob Gross, —. Lived in Ohio.

IV. Abraham Shaddinger, bn. Jan. 8, 1789; died —. Mrd. Agnes Landis, Oct. 20, 1812. She was bn. July 29, 1791; died Apr. 28, 1852. Weaver. Menn. Children: Jacob, Mary, John, Hannah, Magdalena, Sarah.

V. Jacob L. Shaddinger, bn. July 22, 1813. Mrd. Mary Leatherman, Mar. 8, 1842. She died —. P. O., Dublin, Pa. Retired farmer. Menn. Children: Sophia, Mary, Charles, Edward, Sallie, Elias.—Jacob mrd. second wife Sarah Fretz, Mar. 23, 1875.

VI. Sophia Shaddinger, bn. Apr. 12, 1844. Mrd. Henry M. Kratz. (See Index of References No. 83.)

VI. Mary Ann Shaddinger, bn. July 18, 1847. Mrd. Rev. Henry B. Rosenberger, Dec. 19, 1868. Farmer and minister. Mr. Rosenberger was ordained to the ministry of the Mennonite church at Blooming Glen, Pa., where he has since served as one of the ministers. No issue.

VI. Charles F. Shaddinger, bn. June 15, 1850; died June 2, 1876. Carpenter. Menn.

VI. Edward E. Shaddinger, bn. Dec. 21, 1852; died Oct. 29, 1884. Mrd. Anna Rosenberger, Nov. 23, 1879. Farmer. Menn. One child: (**VII.**) Henry Shaddinger. bn. May 23, 1881.

VI. Sallie Shaddinger, born Sept. 30, 1855; died Aug. 20, 1879. Menn.

VI. Elias F. Shaddinger, born Sept. 11, 1858; died Feb. 4, 1863.

V. Mary L. Shaddinger, bn. Aug. 31, 1815. Mrd. Christian Gayman, Sept. 30, 1845. Farmer near Fountainville, Penna. Menn. Children: Abraham, Harvey.

VI. A. James Gayman, bn. Oct. 12, 1847. Mrd. Lydia Swartzlander, June 14, 1877. Mr. G. began teaching school in 1866 and has followed that profession ever since. One child: (**VII.**) Paul Swartzlander Gayman, bn. May 13, 1885.

VI. Harvey Gayman, born Apr. 12, 1849. Mrd. Sarah Gross, in Sept. 1876. Formerly school-teacher, now farmer. P. O., Fountainville, Pa. Children:

(VII.) Bertha Gayman, bn. July 23, 1879. (VII.) J.
Willis Gayman, born Sept. 4, 1882; died Feb. 23,
1889. (VII.) George G. Gayman, bn. Mar. 1, 1886.
V. John L. Shaddinger, bn. July 16, 1818. Mrd.
Catharine Seblotter, Oct. 8, 1840. P. O., Blooming
Glen, Pa. Carpenter. Menn. Children: William,
Mary, Harvey, John, Susanna.
VI. William J. Shaddinger, bn. Sept. 24, 1841. He
enlisted in 1862 in the 104th Reg't, Co. A. Penna. Inf.,
and was killed by a bomb on Morris Island, at the
siege of Fort Wagner, Aug. 21, 1863.
VI. Mary Elizabeth Shaddinger, bn. Dec. 4, 1844;
died —. Mrd. William M. Kratz, —. Menn. No
issue.
VI. Harvey Shaddinger, bn. July 15, 1848. Mrd.
Annie Fretz, Nov. 23, 1872. Saddler, painter and
paper-hanger. P. O., Kansas City, Mo. Baptists.
Children: (VII.) Willie Ira Shaddinger, bn. Apr. 24,
1876. (VII.) John Alvin Shaddinger, bn. Jan. 1,
1883. (VII.) Anna Laura Shaddinger, bn. Dec. 18,
1884. (VII.) Ina May Shaddinger, bn. May 1, 1887.
VI. John Henry Shaddinger, bn. Aug. 14, 1853.
Paper-hanger at Little Rock, Ark.
VI. Susanna Shaddinger, bn. Feb. 22, 1859. Mrd.
William D. Bishop, Oct. 31, 1878. Merchant of the
firm Bishop and Bro., Blooming Glen, Pa. Menn.
Children: (VII.) Katie Florence Bishop, bn. Mar. 4,
1880. (VII.) Lizzie Cora Bishop, born, Nov. 4, 1881.
(VII.) Walter S. Bishop, bn. Dec. 29, 1885.
V. Hannah Shaddinger, born Dec. 2, 1821. Mrd.
Joseph Leatherman,—. Farmer. Menn. Children:
Abraham, William.
VI. Abraham S. Leatherman, born, June 14, 1847.
Mrd. Ella Snyder, Feb. 5, 1874. Veterinary Surgeon
at Clinton, N. J. One child: (VII.) Maud Leatherman,
bn. May 25, 1875.
VI. William S. Leatherman.
V. Magdalena Shaddinger, bn. June 17, 1826. Mrd.
Samuel A. Detweiler, Sept. 10, 1845. He died Oct.
23, 1873, in Ill. Christian ch. Children: Joseph,
Clayton, Mary, Hannah, Edwin, Abia, Henry, Anna,
Harvey.

VI. Joseph S. Detweiler, bn. in Bucks Co., Pa., Aug. 21, 1847. Mrd. Fannie R. Rutt, Sept. 12, 1872. P. O., Sterling, Ill. Merchant. Christians. Children: **(VII.)** Ira Grant Detweiler, bn. Oct. 17, 1873. **(VII.)** Harry Detweiler, bn. Aug. 31, 1875. **(VII.)** Guy Leroy Detweiler, bn. June 8, 1880. **(VII.)** Anna Pearl Detweiler, bn. July 10, 1888.

VI. Clayton S. Detweiler, bn. Aug. 29, 1850. Mrd. Cora A. Noble, Dec. 27, 1883. P. O., Clay Centre, Neb. Farmer. Christian. Wife Cong. Children: **(VII.)**Fannie Lucile Detweiler, bn. June 4, 1885. **(VII.)** Verne Noble Detweiler, bn. May 8, 1887.

VI. Mary Ann Detweiler, born May 12, 1852; died Dec. 14, 1864.

VI. Hannah Detweiler, bn. Dec. 23, 1854. Mrd. Christian R. Rutt, Sept. 12, 1872. Wheelwright in Whiteside Co., Ill. Christians. Children: **(VII.)** Martin Elwood Rutt, bn. Mar. 11, 1874; died Aug. 20, 1879. **(VII.)** Ida May Rutt, bn. Nov. 22, 1877; died Aug 21, 1879. **(VII.)** John Clayton Rutt, bn. Mar. 15, 1879. **(VII.)** Albert Leroy Rutt, bn. Sept. 10, 1880; died Nov. 26, 1884. **(VII.)** Samuel Urr Rutt, bn. Oct. 21, 1882; died Dec. 27, 1882. **(VII.)** William Lloyd Rutt, bn. Feb. 15, 1886.

VI. Edwin S. Detweiler, M. D. bn. May 9, 1856. Physician in Chicago, Ill. Cong.

VI. Abia John Detweiler, bn. at Sterling, Ill., Feb. 27, 1860. Mrd. Lena Brooks, Dec. 21, 1882. P. O., Clay Centre, Neb. Farmer. Christians. Children: **(VII.)** Bertha Detweiler, bn. Oct. 15, 1883. **(VII.)** Magdalena Detweiler, bn. Mar. 4, 1885. **(VII.)** Edwin Detweiler, bn. Aug. 24, 1886. **(VII.)** Ida Pearl Detweiler, bn. Sept. 19, 1888.

VI. Henry Detweiler, bn. Oct. 19, 1863; died Dec. 7, 1864.

VI. Anna Detweiler, bn. May 18, 1866; died Feb. 5, 1867.

VI. Harvey James Detweiler, bn. July 10, 1867. Teacher in Clay Co., Neb. Christian.

V. Sarah Shaddinger, bn. June 7, 1826; died—, aged about 14 years.

IV. Anna Shaddinger, bn.—; died —. Mrd. Samuel Myers,—. He died —. Farmer. Menn. Children: Christian, Abraham, Joseph, Hannah, Sarah, John, Levi.

V. Christian S. Meyer, bn.—. Mrd. —Detweiler,—. P. O., Dublin, Pa. Farmer. Menn. Children: Sophia, Mary, Anna, Lizzie.

VI. Sophia Meyers, bn.—. Mrd. Abraham K. Meyer, Jan. 23, 1863. Farmer. Menn. Children: (VII.) Tillman Meyer, bn. Dec. 10, 1865. (VII.) Lydia Meyer, bn. Oct. 14, 1869. (VII.) Edwin M. Meyer, bn. Nov. 20, 1873. (VII.) Abraham Meyer, bn. Mar. 5, 1880.

VI. Mary Meyers, bn.—. Mrd. Rev. John Leatherman. (See Index of References No. 19.)

VI. Anna Meyers, bn.—. Mrd. Jacob Leatherman. (See Index of References No. 20.)

VI. Lizzie Meyers, bn.—. Mrd. John O. Overholt. P. O., Plumsteadville, Pa.

V. Abraham S. Meyers, bn.—. Mrd. Elizabeth Leatherman,—. P. O., Bedminster, Pa. Farmer. Menn. Children: (VI.) Christian L. Meyers, bn.—. P. O., Plumsteadville, Pa. (VI.) Abraham L. Meyers, bn.—. (VI.) Anna Meyers, bn.—. Mrd. Jacob High, —. P. O., Bedminster, Pa. (VI.) Sallie Meyers, bn. —. Mrd. Jacob Angeny. (See Index of References No. 21.) (VI.) Lizzie Meyers, bn.—. P. O., Bedminster, Pa. S.

V. Joseph S. Meyer, bn. in Bedminster Twp., Feb. 25, 1838. Mrd. Anna Miller, Nov. 24, 1860. She was bn. in Lehigh Co., Mar. 24, 1838. P. O., Pipersville, Pa. Farmer. Menn. Children: Abraham, Milton, William, Anna, Elizabeth, David.

VI. Abraham M. Meyer, bn. June 28, 1862; died May 28, 1872.

VI. Milton M. Meyer, born Oct. 11, 1864. Mrd. Emma Wisler, —. P. O., Bedminster, Pa. Farmer. One child: (VII.) Joseph Meyer, bn. 1889.

VI. William M. Meyer, bn. Feb. 23, 1867. Mrd. Eliza Meyer,—. P. O., Dublin, Pa. Laborer. One child: (VII.) Anna Meyer, bn. 1889.

VI. Anna M. Meyer, bn. Sept. 22, 1869. Mrd. Tobias Hunsberger,—. P. O., Pipersville, Pa. Farmer.

VI. Elizabeth M. Meyer, bn. Oct. 29, 1871. S.
VI. David M. Meyer, bn. Dec. 29, 1877.
V. Hannah Meyers, bn. —. Mrd. Abraham Gehman, Dec. 20, 1846. P. O., Dublin, Pa. Farmer. Menn. Children: Samuel, John, Elizabeth, Anna, Sarah, Infant, Catharine, Hannah.
VI. Samuel Gehman, bn. Nov. 3, 1848. Mrd. Mary Gross, Feb. 1, 1873. P. O., Plumsteadville, Pa. Farmer. Menn. Children: (**VII.**) John Gehman, bn. Mar. 12, 1874. (**VII.**) Abraham and Samuel Gehman, bn. Aug. 10, 1876. (**VII.**) Daniel Gehman, bn. Nov. 17, 1878.
VI. John Gehman, bn. Mar. 8, 1851; died May 27, 1861.
VI. Elizabeth Gehman, bn. Nov. 8, 1852. Mrd. Henry Rice, Dec. 9, 1878. Farmer. Menn. Children: (**VII.**) Abraham Rice, bn. Oct. 27, 1882. (**VII.**) Anna Rice, bn. Oct. 13, 1884. (**VII.**)Hannah Rice, bn. Sept. 7, 1886. (**VII.**) Samuel Rice, bn. Aug. 23, 1888.
VI. Anna Gehman, bn. Feb. 8, 1855. Mrd. Martin M. Leatherman. (See Index of References No. 22.)
VI. Sarah Gehman, bn. Oct. 10, 1857. Mrd. Jacob Y. Leatherman, Feb. 1876. Farmer. Menn. Children: (**VII.**) Elizabeth Leatherman. (**VII.**) —Leatherman.
VI. Infant bn. and died unnamed.
VI. Catharine Gehman, bn. Sept. 24, 1860. Mrd. Samuel Leatherman, in 1880. Menn. Children: (**VII.**) Abraham, (dec'd). (**VII.**) David. (**VII.**) Jacob. (**VII.**) Hannah. (**VII.**) Anna.
VI. Hannah Gehman, bn. June 7, 1864. Mrd. Henry Y. Leatherman in 1884. Farmer. Menn. One child: (**VII.**) Sarah Leatherman, bn. Oct. 10, 1889.
V. Sarah Meyers, bn.—. Mrd. Aaron Tyson,—. One child: (**VI.**) Joseph M. Tyson, bn.—. Mrd. Elizabeth Leatherman,—.
V. John S. Myers, bn. in Bedminster Twp., Pa., Nov. 20, 1813; died Mar. 6, 1887. Mrd. Mary Holdeman in 1835. She was bn. Oct. 28, 1810; died Apr. 7, 1845. Children: Anna, Cornelius, Hannah.—John mrd. second wife —Hunsicker (a widow Derstine). Farmer. Menn. Children: Lydia, Sophia, John, Mary.

VI. Anna Myers, bn. Oct. 8, 1837. Mrd. Daniel Myers,—. He died —. P. O., Pipersville, Pa. Children: Peter, Mary, Lydia, Daniel.

VII. Peter Myers, bn.—. Mrd.—. P. O., Pipersville, Pa.

VII. Mary Myers, bn.—. Mrd. Albert Rice in 1882. P. O., Pipersville, Pa. Farmer. Menn. Children: **(VIII.)** Daniel Rice, bn. Mar. 1883. **(VIII.)** Harvey Rice, bn. in 1885. **(VIII.)** Twins died unnamed. **(VIII.)** Noah Rice, bn. July 1888.

VII. Lydia Myers, bn. —; died—. Mrd. Isaac M. Mill. Two children: —. —.

VII. Daniel Myers, bn.—. S.

VI. Cornelius Myers, bn. in Bedminster Twp., Pa. Oct. 24, 1839. Mrd. Anna Wismer, Mar. 20, 1869. P. O., Plumsteadville, Pa. Farmer. Menn. Children: **(VII.)** Libbie Myers, bn. Aug. 7, 1870. S. **(VII.)** Mary Myers, bn. Dec. 23, 1871. S. **(VII.)** Ella Myers, bn. Dec. 20, 1873. S. **(VII.)** Cornelius Myers, bn. May 3, 1876. **(VII.)** Eli Wismer Myers, bn. Apr. 18, 1878. **(VII.)** Sophia Myers, bn. Apr. 29, 1880. **(VII.)** Annie Myers, bn. May 21, 1885.

VI. Hannah Myers, bn. Dec. 4, 1843; died May 27, 1844.

VI. Lydia Myers, bn. —. Mrd. Jacob M. High. (See Index of References No. 23).

VI. Sophia Myers, bn. Oct. 9, 1855. Mrd. John L. Fretz, Oct. 9, 1875. P. O., Gardenville, Pa. Farmer. Menn. Children: **(VII.)** Wilson L. Fretz, bn. Apr. 15, 1878. **(VII.)** Ella Nora Fretz, bn. Aug. 5, 1884. **(VII.)** Mary Etta Fretz, bn. Sept. 6, 1886. **(VII.)** Flora Fretz, bn. May 20, 1888.

VI. John A. Myers, bn. —. Mrd. Mary Myers —. Menn. Have Issue.

VI. Mary Meyers, bn. —. Mrd. Daniel G. Gross —. P. O., Fountainville, Pa.

V. Levi S. Meyers, bn. —. Mrd. —. No issue.

IV. John Shattinger, bn. Aug. 13, 1799; died Mar. 5, 1861. Mrd. Catharine Myers,—. She was bn. Sept. 1810. Farmer. Mrs. S. Menn. Children: Mary, Rachel, Jacob, Ephraim, Joseph, Eliza, Hannah, Samuel, John, Wilson, Levi.

V. Mary W. Shaddinger, bn. in Bucks Co., Pa., Apr.
30, 1829. Mrd. Geo. Hoverstick, May 17, 1849. He
died Apr. 19, 1891. They lived in Pennsylvania six
years, then purchased a farm in Indiana on which
they lived from 1864 to 1889, when they sold it and
bought a home in Nappanee, Ind. Shoemaker and
Farmer. Mr. H. member Ch. of God. Mrs. H. Meth.
Ep. Children: Washington, Caroline, Emma.

VI. Washington Hoverstick, bn. in Bucks Co., Pa.,
June 18, 1852. Mrd. Annie Kauffman, Sept. 12,
1874. She was born at Fish Lake, Ind., Sept. 10,
1855. P. O., Waukesha, Wis. Engineer on Wisconsin Central R. R. Meth. Children: **(VII.)** Zulah
Hoverstick, bn. June 24, 1879. **(VII.)** Gracie Hoverstick, bn. Feb. 5, 1885. **(VII.)** Della Hoverstick, bn.
Aug. 23, 1886. **(VII.)** Frank W. Hoverstick, bn. Oct.
5, 1888.

VI. Caroline Hoverstick, bn. in Bucks Co., Pa., Aug.
6, 1854. Mrd. Samuel J. Winder, May 5, 1873. He
was bn. at Portage, O., Dec. 17, 1848. P. O., Ottawa, Kan. Carpenter in employ of Sante Fee R. R.
shops. Mrs. W. Meth. Children: **(VII.)** Frank Alda
Winder, bn. Nov. 23, 1874. Meth. **(VII.)** Harry Leander Winder, bn. Aug. 26, 1877. Meth. **(VII.)** Willis Nelson Winder, bn. Jan. 6, 1881. **(VII.)** Charles
Earl Winder, bn. Aug. 28, 1885; died Feb. 2, 1892.
(VII.) Nellie Elsie Winder, bn. Feb. 7, 1889.

VI. Emma Hoverstick, bn. in Bureau Co., Ill., June
20, 1858. Mrd. Fred. J. Bryson, son of Rev. George
Bryson, Sept. 12, 1875. He was bn. in Elkhart Co.,
Ind., Nov. 8, 1851. P. O., Waukesha, Wis. Fireman
on Wisconsin Central R. R. Children: **(VII.)** Nellie
Irene Bryson, bn. Aug. 15, 1878. **(VII.)** Louis Leroy
Bryson, bn. May 9, 1880.

V. Rachel Shaddinger, bn. Mar. 7, 1831. Mrd. Nathan Fretz, —. P. O., Gardenville, Pa. Farmer.
Drover. Children: Laura, Lizzie, Ella, Eddie, Daniel, Willis, Clara.

VI. A. Laura Fretz, bn. —. Mrd. Absalom Fretz,
Dec. 27, 1883. Grocery business at 1430 Norris St.,
Philadelphia, Pa. Baptists. Children: **(VII.)** Herbert

S. Fretz, bn. Dec. 20, 1886. (VII.) Walter L. Fretz, bn. June 12, 1889.

VI. Lizzie F. Fretz, bn. Aug. 10, 1861. Mrd. Montgomery Miller, Nov. 16, 1881. Machinist. Baptists. Children: (VII.) Pearl F. Miller, bn. Sept. 16, 1885. (VII.) Willis F. Miller, bn. Jan. 20, 1888; died Aug. 18, 1888.

VI. Ella Fretz, bn. —.

VI. Eddie Fretz, bn. —. Mrd. Miss Black. One Child: (VII.) —.

VI. Daniel Fretz.

VI. Willis Fretz.

VI. Clara Fretz.

V. Jacob Shaddinger, bn. Dec. 7, 1833. Mrd. Mary J. Wismer, —. P. O., Lahoska, Pa. Mason. Baptists. Children: Hannah, Theodosia, Addie, Theodore, Lidie, Harry.

VI. Hannah A. Shaddinger, bn. at Richboro, Pa., June 5, 1865. Mrd. Charles Lawson Pierson, Sr., —. He was bn. in Philadelphia, Pa., May 30, 1868. P. O., Philadelphia, Pa. Carpenter and builder. Children: (VII.) Ida Myrtle Pierson, bn. Mar. 4, 1890. (VII.) Charles Lawson Pierson, Jr., bn. Jan. 13, 1892; died July 15, 1892. (VII.) Earl Leslie Pierson, bn. Jan. 12, 1893.

VI. Theodosia C. Shaddinger, bn. in Plumsteadville, Pa., Sept. 4, 1867. Mrd. Isaac Peters, —. He was bn. in N. J., Jan. 1, 1858. Laborer. Children: (VII) Isaiah P. Peters, bn. Nov. 21, 1888; died Oct. 25, 1890. (VII.) Agnes E. Peters, bn. Apr. 16, 1891.

VI. Addie G. Shaddinger, bn. in Bucks Co., Nov. 13, 1870.

VI. Theodore Shaddinger, bn. Nov. 7, 1873; died Apr. 25, 1885.

VI. Lidie Shaddinger, bn. in Solebury, Oct. 11, 1876.

VI. Harry G. Shaddinger, bn. in Solebury, Oct. 21, 1881.

V. Ephraim M. Shadinger, bn. Mar. 31, 1835. Mrd. Kate W. Cope, Mar. 30, 1865. P. O., Pemberton, N. J. School-teacher. Baptists. Children: (VI.)

Spencer C. Shadinger, bn. Jan. 9, 1874. Baptist. S.
(VI.) John Hervey Shadinger, bn. —; died May 1877.
V. Joseph Shadinger, bn. Aug. 27, 1837; died —.
Mrd. Hannah Hanway, —. She died —. Children:
(VI.) William Sbaddinger, bn. —; died —. (VI.) David
Shaddinger, bn. —.
V. Eliza Shaddinger, bn. Jan. 1, 1840; died Mar. 17,
1863. Mrd. Joseph Nash, - . Had one child, (VI.) —
Nash, bn. —; died - .
V. Hannah Shaddinger, bn. Dec. 1, 1842. P. O.,
Gardenville, Pa. S.
V. Samuel Shaddinger, bn. Nov. 5, 1843.
V. John Shaddinger, bn. in Bucks Co., Pa., Nov.
14, 1845. Mrd. Jennie R. Titus, of Philadelphia, Pa.,
May 7, 1874. P. O., Goshen, Ind. Book-keeper.
Baptists. Children: (VI.) Jennie Louisa Shaddinger,
bn. Nov. 1, 1876; died Feb. 10, 1889. (VI.) Howard
Shaddinger, bn. Mar. 5, 1887; died Sept. 13, 1887.
(VI.) Wilson Whitney Shaddinger, bn. Feb. 6, 1889.
V. Wilson Shaddinger, bn. Oct. 5, 1847. S.
V. Levi Shadinger, bn. Sept. 27, 1849. P. O., Gar-
denville, Pa. Studied medicine. Graduated M. D. at
University of Pennsylvania. Baptist. S.
IV. Mary Shattinger, bn. about 1804; died 1864.
Mrd. David Weirman, —. He was bn. about 1800;
died in Philadelphia, Pa., about 1832. Hotel keeper.
Mr. W. Menn. Mrs. W. Baptist. Children: John,
Joseph, Charles, Cordelia.
V. John Weirman, bn. about 1824; died 1875. Mrd.
Wilhelmina Lukins, —. Family live at 2310 Fairhill
St., Philadelphia.
V. Joseph Weirman, bn. about 1827; died in 1873.
Mrd Martha Yothers, —. Free Christian. Res.
Philadelphia, Pa.
V. Charles Weirman, bn. near Milford, Pa., in 1829.
Mrd. Amanda Jones, —. P. O., Vineland, N. J.
Formerly coach-maker. Baptist. Children: Emma,
Carrie, Annie, George.
VI. Emma Weirman, bn. 1855. Mrd. John Livezey,
—. Painter. Baptist. Children: (VII.) Bertha Live-
zey, bn. in 1876. (VII.) Carrie Livezey, bn. in 1879;
died in infancy. (VII.) Annie Livezey, bn. in 1879

(twin); died in infancy. (VII.) Elsie F. Livezey, bn. in 1882.

VI. Carrie Weirman, bn. 1858. P. O., Vineland, N. J. Baptist. S.

VI. Annie Weirman, bn. 1860. Mrd. Wm. Coulter. Hosiery M'f'g in Phila. Baptist. Children: (VII.) Annie A. Coulter, bn. in 1881. (VII.) Emma F. Coulter, bn. in 1888. (VII.) Ruth E. Coulter, bn. in 1891.

VI. George Weirman, bn. in 1862; died 1882. Baptist. One child: (VII.) Charles Weirman, bn. in 1882; died in infancy.

V. Cordelia Weirman, bn. about 1831; died 1862. Baptist.

IV. Henry Shattinger, bn. in Bucks Co., Pa., June 12, 1800; died Mar. 22, 1841. Mrd. Mary A. Shaddinger, daughter of Jonathan and Susanna Shaddinger, Mar. 25, 1825. She was bn. Aug. 4, 1804; died in Phila., Pa., May 15, 1884. Farmer. Baptists. Children: Margaret, Susanna, Caroline, Samuel, Joseph, Hannah, Henry, Matthias.

V. Margaret G. Shattinger, born July 29, 1826; died Dec. 23, 1861. Mrd. Reading Lewis, M. D., Jan. 18, 1848. He died in Caldwell, Kan., Jan. 4, 1888. Children: Granville, Byron, Mary.

VI. S. P. Granville Lewis, bn. in Dublin, Bucks Co., June 24, 1849. Mrd. Mary A. Griffin, Oct. 19, 1875. She was born Aug. 1, 1848. P. O., Caldwell, Kan. Real estate and insurance. Mrs. L., Baptist. Children: (VII.) Sydney Caroline Lewis, bn. and died Jan. 11, 1877. (VII.) Edna Bell Lewis, bn. Mar. 30, 1880. (VII.) Ralph Granville Lewis, Eugene Neal Lewis, bn. Feb. 15, 1882, twins. (VII.) Francis Clay Lewis, bn. Apr. 16, 1884; died Oct. 22, 1888. (VII.) Ernest Lewis, bn. Aug. 15, 1888.

VI. Byron Lewis, bn. Feb. 3, 1853.

VI. Mary Caroline Lewis, bn. at Dublin, Pa., Dec. 13, 1854. Mrd. Titus Eugene Neal, Jan. 17, 1877. He was bn. in Knoxville, Iowa. P. O., Caldwell, Kan. Banker. Baptists. Children: (VII.) Mabel Gertrude Neal, bn. May 23, 1880. (VII.) Frances

Inez Neal, bn. June 26, 1882. (VII.) Alice Neal, bn. Mar. 25, 1891.

V. Susanna Shattinger, born July 29, 1826; died Oct. 2, 1841.

V. Caroline Shattinger, bn. June 29, 1830. Mrd. Rev. C. C. Bitting, D. D., Dec. 5, 1855. Res. 1420 Chestnut St. Phila., Pa. Dr. Bitting was bn. in Philadelphia, Pa., graduated from the Central High School in 1850. Baptized Feb. 1847 and united with the Broad Street Baptist Church. Prosecuted his studies at the University at Lewisburg, Pa., and the Hamilton N. Y. Madison University. Taught in the Baptist Female College of Tenn., and was ordained at Murfreesboro, Tenn. He was pastor of the Mount Olivet and Hopeful Baptist churches, in Hanover county, Va., 1855–1859. At Alexandria, Va., 1859–1866. Secretary of the Sunday-school Board of the Southern Baptist Convention 1866–1868. Pastor in Linchburg, Va., 1868–1872, where the results were most successful. He was District Secretary for the Southern states of the American Baptist Publication Society, then became pastor of the Second Baptist Church, Richmond, Va., 1873–1876, and the Franklin Square Baptist Church, Baltimore, Md., 1876-1883. Since that time he has been the Bible and Missionary Secretary of the American Baptist Publication Society in Phila., Pa.

In 1874, Dr. Bitting visited Europe, Palestine and Egypt, during which time he baptized two persons in the river Jordan at the traditional baptizing place of the Redeemer. He has made valuable additions to the literature of the denomination. Children: William, Charles, Linnaeus, Carrie, Miriam, Ruth, Naomi.

VI. Rev. William Coleman Bitting, M. A., born in Hanover Co., Va., Feb. 5, 1857. Mrd. Anna Mary Biedler of Page Co., Va., Nov. 17, 1886.

Mr. Bitting was graduated M. A. by Richmond College, Richmond, Va., June 1877. He was Final Orator *Mu Sigma Rho* Literary Society, of his alma mater, June 1876; Gwin Medallist, School of Philosophy, session 1876-'77; Orator of Society of Alumni.

June 1885. He was licensed to preach by Franklin Square Baptist Church; Baltimore, Md., Sept. 2, 1877; the same month matriculated at Crozer Theological Seminary, Chester, Pa., by which he was graduated June 1880, after pursuing full course. He was stated supply for Lee Street Baptist Church, Baltimore, Md., July 1 to Dec. 31, 1880. Became pastor of the Baptist Church at Luray, Va., Feb. 5, 1881, where he was ordained May 15, 1881, and continued until Dec. 31, 1883. While serving the church at Luray, he was also pastor at Front Royal, Va., Feb. 27, 1881 to Jan. 31, 1882; and at Riverton, Va., Feb. 1882 to Dec. 31, 1883. On Jan. 1, 1884, he became pastor of the Mount Morris Baptist Church, New York City, which during his nine years of service has increased in membership from 253 to 750, besides building an edifice costing $90,000. He edits a church paper, issued weekly; is the New York correspondent of *The National Baptist* of Philadelphia, Pa.; *The Watchman* of Boston, Mass.; and *The Central Baptist* of St. Louis, Mo.; has contributed to various newspapers, magazines, and volumes of sermons. He has been President of the Baptist City Mission of New York City, since Oct. 1890; President of the Baptist Ministers' Home Society since Dec. 1887; member of Executive Committee New York Baptist State Convention since 1889. One child: (VII.) William Charles Bitting, bn. Aug. 17, 1887.

VI. Charles C. Bitting, Jr., bn. in Va., July 14, 1858. Mrd. Eva H. Rayfield —. Graduate from Maryland University Law School, Baltimore, Md., 1878. Lawyer. Res. 1420 Chestnut St., Phila., Pa. Children: (VII.) Carrie R. Bitting, bn. in Baltimore, Md., Oct. 5, 1881. (VII.) Hattie Ruth Bitting, bn. in Abilene, Kan., Jan 1, 1887.

VI. Linnaeus L. Bitting, bn. in Virginia, Oct. 14, 1859; died in Baltimore, Md., Aug. 21, 1886. Physician. Graduate of the College of Physicians and Surgeons, Baltimore, Md.

VI. Carrie Bitting, bn. in Va., Dec. 8, 1862; died May 28, 1864.

VI. Miriam Bitting M. D. bn. in Alexandria, Va., Sept. 22, 1864. Physician. Graduate of the woman's Medical College, Philadelphia, Pa., the woman's and children's Hospital; Belleview Medical College, N. Y. and Philadelphia Hospital, Pa.

VI. Ruth Bitting, bn. in Alexandria, Va., Feb. 12, 1866. Graduated in Philadelphia.

VI. Naomi Bitting, bn. in Linchburg, Va., Nov. 21, 1869. Student at University of Pennsylvania.

V. Samuel M. Shattinger, bn. May 16, 1832; died Sept. 13, 1853.

V. Joseph S. Shattinger, bn. Aug. 17, 1834. Mrd. Margaret Dudgeon, of Ill., —. She died —, leaving five children. — Joseph married second wife Susan McCound, —. P. O., Abilene, Kan., five children by this marriage.

V. Hannah Shattinger, bn. July 19, 1836. Mrd. Prof. Thomas O'Neill, of Philadelphia, Apr. 24, 1856. Res. 2405 Master St., Phila., Pa. Professor of Music. Prof. Thomas O'Neill was born in Philadelphia, Pa., Dec. 14, 1829. At a very early age he evinced a talent for music which he gratified by writing notes to any thing in the form of a melody that he heard whistled or sung. A talent, however, which his father thought not to encourage. In 1856 he became organist and choirmaster of the Broad Street Baptist church in Philadelphia. He was subsequently induced to remove to Norristown, where for many years the music at the Frest Presbyterian church of which he was organist and choirmaster, was an attractive feature of the services. After ten consecutive years of service as principal of the music department at the Oakland Female Institute, at Norristown, then a flourishing school for young ladies, he voluntarily resigned the position at the seminary in order to attend to outside teaching. Quite a number of his pupils occupy prominent positions.

Mr. Elnord Beaver, a competent church organist of Norristown, was under his instruction for five years, and Miss Anna L. Cressinan, who succeeded him as organist at the F. P. ch. was his pupil for a like term of years. Among his brightest pupils is

H. E. Kratz, Ph. D.

(See page 151.)

his daughter, Mrs. J. Jay Gheen, of West Chester, who is a pianist of such signal ability that her music is not only a joy to her, but is an unfailing source of pleasure to her large circle of friends.

Mr. O'Neill's compositions are characterized by an originality and depth of feeling which proclaim him to be a composer of decided talent. His "Morning Song" and "Among the Birds" are little *gems*, while his "Good-bye, Sweet Day" has been described as "a charming little bit of music, of that plaintive tone that never fails to touch a responsive chord in the heart of the listener." As a *lecturer* and *writer*, Mr. O'Neill also deserves mention, his letters (as special correspondent) to the *Norristown Herald*, are graphic, complete and interesting in the extreme, he possesses that rare faculty of putting into words the impression conveyed to his own poetic soul by beautiful music and brilliant effects, and some of his letters on this subject are the most charming we have ever read. Mr. O'Neill, Presby. Mrs. O'Neill, Baptist. Children: Carrie, Margarette, Thomas, Samuel.

VI. Carrie O'Neil, bn. in Phila. Jan. 20, 1857. Mrd. John Jay Gheen, of West Chester, Pa., Oct. 8, 1885. He was born in E. Bradford, Chester Co., Pa., Feb. 19, 1855. P. O., West Chester, Pa. Lawyer. Presby. Children: **(VII.)** John Edward Gheen, bn. July 2, 1886. **(VII.)** Thomas Stanley Gheen, bn. June 14, 1887. **(VII.)** Evan Pennock Gheen, bn. Mar. 4, 1890.

VI. Margarette O'Neil, born in Norristown, Pa., Oct. 2, 1858. Mrd. Rev. Thomas R. Evans, Nov. 9, 1886. He was bn. in Beaufort, Wales, Aug. 7, 1839. P. O., Azusa, Cal. Minister of the Baptist church. One child: **(VII.)** Emily Evans, bn. Sept. 6, 1888.

VI. Thomas Ralph O'Neil, born in Norriston, Pa., Dec. 4, 1863. Engraver on wood.

VI. Samuel H. O'Neil, born in Norristown, Pa., Feb. 11, 1868. Engraver on wood.

V. Henry S. Shattinger, bn. Oct. 3, 1839. Mrd. Nellie Parks of Ill. P. O., Abilene, Kan. Two children.

7

V. Matthias Shattinger, born Aug. 24, 1841; died Feb. 6, 1853.

IV. Joseph Shaddinger, bn. —; died —, 1892. Mrd. Anna Shaffer, —. Farmer. Baptists. Children: Maria, William, Amanda, Annie.

V. Maria Shaddinger, bn. —. Mrd. Cyrus S. Black. (See Index of References No. 24.)

V. William Shaddinger, bn. —. Mrd. —. Reside in Philadelphia.

V. Amanda Shaddinger, bn. —. Mrd. Amos Wismer. (See Index of References No. 25.) — Amanda mrd. second husband Jacob Handy, —. P. O., New Hope, Pa. One child: **(VI.)** — Handy.

V. Annie Shaddinger, bn. —. Mrd. Lewis Wismer. (See Index of References No. 26.)

IV. Jacob Shaddinger, bn. —; died. S.

III. Margaret Wismer, bn. June 4, 1768; died July 23, 1822. Mrd. Anthony Fretz, Apr. 16, 1795. He was bn. Feb. 1, 1774; died Jan. 26, 1856. He mrd. second wife a Quaker lady. He lived on a farm of 60 acres at the "Old Burnt Mill," in Plumstead Twp. Farmer and miller. He was known as "Lame Anthony," having received an injury to one of his legs by a scythe or cradle, making amputation necessary. Children: Samuel, Anna, Mary, Mark, Elizabeth, Joseph, Catharine.

IV. Samuel Fretz, bn. Jan. 17, 1796. Mrd. Elizabeth Fretz in 1824. Miller. In 1832 they moved to Clinton, N. J. from whence 17 years later they moved to Medina Co., O. where he died, Apr. 6, 1852. Sawyer. Children: Lewis, Anthony, Christian, Mahlon, Anna.

V. Lewis Fretz, bn. in Bucks Co., Pa., Oct. 26, 1826. Farmer, sawyer and builder, now retired. He enlisted under the call of President Lincoln for 75,000 men, and was commissioned Captain of the first company of Vol's raised in Medina Co. After expiration of enlistment, he again enlisted in the 166 O. N. G., the last company raised in Medina Co., serving as first Lieutenant with Captain's duties. This company was sent to Washington as National Guards, to guard the forts on Arlington Heights, near Alexandria. For honorable services rendered he received a certificate of thanks from President Lincoln. Some of the principal battles engaged in were Fort Henry, Fort Donaldson, Pittsburgh Landing, Shiloh, etc. He has served in various Twp. offices, among them Justice of the Peace. Unmrd.

V. Anthony Fretz, bn. in Bucks Co., Pa., Jan. 5, 1829. Mrd. Emily Hosmer in 1855. She died soon after, leaving one child—Ida. Anthony mrd. second wife Hannah A. Crawford, Sept. 19, 1863. One child: Clair. Mr. Fretz was formerly in partnership with his brother Lewis, as farmer, sawyer and builder. At the outbreaking of the war he enlisted in the 12th Ill. V. I. as musician. He enlisted a second time in 166 O. N. G. as principal musician, and received from President Lincoln a certificate of honorable service. P. O., Wooster, O. Presbyterian elder.

VI. Ida E. Fretz, bn. Jan. 17, 1856. Mrd. Melvin S. Flickinger, Feb. 14, 1878. P. O., Chippewa Lake, O. Farmer. Meth. Children: **(VII.)** Anna Fern Flickinger, bn. May 4, 1884. **(VII.)** Lulu Hope Flickinger, bn. Mar. 31, 1889.

VI. Clair W. Fretz, bn. Oct. 3, 1870.

V. Christian Fretz, bn. Oct. 18, 1831; died Nov. 19, 1836.

V. Mahlon Fretz, bn. at Clinton, N. J., —. Mrd. —. Enlisted in the 12th Ill. V. I. as musician, and while in the army contracted a disease from which he died soon after his return. One child: **(VI.)** Mahlon D. Fretz, bn. —. Mrd. —.

V. Anna W. Fretz, bn. at Clinton, N. J. May 21, 1841. Mrd. Chester W. Abbott, Aug. 9, 1861. Farmer in Medina Co., O. He enlisted in the 103d Reg't O. V. I. for three years and participated in the battles of East Tennesee, Knoxville, Armstrong, Atlanta, Franklin, Nashville, Wilmington, Goldesborough, and Raleigh. Mrs. A. Presby. Children: **(VI.)** Lewis Fretz Abbott, bn. in Medina Co., O., in 1862. Mrd. Philena Bowman, Sept. 12, 1882. Farmer and miller. He Presby. She Disciple. No issue. **(VI.)** Cora L. Abbott, bn. in 1866. Mrd. Clifford V. Matter-

son. P. O., Seville, O. Merchant. Presby. **(VI.)** Ida
E. Abbott, bn. in 1873; died Dec. 12, 1881.
IV. Anna Fretz, bn. in Bucks Co., Aug. 10, 1797;
died in 1885. Mrd. Joseph Solliday, Dec. 11, 1817.
Children: Joseph, Mary, Lucy, Lewis. —Anna mrd.
second husband Tobias Weisel, —. Children: Lucinda,
Caroline, Anthony.
V. Joseph Solliday, bn. Oct. 24, 1818.
V. Mary Solliday, bn. Mar. 3, 1820; died Jan. 25,
1821.
V. Lucy Ann Solliday, bn. Mar. 18, 1822; died Nov.
11, 1822.
V. Lewis C. Solliday, bn. Nov. 14, 1823. Mrd. Mary
Ann Solliday, Nov. 2, 1845. Farmer. Ger. Ref.
Children: Morris, Catharine, Elwood.
VI. Morris Solliday, bn. Oct. 14, 1849. Mrd. Emma
Moyer, Nov. 7, 1878. P. O., Erwinna, Pa. Farmer.
Ger. Ref. One child. **(VII.)** Gertrude Solliday.
VI. Catharine Ann Solliday, bn. Apr. 7, 1845; died
May 3, 1876. Mrd. Newberry Sassaman, —. One
child: **(VII.)** Mary May Sassaman.
VI. T. Elwood Solliday, bn. —. Mrd. Emma Yost, —.
V. Lucinda Weisel, bn. —. Mrd. Joshua Evans, M.
D. —. He died —. Children:
VI. Olive Evans, —; died young.
VI. William Evans, —; died young.
VI. Carrie Evans, —. Mrd. George E. Wagner, —.
Children: **(VII.)** Carrie Wagner. **(VII.)** Florence Wag-
ner.
VI. Annie Evans, mrd. William T. Beans, —.
VI. Wilbur C. Evans.
VI. Edward S. Evans.
V. Caroline Augusta Weisel, bn. in Bucks Co., Pa. S.
V. Anthony Fretz Weisel, bn. in Bucks Co., Pa.
Mrd. Hannah E. Delp, —. P. O., Doylestown, Pa.
Dealer in fancy coach and driving horses. Children:
(VI.) Debbie D. Weisel. **(VI.)** H. Ross Weisel. **(VI.)**
Augusta Weisel.
IV. Mary Fretz, born, Apr. 26, 1799; died —. Mrd.
Samuel Solliday, May 17, 1821. He died Oct. 3, 1830.
Children: Eli, Rachel, Joseph, Clarissa, Wilson, Sarah.

—Mary mrd. second husband John Bissey, Nov. 10, 1846. He died Oct. 3, 1870.

V. Eli K. Solliday, bn. Dec. 22, 1821;died in 1887.

V. Rachel E. Solliday, born May 14, 1823. Mrd. Robert A. Bayard, - -. He died July 21, 1854. Attends Presbyterian ch. Children: Mary, Armstrong, Martha, Sarah, Elizabeth, Joseph.

VI. Mary A. Bayard, bn. May 10, 1842; died —.

VI. Armstrong Bayard, bn. Dec. 10, 1843; died —.

VI. Martha A. Bayard, born, Dec. 8, 1846. Mrd. William H. Gandey, Oct. 25, 1865. P. O., Lambertville, N. J. Paper manufacturer. Presby. Children: **(VII.)** James C. W. Gandey, born July 17, 1866; drowned July 17, 1879. **(VII.)** Minnie B. Gandey, bn. May 10, 1868. **(VII.)**Ann B. W. Gandey, bn. Sept. 28, 1870. **(VII.)** Lizzie L. Gandey, bn. Sept. 28, 1872; died Nov. 11, 1877. **(VII.)** Sallie Gandey, bn. Sept. 18, 1874; died Dec. 29, 1887. **(VII.)** Mattie B. Gandey, bn. Nov. 1, 1875. **(VII.)** Hannah E. H. Gandey, bn. Oct. 24, 1880.

VI. Sarah L. Bayard, bn. Aug. 16, 1848; died Aug. 1873. Mrd. Alfred C. Gandey, Dec. 28, 1869. One child: **(VII.)** Harry B. Gandey, bn. Oct. 1870; died Sept. 1876.

VI. Elizabeth Bayard, bn. Aug. 29, 1850; died —.

VI. Joseph Ely Bayard, bn. Nov. 2, 1853. Married Lizzie A. Holcomb, Feb. 2, 1873.

V. Joseph Solliday, bn. Sept. 5, 1824. Mrd. Annie C. Atkinson, Feb. 17, 1846. P. O., Hawley, Pa. Merchant. Presby. No issue.

V. Clarissa A. Solliday, bn. Aug. 20, 1826. S.

V. Wilson A. Solliday, bn. Mar. 4, 1828; died —.

V. Sarah Solliday, bn. Apr. 28, 1830. Mrd. J. B. Longshore, M. D. of Camden, N. J. Apr. 12, 1854. Presby. No living issue.

IV. Mark Fretz, born Mar. 17, 1801; died July 24, 1849. Mrd. Julia A. Bissey, Dec. 20, 1825. Miller. Children: Silas, Margaret, Mary, Wilson, Julia, Nelson, Jonas, Justus, Clarissa, Sarah.

V. Silas Fretz, bn. Dec. 1, 1826; died in Michigan, May 19, 1878. Mrd. Catharine Ann Johnson. Millwright. Meth. Ep. Children: Lucinda, Anna, Alice, George, Kittie.

VI. Lucinda Fretz, bn. at Frenchtown, N. J. Sept. 14, 1853. Mrd. Joseph Swails, Aug. 15, 1872. P. O., Charlevoix, Mich. Sea carpenter. Meth. Ep. Children: **(VII.)** Eva Swails. **(VII.)** Alice Swails. **(VII.)** Silas Swails. **(VII.)** Lillie Swails. **(VII.)** Maggie Swails. **(VII.)** John Swails. **(VII.)** Flora Swails.

VI. Anna E. Fretz, bn. in Wayne Co., O. Apr. 11, 1857. Mrd. Frank W. Swails, Dec. 27, 1876.

VI. Alice Amelia Fretz, bn. in Defiance Co., Ohio, May 26, 1863. Mrd. C. P. House, May 9, 1882. P. O., Puyallup, Washington. Barber.

VI. George H. Fretz, bn. in Williams Co., O., Apr. 23, 1867. Seaman at South Haven, Mich.

VI. Kittie Louisa Fretz, bn. and died Aug. 10, 1873.

V. Margaret Fretz, bn. Sept. 22, 1828. Mrd. James Wells in 1850. He died in 1875. Sail-maker. Presby. Children: Susan, Ida, Harry.

VI. Susan Wells, bn. July 24, 1856. Mrd. James A. McCaughan, May 1, 1879. Merchant. Presby. Children: **(VII.)** Margaret Sarah McCaughan. **(VII.)** James Stewart McCaughan. **(VII.)** Mary Emily McCaughan. **(VII.)** Susie A. McCaughan. **(VII.)** Harry Wells McCaughan.

VI. Ida Wells, bn. Apr. 4, 1860.

VI. Harry Wells, bn. Aug 24, 1862.

V. Mary Fretz, bn. Sept. 26, 1830. Mrd. Mahlon Hendricks in 1850. No issue.

V. Wilson Fretz, bn. Feb. 14, 1832. Mrd. Mary Saville. She died Dec. 10, 1869. Lumberman. Res. 9 Wilson St. Phila., Pa. Children: Mark, Lydia, Mary.

VI. Mark Fretz, bn. Sept. 14, 1857. Mrd. Alice Kurtz, Sept. 12, 1877. She died Feb. 7, 1884. Blacksmith. One child: **(VII.)** Charles Fretz, bn. June 30, 1880.

VI. Lydia Fretz, bn. May 7, 1859. Mrd. William H. Servos, June 13, 1881. Children: **(VII.)** William H. Servos. **(VII.)** Gertrude Servos. **(VII.)** Edna May Servos died Oct. 24, 1888. **(VII.)** Viola Moore Servos.

VI. Mary Louisa Fretz, bn. Nov. 10. 1861; died Jan. 19, 1885.
V. Julia A. Fretz, bn. Nov. 2, 1834. No. 9 Wilson St. Phila., Pa. Presby. S.
V. Nelson Fretz, bn. Sept. 12, 1836; died in infancy.
V. Jonas Fretz, bn. June 11, 1838; died in infancy.
V. Justus Fretz, bn. July 29, 1839; died in infancy.
V. Clarissa Fretz, bn. May 24, 1842; died in infancy.
V. Sarah E. Fretz, bn. Sept. 7, 1843; died Aug. 24, 1860. S.
IV. Elizabeth Fretz, bn. Nov. 9, 1803; died young.
IV. Joseph Fretz, bn. Mar. 23, 1807; died Mar. 17, 1854. Mrd. Catharine Fretz, daughter of "Big Joe," in 1833. Cabinet maker and miller. Menn. Children: Nathan, Isaiah, Reuben, Moses, Ely, Aaron.
V. Nathan Fretz, bn. in Bucks Co., Pa. May 3, 1834. Mrd. Catharine Longenecker, June 24, 1854. She died Dec. 1884. P. O., Indianapolis, Ind. Children: **(VI.)** Infant, died aged 5 days. **(VI.)** Lavina Fretz, mrd. — Miller —. He died —. **(VI.)** Mary Fretz. **(VI.)** Noah Fretz. **(VI.)** Martha Fretz. **(VI.)** Susan Fretz. **(VI.)** Jacob Fretz. **(VI.)** Rhoda Fretz.
V. Isaiah Fretz, bn. Mar. 3, 1836; died Mar. 8, 1839.
V. Reuben Fretz, bn. in Bucks Co., Pa., Sept. 27, 1837. Mrd. Fannie Holley, Nov. 15, 1868. Aug. 14, 1862 he enlisted for 3 years in the 103 O. V. I. was in the command of Gen. A. E. Burnside, in the siege of Knoxville, Tenn. and with Gen. Sherman in the Atlanta Campaign. Farmer in Clay Co., Ind. He attends Meth. Ep. ch. Wife, Menn. Children: **(VI.)** Catharine Fretz, bn. Aug. 14, 1869. **(VI.)** Laura Fretz, bn. Dec. 4, 1870; died Oct. 16, 1876. **(VI.)** Cyrus Fretz, bn. Jan. 20, 1873; died Jan. 12, 1875. **(VI.)** Rachie Fretz, bn. Sept. 24, 1874. **(VI.)** Emma Fretz, bn. Aug. 19, 1876. **(VI.)** Anthony Fretz, bn. Sept. 21, 1878. **(VI.)** Mattie Fretz, bn. in Feb. and died Mar. 26, 1881. **(VI.)** Dorothea Fretz, bn. Aug. 18, 1882. **(VI.)** William Abram Fretz, bn. Dec. 15, 1884. **(VI.)** Maud Fretz, bn. Dec. 1886; died Feb. 12, 1887. **(VI.)** Clara Hope Fretz, bn. June 14, 1888.
V. Aaron Fretz, bn. in Bucks Co., Pa., Jan. 11, 1840. Mrd. Ella Chase, Dec. 31, 1873. In 1861 he

enlisted in the U. S. I. 1st Battalion, and served his country three years. P. O., Edmund, Oklahoma. Meth. Ep. Children: **(VI.)** Lulu Ella Fretz. **(VI.)** Hazzard D. C. Fretz. **(VI.)** Maud Leno Fretz.

V. Moses Fretz, bn. in Bucks Co., Pa., Sept. 14, 1841. Mrd. Elizabeth C. Henney, July 3, 1866. In April 1861, he enlisted for three months, and Sept. 1, 1861, re-enlisted in Co., D. 15th U. S. Regulars. Was appointed Corporal Nov. 26, 1861, served in the engagements of Green River, Ky., Corinth, Miss. P. O., Jackson, Mich. Foreman in Knickerbocker Packing Co. Establishment. Children: Anna, William, Lulu.

VI. Anna Marilla Fretz, bn. in Steuben Co., Ind., Feb. 4, 1868. Mrd. Grant Bennett, July 5, 1884. Machinist. One child: **(VII.)** Arty Eugene Bennett, bn. Aug. 10, 1885.

VI. William F. Fretz, bn. Sept. 20, 1870; died in 1873.

VI. Lulu C. Fretz, bn. Feb. 11, 1877.

V. Ely Fretz, bn. in Bucks Co., Pa., Sept. 27, 1843. Mrd. Mary E. Simerman, Dec. 23, 1869. She died May 28, 1883. Children: **(VI.)** Jennie D. Fretz, bn. Oct. 13, 1870. **(VI.)** Arthur W. Fretz, bn. Dec. 12, 1872. — Ely mrd. second wife Katie Yohey, Dec. 30, 1884. Foreman of Siberling Reaper and Mower Co., Doylestown, Ohio. Meth. Ep. One child: **(VI.)** George C. Fretz, bn. Feb. 14, 1886.

IV. Catharine Fretz, bn. in Bucks Co., Pa., Sept. 20, 1813. Mrd. Samuel Solliday. Jeweler and lumber and coal merchant. P. O., New Hope, Pa. Presby. Children: Silas, Willie, Caroline, Wilson, Edward, Charles, Amanda, Mary, Samuel, Calvin, Harry, Ella.

V. Silas Solliday, bn. in 1834; died in 1835.

V. Willie Solliday, bn. in 1836; died Feb. 27, 1885. Mrd. J. Howard Murray in 1860. Mrs. M. Presby. Children: Carrie, Edward, Anita, Howard.

VI. Carrie A. Murray, bn. —. Mrd. Richard Whitehead, in 1885. Manufacturer of rubber goods. Mrs. W. Episcopalian. Children: **(VII.)** Richard R. Whitehead. **(VII.)** J. Murray Whitehead.

VI. J. Edward Murray.
VI. Anita R. Murray.
VI. Howard Murray.
V. Caroline Solliday, bn. in 1838. Presby. S.
V. Wilson Solliday, bn. in 1839. Mrd. Lizzie Crook in 1861. Book-keeper for Lehigh Valley Shops at South Easton, Pa. Children: (**VI.**) Charles Solliday. (**VI.**) William Solliday. (**VI.**) Clara Solliday. (**VI.**) Harry Solliday. (**VI.**) Lida Solliday. (**VI.**) Roy and Russel Solliday, (twins).
V. Edward Solliday, bn. in 1841. Mrd. Mary Reading, Feb. 6, 1864. Special agent in Legal Dept. of Penna. R. R. Co. Presby. Children: (**VI.**) Ollie Solliday. (**VI.**) Howard Solliday.
V. Charles Solliday, bn. in 1843: died in 1844.
V. Amanda Solliday, bn. in 1845; died in 1847.
V. Mary Solliday, bn. in 1847. S.
V. Samuel Solliday, bn. 1849; died 1877. Presby.
V. Calvin Solliday, bn. 1851. Mrd. Louisa Hoppock, in 1877. Jeweler, lumber and coal merchant at New Hope, Pa. Presby. One child: (**VI.**)Chrissie Solliday.
V. Harry Solliday, bn. 1857. Mrd. Sylvia Curtis in 1883. Ticket receiver for the Pa. R. R. at Indianapolis, Ind. Presby. One child: (**VI.**) Raymond Solliday.
V. Ella Solliday, bn. in Bucks Co., Pa., in 1857.

II. Mary Wismer, daughter of Jacob Wismer, **I.** date of birth not known, but probably born about 1723. Mrd. Christopher Angeny, —. At the time she received her legacy from her father's estate June 14, 1791, she was a widow. No descendants of her's have been found.

DESCENDANTS OF ELIZABETH WISMER
DAUGHTER OF JACOB WISMER, I.

II. Elizabeth Wismer, bn. Apr. 29, 1725; died —.
Mrd. Jacob Angeny, Nov. 11, 1762. He was bn. in
1740; died —. Farmer and miller. He built the mill
known as Angeny's mill, on the Deep Run, one mile
east of Dublin, and includes the places now owned
and occupied by Abraham K. Meyer, Joseph Tyson,
a portion of Ephraim Detweiler's farm, and where the
Old Mill stood with about 3 acres belonging to Abraham K. High. Children: Elizabeth, Mary, Barbara,
Jacob.

III. Elizabeth Angeny, bn. Nov. 19, 1763; died —.
Mrd. Abraham Moyer —. Farmer. Lived in Spring-
field Twp., Bucks Co. Menn. Children: Elizabeth,
Mary, Catharine, Henry.

IV. Elizabeth Moyer, bn. —; died —. Mrd. Jacob
Moyer, —. He died —. Farmer. Menn. Children:
Abraham, Nancy, Elizabeth, Sarah.

V. Abraham Moyer, bn. Nov. 14, 1820; died Nov.
19, 1879. Mrd. Catharine Ann Fretz in 1848. She
was bn. July 29, 1827; died July 29, 1853. Children:
Elizabeth, Henry.—Abraham mrd. second wife Elizabeth, daughter of John and Anna Lapp, May 1856.
She was bn. Nov. 5, 1831; died Dec. 14, 1888. Farmer.
Menn. Children: Jacob, John, Sallie, Mary, and two
died.

VI. Elizabeth Moyer, bn. Jan. 21, 1850. Mrd. Jacob
H. Myers, Nov. 28, 1874. P. O., Dublin, Pa.
Farmer. Menn. Children: **(VII.)** Flora M. Myers, bn.
June 18, 1876. **(VII.)** Abraham Linford Myers, bn.
Nov. 6, 1879.

VI. Henry F. Moyer, bn. Jan. 18, 1852. Mrd. A. Eliza Swartley Nov. 18, 1882. P. O., Line Lexington, Pa. Farmer. Menn. Children: (**VII.**) Martha Moyer, bn. Mar. 2, 1889. (**VII.**) Laura Moyer, bn. —; died —. (**VII.**) Harvey Moyer, bn. —.

VI. Jacob L. Moyer, bn. Res. 1429 Kay St. Phila., Pa.

VI. John L. Moyer, bn. —. P. O., Line Lexington, Pa.

VI. Sallie Moyer, bn. —. Mrd. John Garges. P. O., Line Lexington, Pa.

VI. Mary L. Moyer, bn. Mar. 8, 1867. Mrd. Isaac M. Swartley. He was bn. Jan. 16, 1865; died May 21, 1892. P. O., Line Lexington, Pa. Menn. Children: (**VII.**) Bertha M. Swartley, bn. Aug. 22, 1890. (**VII.**) Harvey M. Swartley, bn. Jan. 17, 1892; died Feb. 17, 1892.

V. Anna Moyer, born —. Mrd. Jacob H. High. (See Index of References No. 28.)

V. Elizabeth Moyer, born —. Mrd. William F. Myers, in 1849. He was bn. Nov. 20, 1819; died —. Farmer. Menn. Children: Catharine, Sarah.

VI. Catharine Myers, bn. —; died infant.

VI. Sarah Myers, bn. in 1852. Mrd. Jacob B. Rosenberger, in 1873. Merchant. Menn. Children: (**VII.**) William M. Rosenberger, bn. 1875. (**VII.**) Allen M. Rosenberger, bn. 1881. (**VII.**) Susie May Rosenberger, bn. 1886.

V. Sarah Moyer, bn. —. Mrd. Daniel Kaisinger, —.

IV. Mary Moyer, bn. —; died —. Mrd. Abraham Meyers, —. Farmer. Menn. (Author of Hymns printed in German.) Children: David, Elizabeth, Nancy.

V. David D. Meyers, born Apr. 30, 1821. Mrd. Annie Benner, Sept. 19, 1847. P. O., Plumsteadville, Pa. Retired farmer. Menn. No issue.

V. Elizabeth Meyers, bn. —. Mrd. Jacob O. Leatherman. (See Index of References No. 29.)

V. Nancy Meyers, bn. —. Mrd. Martin Leatherman. (See Index of References No. 30.)

IV. Catharine Moyer, bn. Dec. 24, 1805; died Nov. 8, 1879. Mrd. Henry Leatherman, Oct. 18, 1829.

He was born June 17, 1806; died Dec. 21, 1859.
Farmer. Menn. Children: Elizabeth, Abraham,
Sarah, Henry, Joseph.

V. Elizabeth Leatherman, bn. Aug. 20, 1831. Mrd.
Isaac M. Wismer. (See Index of References No. 31.)

V. Abraham Leatherman, bn. June 12, 1834. Watchman in Phila., Pa. S.

V. Sarah Leatherman, born May 10, 1837. Mrd.
Peter Bean. Carpenter in Phila., Pa. Menn's.
Children: Emma. William, Laura.

VI. Emma Bean, bn. Jan. 3, 1864. Mrd. Ambrose
Moyer, Dec. 25, 1882. Provision dealer in Phila.,
Pa. Menn. One child: (**VII.**) Elwood Moyer, born
Sept. 29, 1883.

VI. William H. Bean, bn. July 22, 1866. Stair-
builder. Menn.

VI. Laura Bean, bn. Apr. 22, 1869; died July 16,
1869.

V. Henry Leatherman, bn. Nov. 25, 1840. Mrd.
Sarah Fegley, Nov. 3, 1881. Whiting manufacturer
in Phila., Pa. Mrs. L. Ger. Ref. No issue.

V. Joseph Leatherman, bn. Mar. 16, 1847. Mrd.
Amanda Smith, Jan. 7, 1870. Whiting manufact-
urer in Phila., Pa. Menn. One child: (**VI.**) Charles
Leatherman, bn. Aug. 28, 1873.

IV. Henry A. Moyer, bn. in Bucks Co., 1812; died
Jan. 18, 1891. Mrd. Anna Moyer, —. Farmer.
Menn's. Children: Sarah, Elizabeth, Nancy, Lana,
Maria, Catharine.

V. Sarah Moyer, bn. — . Mrd. Samuel S. Beidler,
—. P. O., Shelly Station, Pa. Menn. Children:
Annie, Amanda.

VI. Annie Beidler, bn. —. Mrd. Tobias Shelly, —.
P. O., Shelly Sta., Pa. Farmer. Ref. ch. Three
children —.

VI. Amanda Beidler, bn. —. Mrd. Allen H. Erd-
man, —. P. O., Shelly Sta., Pa. Carpenter. Luth.
One child: —.

V. Elizabeth Moyer, bn. —. Mrd. Wm. H. Landis.
P. O., Richland Centre, Pa. One child: (**VI.**) Henry
Landis, bn. --. Mrd.

V. Nancy Moyer, bn. Feb. 24, 1840. Mrd. Enos S. Beidler, Mar. 23, 1862. P. O., Shelly Station, Pa. Menn. Children:
VI. William M. Beidler, born Aug. 16, 1863; died Sept. 13, 1887.
VI. Amanda M. Beidler, bn. July, 28, 1866. Mrd. William L. Lapp, May 11, 1888. P. O., Hilltown, Pa. One child: (VII.) Laura B. Lapp, bn. Oct. 16, 1891.
VI. Climena M. Beidler, born Feb. 7, 1869; died June 14, 1887.
VI. Lizzie M. Beidler, born Sept. 17, 1871; died Aug. 13, 1887.
VI. Katie M. Beidler, bn. Apr. 27, 1874.
VI. Ida M. Beidler, bn. Dec. 13, 1877.
VI. Henry M. Beidler, bn. Oct. 30, 1879.
V. Magdalena Moyer, born in Springfield, Twp., Bucks Co., Pa., Oct. 1, 1843; died Apr. 27, 1880. Mrd. Christian L. Rosenberger. He was bn. in Richland Twp., Oct. 27, 1838. P. O., Zion's Hill, Pa. Farmer. Menn. Children: Anna, William, Elmer, Lizzie, Harvey, Samuel, Catharine.
VI. Anna Mary Rosenberger, bn. Sept. 14, 1866.
VI. William Henry Rosenberger, bn. Aug. 9, 1868. Mrd. Alice Schlifer, —. P. O., Centre Valley, Pa. Butcher. Menn. One child: (VII.) Violet Rosenberger, bn. Feb. 6, 1891.
VI. Elmer Rosenberger, bn. Jan. 25, 1871. Mrd. Elemina Young, —. P. O., Zion's Hill, Pa. Farmer. Menn. One child: (VII.) Henry Rosenberger, born Nov. 23, 1889.
VI. Lizzie Rosenberger, bn. Apr. 10, 1875.
VI. Harvey Rosenberger, bn. Aug. 14, 1877.
VI. Samuel Rosenberger, bn. Feb. 28, 1873; died Apr. 21, 1873.
VI. Catharine Rosenberger, bn. Apr. 4, 1880; died Sept. 10, 1880.
V. Maria Moyer, bn. Sept. 28, 1847. Mrd. William Stauffer, in 1866. P. O., Zion's Hill, Pa. Farmer. Menn. Children: (VI.) Emma Stauffer, born Mar. 1868. Mrd. Harvey S. Rummery, —. P. O., Allentown, Pa. Clerk. (VI.) John Stauffer, bn. 1870.

Menn. S. (VI.) Henry Stauffer, born 1872; died 1875. (VI.) Howard Stauffer, born 1875. Menn. (VI.) Oliver Stauffer, bn. 1878. Menn. (VI.) Clarence Stauffer, bn. 1885. Menn.

V. Catharine Moyer, born Sept. 24, 1852; died Apr. 25, 1878. Mrd. William M. Geisinger, Jan. 15, 1873. P. O., Centre Valley, Pa. Farmer. Menn. Children: (VI.) Abraham Geisinger, bn. Dec. 5, 1874. (VI.) Henry Geisinger, bn. Jan. 18, 1878.

III. Mary Angeny, bn. Mar. 12, 1765; died —. Mrd Jacob Oberholtzer, May 17, 1791. He was born Mar. 12, 1767. Farmer. Menn. Children: Jacob, Elizabeth, Martin, Barbara, Infant, Anna, Maria, Sarah.

IV. Jacob Overholt, bn. Apr. 6, 1792; died —. Mrd. Anna Shutt, —. Farmer. Menn. No issue.

IV. Elizabeth Overholt, bn. Dec. 5, 1793; died —. Mrd. Christian Fretz, Mar. 6, 1817. He was born Sept. 5, 1787; died —. Mason. Menn. Children: Christian, Enos.

V. Christian Fretz, bn. Nov. 5, 1821; died Sept, 5, 1866. Mrd. Maria Moyer, Mar. 7, 1847. Farmer. Menn. Children: Elizabeth, Annie, Abraham, Sallie, Jacob, Henry, Isaiah.

VI. Elizabeth Fretz, bn. Mar. 15, 1848. Mrd. Joseph D. Bishop, Feb. 20, 1869. P. O., Blooming Glen, Pa. Farmer. Menn. Three children died unnamed.

VI. Annie Fretz, bn. Oct. 24, 1850. Mrd. William Beidler, June 4, 1870. Salesman. Children: (VII.) Ella Beidler, bn. Feb. 24, 1871. (VII.) Maria Beidler, bn. June 15, 1872.

VI. Abraham M. Fretz, bn. May 15, 1853. Mrd. Sarah Ann Hendricks, Nov. 22, 1873. P. O., Blooming Glen, Pa. Menn. Children: (VII.) Ulysses G. H. Fretz, bn. June 20, 1875. (VII.) Albertha H. Fretz, bn. Nov. 26, 1885. (VII.) Mabel May Fretz, bn. Apr. 6, 1888. (VII.) Anna Myra Fretz, bn. Aug. 23, 1891.

VI. Sallie Fretz, bn. May 10, 1855. Mrd. A. E. Detweiler, Jan. 20, 1877. Tinsmith. Menn. Children: (VII.) Manerva Detweiler, born Oct. 6, 1878. (VII.) Preston Detweiler, bn. Jan. 18, 1883. (VII.) Sarah Alma Detweiler, bn. Mar. 2, 1892.

VI. Jacob M. Fretz, bn. Feb. 6, 1860. Mrd. Lizzie Geisinger, —. Children: (VII.) Emma G. Fretz, bn. May 1, 1886. (VII.) Allen G. Fretz, bn. Aug. 1888. (VII.) Cora G. Fretz, bn. —.

VI. Henry M. Fretz, bn. Apr. 8, 1863. Farmer in Marshall Co., Kans.

VI. Isaiah M. Fretz, bn. Jan. 27, 1866. Mrd. Lizzie Moyer, —.

V. Enos Fretz, bn. —; died —, aged 24 years.

IV. Martin Overholt, born Oct. 13, 1796; died —. Mrd. Anna Kulp, Dec. 20, 1825. She died 1885. Farmer. Menn. One child: Jacob.

V. Jacob K. Overholt, bn. Sept. 14, 1826; died —. Mrd. Hannah Baum, Nov. 25, 1849. Farmer. Mennonite deacon for 30 years. Children: Martin, Hetty, Anna, Sarah, Joseph, Kate, Jacob.

VI. Martin Overholt, bn. Jan. 26, 1851. Mrd. Kate Hunsberger, Mar. 17, 1888. P. O., Benjamin, Pa. Miller. Menn.

VI. Hetty Overholt, bn. Jan. 21, 1853. Mrd. Levi L. Meyer, Dec. 20, 1873. P. O., Bedminster, Pa. Farmer. Menn. Children: (VII.) Emma Meyer, bn. Oct. 8, 1876. (VII.) Annie Meyer, bn. Nov. 12, 1880. (VII.) Jacob Meyer, bn. Apr. 6, 1887.

VI. Anna Overholt, bn. Mar. 29, 1855. Mrd. Abraham M. Hunsicker, May 27, 1876. Miller. Menn. Children: (VII.) Sallie Hunsicker. (VII.) Katie Hunsicker. (VII.) Jacob Hunsicker. (VII.) Hannah B. Hunsicker.

VI. Sallie Overholt, bn. Jan. 2, 1858. Mrd. George A. Schriver, Nov. 27, 1881. Farmer in Harvey Co., Kan. Luth. Children: (VII.) Richard Schriver. (VII.) Nola Schriver, (and two died).

VI. Joseph B. Overholt, bn. July 29, 1860. Mrd. Sallie Leatherman, Sept. 29, 1883. P. O., Dublin, Pa. Farmer. Menn. Children: (VII.) Hannah Overholt. (VII.) Lizzie Overholt.

VI. Kate Overholt, bn. —. P. O., Dublin, Pa. S.

VI. Jacob Overholt, bn. Aug. 17, 1867. Mrd. — Herr.
IV. Barbara Oberholtzer, bn. Aug. 8, 1798; died —.
Mrd. John Leatherman (known as "thick John") —.
Farmer. Menn. Children: Jacob, Martin, Mary,
Elizabeth, Barbara, Nancy.
V. Jacob O. Leatherman, bn. —; died —. Mrd.
Elizabeth Myers. Farmer. Menn. Children: John,
Martin, Samuel, Elizabeth, Abraham, David, Anna,
Jacob, &c.
VI. Rev. John Leatherman, bn. —. Mrd. Mary
Myers. P. O., Dublin, Pa.
VI. Martin Leatherman, bn. —. Mrd. —. P. O.,
Bedminster, Pa.
VI. Samuel Leatherman, bn. —. Mrd. —. P. O.,
Bedminster, Pa.
VI. Elizabeth Leatherman, bn. Mrd. Joseph M.
Tyson. (See Index of References No. 32.)
VI. Abraham Leatherman, bn. —; died. —. S.
VI. David Leatherman, bn. —; died —. S.
VI. Anna Leatherman, bn. —; died —. S.
VI. Jacob Leatherman, bn. —; died —. Mrd. Anna
Myers, —. Two children: (**VII.**) —. S. (**VII.**) —. S.
V. Martin Leatherman, bn. —. Mrd. Nancy Myers,
—. P. O., Bedminster, Pa. Farmer. Menn. Chil-
dren: (**VI.**) John M. Leatherman, bn. —. Mrd. —
Kulp. P. O., Bedminster, Pa. (**VI.**) Eli Leather-
man, bn. —; died —. S.
V. Mary Leatherman, bn. —. Mrd. John Detweiler,
—. He died —. Farmer. Menn. Children: Peter,
Jacob, Anna.
VI. Peter Detweiler, bn. —. Mrd. Catharine God-
shall (dau. of Rev. Samuel Godshall). P. O., Dub-
lin, Pa.
VI. Jacob M. Detweiler, bn. Sept. 25, 1848; died
Dec. 8, 1892. Mrd. Mary Myers, Nov. 25, 1871.
Farmer. Menn's. One child: Emma.

In his youth Mr. Detweiler attended school in
winter, and assisted his father on the farm along the
headwaters of Deep Run.

The year following his marriage he took charge of
his father's farm, of which he later became the owner,
and on which he resided until the date of his tragic

H. E. Kratz, (See page 176.)

death. On December 8, 1892, between the hours of six and seven in the evening, he left his home on foot to transact some business affairs with a neighbor, distant about one mile. He did not return at the expected hour, and about midnight members of the family went to the place he had intended to visit and learned he had not been there. A searching party immediately started over the rout, through woods and fields, supposed to have been taken.

Between two and three o'clock his lifeless body was found in a shallow pond of water, in his own woods, about fifty rods from his house. His coat and vest were open, his watch and money were missing. Suspicions of foul play were fully aroused, and were confirmed by further investigations. In a line from the spot where the body was found, about one fourth of a mile in length, along the trail of strange and peculiar footprints, were found an account book, and a purse and wallet from which the contents had been removed, all of which were identified as belonging to the deceased. An autopsy also revealed a number of contusions, caused by blows on the head. Great excitement prevailed in the vicinity, and hundreds of people visited the spot and surroundings daily. Detectives were immediately employed. The county authorities offered a reward of $500 and a citizens' meeting of the surrounding vicinity an additional reward of $1000 for the apprehension and conviction of the guilty person or persons.

His remains were interred at the Deep Run Mennonite church of which he was a member. On Dec. 12, an immense throng assembled to pay their last tribute of respect. By actual count over 325 carriages left his late residence in the funeral procession. He was much esteemed and highly respected by hosts of relatives, friends and acquaintances.

VII. Emma Detweiler, bn. Dec. 28, 1872. Mrd. Oscar A. Rufe, Sept. 19, 1891. P. O., Dublin, Pa. Farmer. Lutherans.

VI. Anna Detweiler, bn. —. Mrd. Mahlon F. High. (See Index of References No. 33.)

8

V. Elizabeth Leatherman, bn. —. Mrd. Joseph G. Overholt. (See Index of References No. 34.)

V. Barbara Leatherman, bn. —. Mrd. Abraham K. High, —. P. O., Dublin, Pa. Farmer. Menn. Children: John, etc. **(VI.)** John L. High, bn. —. Mrd. Mary Moyer, —. P. O., Dublin, Pa.

V. Nancy Leatherman, bn. —; died —. Mrd. Abraham Kulp. P. O., Bedminster, Pa. Farmer, shoemaker. Menn. Children: Mary, Anna, John, Abraham, Barbara.

VI. Mary Kulp, bn. —. Mrd. Aaron M. Kulp, —. P. O., Bedminster, Pa. Farmer. Menn. No issue.

VI. Anna Kulp, bn. —. Mrd. Isaac O. Yothers, —. P. O., Dublin. Farmer. Menn. Children: Ed, Abraham, &c.

VI. John L. Kulp, bn. —. Mrd. Hannah Barndt, —. P. O., Bedminster, Pa. Farmer. Children: **(VII.)** Henry Kulp. **(VII.)** Isaac Kulp. **(VII.)** Ellen Kulp. **(VII.)** Mary Kulp. **(VII.)**(Baby) Kulp.

VI. Abraham L. Kulp, bn. —. Mrd. Emma Rohr. P. O., Bedminster, Pa. Farmer. Children: **(VII.)** —. —.

VI. Barbara Kulp, bn.—; died young.

VI. — Kulp, bn. —; died young.

IV. Anna Oberholtzer, bn. May 15, 1801; died Sept. 15, 1888. Mrd. Peter Loux, May 12, 1836. He was bn. June 27, 1776; died July 24, 1871. Farmer. Menn. One child:

V. Mary Loux, bn. Mar. 3, 1837. Mrd. Enos Hunsberger, Nov. 5, 1859. P. O., Plumsteadville, Pa. Farmer. Menn. Children: **(VI.)** Anna L. Hunsberger, bn. Feb. 26, 1861; died Mar. 29, 1863. **(VI.)** Sarah Hunsberger, bn. Nov. 11, 1862; died Apr. 8, 1863. **(VI.)** Emma L. Hunsberger, bn. June 12, 1864. Mrd. Samuel W. Gross. (See Index of References No. 35.) **(VI.)** Peter L. Hunsberger, bn. Nov. 9, 1869. S. **(VI.)** Harvey D. Hunsberger, bn. Oct. 8, 1873.

IV. Maria Oberholtzer, bn. Sept. 17, 1803. (living '92.) Mrd. John Leatherman, (known as "little John") —. Farmer. Menn. Children: Elizabeth, Anna, Mary, Catharine, Hannah.

V. Elizabeth Leatherman, bn. —. Mrd. Abraham S. Meyers. (See Index of References No. 36.)

V. Anna Leatherman, bn. —; died Mar. 10, 1890. Mrd. Aaron Fretz, Oct. 30, 1858. He died —. Justice of the Peace and auctioneer. Presby. Children: Susanna, Tobias, Harvey, Marietta, Franklin, Anna, Theodore.

VI. Susanna Fretz, bn. Sept. 17, 1860; died Jan. 19, 1871.

VI. Tobias Fretz, bn. May 18, 1862. Mrd. Millie Strouse, —. Res. Phila. Presby. Children: **(VII.)** Charles Fretz. **(VII.)** Aaron Fretz. **(VII.)** Mabel Fretz.

VI. Harvey Fretz, bn. Jan. 30, 1864. Presby. S.

VI. Marietta Fretz, bn. June 8, 1865; died Mar. 21, 1869.

VI. Franklin Fretz, bn. Aug. 28, 1867; died July 20, 1878.

VI. Anna Fretz, bn. Nov. 27, 1869.

VI. Theodore Fretz, bn. Feb. 20, 1872; died Aug. 27, 1872.

V. Mary Ann Leatherman, bn. —. Mrd. David B. Myers in 1852. He died —. Farmer. Menn. Children: Catharine, Barbara, Harvey, Mary.

VI. Catharine Myers, bn. Dec. 19, 1854. Mrd. William H. Myers, Oct. 13, 1877. Farmer. Menn. Children: **(VII.)** Franklin Myers, bn. Jan. 18, 1879. **(VII.)** Rosa May Myers, bn. Jan. 26, 1881. **(VII.)** Clara Myers, bn. July 19, 1884.

VI. Barbara Myers, bn. Nov. 1, 1856. Mrd. Calvin Lear, —. Farmer. Menn. Have issue.

VI. Harvey Myers, bn. Oct. 9, 1858. Mrd. Annie Lear, —. Farmer. Menn. Have issue.

VI. Mary Myers, bn. Apr. 5, 1861. Mrd. John A. Myers, —. Menn. Have issue.

V. Catharine Leatherman, bn. —. Mrd. Samuel Shelly, —. P. O., Plumsteadville, Pa. Farmer. Menn. Children: John, Kate, Mary, Emma, Harvey, Levi, Frank, Lizzie, Edwin.

VI. John Shelly, bn. —. Mrd. Lizzie Leatherman, —. P. O., Plumsteadville, Pa.

VI. Kate Shelly, bn. —. Mrd. Christian Crouthamel —. P. O., Fountainville, Pa.

VI. Mary Shelly, bn. —; died —. Mrd. Edward Schmell, —.

VI. Emma Shelly, bn. —. Mrd. Wilson Lear —. P. O., Gardenville, Pa.

VI. Harvey Shelly, bn. Mar. 1, 1864. Mrd. Mary E. Godshall, Dec. 18, 1887. Laborer. Menn. One child: **(VII.)** Walter G. Shelly, bn. Dec. 22, 1888.

VI. Levi Shelly, bn. —.

VI. Frank Shelly, bn. —.

VI. Lizzie Shelly, bn. —.

VI. Edwin Shelly, bn. —.

.V. Hannah Leatherman, bn. —. Mrd. Samuel Derstine —. Farmer. Menn. Children: **(VI.)** John Derstine, bn. —. Mrd. Lydia M. Mill, —. **(VI.)** Isaac Derstine, bn. —; died aged 15 years. **(VI.)** Mary Derstine. **(VI.)** Samuel Derstine. **(VI.)** Abraham Derstine. **(VI.)** Lizzie Derstine. **(VI.)** Anna Derstine.

IV. Sarah Overholt, bn. Aug. 25, 1808. Mrd. Rev. Samuel Leatherman, Apr. 12, 1836. He was bn. May 1, 1815. P. O., Line Lexington, Pa. Farmer and minister. Ordained minister of the Mennonite church at Line Lexington in 1843. Children: Jacob, Elizabeth, Henry.

V. Jacob Leatherman, bn. Apr. 30, 1837. Mrd. Sarah Musselman, Jan. 1861. Menn. Children: **(VI.)** Samuel Leatherman. **(VI.)** John Leatherman.

V. Elizabeth Leatherman, bn. Jan. 5, 1840. Mrd. Charles Taylor, Oct. 7, 1877. He died Aug. 12, 1889. Farmer. Menn. No issue.

V. Henry Leatherman, bn. Jan. 13, 1845. Mrd. Catharine Lapp, Dec. 7, 1871. P. O., Line Lexington, Penna. Farmer. Menn. Children: **(VI.)** Emma Leatherman, born May 28, 1873. **(VI.)** Abraham Leatherman, bn. Sept. 17, 1876. **(VI.)** Sallie Leatherman, bn. Jan. 24, 1879. **(VI.)** William Leatherman, bn. Sept. 3, 1882. **(VI.)** Henry Leatherman, bn. July 20, 1884; died Sept. 17, 1884.

III. Barbara Angeny, bn. Apr. 8, 1770; died —. Mrd. Joseph Moyer of Hilltown, Pa., —. Farmer. Menn. Children: Samuel, Joseph, William, Henry, Jacob, Elizabeth, Mary.

IV. Samuel Moyer, bn. —; died —. Mrd. — Hun-
sicker. Farmer. Menn. Children: Isaac, Samuel,
Jacob, Joseph, Lydia, Maria.
   V. Isaac H. Moyer, born. —. Mrd. —. P. O.,
Blooming Glen, Pa. Children: (VI.) Mary Moyer, bn.
—. Mrd. John L. High. (See Index of References
No. 37.) (VI.) William M. Moyer, Jr. bn. —. P. O.,
Blooming Glen, Pa. (VI.) Samuel Moyer, bn. —. P.
O.. Blooming Glen, Pa. (VI.) Sybilla Moyer, bn. —.
Mrd. —.
   V. Samuel H. Moyer, bn. —. Mrd. Mary Ann
Moyer, daughter of Rev. Abraham F. Moyer, in 1862.
She was born June 2, 1845. P. O.. Dublin, Penna.
Farmer. Menn's. Children: (VI.) Milton Moyer, bn.
Sept. 9, 1863; died Oct. 5, 1863. (VI.) Esther Ellen
Moyer, bn. Apr. 27, 1865; died Jan. 20, 1877. (VI.)
Abram Moyer, bn. Oct. 5, 1867. (VI.) Anna Mary
Moyer, bn. Nov. 10, 1869; died Sept. 9, 1877. (VI.)
Amanda Moyer, bn. Aug. 6, 1871; died Apr. 1, 1877.
(VI.) Ellen Moyer, bn. May 2, 1874. (VI.) Harriet
Moyer, bn. July 6, 1875. (VI.) Lizzie Moyer, born
July 1, 1877. (VI.) Della Moyer, bn. Mar. 20, 1880.
(VI.) Emma Moyer, born Oct. 31, 1882. (VI.) Ida
Moyer, bn. Aug. 19, 1885; died Aug. 17, 1886.
   V. Jacob H. Moyer, bn. —. P. O.. Dublin, Pa.
   V. Joseph H. Moyer, bn. in Bucks Co., Pa.. May 22,
1840; died Feb. 27, 1886. Mrd. Elizabeth George,
Feb. 8, 1862. She was bn. Dec. 1, 1839. Farmer.
Menn's. Children: Mary, Emma, Abraham, Daniel,
Lizzie, Kate, Addie, Joseph.
   VI. Mary G. Moyer, bn. —. Mrd. Jacob M. Rush,
Aug. 4, 1883. P. O., Plumsteadville, Pa. Farmer.
Menn's. Child: (VII.) Nora Lizzie Rush, bn. Feb. 20,
1885.
   VI. Emma Moyer, bn. in Hilltown Twp., Bucks Co.,
May 24, 1865. Mrd. John Bergstresser, Apr. 2,
1887. P. O., Pipersville, Pa. Merchant. Mrs. B.
Menn. Children: (VII.) Abel Bergstresser. (VII.)
Howard Bergstresser. (VII.) Daniel Bergstresser.
   VI. Abraham G. Moyer, bn. Apr. 4, 1867. Mrd.
Hannah Fretz, Oct. 27, 1887. P. O.. Milford Square,
Pa., Merchant. Menn. Children: (VII.) Willis Moyer,

bn. Apr. 23, 1891. **(VII.)** Pearl Moyer, bn. Feb. 12, 1893.

VI. Daniel G. Moyer, bn. —. Mrd. Maggie Souder. P. O., Telford, Pa.

VI. Lizzie Moyer, bn. —. S.

VI. Katie Moyer, bn. Apr. 15, 1874. Mrd. Henry C. Beidler, Mar. 24, 1892. P. O., Milford Square, Pa. Clerk. No issue. (1893.)

VI. Addie Moyer, bn. —. S.

VI. Joseph Wilson Moyer, bn. —; died May 24, 1882.

V. Lydia Moyer, bn. May 13, 1831; died Oct. 19, 1856. Mrd. Henry H. High. (See Index of References, No. 82.)

V. Maria Moyer, bn. —. Mrd. Samuel Godshall. P. O., Blooming Glen, Pa.

IV. Joseph Moyer, bn. Dec. 29, 1802; died Nov. 4, 1842. Mrd. Elizabeth Hunsberger, Oct. 31, 1826. She died —. Farmer. Menn. Children: Barbara, John, Elizabeth.

V. Barbara Moyer, bn. Sept. 20, 1827. Mrd. Francis Gerhart, Nov. 9, 1845. P. O., Dublin, Pa. Tailor and farmer. Children: **(VI.)** Maria Gerhart, bn. —; died —. **(VI.)** Abraham M. Gerhart, bn. —. Mrd. Amanda Springer, —. **(VI.)** Emma Gerhart, bn. —. Mrd. Harry Leatherman, —. **(VI.)** Joseph Gerhart, bn. —. Mrd. Adda Derr, —. **(VI.)** Samuel Gerhart, bn. —. Mrd. Mattie Swartz.

V. John Moyer, bn. Apr. 25, 1829; died about 1867. Mrd. Barbara Benner, —. Children: **(VI.)** Milton. **(VI.)** Reuben. **(VI.)** Lizzie. **(VI.)** Mary (dec'd.)

V. Elizabeth Moyer, bn. Nov. 30, 1837; died Nov. 18, 1890. Mrd. Abraham Landis, —. Children: **(VI.)** John. **(VI.)** Reuben. **(VI.)** Emma. **(VI.)** Edmund (dec'd.)

IV. William A. Moyer, bn. —; died —. Mrd. Sarah Clymer. She died —. Children: Henry, Samuel, Barbara, John, Mary.

V. Henry Moyer, bn. —; died —. Mrd. —.

V. Samuel C. Moyer, M. D., bn. —. Mrd. —. P. O., Lansdale.

V. Barbara Moyer, bn. Mar. 12, 1840. Mrd. George R. Landis, Nov. 15, 1860. P. O., Dublin, Penna. Farmer. Menn. Children: Sarah, Daniel, William, John, Samuel.

VI. Sarah Landis, bn. 1861, Mrd. Daniel O. Landis, 1880. Fireman on train. Children: **(VII.)** Abraham. **(VII.)** Barbara. **(VI.)** Ida. **(VII.)** Samuel.

VI. Daniel M. Landis, M. D., bn. in Milford Twp., Bucks Co., Pa., April 17, 1864. Soon after his birth his parents moved to Hilltown Twp., where he was brought up on the farm. He was always fond of going to school, and always had the good fortune to be at the head of his class. In 1879 one of his teachers, Mr. A. R. Moyer, imbued him with the spirit to go to a high school, and accordingly in March, 1881, he was sent to the Quakertown High School. In the summer he worked on the farm again with his father. The next winter, 1882, he resided with his uncle, Dr. S. C. Moyer, and attended the Lansdale High School. His residence here no doubt had something to do with his future profession. In the fall of 1883 he began teaching school, and taught for three successive winters. In the spring of 1884 he went to the North Wales Academy one course. He took up the study of medicine in the summer of 1886, with his uncle, Dr. S. C. Moyer. In the fall of that same year he entered the Hahnemann Medical College of Philadelphia, Pa., from which he graduated in April 1889 as Doctor of Medicine, and Doctor of Homeopathic Medicine. In April of the same year of graduation he located at Perkasie, Pa., where he is still practicing his profession. He was mrd. to Lizzie Hedrick, daughter of David and Sarah Hedrick, of near Chalfont, Pa., in 1889. Menn's. One child: **(VII.)** Joycelin Landis, bn. May 2, 1892; died July 16, 1892.

VI. William M. Landis, bn. July 4, 1869. Mrd. Lizzie Detweiler, Nov. 10, 1892. P. O., Dublin, Pa. Farmer.

VI. John M. Landis, bn. 1878.

VI. Samuel M. Landis, bn. Nov. 1883.

V. John Moyer, bn.—; died—. Mrd.—.

V. Mary Moyer, bn.—. Mrd. John Christman,—.
P. O., Milford Square, Pa.
IV. Henry A. Moyer, bn. in Bucks Co., Pa., Oct.
26, 1807; died Aug. 4, 1875. Mrd. Sarah Gerhart,
Dec. 8, 1833. She was bn. Aug. 20, 1814; died Feb.
28, 1890. Farmer. Menn. Children: Lydia, Abra-
ham, Barbara, Joseph, Sarah, Henry, Jacob, Isaiah.
V. Lydia Moyer, bn. Feb. 22, 1835. Mrd. Samuel
M. Gerhart, Oct. 22, 1852. P. O., Perkasie, Pa. Re-
tired farmer. Ref. ch. Children: Mahlon, Sallie,
John, Albert, Frank.
VI. Mahlon M. Gerhart, bn. Oct. 7, 1853. Mrd.
Susan Kramer,—. P. O., Hilltown, Pa. Farmer.
Ref. ch. Children: **(VII.)** Sallie Gerhart. **(VII.)** Har-
vey Gerhart. **(VII.)** Lydia Gerhart.
VI. Sallie A. Gerhart, bn. Oct. 28, 1856. Mrd. Jesse
L. Stump,—. P. O., Ridge, Pa. Blacksmith. Ref.
ch. Children: **(VII.)** Tiras (dec'd). **(VII.)** Jennie. **(VII.)**
Ira.
VI. John H. Gerhart, bn. Dec. 17, 1859. Mrd.
Emma Leatherman,—. P. O., Fountainville, Pa.
Farmer. Ref. ch. Children: **(VII.)** Howard. **(VII.)**
Elsie.
VI. Albert M Gerhart, bn. Mar. 10, 1863. Mrd.
Laura Loux,—. P. O., Pipersville, Pa. Creamery-
man. Ref. ch. One child: **(VII.)** Wilmer Clarence
Gerhart.
VI. A. Frank Gerhart, bn. Dec. 12, 1866. P. O.,
Mauch Chunk, Pa. Printer. Ev. Ass'n.
V. Abraham G. Moyer, bn. Sept. 26, 1837; died—.
Mrd. Annie Hunsberger,—. P. O., Blooming Glen,
Pa.
V. Joseph G. Moyer, bn. Feb. 10, 1840. Mrd. Mary
Ann Kratz, Dec. 23, 1862. P. O., Perkasie, Pa.
Lumber and coal merchant. Ger. Ref. Children:
Madora, Irwin, Elmer, Mary, Lyre, Gertie.
VI. S. Madora Moyer, bn. Apr. 3, 1864. Mrd. B.
Frank Hartzell, Feb. 23, 1883. P. O., Chalfont, Pa.
Merchant miller. Ger. Ref. Children: **(VII.)** Russel
M. Hartzell, bn. Mar. 11, 1885. **(VII.)** Percy M.
Hartzell, bn. Mar. 15, 1887.

VI. H. Irwin Moyer, bn. Aug. 2, 1865. Mrd. Eliza, daughter of David K. Moyer, of Hilltown, Sept. 29, 1887. P. O., Perkasie, Pa. Clerk. Ger. Ref. Children: **(VII.)** Marion Moyer. **(VII.)** Joseph Nevin Moyer.

VI. Elmer K. Moyer, bn. July 22, 1867. Mrd. Laura Wickert,—. Res. 2111 Percy St., Phila., Pa. Ger. Ref. Children: **(VII.)** Ernest Wickert Moyer. **(VII.)** Grace Evelyn Moyer.

VI. Mary Delilah Moyer, bn. Nov. 2, 1872. P. O., Perkasie, Pa. Ger. Ref.

VI. J. Dyre Moyer, bn. Sept. 14, 1875.

VI. Gertie K. Moyer, bn. Mar. 4, 1882.

V. Barbara Moyer, bn. Aug. 28, 18—. Mrd. Samuel G. Kramer. P. O., Church Hill, Pa.

V. Sarah Jane Moyer, bn. Oct. 15, 1845. Mrd. Henry O. Moyer. P. O., Bedminster, Pa.

V. Henry G. Moyer, bn. in Bucks Co., Aug. 28, 1848. Mrd. Emeline Seiple, of Allentown,—. P. O., Perkasie, Pa. Mr. Moyer spent his boyhood days on his father's farm in Hilltown Twp., and attended the common schools of the township and several terms at the Leondonian Seminary, and graduated in the Philadelphia Business College at the age of 20 years. He spent the next 15 years as clerk in store, three years at Blooming Glen and several years in Philadelphia, in the wholesale notion house of Mackey, Bodder & Co., and 10 years with J. A. Hendricks at Perkasie. In 1879, when Perkasie Borough was founded, he was elected to the office of Justice of the Peace, and on May 10, 1890, he entered upon his third term, having now served about 13 years in that capacity.

The latter part of 1881, he engaged in the newspaper business, and in company with Mahlon H. Sellers, under the firm name of M. H. Sellers & Co., established the "Central News," a local weekly paper. In Feb. 1882 Mr. Sellers died, and his interest in the paper was purchased by Samuel R. Kramer, and since then the firm name has been Moyer and Kramer. The "News," after hard struggling in the beginning, soon obtained a firm footing and is now recognized as one of the leading papers of upper Bucks

Co., with a circulation of over 2000 copies weekly.
Mr. and Mrs. Moyer are members of the Evangelical
Association church at Perkasie, of which he is a class-
leader, and in this capacity has done considerable
public speaking. Children: (VI.) Bertha May Moyer,
bn. May 13, 1871; died Dec. 16, 1877. (VI.) Wallace
B. Moyer, bn. Dec. 10, 1873; died Apr. 8, 1875.
(VI.) Henrietta Moyer, bn. Apr. 21, 1876; died Jan.
18, 1882. (VI.) Jennie Moyer, bn. Dec. 16, 1877; died
Jan. 9, 1882. (VI.) Mabel Rebecca Moyer, bn. Oct.
10, 1882. (VI.) Emilie Moyer, bn. Mar. 2, 1886; died
July 25, 1887. (VI.) Henry Clayton Moyer, bn. Mar.
5, 1888.

V. Jacob G. Moyer, bn. Feb. 23, 1852. Mrd. Susan
B. Dill, June 20, 1874. P. O., Bedminster, Pa. Ba-
ker. Ev. Ass'n. Children: (VI.) Charles Linford
Moyer. (VI.) Wesley D. Moyer. (VI.) G. Ida Moyer.
(VI.) Cora May Moyer. (VI.) Annie Letitia Moyer.
(VI.) Emma Floyd Moyer. (VI.) Paul Stanley Moyer.

V. Isaiah G. Moyer, bn. Nov. 12, 1853; died—.

IV. Jacob Moyer, bn.—; died in Canada. S.

IV. Elizabeth Moyer, bn.—. Mrd. Abraham Gerhart. He died—. Children: (V.) Mary Ann Gerhart,
bn.—; died—. Mrd. Abraham Zeigenfuss. (V.) Rebecca Gerhart, bn.—. Mrd. Elias Weikler. (V.) Abraham Gerhart, bn.—; died. Mrd. —. (V.) Elizabeth
Gerhart, bn.—. P. O., Perkasie, Pa. S.

IV. Mary Moyer, bn.—. Mrd. Abraham K. Hunsberger, Apr. 11, 1833. He was bn. Mar. 1, 1811;
died Aug. 23, 1865. Farmer. Menn. Children: Barbara, Joseph, Veronica, Maria, Lucy, Eliza, Isaiah,
Lydia.

V. Barbara Hunsberger, bn. Apr. 5, 1834. Mrd.
Levi Loux, 1855. He died Mar. 15, 1863. Wheelwright. Children: (VI.) Abraham F. Loux, bn. May
14, 1856; died Mar. 8, 1863. (VI.) Oliver S. Loux
and Alfred H. Loux, twins, bn. Sept. 6, 1857; died
Mar. 8, 1863. (VI.) William M. Loux, bn. Sept. 17,
1859; died Mar. 3, 1863. (VI.) H. Erwin Loux, bn.
Feb. 4, 1862; died Apr. 22, 1863.—Barbara mrd. second husband, Samuel T. Morris, Oct. 14, 1865.
P. O., Dublin, Pa. Farmer. Ref.

V. Joseph Hunsberger, bn. Feb. 15, 1836; died aged about 3 years.

V. Veronica Hunsberger, bn. Dec. 31, 1837; died aged about 2 years.

V. Maria Hunsberger, bn. Feb. 15, 1840. Mrd. William H. Fretz, Dec. 25, 1873. He died May 13, 1888. Carpenter. Menn. Children: **(VI.)** Edmund Fretz, bn. Oct. 19, 1874. **(VI.)** Mary Lizzie Fretz, bn. July 16, 1876. **(VI.)** Leah Anna Fretz, bn. Mar. 17, 1879.

V. Lucy A Hunsberger, bn. Mar. 23, 1843. Mrd. Joseph Loux, Aug. 14, 1869. P. O., Plumsteadville, Pa. Carriage trimmer. Ger. Ref. Children: **(VI.)** Ulysses G. Loux, bn. Nov. 5, 1872. **(VI.)** Abraham W. Loux, bn. Feb. 26, 1877.

V. Eliza Hunsberger, bn. July 1, 1846. Mrd. Peter B. Loux, Dec. 24, 1871. Farmer. Menn. No issue.

V. Isaiah Hunsberger, bn. Apr. 5, 1850; died May 31, 1877. Mrd. Emily Giek, —. No issue.

V. Lydia A. Hunsberger, bn. Nov. 1, 1853; died Mar. 24, 1863.

III. Jacob Angeny, bn. Dec. 2, 1773; died —. Mrd. Barbara Gehman, —. Farmer and miller. Owned the old Angeny homestead. Children: Jacob, Elizabeth, Abraham, Samuel, William, David.

IV. Jacob Angeny, bn. —; died —. Mrd. Mary Slifer, —. She died —. Farmer, owned greater portion of the old homestead. Children: Joseph, Jacob, Catharine, Nancy.

V. Joseph S. Angeny, bn. Mar. 10, 1828. Mrd. Sarah Detweiler, Feb. 15, 1851. P. O., New Britain, Pa. Farmer. Children: **(VI.)** Josephine Angeny, bn. —; died Nov. 14, 1881. **(VI.)** Mary Angeny, bn. Aug. 21, 1854. Mrd. Benevil F. Markley, Oct. 22, 1890. Res. Phila., Pa. Mrs. M. Baptist. **(VI.)** Leidy Angeny, bn. —; died Apr. 17, 1862. **(VI.)** Wilson H. Angeny, bn. —. Mrd. Amanda Brunner, —. Res. Phila., Pa. **(VI.)** Emma Angeny. **(VI.)** John D. Angeny. **(VI.)** Edwin Angeny. **(VI.)** Joseph S. Angeny. **(VI.)** Ida Angeny. **(VI.)** Sarah E. Angeny. **(VI.)** Granville Angeny. **(VI.)** Ferdinand G. Angeny.

V. Jacob S. Angeny, bn. —. Mrd. Garner. P. O., Dublin, Pa.

V. Catharine Angeny, bn. —. Mrd. Abraham F. Hunsberger, Dec. 9, 1858. P.O., Dublin, Pa. Farmer. Menn. Children: **(VI.)** Mary Ann Hunsberger, bn. 1860. **(VI.)** Remandes Hunsberger, bn. 1863. **(VI.)** Jacob Hunsberger, bn. 1867. **(VI.)** Leidy and Edwin Hunsberger (twins), bn. 1877.

IV. Elizabeth Angeny, bn. —; died S.

IV. Abraham Angeny, bn. Oct. 27, 1802; died May 14, 1880. Mrd. Leah Fretz, daughter of Martin Fretz, of Hilltown, Oct. 21, 1828. They lived on the property known as Angeny's Mill, in Bedminster Twp., until the spring of 1848, when they moved to Union Co., Pa., and later (1859) to Milton, Northumberland Co., Pa., where Mr. Angeny perished in the great fire of 1880 in his 78th year. Carpenter and cabinet-maker. Menn. Children: Anna, Barbara, Eva, Martin, Leah, Rachel, Abbie, Katharine, Minerva.

V. Anna Eliza Angeny, bn. Dec. 21, 1829; died Jan. 13, 1850. S.

V. Barbara Angeny, bn. Aug. 29, 1831. Mrd. Jacob Gehman, Oct. 2, 1849. P. O., Beatrice, Nebr. Farmer. Menn. Children: Abraham, Jacob, Elizabeth, Fannie, Rachel, Sarah, Lillie, Emma, Benjamin, Samuel, Mary.

VI. Abraham A. Gehman, bn. in Bucks Co., Pa., Aug. 26, 1850. Music teacher at Hutchinson, Kans.

VI. Jacob Gehman, bn. Mar. 24, 1852; died Oct. 26, 1860.

VI. Elizabeth Gehman, bn. Jan. 19, 1854; died Oct. 20, 1860.

VI. Menno S. Gehman, bn. in Bucks Co., Pa., May 17, 1856. Running a stock range in Wyo.

VI. Fannie Gehman, bn. in Bucks Co., Pa., Feb. 19, 1858. Mrd. Samuel Horning, of Clarinda, Ia., Oct. 31, 1878. P. O., Pickrell, Nebr. Farmer. Disciples. Children: **(VII.)** Benjamin F. Horning, bn. Apr. 19, 1880. **(VII.)** Jacob Lee Horning, bn. Apr. 12, 1881. **(VII.)** Edwin G. Horning, bn. Aug. 2, 1882. **(VII.)**

Jennie Agatha Horning, bn. Jan. 5, 1884. (VII.) Alice Horning, bn. Jan. 19, 1888.

VI. Rachel A. Gehman, bn. in Bucks Co., Pa., Feb. 17, 1860. Mrd. Henry Wm. Smith, of Rockford, Mo., Oct. 21, 1886. Mrs. S. Baptist. Mr. S. Luth. Children: (VII.) Arthur Raymond Smith, bn. July 23, 1887. (VII.) — Smith, bn. —.

VI. Sarah Gehman, bn. in Fayette Co., Ia., Aug. 10, 1862. Mrd. William G. Grebe, Dec. 25, 1883. Farmer in Atchison Co., Mo. Meth. Ep. Children: (VII.) Elsie Grebe, bn. Sept. 27, 1884. (VII.) Guy Grebe, bn. Mar. 28, 1886. (VII.) Herbert Grebe, bn. June 12, 1888. (VII.) — Grebe (a daughter), bn. —.

VI. Samuel Gehman, bn. in Fayette Co., Ia., July 6, 1864. Running a stock ranch in Wyo.

VI. Lillie A. Gehman, bn. in Fayette Co., Ia., Apr. 15, 1868. Teacher. S.

VI. Emma B. Gehman, bn. in Fayette Co., Ia., Sept. 27, 1870. Mrd. Rev. H. R. Murphy, Sept. 1, 1891. P. O., Beatrice, Nebr. Minister of Free Baptist ch.

VI. Benjamin F. Gehman, bn. in Fayette Co., Ia., Aug. 1, 1873.

VI. Mary Anna Gehman, bn. Aug. 6, 1876.

V. Eva Angeny, bn. in Bucks Co., Pa., Oct. 25, 1833. Mrd. Reuben L. Hatfield, Dec. 4, 1851. P. O., Milton, Pa. Tinner. Baptists. Children: Annetta, Ella, Lillian, Carroll, Edgar, William, Minnie, Grace, Mabel.

VI. Annetta V. Hatfield, bn. May 29, 1853. Mrd. William I. Webb, Apr. 27, 1880. P. O., Milton, Pa. Clerk and book-keeper. Meth. Ep. Children: (VII.) John Webb, bn. Mar. 10, 1881; died Sept. 7, 1881. (VII.) Fannie B. Webb, bn. July 18, 1883.

VI. Ella E. Hatfield, bn. Aug. 9, 1855.

VI. Lillian V. Hatfield, bn. Dec. 1, 1857. Mrd. John H. Krauser, Mar. 27, 1879. P. O., Milton, Pa. Traveling salesman. Children: (VII.) Webb Guy Krauser, bn. May 31, 1880. (VII.) James B. Krauser, bn. July 5, 1883.

VI. Carroll D. Hatfield, bn. Dec. 1, 1859. Mrd. Laura Quick, Mar. 29, 1881. P. O., Huntsville, Mo. Carriage maker. Baptists. Children: **(VII.)** Walter Hatfield, bn. Dec. 14, 1882. **(VII.)** Annetta Jennie Hatfield, bn. Jan. 25, 1885.

VI. Edgar A. Hatfield, bn. Feb. 16, 1862. Mrd. Anna M. Brigg, Nov. 30, 1886. P. O., La Junta, Colo. Machinist.

VI. William S. Hatfield, bn. Sept. 2, 1864. Painter and paper-hanger.

VI. Minnie E. Hatfield, bn. Feb. 7, 1869.

VI. Grace C. Hatfield, bn. Jan. 24, 1872.

VI. M. Mabel Hatfield, bn. Jan. 17, 1877.

V. Martin F. Angeny, bn. Nov. 27, 1835; died Oct. 30, 1865. Mrd. Clara F. Hagner, Mar. 3, 1864. Carpenter. Baptists. One child: **(VI.)** Harry R. Angeny, died Oct. 5, 1865, aged 7 mo.

V. Leah Angeny, bn. Dec. 9, 1837; died Jan. 13, 1866. S.

V. Rachel Angeny, bn. Feb. 24, 1840. Mrd. Seth Comly Hill, Oct. 3, 1861. P. O., Milton, Pa. Farmer. Baptists. Children: **(VI.)** Raymond C. Hill, bn. Aug. 31, 1862; died Aug. 11, 1864. **(VI.)** Clara R. Hill, bn. May 29, 1864. **(VI.)** Kate E. Hill, bn. Aug. 21, 1866. **(VI.)** Alice Hill, bn. June 19, 1869. **(VI.)** Bessie Hill, bn. Oct. 24, 1872. **(VI.)** Herbert Hill, bn. Apr. 16, 1874. **(VI.)** Harry M. Hill, bn. Apr. 30, 1878.

V. Abbie C. Angeny, bn. June 26, 1842. Mrd. Thomas Shuler, in 1866. P. O., Grand Junction, Ia. Machinist. Meth. Ep. Children: **(VI.)** Elmer E. Shuler, bn. Nov. 26, 1867. Druggist at Omaha, Nebr. **(VI.)** Charles C. Shuler, bn. July 2, 1869. Groceryman at Grand Junction, Ia. **(VI.)** J. Eugene Shuler, bn. Mar. 28, 1871. Clerk in Chicago. **(VI.)** Martin A. Shuler, bn. May 27, 1872. **(VI.)** Bessie M. Shuler, bn. Oct. 3, 1875. **(VI.)** Willie T. Shuler, bn. Jan. 16, 1878. **(VI.)** Robert A. Shuler, bn. Aug. 14, 1880. **(VI.)** David O. Shuler, bn. Oct. 8, 1883; died Nov. 28, 1886. **(VI.)** Ben Harrison Shuler, bn. July 18, 1888.

V. Katharine Angeny, bn. Sept. 18, 1844. Mrd. William Shields, Dec. 26, 1867. P. O., Kelly Point, Pa. Wheel-wright. Mrs. S. Baptist. Children: **(VI.)**

Esther Lucas Shields, bn. Dec. 26, 1868. Presby. (VI.) Lillian Angeny Shields, bn. Dec. 12, 1870. Baptist. (VI.) Ellen Harris Shields, bn. Jan. 31, 1873. Presby. (VI.) William Scott Shields, bn. Apr. 11, 1875. (VI.) Edgar Thomson Shields, bn. Sept. 24, 1877. (VI.) Charlotte Elliott Shields, bn. May 4, 1880. (VI.) James Leigh Shields, bn. Jan. 27, 1885.

V. Minerva Angeny, bn. in Union Co., Pa., June 26, 1852. S.

IV. Samuel Angeny, bn. —. Mrd. Anna Kulp, Apr. 2, 1832. She was bn. Apr. 12, 1812; died Feb. 19, 1876. P. O., Perkasie, Pa. Farmer. Menn. Children: Hester, Barbara, Tillman.

V. Hester Angeny, bn. Dec. 14, 1833. Mrd. Jacob Hockman, Oct. 15, 1859. Carpenter. Children: Reuben, Annie.

VI. Reuben Hockman, bn. Feb. 21, 1862. Mrd. Elizabeth Strouse, 1883. P. O., Hatboro, Pa. Tonsorial artist. Meth. Ep. Children: (VII.) Lillian Hockman, bn. Jan. 5, 1884. (VII.) Gertrude Hockman, bn. July 13, 1886.

VI. Anna Hockman, bn. Feb. 11, 1865.

V. Barbara Angeny, bn. May 28, 1835. Mrd. Henry M. Kramer, Sept. 29, 1864. Carpenter. Luth. Children: (VI.) Emma Kramer, bn. Jan. 18, 1867. Mrd. C. F. Follmer, Oct. 27, 1888. Machinist. Luth. (VI.) William H. Kramer, bn. Apr. 15, 1873; died Mar. 30, 1876. (VI.) Anna E. Kramer, bn. Apr. 9, 1875; died July 18, 1876. (VI.) S. Linford Kramer, bn. Sept. 18, 1879.

V. Tillman Angeny, bn. Apr. 28, 1844. Mrd. Victoria Grace Wickert, June 17, 1886. Salesman in general store. Lutherans No issue.

IV. William Angeny, bn. Aug. 24, 1808. Mrd. Catharine Nonamaker, Mar. 1, 1836. She was bn. May 24, 1817; died Apr. 14, 1886. P. O., Gardenville, Pa. Farmer. Menn. Children: (V.) Sarah Angeny, bn. July 2, 1840; died Feb. 27. 1845. (V.) Abraham Angeny, bn. Nov. 2, 1841; died June 7, 1862. (V.) Samuel Angeny, bn. Feb. 21, 1846. S. (V.) Anna Angeny, bn. Oct. 15, 1851. S.

IV. David Angeny, bn. —; died —. Mrd. Elizabeth Kulp, Nov. 14, 1841. She was bn. June 30, 1815. P. O., Blooming Glen, Pa. Farmer. Menn. Children: Henry, Jacob, Anna, Mary.
V. Henry Angeny, died in infancy.
V. Jacob K. Angeny, bn. Dec. 11, 1845. Mrd. Catharine Shelly, Apr. 12, 1873. Farmer. Menn. Children: **(VI.)** Elizabeth S. Angeny, bn. July 23, 1875. **(VI.)** Henry S. Angeny, bn. Oct. 26, 1876. **(VI.)** David S. Angeny, bn. Mar. 10, 1879. **(VI.)** Jacob S. Angeny, bn. Apr. 1, 1881. **(VI.)** Mary S. Angeny, bn. Mar. 5, 1883. **(VI.)** Katie S. Angeny, bn. May 9, 1886. **(VI.)** Anna S. Angeny, bn. Oct. 27, 1888.
V. Anna Angeny, bn. Sept. 1, 1850. Mrd. Henry K. Detweiler, Feb. 28, 1874. P. O., Blooming Glen, Pa. Farmer. Menn. Children: **(VI.)** Samuel A. Detweiler, bn. Mar. 17, 1875; died Aug. 20, 1875. **(VI.)** David A. Detweiler, bn. May 2, 1876. **(VI.)** Mary A. Detweiler, bn. Aug. 1, 1878; died —. **(VI.)** Elizabeth A. Detweiler, bn. Nov. 19, 1879. **(VI.)** Annie A. Detweiler, bn. Aug. 7, 1882. **(VI.)** Mary A. Detweiler, bn. Mar. 20, 1884; died Mar. 30, 1885. **(VI.)** Jacob A. Detweiler, bn. Dec. 21, 1886. Still-born. **(VI.)** Emma A. Detweiler, bn. Jan. 19, 1888.
V. Mary Angeny, bn. Apr. 18, 1857. Mrd. Isaac H. Kulp. (See Index of References No. 38.)

Reuben Z. Kratz.

(See page 177)

DESCENDANTS OF JOSEPH WISMER SON OF JACOB WISMER.

II. Joseph Wismer, bn. in Bucks Co., —; died before his father made his will. His portion of his father's estate, was paid to his two sons in 1791. Mrd. —. Children: Jacob, Joseph.

III. Jacob Wismer, bn. Dec. 3, 1751; died Apr. 18, 1837. Mrd. Susan Delp, —. She was bn. about 1761; died Dec. 15, 1827, aged 66 years. Lived at Weavertown, and is known as "Weavertown Jacob." Farmer. Children: Mary, Catharine, Nancy, Elizabeth.

IV. Mary Wismer, bn. —; died —. Mrd. Michael Bissey, —. Moved to Ohio. Had issue, a son: **(V.)** Adna.

IV. Catharine Wismer, bn. Mrd. Joseph Fredericks —. Farmer. Menn's. Children: Isaac, Jonathan, Jacob, Abraham, Henry.

V. Isaac Fredericks, bn. —; died young.

V. Jonathan Fredericks, born —. Mrd. Rebecca Morris, —. Carpenter in Camden, N. J. Children: **(VI.)** Joseph. **(VI.)** Jacob. **(VI.)** Cornelia. **(VI.)** Emma. **(VI.)** Susan.

V. Jacob W. Frederick, bn. in Plumstead Twp., Bucks, Co., Nov. 7, 1820. Mrd. Esther L. Morris, daughter of Joseph and Dorothy Morris of Wrightstown, Pa., Mar. 26, 1846. Farmer. Children: Joseph, Henry, Edward, Emily.

VI. Joseph M. Frederick, bn. —. Mrd. Lizzie Ely, —. One child: **(VII.)** Linford K.

VI. Henry S. Fredericks, bn. —. Mrd. Lizzie H. Betts, —. P. O., Carversville, Pa. Children: **(VII.)** Edward C. **(VII.)** Flora L.

VI. W. Edward Fredericks, bn. —. S. P. O., Carversville, Pa.

9

VI. S. Emily Fredericks, bn. —. P. O., Carvers
ville, Pa. S.
V. Abraham Fredericks, bn. Nov. 14, 1824. Mrd.
Louisa Van Hart in 1854. Laborer. Children:
Amanda, Mary, Hannah.
VI. Amanda Fredericks, bn. Feb. 18, 1855. Mrd.
Thornton Worthington, Jan. 1, 1873. P. O., Dublin,
Pa. Farmer. Children: **(VII.)** Mary Worthington,
bn. Mar. 5, 1876. **(VII.)** Charles Worthington, bn.
Nov. 11, 1879. **(VII.)** Anson Worthington, bn. Dec.
2, 1881; died aged 6 years. **(VII.)** Taylor Worthing-
ton, bn. Feb. 5, 1884. **(VII.)** Levi Worthington, bn.
June 14, 1886, **(VII.)** Laura Worthington, bn. July
12, 1889.
VI. Mary Fredericks, bn. Oct. 8, 1856, Mrd. Taylor
Worthington. P. O., Levin, Pa. Farmer. Children:
(VII.) L. Ellen Worthington, bn. Aug. 9, 1878; died
Oct. 27, 1879. **(VII.)** Arthur C. Worthington, bn.
Sept. 19, 1880. Killed while trimming a fallen tree,
Apr. 5, 1892. **(VII.)** Lewis W. Worthington, bn.
Apr. 20, 1883. **(VII.)** Alonzo F. Worthington, bn.
Mar. 20, 1886, **(VII.)** Edith Worthington, bn. July 7,
1889. **(VII.)** Eva B. Worthington, bn. Sept. 20, 1891.
VI. Hannah Fredericks, bn. July 5, 1859. Mrd.
Alonzo Fesmire. P. O., Hopewell, N. J. Foreman
and engineer of Hopewell Stone Crusher. Children:
(VII.) John B. Fesmire, bn. Nov. 10, 1878. **(VII.)**
Bertha L. Fesmire, bn. Mar. 23, 1880. **(VII.)** A. Fred-
die Fesmire, bn. Dec. 16, 1881; died Sept. 6, 1882.
(VII.) Nora Fesmire, bn. May 8, 1882; died Mar. 3,
1885. **(VII.)** George Fesmire, bn. Oct. 26, 1884; died
Feb. 22, 1885. **(VII.)** Frank Fesmire, bn. Jan. 25,
1885. **(VII.)** Harry Fesmire, bn. Apr. 15, 1887. **(VII.)**
Raymond Fesmire, bn. May 27, 1888; died Aug. 20,
1888. **(VII.)** Martha B. Fesmire, bn. Sept. 22, 1889.
(VII.) Alonzo Fesmire, Jr. bn. June 8, 1891.
V. Henry Fredericks, bn. —. Mrd. —. Lives in
Ohio.
IV. Nancy Wismer, bn. —; died —. Mrd. Charles
Rice, —. He was bn. Jan. 2, 1800; died July 16, 1884.
Carpenter 25 years then farmer. Children: Susan,
Margery, Elizabeth, Jacob, James, Abagail.

V. Susan Rice, bn. in Bucks Co., May 11, 1829; died Dec. 17, 1892. Mrd. William Mitchell, Dec. 14, 1850. He was bn. Jan. 26, 1819; died Jan. 22, 1890. Blacksmith. Children: Edgar, Marques, Morris, Abby, Charles, William, Augustus, Glenville, Anna, Henry, Alfred, Albert, Keziah.

VI. Edgar Lehman Mitchell, bn. Sept. 12, 1851. P. O., Flourtown, Pa.

VI. Marques DeLafayette Mitchell, bn. Nov. 3, 1853; died July 16, 1854.

VI. Morris Harvey Mitchell, bn. Jan. 21, 1855. Mrd. Mary Lake in 1880. P. O., New Hope, Pa. Drives mill team. One child: (**VII.**) Harriet W. Mitchell, bn. 1881.

VI. Abby Ann Mitchell, bn. July 6, 1856; died July 25, 1856.

VI. Charles Henry Mitchell, bn. June 4, 1857; died June 7, 1857.

VI. William Worthington Mitchell, bn. Feb. 6, 1859. Mrd. Mary Smith, Feb. 28, 1884. Res. 2005 Madison Ave., Phila. Car builder. One child: (**VII.**)Earl Mitchell, bn. Feb. 27, 1891; died June 27, 1891.

VI. Augustus Ludlow Mitchell, bn. Aug. 5, 1860. Mrd. Anna Wilson. P. O., Penns Park, Pa. Children: (**VII.**) Walter Mitchell. (**VII.**) Nellie Mitchell. (**VII.**) Howard Mitchell.

VI. Glenville Lear Mitchell, bn. Nov. 28, 1861. Mrd. Sallie Foster. P. O., Pinesville, Pa. One child: (**VII.**) Lehman Mitchell.

VI. Anna Louisa Mitchell, bn. Mar. 17, 1863. Mrd. J. Frank Johnson. Res. 2120 Darien St., Phila. One child: (**VII.**) Cora Johnson.

VI. Henry Levi Mitchell, bn. —; died Aug. 24, 1865.

VI. Alfred Ross Mitchell, bn. Jan. 6, 1866; died May 23, 1866.

VI. Albert Printz Mitchell, bn. Sept. 6, 1867; died Oct. 7, 1867.

VI. Keziah Printz Mitchell, bn. Sept. 6, 1867; Mrd. Charles Clinton McEntyre. P. O., Carversville, Pa. Children: (**VII.**) Alice Ross McEntyre, bn. May 31, 1890. (**VII.** Elmer McEntyre, bn. June 3, 1891.

V. Margery Rice, bn. —; died —. Mrd. Levi Munday, —. Children: Cornelia, Samuel, George, —.
VI. Cornelia Munday, bn. —. Mrd. Alfred Ross.
V. Elizabeth Rice, bn. —. Mrd. John Magee. P. O., Somertown, Pa. Children: **(VI.)** Charles. **(VI.)** Anna.
V. Jacob Rice, bn. —. Mrd. —. P. O., Lawrence, Kansas. Children: Cornelia, Charles, Hannah, Mary.
V. James Rice, bn. —. Mrd. Kate Flack, —. P. O., Hestonville, West Phila. Son: **(VI.)** Samuel Rice.
V. Abagail Rice, bn. —; died when about 2 yrs. old.
IV. Elizabeth Wismer, mrd. John Shaddinger.

III. Joseph Wismer, bn. —; died —. Mrd. Barbara Wismer, daughter of Henry Wismer of Hilltown, Pa. —. Farmer in Bedminster Twp. Children: Elizabeth, Barbara, Catharine, Esther, Henry, Henry, Joseph, Jacob, Mary, Anna.
IV. Elizabeth Wismer, bn. Dec. 8, 1782; died in Mar. 1836. Mrd. Jacob Ruth in 1801. Children: Henry, Catharine, Barbara, Michael, Hettie, Elizabeth, Mary, Joseph, Anna, John.
V. Catharine Ruth, bn. in 1804. Mrd. John G. Myers. One son: **(VI.)** Levi Myers. P. O., Wismer, Pa.
V. Barbara Ruth, bn. Feb. 10, 1806; died Feb. 20, 1893. Mrd. George Lear, —. Children: Jacob, John, Elizabeth, Joseph, Mary, Peter, Isaac.
VI. Jacob R. Lear, bn. —. Mrd. —. P. O., Wismer, Pa. Children: **(VII.)** Anson Lear. P. O., Phillipsburgh, N. J. **(VII.)** Smith Lear. P. O., Philadelphia, Pa. **(VII.)** Harvey Lear. P. O., Wismer, Pa. **(VII.)** Calvin Lear. P. O., Plumsteadville, Pa. **(VII.)** Ellen Lear, bn. —. Mrd. — Nichols, —. P. O., Wismer, Pa. **(VII.)** Cadie Lear, bn. —. Mrd. —Trauger, —. P. O., Ottsville. Pa. **(VII.)** Mary Lear, bn. Mrd. — Riegel, —. P. O., Pipersville, Pa.
VI. John R. Lear, bn. —. Mrd. Susan W. Nash, in 1857. P. O., Doylestown, Penna. Contractor and member of the council of Doylestown Borough. In 1873 he was nominated by the Republican party for County Commissioner. Presby. Children: Rosa, Minnie.

VII. Rosa Lear, bn. —. Mrd. Martin Hulshizer, June 12, 1884. P. O., Doylestown, Pa. Druggist. Mr. Hulshizer is organist of the Presbyterian church of Doylestown, a position he has held for over 25 years, and a member of Brock's Orchestra since its organization in 1876.

VII. Minnie Dora Lear, bn. —; died Mar. 8, 1872.

VI. Elizabeth Lear, bn. in Bucks Co., July 20, 1834. Mrd. Samuel F. Welden, Oct. 1, 1854. P. O., Danboro, Pa. Presby. Children: Martha, Mary, Curtin, Kate, Anna, George, Jennie, Lizzie.

VII. Martha L. Welden, bn. June 5, 1856. Mrd. James M. Reigle, —. P. O., Danboro, Pa. Presby. One child: (**VIII.**) Samuel W. Reigle.

VII. Mary Ellen Welden, bn. June 21, 1858. Mrd. Henry F. Bisson, —. P. O., Solebury, Pa. Presby. Children: (**VIII.**) Anna May Bisson. (**VIII.**) Florence Bisson. (**VIII.**) Lizzie W. Bisson.

VII. A. G. Curtin Welden, bn. Nov. 27, 1860. Mrd. Annie Leatherman, —. Res. 2550 Germantown Ave., Phila., Pa. Groceryman. Baptist. Children: (**VIII.**) Mabel Welden. (**VIII.**) Russel Welden. (**VIII.**) Grace Welden, bn. —; died —.

VII. Kate L. Welden, bn. Jan. 1. 1863. Mrd. Amos' Fretz, Oct. 27, 1886. Res. 2550 Germantown Ave., Phila., Pa. Groceryman. Baptists. Children: (**VIII.**) Elsie W. Fretz. (**VIII.**) Florence Fretz.

. **VII.** Anna B. Welden, bn. July 29, 1865. Presby. S.

VII. George L. Welden, bn. Sept. 27, 1867. S.

VII. Jennie L. Welden, bn. May 12, 1870; died July 22, 1890.

VII. Lizzie Welden, bn. Oct. 2, 1872. Presby. S.

VI. Joseph R. Lear, bn. Mar. 5, 1837; died Feb. 21, 1885. Mrd. Mary Ann Wismer, —. P. O., Wismer, Pa. Carpenter, undertaker, farmer, merchant. Mrs. L. Baptist. One child: (**VII.**) Lincoln Lear, bn. Nov. 9, 1866. Mrd. Anna Hunsberger, —. P. O., 11 & Mifflin St., Phila., Pa. Merchant grocer. Baptist.

VI. Mary Lear, bn. in Bucks Co., July 5, 1840. Mrd. Jacob M. Steineback, —. P. O., Shelly, Pa. Farmer. Luth's. Children: (**VII.**) Howard Steineback, bn. Dec. 9, 1864. Mrd. Ida Benner, Feb. 28,

1891. P. O., Zionsville, Pa. Merchant. Luth's.
(VII.) Annie Steineback, bn. May 2, 1881.
VI. Peter R. Lear, bn. in Bucks Co., Pa., Mar. 4,
1844. P. O., Clear Water, Cal. Stone mason. S.
VI. Isaac R. Lear, bn. June 1, 1847. Mrd. Emma
Bissey, Sept. 28, 1872. P. O., Tinicum, Pa. Mason.
No issue.
V. Michael Ruth, bn. 1808. Mrd. Catharine Ders-
tine. P. O., Lansdale, Pa. Children: (VI.) Henry D.
Ruth, bn. —. P. O., Lansdale, Pa. (VI.) Abraham
D. Ruth, bn. —. P. O., Lansdale, Pa. (VI.) Annie
Ruth, bn. —. Mrd. —.
V. Hettie Ruth, bn. 1810; died —.
V. Elizabeth Ruth, bn. 1811; died —. Mrd. Isaac
Cassel (dec'd), —.
V. Mary Ruth, bn. 1815; died —.
V. Joseph Ruth, bn. 1818; died —.
V. Anna Ruth, bn. 1819; died —. Mrd. Samuel
Ebert (dec'd).
V. John Ruth, bn. 1821. Mrd. Catharine Derstine,
Dec. 25, 1852. She was bn. May 11, 1830. P. O.,
Lansdale, Pa. Shoemaker. Children: (VI.) Mary
Ann Ruth, bn. Dec. 23, 1853; died Oct. 18, 1856.
(VI.) Henry Ruth, bn. —. Mrd. —. P. O., Lansdale,
Pa. (VI.) Abraham Ruth, bn. —. Mrd. —. P. O.,
Lansdale, Pa.
IV. Barbara Wismer, bn. June 13, 1785; died Mar.
14, 1870. Mrd. Mark Fretz (son of "Shoemaker"
Henry Fretz). Children: Joseph, Henry, John,
Mary, Barbara, Elizabeth.
V. Joseph Fretz, bn. —.
V. Henry Fretz, bn. Nov. 27, 1811; died Sept. 12,
1864. Mrd. Elizabeth Landis, Dec. 12, 1859.
Farmer. Menn. Children: Maria, Catharine, Eliza,
Sarah, Barbara.
VI. Maria Fretz, bn. Jan. 6, 1855; died May 12, 1855.
VI. Catharine Fretz, bn. Oct. 30, 1856. Mrd. Isaac
M. Swartz, Sept. 7, 1878. Farmer. Menn. Children:
(VII.) Elizabeth Swartz, bn. May 10, 1879; died Aug.
3, 1879. (VII.) — Swartz, bn. June 3, 1880; died May
20, 1885. (VII.) Annie Swartz, bn. Oct. 4, 1882.
(VII.) Ida Swartz, bn. Aug. 15, 1886.

VI. Eliza Fretz, bn. Sept. 27, 1858. Mrd. Mahlon Moyer, —.

VI. Sarah Fretz, bn. July 1, 1860. Mrd. Samuel L. Myers, Oct. 26, 1878. He died Feb. 25, 1889. Farmer. Menn's. One child: (**VII.**) Anna Myers, bn. Jan. 26, 1885; died Jan. 16, 1887.

VI. Barbara Fretz, bn. Jan. 7, 1863. Mrd. Jacob Y. Moyer, May 24, 1884. Farmer. Menn. One child: (**VII.**) Lizzie Moyer, bn. Jan. 31, 1887; d. Feb. 9, 1887.

V. John Fretz, bn. —; died —. Mrd. Catharine Moyer, Feb. 4, 1849. Farmer. Menn. Children: Amanda, Henry, Barbara.

VI. Amanda Fretz, bn. Nov. 15, 1849. Mrd. John Keller, Jan. 12, 1878. Farmer. Luth. Children: (**VII.**) Ervin Keller, bn. July 7, 1881. (**VII.**) Jacob Keller, bn. June 13, 1886.

VI. Henry Fretz, bn. July 22, 1852. Mrd. Susan Keller, —. Farmer. Luth. Children: (**VII.**) Wilmer. (**VII.**) Phares. (**VII.**) Harvey. (**VII.**) Ida. (**VII.**) Della.

VI. Barbara Fretz, bn. Jan. 9, 1855. Mrd. Aaron Swartz, Nov. 17, 1877. Menn. Children: (**VII.**) Katie Swartz, bn. Nov. 2, 1878. (**VII.**) Ella Swartz, bn. Nov. 17, 1880. (**VII.**) Isaac Swartz, bn. May 11, 1883. (**VII.**) Amanda Swartz, bn. May 17, 1885. (**VII.**) Samuel Swartz, bn. Dec. 26, 1886. (**VII.**) Anna Swartz, bn. Jan. 26, 1889.

V. Mary Fretz, bn. --; died 1889. Mrd. Henry Shelly, —. He died —. Had issue. Mrd. second husband, — Frick.

VI. Catharine F. Shelly, bn. —. Mrd. Jacob K. Angeny. (See Index of References No. 39.)

V. Barbara Fretz, bn. —; died —. Mrd. George Wismer. (See Index of References No. 40.)

V. Elizabeth Fretz, bn. -; died —. S.

IV. Catharine Wismer, bn. in Bucks Co., Jan. 23, 1787; died Sept. 23, 1859. Mrd. John Althouse in 1803. He was bn. in 1772; died in 1848. Farmer. Ger. Ref. Children: Sarah, Mary, Joseph, Enos.

V. Sarah Althouse, bn. Jan. 12, 1805; died infant.

V. Mary Althouse, bn. June 9, 1806. Mrd. Jacob Weidner, —. He died —. Luth's. No issue.

V. Joseph Althouse, bn. Nov. 2, 1807. Went west and was lost sight of.

V. Enos Althouse, bn. Jan. 24, 1811; died July 1, 1890. Mrd. Rosanna Hetzell, Mar. 31, 1853. She was bn. in Wittenburg, Germany, Nov. 7, 1835. Ger. Ref. Children: Mary, Franklin.

VI. Mary C. Althouse, bn in Phila., Pa., Dec. 23, 1856. Mrd. William A. Moock, Nov. 23, 1876. He was bn. June 9, 1855. Res. 1840 N. 8th St., Phila. Ger. Ref. Children: **(VII.)** William Enos Moock, bn. Jan. 10, 1878; died Aug. 17, 1878. **(VII.)** Mary Laura Moock, bn. May 28, 1879. **(VII.)** Alice Rosanna Moock, bn. Mar. 31, 1881; died July 30, 1881. **(VII.)** George Stefles Moock, bn. Sept. 7, 1882.

VI. Franklin B. Althouse, bn in Phila., Jan. 13, 1861. Mrd. Mary Wilhelmina Bruestle. She was bn. July 27, 1862. Res. 1227 Tuckes St., Phila., Pa. Train caller. Ger. Ref. Children: **(VII.)** Franklin Enos Althouse, bn. Jan. 29, 1883. **(VII.)** Mary Rosanna Althouse, bn. Feb. 23, 1885.

IV. Esther Wismer, bn. in Bucks Co., Pa., Jan. 12, 1790; died in Waterloo Co., Ont., Sept. 2, 1881. Mrd. John Cressman, Oct. 3, 1818. He was bn. in Bucks Co., Pa., May 15, 1795; died in Waterloo Co., Ont. Farmer. Menn's. Children: Joseph, Anna, John, Barbara, Henry.

V. Joseph Cressman, bn. —. Mrd. —. Children: **(VI.)** Joseph, bn. —. P. O., Breslau, Ont. **(VI.)** Moses, bn. —. P. O., Breslau, Ont.

V. Anna W. Cressman, bn. in Waterloo Co., Ont., Nov. 18, 1821. Mrd. Eli C. Shantz, May 5, 1840. He was bn. Jan. 23, 1816; died Sept. 19, 1889. Farmer. Menn's. Children: Barbara, Enos, John, Esther, Anna, Eli, Israel, Magdalena, Susanna.

VI. Barbara C. Shants, bn. Mar. 10, 1841; died Dec. 6, 1876.

VI. Enos C. Shantz, bn. in Waterloo Co., Ont., Jan. 26, 1843. Mrd. Elizabeth H. Strickler, Feb. 21, 1883. She was bn. April 29, 1854; died Mar. 7, 1884. P. O., Berlin, Ont. Farmer. Menn's. Visited in Bucks Co., Pa., Sept. 1872, and for some months was employed on a farm near Lansdale, then returned to Canada, Jan. 1873. No issue.

VI. John C. Shantz, bn. July 5, 1846. Mrd. Mary Snyder, Feb. 22, 1874. P. O., Berlin, Ont. Farmer. Menn. Children: (VII.) Israel S. Shantz, bn. Aug. 31, 1875. (VII.) Norman S. Shantz, bn. Dec. 5, 1876. (VII.) Anna S. Shantz, bn. July 2, 1878. (VII.) Malinda S. Shantz, bn. Nov. 4, 1879. (VII.) Titus S. Shantz, bn. May 17, 1881. (VII.) Alvina S. Shants, bn. Apr. 8, 1883. (VII.) Amza S. Shantz, bn. Apr. 9, 1885. (VII.) Mary Ann S. Shantz, bn. Mar. 2, 1887.

VI. Esther C. Shantz, bn. June 2, 1848. P. O., Berlin, Ont. Menn. S.

VI. Anna C. Shantz, bn. Mar. 10, 1851. Mrd. Ephraim B. Snyder, Oct. 24, 1875. He died May 18, 1880. No issue. Anna mrd. second husband, Samuel B. Snyder, Nov. 2, 1890. P. O., Baden, Ont. Farmer. Menn's.

VI. Eli C. Shantz, bn. Mar. 26, 1854. Mrd. Lucinda Weber, Nov. 9, 1879. She was bn. Sept. 6, 1855. P. O., Berlin, Ont. Farmer. Menn's. Children: (VII.) Valina W. Shantz, bn. Oct. 23, 1880. (VII.) Sylvester W. Shantz, bn. Apr. 10, 1883.

VI. Israel C. Shantz, bn. May 29, 1857; died Nov. 19, 1857.

VI. Magdalena C. Shantz, bn. Sept. 8, 1858. P. O., Berlin, Ont. S.

VI. Susanna C. Shantz, bn. Aug. 2, 1861. Mrd. John H. Schmitt, Jan. 2, 1883. He was bn. July 1, 1858. P. O., Elmira, Ont. Farmer. Menn's. Children: (VII.) Amzi S. Schmitt, bn. dead Sept. 2, 1883. (VII.) Josiah S. Schmitt, bn. Oct. 1, 1884. (VII.) Manasseh S. Schmitt, bn. Dec. 9, 1885. (VII.) Aden S. Schmitt, bn. July 30, 1887; died Aug. 14, 1887. (VII.) Eli S. Schmitt, bn. Aug. 17, 1888; died July 5, 1889. (VII.) John S. Schmitt, bn. Apr. 1, 1891. (VII.) Clayton S. Schmitt, bn. Dec. 24, 1892; died Jan. 4, 1893.

V. John Cressman, bn. Dec. 23, 1822; died Jan. 28, 1845. Mrd. Catharine Shiedel, Oct. 28, 1844. Farmer. Menn. No issue.

V. Barbara Cressman, bn. in Waterloo Co., Ont., July 8, 1823. Mrd. Samuel Cressman, Apr. 13, 1841.

He died —. Farmer. Menn's. Children: Enos, Anna, Abraham, Henry, Esther, Samuel, John, Aaron, Barbara, Mary, Israel, Menno, Lucinda.

VI. Enos Cressman, bn. in Waterloo Co., Ont. Mrd. Elizabeth Shontz, daughter of Bishop Henry Shontz. P. O., New Dundee, Ont.

VI. Anna Cressman, bn. in Waterloo Co., Ont., Jan. 15, 1844. Mrd. Rev. Samuel S. Bowman, Mar. 24, 1887. P. O., Berlin, Ont. Retired. Menn's. Ordained to ministry in 1863. No issue.

VI. Abraham Cressman, bn. at New Dundee, Waterloo Co., Ont., Jan. 31, 1845. Mrd. Veronica Snyder, Feb. 13, 1866. P. O., Berlin, Ont. Farmer. Menn's. Children: Selina, Samuel, Ida, Edgar.

VII. Selina Cressman, bn. Dec. 15, 1867. Mrd. Frank Shantz, Sept. 28, 1886. Children: (**VIII.**) Fanny Violet Shantz, bn. May 8, 1888. (**VIII.**) Esther Estella Shantz, bn. Aug. 26, 1891; died Feb. 14, 1892.

VII. Samuel Cressman, bn. Nov. 24, 1870.

VII. Ida and Edgar Cressman, (twins) bn. Sept. 2, 1882.

VI. Henry Cressman, bn. in Waterloo Co., Ont., June 17, 1846. Mrd. Hannah Bingamin, Jan. 18, 1869. She died Jan. 13, 1870. He mrd. second wife Mary Ann Boorse, Oct. 1871. P. O., Lansdale, Pa. Book-keeper. Ger. Ref. One child: (**VII.**) Essie Ann Cressman.

VI. Esther Cressman, bn. Jan. 20, 1848. Mrd. Amos M. Shantz, Dec. 3, 1872. P. O., Manheim, Ont. Farmer. Menn's. Children: (**VII.**) Jonathan Shantz, bn. Oct. 12, 1873. (**VII.**) Nancy Shantz, bn. Jan. 29, 1875. (**VII.**) Selina Shantz, bn. Mar. 22, 1877. (**VII.**) Addison Shantz, bn. Aug. 22, 1878. (**VII.**) Samuel Shantz. bn. Feb. 29, 1880. (**VII.**) Magdalena Shantz, bn. May 9, 1882. (**VII.**) Barbara Shantz, bn. Sept. 22, 1884. (**VII.**) Elminda Shantz, bn. Jan. 6, 1889. (**VII.**) Silva Shantz, bn. Mar. 26, 1891; died June 2, 1892.

VI. Samuel C. Cressman, bn. in Waterloo Co., Ont., Apr. 9, 1849. Mrd. Angeline Bingeman in 1873. P. O., Baden, Ont. Farmer. Children: (**VII.**) Elma Cressman, bn. Mar. 30, 1874. (**VII.**) Laura Cressman,

bn. Nov. 18, 1875. (VII.) Millo Cressman, bn. Feb.
10, 1878. (VII.) Morgan Cressman, bn. Mar. 3, 1880.
(VII.) Nellie Cressman, bn. Apr. 4, 1882. (VII.) Alice
Cressman, bn. Aug. 6, 1884. (VII.)Harry Cressman, bn.
Oct. 28, 1885. (VII.) Zillah Cressman, bn. Mar. 26,
1887. (VII.) Bruce Cressman, bn. Jan. 5, 1889. (VII.)
Douglass Cressman, bn. Sept. 26, 1890. (VII.) Thel-
bert Cressman, bn. Nov. 17, 1892.

VI. John Cressman, bn. in Waterloo Co., Ont., Oct.
24, 1851. Mrd. Mary Horlacher, Dec. 26, 1876. P.
O., New Dundee, Ont. Farmer. Menn's. Children:
(VII.) Ida Cressman, bn. Nov. 18, 1877. Menn. (VII.)
Nina Cressman, bn. Jan. 18, 1880. (VII.) Ivan Cress-
man, bn. Jan. 4, 1883.

VI. Aaron Cressman, bn. in Waterloo Co., Ont.
Apr. 8, 1854. Mrd. Magdalena Betzner. P. O.,
Strasburg, Ont. Farmer. Menn. Children: (VII.)
Barbara Cressman, bn. July 7, 1878. (VII.) Ida Mi-
nerva Cressman, bn. Apr. 19, 1880. (VII.) Maria
Cressman, bn. Apr. 30, 1884. (VII.) Lanora Cress-
man, bn. Oct. 10, 1886. (VII.) Mabel Cressman, bn.
Oct. 8. 1888. (VII.) Wilfred Solon Cressman, bn. Feb.
14, 1891. (VII.) Alvina Cressman, bn. Mar. 19, 1893.

VI. Barbara Cressman, bn. —; died —, aged 5 years.

VI. Mary Cressman, bn. in Waterloo Co., Ont., Jan.
26, 1858. Mrd. Titus Bingaman, Dec. 12, 1882. P.
O., New Dundee, Ont. Farmer. Children: (VII.)
Olive Bingaman, bn. Dec. 6, 1883. (VII.) Essie Bingaman, bn. May 23. 1885. (VII.) Ada Bingaman, bn.
May 3, 1886. (VII.) Elmer Bingaman, bn. Sept. 14,
1887; died Nov. 18, 1887. (VII.) Roy Bingaman, bn.
Sept. 20, 1888, (VII.) Moral Bingaman, bn. Sept. 10,
1890. (VII.) Ina Bingaman, bn. Sept. 15, 1892.

VI. Israel Cressman, bn. in Waterloo Co., Ont., Jan.
2, 1860. Mrd. Sarah Bowman, June 16, 1886. P. O.,
New Dundee, Ont. Farmer. Menn's. Children: (VII.)
Ethelbald Cressman, bn. Jan. 13, 1888. (VII.) Orkney
Cressman, bn. Dec. 17, 1889.

VI. Menno Cressman, bn. in Waterloo Co., Ont.,
Nov. 5, 1861. Mrd. Mary Ann Nahrgang, June 28,
1887, P. O., Berlin, Ont. Dry goods merchant.

Menn's. One child: (VII.) Grace Geraldine Cressman, bn. Jan. 30, 1892.

VI. Lucinda Cressman, bn. —. S.

V. Henry Cressman, bn. in Waterloo Co., Ont., Feb. 27, 1825. Mrd. Sarah Woolner, Mar. 4, 1851. P. O., Berlin, Ont. Retired farmer. Menn's. Children: Esther, Adaline, Susannah, Louisa, Phillis.

VI. Esther Cressman, bn. Apr. 29, 1852; died Mar. 5, 1856.

VI. Adaline Cressman, bn. Mar. 25, 1855; died Aug. 21, 1862.

VI. Susannah Cressman, bn. July 25, 1857. Mrd. John K. Devitt, --. P. O., Berlin, Ont. Farmer. Menn's. Children: (VII.) Elsie Selina Devitt. (VII.) Clarissa Leda Devitt. (VII.) Alice Adelia Devitt. (VII.) Bernice May Devitt. (VII.) Sarah Magdalena Devitt.

VI. Louisa Cressman, bn. June 1, 1860. Mrd. Dilman Brubacker, —. P. O., St. Jacobs, Ont. Farmer. Menn's. Children: (VII.) Magdalena Brubacker. (VII.) Irvin Brubacker. (VII.) Adina Brubacker. (VII.) Henrietta Brubacker. (VII.) Ida Brubaker. (VII.) Stanley Brubacker.

VI. Phillis Cressman, born Aug. 25, 1863. Mrd. George S. Weber, —. P. O., Berlin, Ont. Farmer. Menn's. Children: (VII.) Irvin Weber. (VII.) Ida Adelia Weber.

IV. Henry Wismer, bn. Mar. 11, 1792; died an infant.

IV. Henry Wismer, bn. Mar. 10, 1794; died June 11, 1876. Mrd. Mary Cressman. Lived in Waterloo Co., Ont. Children: Daniel, Henry, Barbara, Esther, Elizabeth, Mary.

V. Rev. Daniel Wismer, bn. —. Mrd. —. P. O., Berlin, Ont. Children: Moses, Esther.

VI. Moses Wismer, bn. —. P. O., Preston, Ont.

VI. Esther Wismer, bn. in Waterloo Co., Ont. Mrd. John B. Kraft. He was bn. in Waterloo Co., Ont., Apr. 6, 1844. P. O., Caledonia, Mich. Farmer. Children: Lydia, Urias, Noah, Elsie, Alfred, George, Robert, John, Eddie, Sarah, Laura.

VII. Lydia Ann Kraft, bn. in Waterloo Co., Ont., Nov. 1, 1868. Mrd. Wesley Break, Sept. 16, 1889. P. O., Crosby, Mich. Blacksmith. Children: **(VIII.)** Clinton Break, bn. July 14, 1890. **(VIII.)** Myrl Break, bn. Sept. 7, 1891.

VII. Urias Kraft, bn. Feb. 22, 1870, in Waterloo Co., Ont.

VII. Noah Kraft, bn. Dec. 14, 1871, in Waterloo Co., Ont.

VII. Elsie Kraft, bn. Apr. 4, 1873; died Nov. 30, 1873.

VII. Alfred Kraft, bn. Nov. 4, 1874, in Oxford Co., Ont.

VII. George Kraft, bn. Oct. 26, 1876, in Oxford Co., Ont.

VII. Robert Kraft, bn. Nov. 6, 1877, in Oxford Co., Ont.

VII. John Kraft, bn. Feb. 22, 1880, in Kent Co., Mich.

VII. Eddie Kraft, bn. Sept. 4, 1882, in Kent Co., Mich.

VII. Sarah Kraft, bn. Apr. 12, 1884, in Kent Co., Mich.

VII. Laura Kraft, bn. Sept. 16, 1886.

V. Henry Wismer, bn. —; died —. Mrd. —.

V. Barbara Wismer, bn. in Waterloo Co., Ont., Oct. 25, 1816; died in Clinton Co., Mich., Aug. 28, 1889. Mrd. David Baer, Jan. 30, 1838. He was bn. Nov. 24, 1810; died in Oxford Co., Ont., July 6, 1881. Farmer. Menn's. Children: Amos, Henry, Mary, Abraham, Daniel, Elizabeth, Esther, John, Martin, Sallie.

VI. Amos Baer, bn. Nov. 27, 1838. Mrd. —. P. O., Bright, Ont.

VI. Henry Baer, bn. in Waterloo Co., Ont., Oct. 21, 1842. Mrd. Leah Bowman, Feb. 27, 1868. P. O., Mannheim, Ont. Carpenter and farmer. Menn's. Children: **(VII.)** Angeline Baer, bn. July 7, 1869. **(VII.)** Elvina Baer, bn. Mar. 12, 1871. **(VII.)** Moses Baer, bn. July 25, 1872. **(VII.)** Henry Baer, bn. Feb. 27, 1874; died June 14, 1874. **(VII.)** Fidia Baer, bn. May 4, 1875; died Oct. 14, 1880. **(VII.)** Ephraim

Baer, bn. Jan. 24, 1877. (VII.) Simon Baer, bn. Dec. 22, 1879. (VII.) Louisa Baer, bn. Feb. 18, 1881. (VII.) Josiah Baer, bn. Oct. 9, 1882. (VII.) Noah Baer, bn. Oct. 26, 1884. (VII.) Eva Baer, bn. May 15, 1886. (VII.) Edon Baer, bn. Sept. 22, 1887; died Oct. 21, 1887. (VII.) Norman Baer, bn. Sept. 21, 1888. (VII.) Ezra Baer, bn. Nov. 20, 1890.

VI. Mary Baer, bn. Dec. 21, 1844.

VI. Abraham Baer, bn. July 30, 1846; died June 25, 1868.

VI. Daniel Baer, bn. July 5, 1848; died Nov. 30, 1852.

VI. Elizabeth Baer, bn. July 24, 1850. Mrd. Henry Miller. P. O., St. Johns, Mich.

VI. Esther Baer, bn. —. Mrd. Samuel Bauman. P. O., Rosina, Ionia Co., Mich.

VI. John Baer, bn. Dec. 18, 1853.

VI. Martin Baer, bn. Oct. 17, 1855; died Oct. 13, 1861.

VI. Sallie Baer, bn. Sept. 17, 1859; died July 27, 1878.

V. Elizabeth Wismer, bn. in Waterloo Co., Ont., Mar. 28, 1824. Mrd. Moses B. Snyder. He was bn. Mar. 12, 1826; died Feb. 16, 1868. Farmer. Menn's. Children: Mary, Amos, Abram, Magdalena, Jacob, Henry, Ephraim, Isaac, Menno.

VI. Mary Snyder, bn. Nov. 28, 1847. Mrd. John C. Shantz, Feb. 22, 1874. P. O., Breslau, Ont. Menn's. Children: (VII.) Hettie Shantz, bn. at Bloomingdale, Ont. Mrd. Moses Eby, Mar. 9, 1890. P. O., Moorfield, Ont. Farmer. Menn. Bre. in Christ. (VII.) Israel Shantz. (VII.) Norman Shantz. (VII.) Annie Shantz. (VII.) Malinda Shantz. (VII.) Titus Shantz. (VII.) Elvina Shantz. (VII.) Amzi Shantz. (VII.) Mary Shantz.

VI. Amos W. Snyder, bn. Apr. 16, 1849. Mrd. Lydia Shantz, Feb. 15, 1874. P. O., Bloomingdale, Ont. Farmer. United Brethren. Children: (VII.) Urban Snyder, bn. Mar. 24, 1875. (VII.) Lizzie Snyder, bn. June 2, 1877. (VII.) Alvin Snyder, bn. Feb. 27, 1879.

VI. Abraham Snyder, bn. Dec. 19, 1852; died Jan. 11, 1853.

VI. Magdalena Snyder, bn. in Waterloo Co., Ont., Jan. 1, 1854. Mrd. John S. Frey, Feb. 21, 1875. P. O., Breslau, Ont. Farmer. Menn's. Children: (VII.) Ephraim Frey, bn. Feb. 28, 1876. (VII.) Abram Frey, bn. Jan. 18, 1877. (VII.) John Henry Frey, bn. Feb. 10. (VII.) Catharine Frey, bn. Mar. 31, 1880. (VII.) Elizabeth Frey, bn. Jan. 14, 1882. (VII.) Susanna Frey, bn. Mar. 18, 1884. (VII.) Isaac Frey, bn. Oct. 6, 1885. (VII.) Benjamin Frey, bn. Nov. 15, 1887. (VII.) Josiah Frey, bn. Mar. 28, 1890. (VII.) Jackniah Frey, bn. Oct. 27, 1881. (VII.) — Frey, bn. 1893.

VI. Jacob Snyder, bn. May 4, 1856. Mrd. Mary Ann Snyder, June 1878. P. O., Freeport, Ont. New Menn's. Children: (VII.) Alberta Lorena Snyder. (VII.) Luella Florence Snyder. (VII.) Harvey Alton Snyder.

VI. Henry Snyder, bn. Feb. 11, 1857. Mrd. Sarah Shantz, June 1875. She died June 10, 1878. United Bre. One child: (VII.) Elah Snyder, bn. May 3, 1876. —Henry mrd. second wife, Elizabeth Snyder, Feb. 3, 1879. She died Jan. 20, 1883. One child: (VII.) Elton Snyder, died infant.—Henry mrd. third wife, Lena Moss, May 1885. P. O., Caledonia Station, Mich. One child: (VII.) Ira Alvin Snyder.

VI. Ephraim Snyder, bn. Mar. 5, 1858. Mrd. Susanna Eby, Mar. 14, 1880. P. O., Bloomingdale, Ont. Gardener. New Menn's. Children: (VII.) Hannah Snyder, bn. Jan. 16, 1881; died Jan. 18, 1881. (VII.) Hiram Snyder, bn. Jan. 29, 1882; died Oct. 26, 1883. (VII.) Jeremiah Snyder, bn. Aug. 20, 1884.

VI. Isaac Snyder, bn. Aug. 7, 1860. P. O., Hespeler, Ont. Carpenter. S.

VI. Menno Snyder, bn. Oct. 6, 1864. P. O., Grand Rapids, Mich. Farm laborer. S.

V. Esther Wismer, bn. in Waterloo Co., Ont., June 1, 1826; died Nov. 20, 1881. Mrd. Daniel Shantz, Oct. 30, 1849. He was bn. Mar. 30, 1827. P. O., Bloomingdale, Ont. Farmer. Menn's. Children: Jacob, Henry, Noah, Maria, Daniel, Esther, Barbara, Menno.

VI. Jacob W. Shantz, bn. Sept. 3, 1850. Mrd. Magdalena Cressman, Jan. 19, 1873. P. O., Wallace, Ont. Farmer. Menn's. Children: **(VII.)** Ananias Shantz, bn. Oct. 21, 1873. **(VII.)** Esther Shantz, bn. Aug. 7, 1875. **(VII.)** Addison Shantz, bn. Sept. 24, 1877. **(VII.)** Nathan Shantz, bn. Sept. 13, 1879. **(VII.)** Emma Shantz, bn. Sept. 2, 1881. **(VII.)** Fanny Shantz, bn. Nov. 17, 1883. **(VII.)** Celina Shantz, bn. June 1, 1887.

VI. Henry Shantz, bn. Feb. 16, 1852; died Aug. 1, 1879. Mrd. Magdalena Bauman, Oct. 29, 1876. Children: **(VII.)** Hannah Shantz, bn. Oct. 10, 1877. **(VII.)** Henry Cyrenus Shantz, bn. June 6, 1879.

VI. Noah W. Shantz, bn. in Waterloo Co., Ont., Aug. 10, 1854. Mrd. Rachel C. Shantz, Feb. 27, 1876. She died Aug. 20, 1890. P. O., Geneva, Ill. Millwright. Menn. Children: **(VII.)** Edmund Shantz, bn. Apr. 12, 1877. **(VII.)** Elah Shantz, bn. Dec. 23, 1878. **(VII.)** Daniel Shantz, bn. Oct. 17, 1880. **(VII.)** Myrtie Shantz, bn. Sept. 3, 1882; died Oct. 13, 1883. **(VII.)** Susannah Shantz, bn. Jan. 2, 1885; died Nov. 12, 1886. **(VII.)** Maurice Shantz, bn. Aug. 13, 1887. **(VII.)** Orvie Shantz, bn. Sept. 20, 1889.

VI. Maria Shantz, bn. May 17, 1858. Mrd. Charles Reichel, Apr. 24, 1885. P. O., Bloomingdale, Ont.

VI. Daniel W. Shantz, bn. Apr. 8, 1861. P. O., Leetsville, Mich. S.

VI. Esther Shantz, bn. Mar. 26, 1863. Mrd. Owen S. Bauman, Jan. 15, 1882. P. O., May City, Iowa. Three children.

VI. Barbara Shantz, bn. June 16, 1865. Mrd. Christian Albemang, Apr. 19, 1885. P. O., Bloomingdale, Ont.

VI. Menno W. Shantz, bn. May 26, 1869. S.

V. Mary Wismer, bn. in Waterloo Co., Ont., June 12, 1831. Mrd. Abraham S. Cressman, Jan. 21, 1877. P. O., Washington, Ont. Retired farmer. Menn's. No issue.

IV. Joseph Wismer, bn. Apr. 9, 1797; died Aug. 25, 1861. Lived in Canada, where he died unmarried.

Jacob C. Wismer, (See page 212.)

IV. Jacob Wismer, bn. Feb. 23, 1799; died in Phila. Apr. 19, 1871. Mrd. Esther Rosenberger, —. She was bn. in Montg. Co., May 10, 1810; died in Phila. Sept. 18, 1877. Produce dealer. Mr. W. Meth. Ep., Mrs. W. Reformed. Children: Mary, Joseph, Ann, Barbara, Emma, Henry, Charles, Jacob, Esther, Allen, Franklin.

V. Mary Ann Wismer, bn. in Phila. Jan. 8, 1830. Mrd. Frederick Theilacker, Feb. 6, 1848. He was bn. in Wurtemburg, Germany, came to the United States when six years of age; died Feb. 27, 1864. Meth. Children: Charlotte, William, Christian, Anna, Esther, Mary, Samuel.

VI. Charlotte Theilacker, bn. —. Mrd. Antone F. Miller, —. Res., 2715 Girard Ave., Phila., Pa. Cigar manufacturer. Children: (**VII.**) Alice E. Miller. (**VII.**) Lottie Miller. (**VII.**) Frank Antone Miller.

VI. William J. Theilacker, bn. Feb. 14, 1850. Mrd. —. Fire Insurance. Children: (**VII.**) Mary Emma Theilacker. (**VII.**) William Theilacker.

VI. Christian F. Theilacker, bn. Mar. 12, 1851; died Mar. 23, 1851.

VI. Anna Eliza Theilacker, bn. Feb. 13, 1853; died Mar. 13, 1854.

VI. Esther Ann Theilacker, bn. May 12, 1854; died Jan. 14, 1856.

VI. Mary Ellen Theilacker, bn. Nov. 28, 1858. Mrd. Mahlon E. Foust, —. Tin-roofer. One child: (**VII.**) Mattie Foust, —.

VI. Samuel Scatergood Theilacker, bn. May 27, 1860.

V. Joseph Wismer, bn. —; died in 1832.

V. Anna Eliza Wismer, bn. Sept. 4, 1833; died Sept. 1848.

V. Barbara A. Wismer, bn. Oct. 5, 1835; died in 1838.

V. Emma Matilda Wismer, bn. in Philadelphia, Jan. 14, 1837. Mrd. Henry Fetters, Jan. 14, 1856. He was bn. Jan. 15, 1830; died Aug. 12, 1886. P. O., 1326 Palmer St., Philadelphia, Pa. Children: James, Esther, Charles, Wilhelmina, Milton, Jacob, Clifford, Walter, Mary, Ella.

VI. James Fetters, bn. in Philadelphia, Pa., Jan. 16, 1857. Res. 1326 Palmer St., Philadelphia. Driver. S.
VI. Esther Ann Fetters, bn. Aug. 8, 1858; died Aug. 17, 1858.
VI. Charles Henry Fetters, bn. in Philadelphia, Sept. 13, 1859. Driver. S.
VI. Wilhelmina Fetters, bn. Sept. 25, 1862. Mrd. Charles H. Royer, Apr. 30, 1889. Children: **(VII.)** Wilhelmina Edna Royer, bn. Apr. 20, 1890. **(VII.)** Mabel Irene Royer, bn. Sept. 8, 1892.
VI. Milton Augustus Fetters, born Feb. 6, 1865. Mrd. Clara Spencer, Oct. 17, 1890. P. O., 2127 Uber St., Philadelphia. Carpenter. Baptist.
VI. Jacob Wismer Fetters, bn. Sept. 27, 1868. 1326 Palmer St., Philadelphia. Salesman. Meth. Ep. S.
VI. Clifford Fetters, bn. Oct. 19, 1870. 1326 Palmer St., Philadelphia. Carpenter. Meth. Ep. S.
VI. Walter Fetters, bn. Oct. 19, 1870; died Nov. 16, 1870.
VI. Mary Emma Fetters, bn. Sept. 20, 1872. Meth. Ep. S.
VI. Ella May Fetters, bn. May 29, 1876.
V. Henry Wismer, bn. Aug. 21, 1839; died Apr. 1874. Mrd. Kate Sweaney, —. Children: **(VI.)** Hester Wismer. **(VI.)** Drusilla Wismer.

V. Charles R. Wismer, bn. in Philadelphia, Nov. 7, 1841. Mrd. Eliza Shuman, Dec. 1, 1867. Res. 2122 Marshall St., Philadelphia, Pa. Clerk. Ref. Children: **(VI.)** Infant, born and died unnamed, Aug. 3, 1868. **(VI.)** Laura Virginia Wismer, bn. Nov. 17, 1869; died July 10, 1888. **(VI.)** Charles Eugene Wismer, bn. July 12, 1872.

V. Allen Wismer, bn. Nov. 2, 1844; died Aug. 20, 1846.

V. Jacob Wismer, bn. in Philadelphia, Pa., Jan. 7, 1847. Mrd. Mary Catharine Sill, July 28, 1870. Res. 1422 Savery St., Philadelphia, Pa. Dealer in delicacies. Children: **(VI.)** Lillian Wismer, bn. June 3, 1871. S. **(VI.)** Amice Wismer, bn. Mar. 18, 1874. S.
V. Esther Wismer (twin), bn. Jan. 7, 1847; died Mar. 10, 1848.

V. Franklin Wismer, bn. Jan. 23, 1851; died Feb. 6, 1856.

IV. Mary Wismer, bn. in Towamencin Twp., Montg. Co., Pa., Dec. 25, 1801; died Dec. 31, 1889. Mrd. George Knipe. Children: Amos, Mary, Joseph, Anna. —Mary mrd. second husband Jacob Overholtzer, — He was bn. 1781; died 1856. Miller. Ger. Ref. Children: Barbara, David, Emma, Henry, Lavina.

V. Amos Knipe, bn. Nov. 18, 1819; died —. Mrd. —. Mason. Son: Lewis W. Knipe, 939 Randolph St., Philadelphia.

V. Mary Knipe, bn. in Montgomery Co., Pa., Jan. 18, 1821. Mrd. William Krupp, Dec. 27, 1840. He was bn. June 14, 1817; died Feb. 7, 1887. Farmer. Menn's. Children: Eliza, David, Isaiah, Annie.

VI. Eliza Krupp, bn. Feb. 23, 1842. Mrd. Samuel D. Hunsberger. P. O., Souderton, Pa. Children: **(VII.)** William E. Hunsberger. **(VII.)** Samuel W. Hunsberger. **(VII.)** Charles O. Hunsberger. **(VII.)** Sylvania K. Hunsberger. **(VII.)** Jonathan Sidney Hunsberger. **(VII.)** Mary Jane Hunsberger, bn. —; died —.

VI. David K. Krupp, bn. Feb. 13, 1844, in Towamencin Twp., Montg. Co., Pa. P. O., Souderton, Pa. S.

VI. Isaiah K. Krupp, bn. Sept. 25, 1846. S.

VI. Annie K. Krupp, bn. Nov. 13, 1849; died Feb. 10, 1870. S.

V. Joseph Knipe, bn. Sept. 13, 1823; died Aug. 7, 1876. Mrd. —. Carpenter. Son: Chester C. Knipe, Hatfield, Pa.

V. Anna Knipe, bn. Aug. 12, 1826; died aged about 8 months.

V. Barbara Amanda Overholtzer, bn. in Montg. Co., Oct. 10, 1834. Mrd. Abraham R. Roth, son of Peter Roth, Aug. 9, 1856. He died Apr. 14, 1879, aged 51 y. 9 m. 10 d. P. O., Lansdale, Pa. Farmer. Menn's. Children: Henry, Isaiah, Abraham, Mahlon, Mary, Emeline, Harvey.

VI. Henry O. Roth, bn. June 10, 1857; died Feb. 18, 1861.

VI. Isaiah O. Roth, bn. Jan. 29, 1860. Mrd. Katie Souder, daughter of Henry Souder. She bn. May 27, 1868. P. O., Telford, Pa. Engineer. Children: **(VII.)** Harry S. Roth, bn. Aug. 7, 1886; died Jan. 18, 1887. **(VII.)** Elsie S. Roth, bn. Oct. 20, 1888; died July 3, 1890. **(VII.)** Erma S. Roth, bn. Dec. 14, 1889. **(VII.)** Edna S. Roth, bn. June 9, 1892.

VI. Abraham O. Roth, bn. Nov. 19, 1861. Mrd. Kate Alderfer, June 16, 1886. Two days after their marriage June 18th, Mr. Roth took his newly made wife back to her parents from the Roth homestead, and while returning to his home he took a friend, Peter Roth, with him in his carriage, and took the road to Sellersville, where they had some business to attend to. As they were crossing the rail-road track at Clymer's Crossing, they were caught by a wreck-train, and the newly made husband was instantly killed, while Peter Roth escaped serious injury. Thus the young couple were married only two days when they were separated by death.

VI. Mahlon O. Roth, bn. Dec. 1, 1862. Mrd. Katie G., daughter of Samuel Derstine, 1884. P. O., Lansdale, Pa. Machinist. Children: **(VII.)** Andrew D. Roth, bn. May 20, 1885. **(VII.)** Laura D. Roth, bn. Oct. 31, 1886. **(VII.)** Annie D. Roth, bn. Dec. 22, 1890: died July 30, 1891.

VI. Mary Lizzie Roth, bn. Oct. 19, 1870. Mrd. Edwin B. Bergey, Nov. 22, 1890. He was bn. July 6, 1863. P. O., Lansdale, Pa. Teamster for bakery. Menn's. One child: **(VII.)** Edwin R. Bergey, bn. Oct. 28, 1892; died Nov. 2, 1892.

VI. Emeline O. Roth, bn. July 22, 1874; died Oct. 16, 1874.

VI. Harvey O. Roth, bn. Nov 25, 1875; died July 4, 1876.

V. David Overholtzer, bn. —. Mrd. Mary Ann Belz. P. O., Souderton, Pa.

V. Emma Overholtzer, bn. —. Mrd. John Oberholtzer, —. P. O., Lansdale, Pa.

V. Henry W. Overholtzer, bn. in Tomensin, Pa., in 1841 Mrd. Catharine Hagey in 1869. 429 Berks St., Philadelphia, Pa. Insurance agent. Presby. Chil-

dren: (VI.) Mary I. Overholtzer, bn. in 1871. Mrd.
Thomas Cressman. Res. 2208 Delhi St., Philadelphia,
Pa. (VI.) Eva E. Overholtzer, bn. in 1873. (VI.) Harry
E. Overholtzer, bn. in 1875. (VI.) Silas G. Overholtzer,
bn. in 1877. (VI.) Flora E. Overholtzer, bn. in 1879.
(VI.) Catharine E. Overholtzer, bn. —; died 1887.
V. Lavina Overholtzer, bn. —; died —.
IV. Anna Wismer, bn. in Montg. Co., Pa., May 10,
1806; died Oct. 6, 1890. Mrd. Isaac B. Tyson, —.
He was bn. in Montg. Co., Oct. 26, 1804; died Jan.
5, 1882. Farmer and miller. Brethren in Christ.
Children: Benjamin, Enos, Isaac, Barbara, Lydia,
Reuben, Emeline, Mary, John, Harriet.
V. Benjamin W. Tyson, bn. —; died young, aged 19
years.
V. Enos W. Tyson, bn. —. Mrd. Sarah Raudenbush, —. P. O., Schwenksville, Pa.
V. Isaac Tyson, bn.—; died young, aged 18 years.
V. Barbara Tyson, bn. —; died young.
V. Lydia W. Tyson, bn. in Montg. Co., Pa., Aug.
11, 1836. Mrd. Henry S. Heisey, Sept 15, 1861.
P. O., William's Mill, Pa. Farmer. Brethren in
Christ. Children: Anna, Reuben, Daniel, Isaac,
Henry, Noah, Emma, Levi.
VI. Anna T. Heisey, bn. Nov. 22, 1863. Mrd. H. B.
Brubaker. Brethren in Christ. One child: (VII.)
Howard Brubaker.
VI. Reuben T. Heisey, bn. July 5, 1864. Mrd. Annie M. Baker. P. O., Shepherdstown, Pa. Children:
(VII.) Fanny Heisey. (VII.) Paul Heisey.
VI. Daniel T. Heisey, bn. near Falmouth, Lancaster Co., Pa., Mar. 21, 1866. Mrd. Catharine A.,
daughter of Jacob and Mary McQuate, of New
Kingston, Cumberland Co., Pa., Sept. 26, 1891.
P. O., Hagerstown, Md. Railway Postal Clerk on
line from Baltimore, Md., to Roanoke, Va. Meth. Ep.
VI. Isaac Heisey, bn. Jan. 20, 1868. Mrd. Cora
Evans. P. O., William's Mill, Pa. One child: (VII.)
J. Henry Heisey.
VI. Henry Heisey, bn. Sept. 20, 1869. S.
VI. Noah Heisey, bn. Dec. 15, 1871. S.
VI. Emma Heisey, bn. Oct. 13, 1873. S.

VI. Levi Heisey, bn. May 2, 1880.
V. Reuben W. Tyson, bn. —. Mrd. Sue Fryer.
P. O., Royer's Ford, Pa.
V. Emeline W. Tyson, bn. in Upper Providence
Twp., Montg. Co., Pa., Mar. 1, 1840. Mrd. Daniel
P. Kinsell, Nov. 24, 1873. P. O., Royer's Ford, Pa.
Farmer. Menn. Bre. in Christ. Children: (VI.)
Emma T. Kinsell, bn. Aug. 28, 1874. P. O., Royer's
Ford, Pa. Tailoress. Menn. Bre. in Christ. (VI.)
Samuel T. Kinsell, bn. Feb. 7, 1876. P. O., Royer's
Ford, Pa. School-teacher. Menn. Bre. in Christ.
(VI.) Eve Ann T. Kinsell, bn. Nov. 8, 1877. P. O.,
Royer's Ford, Pa. Tailoress. Menn. Bre. in Christ.
(VI.) Isaac T. Kinsell, bn. June 28, 1880. Menn. Bre.
in Christ. (VI.) Lydia T. Kinsell, bn. June 4, 1883.
(VI.) Elizabeth T. Kinsell, bn. May 1, 1886.
V. Mary A. Tyson, bn. in Montg. Co., Pa. Mrd.
Levi S. Heisey, Nov. 1868. P. O., Mechanicsburg,
Pa. Farmer. Bre. in Christ. Children: (VI.) Enos T.
Heisey, bn. Mar. 19, 1870; died Sept. 26, 1870. (VI.)
Cyrus T. Heisey, bn. Oct. 10, 1871. (VI.) Ezra T.
Heisey, bn. July 24, 1873. (VI.) Willie T. Heisey,
bn. Dec. 31, 1874. (VI.) Katie A. Heisey, bn. Apr.
26, 1878.
V. John Tyson, bn. —; died young, aged 16 years.
V. Harriet Tyson, bn. in Montg. Co., Pa., Nov. 2,
1844. Mrd. George Detwiler, of Canada, Nov. 27,
1870. P. O., Sherkston, Ont. Farmer. River Breth-
ren. Children: (VI.) Emma Detwiler, bn. Oct. 12,
1871. S. (VI.) Tyson Detwiler, bn. June 6, 1873. S.
(VI.) Henrietta Detwiler, bn. May 14, 1875. S. (VI.)
Irene Detwiler, bn. Aug. 12, 1878; died Oct. 18, 1882.
(VI.) Anna Abigail Detwiler, bn. Mar. 17, 1882. (VI.)
George Leslie Detwiler, bn. Apr. 28, 1885.

DESCENDANTS OF HENRY WISMER, SON OF JACOB WISMER.

II. Henry Wismer, bn. in Bucks Co., Pa., about 1730; died —. Mrd. Barbara Lederach in 1754. He was an enterprising, shrewd and prosperous man. From old documents in the possession of his descendants it can be seen that, of the entire family of Jacob Wismer, he (Henry) was probably the most prominent in wealth and business abilities. Agriculture was his chief pursuit. In 1773 he became owner of his father's farm of 210 acres in Bedminster. At the same time he had a farm in Hilltown of 140 acres, on which he lived and died. In 1793 he sold the homestead with 120 acres to his son Abraham, and the remaining 90 acres to one Ekel, and in 1805 he sold his Hilltown farm to his son-in-law John Funk. He received a life right for himself and wife. Funk was to reside on the farm and take good care of the old couple. He was bound to provide all the necessaries and comforts for old age, even to the point of carrying their firewood into their room and furnish them with five gallons of whiskey yearly as long as either of the old folks lived. Weaving and distilling whiskey were also carried on in connection with farming. Judging from items entered on his Day Book from 1768 to 1800, we are led to believe that persons in need of money and work depended in a great measure on him for assistance. It also appears that a few of his brothers were dependant on him for support towards the close of their lives. In 1803 he ma le a will, which reads as follows:

Jn the name of God. Amen. I, Henry Wismer of
Hilltown township in the county of Bucks and
state of Pennsylvania we were being of old age and
weak in body but of perfect sound mind and memory
thanks be to God therefore calling unto mind the
mortality of my Body Do make and ordain this to be
my last Will and Testament in manner following,
first of all I Reccommend my sould into the hands of
the almighty god that gave it and my body, I Reccommend to the Earth to be buried in a decent Christian manner at the discretion of my Executors hereafter named, and Touching such worldly Effects
which it has pleased God to bless me with in this life,
I Give and dispose of the same in manner following.
First of all after my debts and funeral charges is
paid I do Will all my money that I have in hand and
all my effects to my well beloved Wife Barbery as
much as she pleases to keep of it. then it is my Will
that my Executors hereafter named shall make a
vendue and sell of my Effects what my wife don't
want to keep, & Collect the money and Give it into
the Hands of my widow that she may dow with all
the money that is in hand and what will be made of
the vendue what she pleases during her lifetime and
after her decease my Executors is to make sale of the
effects that is left and pay it to my heirs. Some has
got more away and some less, and so my Executors
must pay to the eleven heirs of the money that is left
and what will be made of the effects after my wifes
decease to make them all alike, only my son Samuel
he is not to Sheer with the rest because he has got
his three hundred pounds aforehand if there is not
anuf of the money that is left and maid out of the effects then my Executors must take of the three hundred pounds which is to be paid down of the planta-

tion and make them all alike. My son-in-law John
Funk is to pay 14 hundred pounds for my plantation,
three hundred pounds in one year after my decease
and then yearly and every year one hundred pounds
is to be paid till the whole is paid and still as the
payments is paid my Executors is to pay it to my
eleven heirs sheer and sheer alike. Notabena my
Daughter Nancy is to have 20 pounds less than the
other heirs, because the 20 pounds goes to her 2 sons
of her first husband. As soon as John Funk pays the
three hundred pounds the first payment I Give my
son Abraham Wismer one of the Executors full and
ample power to make and execute a sufficient Deed
of Conveyance unto the said John Funk clear of all
encumbrance as well as myself could done if I was
living. Notabena, I do will to my two Grandsons
Jacob and Henry Rute ten pounds apiece to be paid
out of their mother Nancy's Portion to be paid out of
the first payment of the plantation if there is anuf
left. And last of all I do hereby Anominate my son
Abraham Wismer of Bedminster Township County
of Bucks and state of Pennsylvania and John Funk
of Hilltown Township my son-in-law and County and
State aforesaid to be my sole Executors of this my
last will and Testament and I do hereby utterly Dis-
alow and Revoke all former Testaments wills Legacies and Executors. Relating this and Confirming
this to be my last will and Testament. In Witness
whereof I have hereunto set my hand and seal this
sixth day of October in the year of our Lord one
thousand eight hundred and six.

Signed Sealed published
pronounced and declared
by the said Henry Wismer
to be his last will and Testament in the presence of
us. Jacob Wismer,
Jacob Landis.

Henry Wismer. {SEAL}

Following is an article of agreement made with his son-in-law, John Funk.

"Articles of agrement made & Concluded the 12th day of September, in the year of our Lord One thousand Eight hundred & Five, Between Henry Wismer, Senior, of the Township of Hilltown, in the County of Bucks, & State of Pennsylvania, of the one part, & John Funk of the Same place, farmer Yeoman, of the other part. WITNESSETH that the Said Henry Wismer, Senior, hath granted, bargained & Sold, released & Confined unto the Said John Funk, his heirs and Assigns forever, all & Singular, that Certain parcel or tract of Land, Situate in the Township & County aforesaid, Containing One hundred & forty acres, be the Same more or Less, & adjoins to Land of Abraham Gudshallies, Isaac Williamsis, Daniel Richardses & others, it being the aforesaid Henry Wismer's Old farm, and Every part & parcel thereof, with the appurtenances, together with all woods & waters thereunto in anywise belonging & the revertion & Revertons remainder & remainders, rents, Isnes & profits thereof.

In Consideration whereof the Said John Funk is to pay fourteen hundred pounds Lawful Money of Pennsylvania in Manner hreinafter Expressed & it is agreed Between both Contracting partyes, that the Said John Funk is to dwell on the above mentioned premises & take Care of the Said Henry Wismer and his wife Barbara, During their Lives; & the Said John Funk is to give & procure them the Said Henry Wismer & barbara his wife, in this present year, 1805, Twenty Bushels of Rye, Six Bushels of Indian Corn, Six Bushels of wheat, Six Bushels Buckwheat & four Bushels of potatoes, two hundred weight of pork, & one hundred weight of Beef, one

Barrel of good Syder & one Barrel of water syder,
& five gallons of Wiskey; and Suffer them to go
into the Orchard to get what fruit they want to
use in the House, & Likewise Keep a Horse and Cow
for them, as he would his own, both Summer & winter,
& when Barbara is not able to Milk her Cow then
Funk must Cause her to be Milked, & the Milk put
up for the Old people's use; and the time their Cow
gos drye he is to Soply them with Milk and Butter.
This all must be given & done in this present year
mentioned, & Likewise in Every Other year, as Long
as Either Shall Live. And Likewise the Said John
Funk is to Suffer them to Dwell in the Little House
adjoining to the gebelend, and Suffer them the poses-
ion of the Little Room adjoining to the same, & Likewise grant them the prevelidge of going through
their Room upon their Loft to Carry thither & hither
what Ever the List of their own property, & Likewise
into the Celler & Likewise grant them the use of the
Little garden adjoining the Little House. & the Said
John Funk is to Carry their grain to Mill, & when
ground, Return the Same again. And Likewise he is
to Soply them with firewood Cut & halled to the
Dore, & Likewise See the Same Cut Small & Caryed
in the House for them. This all must be granted &
Done Whenever required, During Either of their
Lives; & after their Decease, in twelve Month's time
the Said John Funk must pay into the hands of the
aforesaid Henry Wismer's Executors or administra-
tors three hundred pounds good & Lawful Money of
Pennsylvania, aforesaid, Upon which payment the
Said Executors or administraters must Execute unto
the Said John Funk, his heirs, Executors, administraters or assigns A good & Sufficient Deed of Conveyance for the above described premises & Every

part & parcel thereof, & is to be Clear of all Incumberance & after Such Execution the Said John Funk must pay One hundred pounds Lawful Money, as aforesaid, yearly, untill the Said Fourteen hundred pounds are paid, for Which Bonds & good Security must be given, if Required, for the true performance Whereof we bind Ourselves, our heirs, Executors & administraters to Each other, his heirs, Executors, administraters or assigns in the Sum of two thousand Eight hundred pounds Money as aforesaid firmly by these presents, Sealed with our Seals the day & year first above written.

Signed, Sealed & Delivered in the presence of Thomas Darrow, Henry Liscy, Jun., Jacob Landis.	Henry Wismer.	{SEAL}
	John Funk.	{SEAL}

The children of Henry and Barbara Wismer are as follows: Jacob, Abraham, Annie, Maria, Henry, Joseph, Christian, Esther, John, Elizabeth, Samuel, Barbara.

III. Jacob Wismer, bn. in Bucks Co., Pa., Apr. 15, 1755; died —. Mrd. —. Issue: Henry, Jacob, a Mrs. Bradford, and a Mrs. Rittenhouse.—Jacob mrd. second wife —. Issue, one child, Mary. They lived along the Schuylkill in the direction of Royer's Ford, in Montg. Co., on the farm now owned and occupied by Henry Thomas. Miller and farmer.

IV. Henry Wismer, M. D., bn. —; died of yellow fever.

IV. Jacob Wismer, bn. —; died —. Mrd. —. Issue: Henry, John, Ephraim, Eliza.

V. Henry Wismer, bn. —; died —. Mrd. —. Child: **(VI.)** Frank Wismer, P. O., Royer's Ford, Pa.

V. John Wismer, bn. —; died —. Mrd.

V. Ephraim Wismer, bn. —; died —. S.

V. Eliza Wismer, bn. —; died —. Mrd. — Rhodes, —. No issue.

IV. — Wismer, bn. —; died —. Mrd. Hezekiah Bradford —. No issue.

IV. — Wismer, bn. —; died —. Mrd. Henry Rittenhouse, —. Children: Charles, Mary.

V. Charles Rittenhouse, bn. —; died —. Mrd. —.

V. Mary Rittenhouse, bn. —; died —. Mrd. Abel Thomas, —. Children: (**VI.**) Harry Thomas, bn. —. Mrd. —. P. O., Royer's Ford, Pa. (**VI.**) Edwin Thomas, bn. —. P. O., Royer's Ford, Pa.

IV. Mary Wismer, bn. —; died —. Mrd. Daniel Stahl. He died —. No issue. Mary mrd. second husband Isaac Linderman. He died —. No issue.

III. Abraham Wismer, bn. in Bucks Co., Nov. 5, 1756; died in 1844, aged 87 y. 3 m. 27 d. Mrd. Veronica Myers, —. She was bn. Apr. 3, 1757; died about 1818. Mrd second wife Mary, a widow of Detweiler (maiden name Freed). Farmer. Menn. ch. He was the third owner of the Wismer homestead. During the Revolutionary war, his father's teams were pressed into service by the Americans, and Abraham was sent along as teamster, more to take good care of and return the teams. In 1783 Abraham Wismer and one Martin Lowry buried the remains of the notorious outlaw, Moses Doane, who was shot along the Tohickon, on a farm adjoining the Wismer homestead. Mr. Wismer often referred to the mournful appearance of the procession to the grave, composed of a few neighbors, two females, and a small dog. The women wept bitterly, and the dog showed his grief by stepping to the edge of the grave and looking into it. Children: Henry, Samuel, Isaac, Barbara, Catharine, Veronica, Abraham, Elizabeth, Esther.

IV. Henry Wismer bn. Mar. 21, 1778; died Sept. 14, 1828. Mrd. Barbara Ruth, —. Farmer, clock and watch maker, and cattle dealer. Children: Michael, Abraham, Fanny, Elizabeth.

V. Michael Wismer, bn. —; drowned in Virginia. Cattle dealer. S.

V. Abraham Wismer, bn. —; died young.

V. Fanny Wismer. bn. June 13, 1802; died Mar. 17, 1873. Mrd. John Funk. (See Index of References No. 61.)

V. Elizabeth Wismer, bn. —; died —. Mrd. Isaac Stover, —. Children: (**VI.**) Henry W. Stover, bn. —. Mrd. —. P. O., Carversville. Pa. (**VI.**) Oliver Stover, bn. —; died —. S. (**VI.**) Jacob Stover. bn. —. (**VI.**) Newton Stover, bn. —. (**VI.**) Ann Eliza Stover, bn. —. Mrd. —. (**VI.**) Emma Stover, bn. —. (**VI.**) Fannie Stover. bn. —.

IV. Samuel Wismer, bn. Jan. 10, 1780; died Oct. 2, 1851. Mrd. Susanna Detweiler. She was bn. —; died July 16, 1864, of paralysis. She was found prostrate in the yard shortly after breakfast, life extinct. Her age was 83 y. 11 m. 1 d. On the occasion of her funeral 160 carriages accompanied her remains to the place of burial.

Mr. Wismer was a farmer, sawyer, and weaver. He had but three days' English schooling, yet he was a fluent English and German reader, and also wrote both languages, keeping his accounts in the English language. He was a self-educated man, settling up estates, in the neighborhood, and transacting various other public duties in a time when there were but few lawyers to advise and counsel. His six daughters had five spinning-wheels in operation at one time, and the sixth daughter did the reeling, and the father the reading in the evening. His children do not remember of having received a cross word from him. His family government was mild yet firm. Each daughter received a spinning-wheel as part of her "outsetting". Several of the daughters learned to weave and did considerable of it while at home. Five of the daughters had a silk wedding-dress, though most of their every-day wear was homespun. The old time lard lamps were used in the family, hot bricks being put under the lamps to keep the lard warm and thin. Rye bread was the staff of life. All the girls made full hands in the hay and grain fields, and raking leaves in the woods. Some of them also aided at the saw-mill. Menn. Children: Abraham, Elizabeth,

John, Samuel, Barbara, Catharine, Fannie, Susanna, Sarah, Deborah, Henry.

V. Abraham D. Wismer, bn. Aug. 10, 1802; died Aug. 17, 1882, aged 80 y. 7 d. Mrd. Catharine Myers, May 3, 1827. Farmer. Menn. Children: Isaac, Hannah.

VI. Isaac M. Wismer, bn. Oct. 11, 1830. Mrd. Elizabeth Leatherman in 1851. P. O., Hatfield, Pa. Carpenter. Ref. ch. Children: Henry, Catharine, Emma, Sarah, Abraham, Amos, Hannah, Adaline, Ida, Mary.

VII. Henry L. Wismer, bn. May 30, 1852. Ref. ch. S.

VII. Catharine Wismer, bn. May 25, 1854; died Dec. 20, 1862.

VII. Emma Wismer, bn. May 12, 1856. Mrd. John Seibert, May 15, 1875. Farmer. Luth. Children: (**VIII.**) Byron W. Seibert, bn. May 27, 1876. (**VIII.**) Reuben W. Seibert, bn. Sept. 16, 1880.

VII. Sarah Jane Wismer, bn. Feb. 13, 1858; died Dec. 2, 1862.

VII. Abraham L. Wismer, bn. Jan. 20, 1860; died Dec. 9, 1862.

VII. Amos S. Wismer, bn. Dec. 28, 1861. Mrd. Lydia Knipe, Oct. 4, 1884. Merchant tailor. Ref. ch. Children: (**VIII.**) Lottie Wismer. (**VIII.**) Harrison Wismer.

VII. Hannah E. Wismer, bn. Nov. 30, 1863. Mrd. Henry M. Oberholtzer, Nov. 16, 1882. Plasterer. Mrs. O. Ref. ch. Children: (**VIII.**) Maxwell W. Oberholtzer, bn. Apr. 13, 1884. (**VIII.**) Annie E. Oberholtzer, bn. Oct. 18, 1888.

VII. Adaline Wismer, bn. Oct. 14, 1867. Mrd. William F. Kilmer, Dec. 24, 1887. Ref. ch.

VII. Ida Wismer, bn. May 14, 1869. Ref. ch. S.

VII. Mary Ann Wismer, bn. June 11, 1873; died Jan. 10, 1874.

VI. Hannah Wismer, bn. Feb. 18, 1835. Mrd. Amos Scheetz, Jan. 31, 1858. P. O., Dublin, Pa. Farmer. Ger. Ref. ch. No issue.

V. Elizabeth Wismer, bn. Oct. 24, 1804; died Apr. 14, 1886. Mrd. Abraham Hunsberger, son of Bishop

Henry Hunsberger, 1827. He was bn. Aug. 27, 1803; died Feb. 3, 1883. Farmer. Menn. Children: Samuel, Henry, Catharine, Abraham, Simeon, Susan, Elizabeth, Jacob, Joseph, Sarah.

VI. Samuel W. Hunsberger. bn. July 27, 1828. Mrd. Catharine Fretz, Feb. 23, 1854. P. O., Fountainville, Pa. Farmer. Menn. Children: Mary, Elias, Amanda, Kate, Susanna, Anna, Allen, William, Daniel.

VII. Mary F. Hunsberger, bn. Apr. 26, 1855. Mrd. Charles C. Atkinson, Nov. 15, 1879. Shoemaker. One child: **(VIII.)** Samuel Howard Atkinson, bn. Feb. 8, 1882.

VII. Elias F. Hunsberger, bn. Oct. 13, 1856. Mrd. Mrs. Sarah Overholt (maiden name Wismer), —. Teamster. Menn. Children: **(VIII.)** Harvey Samuel Hunsberger. **(VIII.)** Nettie Catharine Hunsberger.

VII. Amanda E. Hunsberger. bn. Mar. 1858. Mrd. Philip Miller, —. Teamster in Phila. No issue.

VII. Kate Hunsberger, bn. May 19, 1860.

VII. Susannah Hunsberger. bn. Aug. 14, 1862; died Sept. 7, 1862.

VII. Annie Hunsberger, bn. Sept. 27, 1863. Mrd. Samuel L. Gross, Mar. 12, 1887. Farmer. Children: **(VIII.)** Warren H. Gross. **(VIII.)** Melvin Gross.

VII. Allen F. Hunsberger. bn. Mar. 28, 1866. Enlisted in the U. S. Army in 1888. Stationed at Fort Hamilton. Battery I., N. Y.

VII. William F. Hunsberger, bn. Apr. 23, 1869.

VII. Daniel Hunsberger, bn. Apr. 28, 1875; died Sept. 11, 1875.

VI. Henry W. Hunsberger, bn. July 13, 1830; died Jan. 24, 1883. Mrd. Mary Rittenhouse, Jan. 1866. She was bn. Apr. 3, 1840; died June 2, 1878. Farmer. Children: **(VII.)** Ida R. Hunsberger, bn. Oct. 8, 1866. S. **(VII.)** Alvah R. Hunsberger, bn. Oct. 16, 1868. Mrd. Maggie Moyer, of Hilltown, Pa., Feb. 1, 1890. P. O., Hilltown, Pa. **(VII.)** Charles L. Hunsberger, bn. Oct. 12, 1871.

VI. Catharine W. Hunsberger, bn. Sept. 25, 1832; died Sept. 10, 1864. Mrd. Jacob B. Overholt, Dec. 1856. P. O., Seville, O. Farmer. Menn. Children: Isaac, Hannah.

Home where Mark Wismer Died (Log Cabin.)

VII. Isaac H. Overholt, bn. Sept. 6, 1857. Mrd. Alice S. Ziegler. Aug. 7, 1881. P. O., Rittman, O. Carpenter. Children: **(VIII.)** Charles Franklin Overholt, bn. June 30, 1882; died June 29, 1883. **(VIII.)** William Henry Overholt, bn. Feb. 20, 1884. **(VIII.)** Effie Elizabeth Overholt, bn. Aug. 13, 1885. **(VIII.)** John Clifford Overholt, bn. Sept. 4, 1887.

VII. Hannah Liby Overholt, bn. July 24, 1859. Mrd. E. E. Pratt, 1888. P. O., Dalton. O. Farmer. Children: **(VIII.)** Iva Irene Pratt, bn. Jan. 18, 1889. **(VIII.)** Ray E. Pratt, bn. Sept. 22, 1890.

VI. Abraham W. Hunsberger, bn. Aug. 29, 1834; died —. Mrd. Sarah Moore, Nov. 27, 1858. Farmer. Menn. Children: Milton, Franklin, Abraham.

VII. Milton M. Hunsberger, bn. Mar. 9, 1860; died Oct. 13, 1863.

VII. Franklin M. Hunsberger, bn. in Bucks Co., Dec. 26, 1861. Mrd. Louisa B. Moyer. P. O., Hilltown, Pa. Carpenter. Luth. Children: **(VIII.)** Lillie Amelia Hunsberger, bn. Aug. 4, 1884. **(VIII.)** Charles Pierson Hunsberger, bn. Oct. 20, 1885. **(VIII.)** Mary Agnes Hunsberger, bn. Jan. 9, 1890. **(VIII.)** Anthony Franklin Hunsberger, bn. Mar. 19, 1891.

VII. Abraham M. Hunsberger, bn. in Bucks Co., Dec. 9, 1863. P. O., Hilltown, Pa. S.

VI. Simeon W. Hunsberger, bn. Oct. 26, 1836. Mrd. Elizabeth Schrauger, Feb. 26, 1860. She was bn. Dec. 15, 1838. P. O., Fountainville, Pa. Farmer. Menn. Children: **(VII.)** Jacob Hunsberger, bn. Mar. 13, 1862; died same day. **(VII.)** Susanna Hunsberger, bn. Apr. 22, 1863; died Mar. 14, 1883. **(VII.)** Jonas Hunsberger, bn. Jan. 12, 1866. Mrd. Kate Heacock, Apr. 24, 1889. She was bn. Dec. 1868. **(VII.)** Tobias Hunsberger, bn. Feb. 16, 1868. Mrd. Anna Meyers, Oct. 17, 1891. She was born Sept. 22, 1869. Laborer. Menn. **(VII.)** John Hunsberger, bn. June 17, 1871; died Mar. 6, 1883. **(VII.)** Elizabeth Hunsberger, bn. June 17, 1871; died same day. **(VII.)** Abraham Hunsberger, bn. Aug. 29, 1874. Saddler. S.

VI. Susanna Hunsberger, bn. Apr. 15, 1839; died Jan. 1, 1848.

11

VI. Elizabeth Hunsberger, bn. Dec. 13, 1841; died Dec. 25, 1843.

VI. Jacob W. Hunsberger, bn. July 13, 1844; died July 21, 1845.

VI. Joseph W. Hunsberger, bn. Mar. 19, 1847. P. O., Fricks.

VI. Sarah Hunsberger, bn. June 19, 1850; died Jan. 10, 1851.

V. John D. Wismer, bn. Aug. 20, 1806; died Oct. 16, 1878. Mrd. Nancy Fly, —. Shoemaker. No issue.

V. Samuel Wismer, bn. Mar. 1, 1809; died aged 6 months.

V. Barbara Wismer, bn. Feb. 1, 1811. Mrd. Samuel Nash. (See Index of References No. 41.)

V. Catharine Wismer, bn. in Bucks Co., Pa., Sept. 20, 1813. Mrd. Jacob Kratz, —. He was bn. in Bucks Co., Aug. 13, 1811; died Feb. 1, 1872. In May 1839 they moved to Wayne Co., O., where they purchased a farm on which they lived until he died. Menn. Children: Samuel, Maria, Reuben, Henry, Jacob, Lee.

VI. Samuel W. Kratz, bn. in Bucks Co., Pa., in 1836. P. O., Acme, O. Retired teacher and farmer. Menn. Single.

VI. Maria Kratz, bn. in Wayne Co., O., Sept. 17, 1840. Mrd. John C. Steiner, in 1863. P. O., Sterling, O. Farmer. Menn. Children: Reuben, Edwin, Kate, Harvey, Alice, Franklin, Lizzie.

VII. Reuben K. Steiner, bn. Dec. 6, 1863.

VII. Edwin L. Steiner, bn. Aug. 3, 1866.

VII. Kate A. Steiner, bn. June 20, 1869. Mrd. Andrew D. Blough, in 1884. P. O., Fredericksburg, O. Druggist. Disciples. One child: **(VIII.)** Walter H. Blough.

VII. Harvey J. Steiner, bn. July 8, 1872.

VII. Alice C. Steiner, bn. Feb. 11, 1876.

VII. Franklin K. Steiner, bn. Apr. 11, 1879; died July 6, 1879.

VII. Lizzie May Steiner, bn. Nov. 10, 1882.

VI. Reuben N. Kratz, bn. in Wayne Co., O., July 2, 1845. In early life Mr. Kratz taught in the public

schools, and also conducted singing-schools in the
vicinity of his former home in Wayne Co., O. He
was married to Amanda M. Miller, of Akron, O.,
Sept. 11, 1873. In 1882 they moved to Mitchell,
South Dakota. He has been variously occupied as
lumber merchant, land office clerk, land attorney,
and at present occupies the position of Register of
U. S. Office at Mitchell. He was also one of the
founders of the University of Dakota, and is a member of its managing board. He is also prominent in
religious circles, and is President of the South Dakota State Sunday School Association. Meth. Ep.
Children: (VII.) Frank E. Kratz, bn. Oct. 11, 1874;
died July 6, 1878. (VII.) Fred M. Kratz, bn. Feb. 21,
1879. (VII.) Carl Samuel Kratz, bn. Feb. 13, 1888.

VI. Henry Elton Kratz, M. A., Ph. D., bn. in Wayne
Co., O., Oct. 14, 1849. He prepared himself for
college in the common and high schools of his native
state, and supported himself by teaching. He first
entered Denison University, Granville, O., where he
remained two years, and then completed his collegiate
course at Wooster University, Wooster O., graduating with the degree of B. S. in 1874. Later the degree of M. A. was granted him by his Alma Mater.
He at once entered upon the work of teaching, and
has been Superintendent and Principal of schools in
several important cities, principally those of Bucyrus,
O., and Dexter, Mich. In both of these states he was
frequently engaged in the institute work by the side
of their best educators. In 1881, he went abroad,
taking his family with him, and during two years
resided in London. While in Europe he made a
special study of systems of education, and methods
of instruction. He met many of the leading educators
of the Old World, and became familiar with their
theories. Opportunities were offered him to observe
school work there which he readily and profitably
availed himself of, and returned to this country. The
year 1885 found him installed in the schools of Mitchell, Dakota, as Superintendent, a position he held for
four years. He organized and graded these schools
and put them in a condition second to none in the

Country. His pupils have found easy admission to
the schools of our leading cities. He promptly
identified himself with the educators of the state, and
has been present at every important educational
meeting in Dakota since 1886. When the Educational
Association organized the reading circle department
he was made the chief officer, and in turn made the
reading circle one of the vital educational forces of
the state. He was three times unanimously chosen
president of the State Educational Association, an
honor not before conferred on any member. He was
also prominently mentioned for the position of Ter-
ritorial Superintendent of Public Instruction. At the
first election for state officers, the leading educators
and teachers all over the state made urgent appeals
for him to consent to become a candidate for the office of State Superintendent of Public Instruction.
Against his better judgment he was finally induced
to make an effort to secure the Republican nomination. Unfortunately preceding nominations on the
ticket, bunched the nominees in his part of the state,
and he was defeated, although even then he received
a large number of votes in the convention.

In the spring of 1889 he was called to the chair
of Pedagogy and principalship of the Normal Department of the University of South Dakota. He
also completed a post graduate course in Philosophy
and Pedagogy in Wooster University, and received
the degree of Doctor of Philosophy.

In November 1891, he was unanimously chosen
Superintendent of the Sioux City, Iowa, schools, to
succeed Prof. Chas. W. Deane. He completed the
year's work in such a satisfactory manner, that he
was unanimously re-elected for two years at a salary
of $2,500 per year. Sioux City has a population of
over 40,000, about 6,000 children are enrolled in her
schools and 140 teachers are required to instruct
them. From this it can be readily inferred that Dr.
Kratz's present field of work is a broad one, and his
responsibilities great.

In addition to his other duties he conducts Teachers' Institutes, lectures from time to time, and occa-

sionally contributes articles on educational topics to the press, and is Director of the Lake Madison Chautauqua Assembly at Lake Madison, South Dakota. Taken altogether, it may readily be seen that Dr. Kratz is an exceedingly busy man. He was married to Lizzie M. Deal of Bucyrus, O., July 19, 1876. Meth. Ep. ch. Children: (VII.) Horace Elton Kratz, bn. Nov. 12, 1877. (VII.) Bessie May Kratz, bn. Jan. 2, 1879. (VII.) Arthur Murray Kratz, bn. Nov. 5, 1880. (VII.) Edward Mars Kratz, bn. Oct. 13, 1891.

VI. Jacob Kratz, bn. in Wayne Co., O., Feb. 7, 1855. Mrd. Acelia Kindig, Mar. 1, 1876. P. O., Shepherd, Mich. Farmer. Meth. Ep. Children: (VII.) Anna M. Kratz, bn. Jan. 1, 1878. (VII.) Harvey D. Kratz, bn. Sept. 27, 1879. (VII.) Infant, bn. July 9; died Sept. 19, 1881.

VI. Lee G. Kratz, bn. in Wayne Co., O., July 27, 1858. He inherited musical tastes from his parents, both of whom were lovers of music, and each possessed gifts and accomplishments exceeding ordinary attainments. He early exhibited marked endowment with these family traits, was diligent at school, and availed himself of high school privileges at Seville, O. After his father's death and breaking up of the old home, he went to live with his brother Reuben in Akron, O., where he entered High School and came under the notice of Prof. N. L. Glover, the instructor in music, under whose influence and counsel he decided to make music his life study and work. For two years he engaged in teaching school, all the time pursuing his study in music. He attended Ohio Normal Music School three terms, and spent one term in Dana's Musical Institute at Warren, O. Later he entered the College of Music at Cincinnati, O., where he graduated in 1882, with second honor of his class. He afterwards engaged in the work of his profession at Davenport, Iowa. Here his influence was felt as a teacher and organizer of Church Choirs, Quartettes, Male Choruses, and as author of musical compositions. His work in building up the Vocal Department of St. Catharine's Hall secured complimentary rec-

ommendation from Bishop Perry, of the Episcopal
church.

In 1887, desiring larger opportunities and fields
he removed to Omaha, where success and prosperity
has invariably attended all his enterprises, making
him a typical Western man in spirit and work. He
is Director of the Vocal Department of the University of Omaha, has three church choirs under training regularly, and is constantly giving concerts. He
organized and is Director of the celebrated "T. K."
Quartette, also the "Owls," a popular male chorus of
40 voices. He has for the last two years given special
attention to musical work in Chautauqua Assemblies.
His compositions are mostly of a sacred character.
His reputation and usefulness is rapidly enlarging.
He was married to Frankie Curtis, of Galva, Ill.,
Nov. 30, 1887. P. O., Omaha, Nebr. Meth. Ep. No
children.

V. Frances Wismer, bn. in Bucks Co., Pa., Nov. 2,
1815; died May 7, 1854. Mrd. Abraham Nash. (See
Index of References No. 42.)

V. Susanna Wismer, bn. Mar. 16, 1818; died aged 3
days.

V. Sarah Wismer, bn. Apr. 30, 1819. Mrd. Joseph
N. Gross. (See Index of References No. 44.)

V. Deborah Wismer, bn. Sept. 2, 1821; died Dec.
15, 1874. Mrd. Isaac Gross. (See Index of References No. 45.)

V. Henry D. Wismer, bn. in Bucks Co., June 2,
1825. Mrd. Elizabeth, daughter of Joseph Leatherman, – . P. O., Gardenville, Pa. Farmer. Menn.
Children: John, Susanna, Joseph.

VI. John L. Wismer, bn. Sept. 29, 1850. Mrd. Kate
Shelly, Sept. 8, 1876. She was bn. Jan. 16, 1856.
P. O., Gardenville, Pa. Farmer. Menn. One child:
(VII.) Walter Wismer, bn. Nov. 28, 1878.

VI. Susanna Wismer, bn. Sept. 13, 1852. Mrd. Tobias F. Shelly, Sept. 3, 1878. He was bn. Jan. 20,
1854. P. O., Gardenville, Pa. Farmer. Menn. One
child: **(VII.)** Bessie May Shelly, bn. Apr. 3, 1883.

VI. Joseph L. Wismer, bn. May 21, 1855. In Jan.
1879 went to Canada, remained two years. After visit-

ing his parents in Bucks Co., in Dec. 1880, he returned
to Canada and remained three years. In March 1886
he took a trip to various parts of the West, visiting
Sterling, Ill., Los Angeles, Cal., and many towns
and villages in California, among them San Francisco. From Los Angeles he took the largest
steamer on the Pacific Ocean for San Francisco,
where he remained some days, then took train for
Sterling, Ill., stopping at Sacramento, Salt Lake
City, Utah, which he represents as the cleanest city
he ever was in, and where he remained a day and a
night. From thence he went to Denver, Colo., and
on through Iowa to Sterling, Ill., remaining until
Oct. 10, when, in company with Albert Myers, of
Hilltown, Pa., he went to Chicago and thence to Elkhart, Ind., where he parted company with Mr. Myers, then went to Buffalo, and arrived in Canada, Oct.
23, 1886. Mrd. Anna H., daughter of Rev. John F.
Rittenhouse, of Jordan, Ont., Jan. 23, 1889. P. O.,
Gardenville, Pa. Farmer. Menn's. Children: (VII.)
Ada Wismer, bn. May 29, 1890. (VII.) Paul Wismer,
bn. Nov. 2, 1892.

IV. Isaac Wismer, bn. in Bucks Co., Pa., May 21,
1782; died in Ont. June 18, 1842. Mrd. Anna High,
of Ont., in the fall of 1802. She died —. He mrd.
second wife, Barbara Martin, —. Farmer. Menn.
Children: Abraham, John, Isaac, Anna, Philip, Daniel, David, Barbara, Catharine, Henry, Elizabeth,
Veronica, Solomon.

V. Abraham Wismer, bn. Aug. 13, 1803. Mrd Susanna Grobb, Dec. 19, 1826. She was bn. Feb. 4,
1809; died Dec. 24, 1883. Farmer. Menn. Children:
Isaac, John, Elizabeth, Anna, Abraham, Susanna,
William, Barbara, Freeman, Sarah, Mary.

VI. Isaac G. Wismer, bn. in Lincoln Co., Ont., Oct.
14, 1827. Mrd. Anna Moyer, Mar. 9, 1852. She was
bn. Oct. 1, 1829; died Sept. 12, 1875. Children: Lavina, Anna, Maria, Jacob, Sarah, Emma, Norman,
Hulda.—Mrd. second wife, Hannah Smith, Apr. 11,
1878. P. O., South Cayuga. Farmer, Blacksmith.
Menn. One child: Robert.

VII. Lavina Wismer, bn. in Lincoln Co., Feb. 6, 1853. Mrd. Michael Dohn, Sept. 19, 1871. P. O., South Cayuga, Ont. Farmer. Ev. Ass'n. Children: **(VIII.)** Albert F. Dohn, bn. Aug. 3, 1875. **(VIII.)** Hattie B. Dohn, bn. Aug. 9, 1877. **(VIII.)** Elsie M. Dohn, bn. May 13, 1880. **(VIII.)** Leslie T. Dohn, bn. Dec. 10, 1883. **(VIII.)** Lavern S. Dohn, bn. June 18, 1888.

VII. Anna M. Wismer, bn. June 6, 1855. Mrd. D. W. Nash. (See Index of References No. 46.)

VII. Maria Wismer, bn. Apr. 22, 1858. Mrd. G. D. Culp, Oct. 20, 1880. P. O., Rainham, Ont. Farmer. Baptists. Children: **(VIII.)** Robert E. Culp, bn. June 30, 1883. **(VIII.)** Anna Nina Culp, bn. Apr. 19, 1885. **(VIII.)** George Ernest Culp, bn. Apr. 6, 1887.

VII. Jacob M. Wismer, bn. Dec. 25, 1860. Mrd. Frances High, Aug. 18, 1886. P. O., Campden, Ont. Blacksmith. One child: **(VIII.)** Harry Wismer, bn. Nov. 7, 1887.

VII. Sarah B Wismer, bn. Oct. 16, 1863. Ev. Ass'n.

VII. Emma Wismer, bn. Nov. 8, 1865. Teacher. Ev. Ass'n.

VII. Norman Wismer, bn. Apr. 3, 1868. P. O., Camville, Manitoba. Farmer.

VII. Huldah Wismer, bn. Mar. 24, 1872. Ev. Ass'n.

VII. Robert D. Wismer, bn. Feb. 1, 1879.

VI. John G. Wismer, bn. Oct. 29, 1829. Mrd. Mary High, Feb. 19, 1861. She died Nov. 18, 1878. Farmer. Menn. Children: **(VII.)** Sarah Wismer, bn. Nov. 18, 1862. Ev. Ass'n. **(VII.)** Martha Wismer, bn. Feb. 25, 1864. Ev. Ass'n. **(VII.)** Sandy Wismer, bn. Oct. 16, 1865. Ev. Ass'n. **(VII.)** Sylvester Wismer, bn. Feb. 27, 1872. Ev. Ass'n. **(VII.)** John Wismer, died at birth. **(VII.)** Mary Wismer, died at birth. — Mrd. second wife, Janet McOmish (a native of Perthshire, Scotland), Dec. 23, 1879. Mrs. W. Presby.

VI. Elizabeth Wismer, bn. Mar. 1, 1832. Mrd. Philip High, Mar. 9, 1852. P. O., South Cayuga, Ont. Farmer. Menn. Children: Mary, Sarah, Emerson, Abraham, Isaac, Susie, Barbara.

VII. Mary Ann High, bn. Mar. 9, 1853; died Dec. 25, 1862.

VII. Sarah High, bn. Feb. 10, 1855. Mrd. Freeman Rittenhouse, Dec. 1, 1878. P. O., Dunnville, Ont. Farmer. Menn. One child: **(VIII.)** Harvey Rittenhouse, bn. Sept. 19, 1880.

VII. Emerson W. High, bn. Dec. 18, 1856. Mrd. Mary Fry, Feb. 27, 1881. She died Jan. 18, 1882. One child: **(VIII.)** Orpha High, bn. Dec. 12, 1881.— Mrd. second wife, Barbara Jane McIntyre (widow), Jan. 27, 1886. P. O., Beamsville, Ont. Farmer. Menn.

VII. Abraham W. High, bn. Nov. 2, 1858. Mrd. Rebecca Jane Beck, Dec. 13, 1882. P. O., South Cayuga, Ont. Farmer. Children: **(VIII.)** Abraham High, bn. Mar. 20, 1886. **(VIII.)** Annie High, bn. Nov. 1, 1887.

VII. Isaac W. High, bn. Dec. 9, 1860. Mrd. Lily Idora Overholt, Dec. 15, 1886. P. O., South Cayuga, Ont. Farmer.

VII. Susie High, bn. Nov. 29, 1864. Mrd. Albert Rittenhouse, Sept. 10, 1882. P. O., Dunnville, Ont. Farmer. Children: **(VIII.)** Henry Rittenhouse, bn. Sept. 15, 1885. **(VIII.)** Elizabeth Rittenhouse, bn. July 23, 1887.

VII. Barbara Jane High, bn. July 4, 1867.

VI. Anna Wismer, bn. May 6, 1834. Mrd. Philip Moyer, June 1857. Children: Norman, Delos, Hattie.

VII. Norman Moyer, bn. Apr. 4, 1858. Mrd. Emma McCurdy, Jan. 3, 1884. Farmer. Ev. Ass'n. One child: **(VIII.)** Burges Moyer, bn. Dec. 17, 1884.

VII. Delos Moyer, bn. Mar. 25, 1866.

VII. Hattie Belle Moyer, bn. Aug. 9, 1872.

VI. Abraham G. Wismer, bn. in Lincoln Co., Ont., Nov. 29, 1836. Mrd. Susanna Nash, May 21, 1870. P. O., South Cayuga, Ont. Children: **(VII.)** Abraham Wismer, bn. Mar. 13, 1871. **(VII.)** Harvey Wismer, bn. July 24, 1873. **(VII.)** Wilford Wismer, bn. Sept. 19, 1875. **(VII.)** Florence Wismer, bn. Dec. 23, 1877. **(VII.)** Delos Wismer, bn. May 9, 1880. **(VII.)** Fannie Wismer, bn. June 24, 1882; died Feb. 17, 1888.

VI. Susanna Wismer, bn. in Lincoln Co., Ont., Mar. 25, 1840. Mrd. Ephraim Grobb. (See Index of References No. 48.)

VI. William G. Wismer, bn. July 21, 1842. Mrd. Huldah Ann Smith, Mar. 31, 1870. P. O., South Cayuga, Ont. Machinist. Children: **(VII.)** Mary Jane Wismer, bn. Aug. 28, 1871. Teacher. **(VII.)** Clara Arminta Wismer, bn. Dec. 4, 1873. **(VII.)** Burges S. Wismer, bn. Mar. 16, 1876. **(VII.)** Bertha May Wismer, bn. Mar. 16, 1876. **(VII.)** Rolland S. Wismer, bn. Aug. 10, 1881. **(VII.)** Lena Alberta Wismer, bn. Aug. 4, 1883.

VI. Barbara Wismer, bn. May 18, 1846. Ev. Ass'n. Single.

VI. Freeman Wismer, bn. June 30, 1848. Presby.

VI. Sarah Wismer, bn. May 24, 1852; died Sept. 23, 1855.

VI. Mary Wismer, bn. July 13, 1854. Presby.

V. John Wismer, bn. in Lincoln Co., Ont., Sept. 20, 1804; died Dec. 27, 1872. Mrd. Agnes Honsberger, Mar. 13, 1832. She was bn. Aug. 14, 1809; died Nov. 23, 1878. Farmer. Menn's. Children: Mary, Annie, Barbara, Agnes, Joseph, Margaret, Christian, John, Abraham, Matilda, Sarah, Adelia.

VI. Mary Wismer, bn. Mar. 18, 1833; died Dec. 16, 1864. Mrd. Ralph Carle, --. Children: Robert, Agnes.

VII. Robert Carle, bn. —. Mrd. Augusta Kratz, Sept. 1883. P. O., Jordan, Ont. Farmer.

VII. Agnes Carle, bn. Dec. 8, 1862. Mrd. James B. High, Dec. 27, 1882. Farmer. Meth. Children: **(VIII.)** Ethel High, bn. Oct. 18, 1883. **(VIII.)** Howard High, bn. Dec. 24, 1885. **(VIII.)** Murrey High, bn. June 9, 1887. **(VIII.)** Carson High, bn. Jan. 17, 1891.

VI. Annie Wismer, bn. July 14, 1834; died Sept. 18, 1847.

VI. Barbara Wismer, bn. Feb. 18, 1836; died Jan. 21, 1872. Mrd. Isaiah Albright. Farmer. Menn's. Children: Henry, Orpha, Agnes, Joshua, John, Joseph, Barbara.

VII. Henry Albright, bn. in Lincoln Co., Ont., Dec. 25, 1858. Mrd. Bella Steakel, Jan. 29, 1890. P. O., Selton, Ont. Farmer. Attend Presby. ch. Children: **(VIII.)** Agnes Robena Albright, bn. Feb. 13, 1891. **(VIII.)** Lottie May Albright, bn. Aug. 3, 1892.

VII. Orpha Albright, bn. in Lincoln Co., Ont., June 5, 1860. Mrd. John Ackroyd, Dec. 5, 1883. P. O., Burton, Mich. Farmer. Meth. Ep. Children: **(VIII.)** Harriet Winnifred Ackroyd, bn. Nov. 22, 1885. **(VIII.)** Mary Barbara Ackroyd, bn. Feb. 14, 1888. **(VIII.)** Jessie Merle Ackroyd, bn. Apr. 1, 1892.

VII. Agnes Albright, born Mar. 6, 1862. Mrd. Charles D. Walker, May 29, 1889. P. O., Dante, Ont. Meth's. One child: **(VIII.)** Meda Walker, bn. July 22, 1890.

VII. Joshua Albright, bn. in Lincoln Co., Ont., Dec. 29, 1864. P. O., Field, B. C. Farmer. Meth. S.

VII. John Albright, bn. July 25, 1868. P. O., Canmore, N. W. T. Farmer. Meth. S.

VII. Joseph Albright, bn. in Middlesex Co., Ont., Feb. 21, 1869. P. O., Calgary, N. W. T. Bookkeeper. Meth. S.

VII. Barbara Albright, bn. Nov. 13, 1870. P. O., Dante, Ont. Meth. S.

VI. Agnes Wismer, bn. Mar. 24, 1838; died Mar. 25, 1865. Mrd. Jacob F. Rittenhouse. (See Index of References No. 49.)

VI. Joseph H. Wismer, bn. in Lincoln Co., Ont., Jan. 1, 1840. Mrd. Hester Ann High, Oct. 28, 1867. P. O., Jordan, Ont. Farmer. Meth. One child: **(VII.)** Camby Wismer, bn. Oct. 14, 1871. P. O., Jordan, Ont.

VI. Margaret Wismer, bn. Oct. 17, 1841; died Jan. 2, 1868.

VI. Christian Wismer, bn. Oct. 4, 1843; died Sept. 3, 1845.

VI. John Wismer, bn. Jan. 1, 1846; died Jan. 13, 1879. Mrd. Eva Valeria Wills, Dec. 27, 1876. Farmer. Disciples. One child: **(VII.)** Sadie Lauretta Wismer, bn. Apr. 9, 1878. P. O., Jordan, Ont. Meth.

VI. Abraham Wismer, bn. May 6, 1848; died Sept. 3, 1848.

VI. Matilda Wismer, bn. Aug. 8, 1849. Mrd. Isaac G. Culp. P. O., Jordan, Ont.

VI. Sarah Wismer, bn. in Lincoln Co., Ont., Dec. 31, 1851. Mrd. John H. Kratz, Feb. 19, 1879. P. O.,

Jordan, Ont. Dealer in hard and soft wood, lumber and timber. Menn's. No issue.

VI. Adelia Wismer, bn. Nov. 19, 1854. Mrd. John G. Stoner, Dec. 31, 1878. He was bn. Apr. 22, 1854. Employed in button factory. P. O., Berlin, Ont. Ref. Menn. Children: **(VII.)** Wilson Stoner, bn. July 18, 1881. **(VII.)** Justus Stoner, bn. May 25, 1886. **(VII.)** Bertha Stoner, bn. Apr. 4, 1889. **(VII.)** Viola Stoner, bn. Apr. 14, 1892.

V. Isaac Wismer, bn. July 31, 1806. Mrd. Magdalena High, daughter of David High, of Bucks Co., Pa.. Sept. 29, 1835. She was bn. —; died May 27, 1892. Emigrated to Canada ——. P. O., Portdalhousie, Ont. Farmer. Menn. Children: Eli, Mary, Tobias, Aaron, Freeman, Alfred, Ephraim.

VI. Eli Wismer, bn. Sept. 18, 1836. Mrd. Catharine High of Louth, Ont., Apr. 15. 1862. She died Feb. 9, 1877. P. O., St. Catharines, Ont. Farmer. Meth. Children: Emma, Ida, Joshua. Franklin, Huldah, James. — Mrd. second wife, Catharine Moyer, of Clinton Twp., Ont., May 21, 1877. Children: Curtis, Vernon.

VII. Emma Amelia Wismer, bn. Feb. 10, 1863. Mrd. —.

VII. Ida Sophia Wismer, bn. Sept. 10, 1864.

VII. Joshua Wismer, born Nov. 3, 1865. Married Emma, daughter of Daniel K. High, Esq., Nov. 18, 1891.

VII. Franklin Wismer, bn. Apr. 10, 1867.
VII. Huldah Orpha Wismer, bn. Nov. 21, 1868.
VII. Curtis Wismer, bn. July 26, 1881.
VII. Vernon Wismer, bn. Feb. 12, 1888; died Feb. 16, 1888.

VI. Mary Wismer, bn. May 9, 1839. Mrd. Henry Grobb, Mar. 31, 1863. He was bn. Sept. 18, 1829. P. O., Beamsville, Ont. Farmer. One child: **(VII.)** Aaron Grobb, bn. Feb. 14, 1870.

VI. Tobias Wismer, bn. Jan. 18, 1841. Mrd. Joanna Emery, of Louth Twp., Ont., Nov. 21, 1866. P. O., St. Catharines, Ont. Farmer. Meth. Children: Susan, Eliza, Ada, Ella, Harry, Minnie, Florence, Isaac.

VII. Susan Alberta Wismer, bn. 1867. Mrd. Samuel Honsberger, —. One child: (**VIII.**) Ina May Honsberger, bn. Mar. 24, 1891.

VII. Eliza Magdalena Wismer, bn. Oct. 8, 1869.

VII. Ada May Wismer, bn. Jan. 11, 1872.

VII. Ella Belle Wismer, bn. Nov. 13, 1873.

VII. Harry Thomas Wismer, bn. Aug. 29, 1875.

VII. Minnie Edney Wismer, bn. Apr. 25, 1878.

VII. Florence Ethel Wismer, bn. Apr. 9, 1881; died Sept. 7, 1881.

VII. Isaac Arthur Wismer, bn. June 18, 1883.

VI. Aaron Wismer, bn. Jan. 7, 1843. Mrd. Mary Margaret Martin, daughter of Abraham and Catharine Martin, Jan. 19, 1876. P. O., Jordan Station, Ont. Farmer. Baptists. No issue.

VI. Freeman Wismer, bn. Oct. 19, 1845. Mrd. Mary Kratz, Jan. 8, 1866. She was born Jan. 23, 1841. P. O., St. Catharines, Ont. Farmer. Menn. Bre. in Christ. Children: (**VII.**) Salina Wismer, bn. Dec. 9, 1866. (**VII.**) Morgan Wismer, bn. July 10, 1869. (**VII.**) Albert Wismer, bn. May 11, 1872. (**VII.**) Archibald Wismer, bn. Oct. 14, 1875. (**VII.**) Hattie Wismer, bn. Feb. 11, 1879. (**VII.**) Mary Wismer, bn. Nov. 8, 1881.

VI. Alfred Wismer, bn. July 15, 1848. Mrd. Barbara Moyer, daughter of Jacob H. Moyer, Jan. 8, 1874. P. O., Portdalhousie, Ont. Farmer. Baptists. Children: (**VII.**) Elsie Maud Wismer, bn. June 3, 1877. (**VII.**) Herbert Stanley Wismer, bn. Mar. 27, 1882. (**VII.**) Eva Florence Wismer, bn. Feb. 20, 1886.

VI. Ephraim Wismer, bn. Aug. 25, 1851. Mrd. Magdalena Moyer, of Louth Twp., Ont., Aug 1, 1872. P. O., St. Catharines, Ont. Book-keeper. Baptists. Children: (**VII.**) Clara Euretta Wismer, bn. Oct. 9, 1873. (**VII.**) Norman Howard Wismer, bn. Dec. 8, 1875. (**VII.**) Cora Mabel Wismer, bn. Oct. 6, 1877. (**VII.**) Effie Gertrude Wismer, bn. Feb. 7, 1880. (**VII.**) Hilliard Grover Wismer, bn. July 11, 1886; died Aug. 21, 1887. (**VII.**) Walter Stanley Wismer, bn. July 21, 1887.

V. Anna Wismer, bn. —, 1808; died —. Mrd. Jacob Detweiler, —. He was bn. in Bucks Co., Pa..

Jan. 20, 1808; died —. Farmer. Menn's. Children: Isaac, Daniel, Benjamin, John, Jacob, Barbara, Susanna, Christian, Enoch, Annie, Mary.

VI. Christian Detweiler, bn. July 22, 1836. Unmrd.

VI. Enoch W. Detweiler, bn. in Waterloo Co., Ont., Sept. 8, 1839. Mrd. Victoria Willits, Nov. 27, 1860. Farmer. United Brethren. Children: Lavina, Rosetta, Alice, Barbara, Elsie, George, Effie.

VII. Lavina Detweiler, bn. Sept. 26, 1861. S.

VII. Rosetta W. Detweiler, bn. Mar. 20. 1865. Mrd. Emanuel Hilborn, Apr. 1886. P. O., Grand Valley, Ont. Miller. United Brethren. Children: (**VIII.**) Ada Hilborn, bn. Feb. 18, 1888. (**VIII.**) Leslie Hilborn, bn. Nov. 3, 1889.

VII. Alice Jane Detweiler, bn. June 1, 1867. Mrd. John W. Battler, Apr. 2, 1890. P. O., New Dundee, Ont. Farmer. United Brethren. No children.

VII. Barbara Annie Detweiler, bn. Feb. 18, 1869. S.

VII. Elsie Eletia Cecilia Detweiler, bn. Aug. 2, 1873. S.

VII. George William Detweiler, bn. Sept. 16, 1875.

VII. Effie Detweiler, bn. Feb. 14, 1879.

VI. Annie W. Detweiler, bn. July 21, 1844. Mrd. Adam B. Cassel, May 21, 1861. P. O., New Dundee, Ont. Farmer. United Brethren. Children: Milton, Oliver, Lavina, John, Jacob.

VII. Milton D. Cassel, bn. May 17, 1862; died same day.

VII. Oliver D. Cassel, bn. June 16, 1863. Mrd. Barbara S. Geiger, Aug. 24, 1886. P. O., New Dundee, Ont. Spinner and carder in wool factory. Children: (**VIII.**) James Lloyd G. Cassel, bn. June 15, 1887. (**VIII.**) Hattie Melissa G. Cassel, bn. Jan. 6, 1890.

VII. Lavina D. Cassel, bn. Nov. 29, 1865. United Brethren. S.

VII. John D. Cassel, bn. Sept. 3, 1871. Farmer.

VII. Jacob D. Cassel, bn. Sept. 3, 1871. Employed in button factory. United Brethren.

VI. Mary Ann Detweiler, bn. Sept. 12, 1850. Mrd. Albert Willits, Feb. 2, 1872. P. O., Wroxeter, Ont. Farmer. Cong. ch. Children: (**VII.**) Jemima Willits, bn. Jan. 25. 1873. (**VII.**) Barbara Anna Willits, bn.

May 19, 1879. **(VII.)** Alberta Willits, bn. Apr. 5, 1881. **(VII.)** Jacob Willits, bn. Apr. 19, 1883. **(VII.)** Alfred Willits, bn. Apr. 22, 1886. **(VII.)** Norman Willits, bn. July 18, 1888. **(VII.)** Gordon Willits, bn. June 28, 1891.

   V. Philip Wismer, bn. in Lincoln Co., Ont., Aug. 31, 1810. Mrd. Margaret High, Jan. 20, 1836. She died —. Farmer. Menn's. Children: Henry, Barbara, Elizabeth, Isaac, Joseph, Mary, William, Sarah, John, Henrietta, Magdalena, Susanna.

   VI. Henry Wismer, bn. Oct. 26, 1836; died Jan. 21, 1837.

   VI. Barbara Wismer, bn. Feb. 12, 1838; died Nov. 16, 1838.

   VI. Elizabeth Wismer, bn. July 9, 1839; died Dec. 19, 1839.

   VI. Isaac Wismer, bn. Mar. 9, 1841; died May 8, 1847.

   VI. Rev. Joseph M. Wismer, bn. July 28, 1842. Mrd. Mary Fretz, Dec. 17, 1867. She was born June 15, 1842. P. O., Jordan, Ont. Farmer, bee-keeper and minister. He was ordained to the ministry of the Mennonite church Nov. 1, 1885. Children: **(VII.)** Philip Henry Wismer, bn. Mar. 26, 1870. **(VII.)** Margaret Elizabeth Wismer, bn. Dec. 17, 1874. **(VII.)** Etta Eltha Wismer, bn. June 25, 1877. **(VII.)** Victoria Catharine Wismer, bn. Feb. 26, 1880; died Jan. 20, 1881.

   VI. Mary Ann Wismer, bn. May 4, 1844. Mrd. Daniel B. Rittenhouse, May 2, 1872. P. O., Jordan, Ont. Baptists. One child: **(VII.)** Thania Ladema Rittenhouse, bn. May 8, 1875.

   VI. William Andrew Wismer, bn. Apr. 19, 1846. Mrd. Alma Alberta Patterson, Mar. 1, 1876. P. O., Jordan, Ont. Farmer. As a believer he has accepted a crucified Savior in the person of Jesus Christ, received water baptism in His name, and worships at (Moyer's) Mennonite church. Children: **(VII.)** Louisa Catharine Wismer, bn. Oct. 21, 1877. **(VII.)** Annalora Margaret Wismer, bn. Mar. 11, 1880. **(VII.)** Jessie Alberta Wismer, bn. Sept. 4, 1882. **(VII.)** Ethel Maryettie Wismer, bn. Nov. 6, 1885. **(VII.)** Beatrice Victoria Wismer, bn. July 18, 1888. (**VII.**) Elma Elmira Wismer, bn. May 12, 1891.

VI. Sarah Catharine Wismer, bn. Aug. 16, 1848; died Dec. 14, 1883. Mrd. Jacob Issler, —. Cabinet maker. She had arranged to join the Presbyterian ch. but death prevented. (**VII.**) One child, still-born.

VI. John Henry Wismer, bn. Dec. 5, 1850. Mrd. Nancy Catharine Tufford, Jan. 23, 1878. P. O., Beamsville, Ont. Farmer. Meth. One child: (**VII.**) Mabel A. Wismer, bn. Jan. 25, 1880.

VI. Henrietta Wismer, bn. Aug. 31, 1852. Mrd. William A. Patterson, Sept. 30, 1880. P. O., Smithville, Ont. Farmer. Presby's. One child: (**VII.**) Emery Ulysses Patterson, bn. June 5, 1883.

VI. Magdalena Wismer, bn. Oct. 19, 1854; died Nov. 9, 1855.

VI. Susanna Wismer, bn. June 4, 1857; died Mar. 8, 1859.

V. Daniel Wismer, bn. in Lincoln Co., Ont., July 20, 1812; died in 1891. Mrd. Barbara High, Jan. 3, 1837. She was born Apr. 23, 1817; died July 23, 1884. In early life farmer, later carpenter and cooper. Methodist. Children: Amos, Henry, Solomon, Francis, Susan, Anna, Mary, Barbara.

VI. Amos Wismer, bn. June 1, 1838; died Mar. 14, 1839.

VI. Henry Wismer, bn. May 29, 1840. Mrd. Nancy Shelly, Dec. 18, 1866. P.O., Suspension Bridge, Ont. Bridge carpenter on Grand Trunk Railway. Meth. Children: (**VII.**) Ida Wismer, bn. Nov. 28, 1867. Mrd. Albert E. Salter, Jan. 6, 1892. P.O., St. Catharines, Ont. Wesleyan Meth. No children. (**VII.**) Hilliard Judson Wismer, bn. Feb. 28, 1869. P. O., Courtice, Ont. Member Salvation army, of which he is an officer. S. (**VII.**) Francis James Wismer, bn. Dec. 10, 1871; died Sept. 3, 1872. (**VII.**) William Henry Wismer, bn. Feb. 23, 1875; died May 3, 1878. (**VII.**) Mary Margaret Wismer, bn. Sept. 22, 1879.

VI. Solomon Wismer, bn. Nov. 24, 1842. Mrd. Susan High, Feb. 13, 1866. P. O., Grimsby, Ont. Carpenter. Mrs.W. Meth. Children: (**VII.**) James Wismer, bn. Aug. 26, 1867; died Oct. 6, 1867. (**VII.**)

Henry Fismer

(See page 326.)

Rolland Wismer, bn. Nov. 12, 1868. (VII.) Della May
Wismer, bn. Jan. 30, 1870. (VII.) Mary Elvora Wismer, bn. May 9, 1874. (VII.) Florence Beatrice Wismer, bn. Mar. 27, 1877. (VII.) Emily and Emerson
Wismer, (twins) bn. Mar. 5, 1880; died May 20, 1880,
and July 30, 1880, respectively. (VII.) Edwin Wismer, bn. Mar. 26, 1882; died Feb. 24, 1884.

   VI. Francis J. Wismer, bn. May 25, 1845; died Sept.
20, 1864.

   VI. Susan Amanda Wismer, bn. May 15, 1849. Mrd.
Charles Phillips, Dec. 22, 1870. P.O., Grimsby, Ont.
Machinist. Meth. Children: (VII.) W. E. Phillips,
bn. Jan. 7, 1872. Printer in the office of "The Inde-
pendent" at Grimsby, Ont. (VII.) Grace D. Phillips,
bn. Mar. 8, 1880.

   VI. Anna Elizabeth Wismer, bn. Mar. 21, 1852.
Mrd. James A. Hewitt, Jan. 5, 1876. P.O., Grimsby,
Ont. Carpenter and builder. Meth. Children: (VII.)
Lillian Orphelia Hewitt, bn. Apr. 8, 1877. (VII.)
James Arthur Hewitt, bn. Dec. 26, 1879. (VII.) Lot-
tie May Hewitt, bn. Mar. 9, 1881. (VII.) Ethel A.
Hewitt, bn. Feb. 17, 1884. (VII.) Albert Roy Hewitt,
bn. Oct. 10, 1890.

   VI. Mary Margaret Wismer, bn. in Lincoln Co.,
Ont., Feb. 12, 1854. Mrd. Edwin George Paradice, of
Bristol, England, Feb. 7, 1878. P.O., Grimsby, Ont.
Children: (VII.) Louisa Maud Paradice, bn. Apr. 28,
1879. (VII.) Edith Mabel Paradice, bn. Aug. 7, 1881.
(VII.) Marguerite Frances Paradice, bn. Feb. 8, 1884.

   VI. Barbara Catharine Wismer, bn. in Lincoln Co.,
Ont., Dec. 26, 1862. Mrd. Alexander Ryckman, 1888.
P.O., Grimsby, Ont. Meth's. Children: (VII.) Charles
Edwin Ryckman, bn. Aug. 5, 1889. (VII.) Albert
Franklin Ryckman, b. Aug. 31, 1891; d. July 15, 1892.

   V. David Wismer, bn. —; died young.

   V. Barbara Wismer, bn. in Lincoln Co., Ont., Aug.
10, 1816; died Apr. 10, 1886. Mrd. Joseph B. Moyer,
Dec. 20, 1836. He was born Apr. 7, 1814; died Aug.
3, 1891. Farmer. Menn's. Children: Anna, Franklin,
William, Solomon, Margaret, Oliver.

   VI. Anna Moyer, bn. in Lincoln Co., Ont., Feb. 8,
1843. Mrd. Abraham C. Moyer, Mar. 28, 1872.

12

P. O., Blooming Glen, Pa. Farmer. Menn's. Children: (VII.) Harvey Moyer, bn. Jan. 21, 1873. S. (VII.) Franklin Moyer, bn. June 2, 1874; died Nov. 29, 1874. (VII.) Madilla Moyer, bn. Sept. 27, 1875. (VII.) Leidy Moyer, bn. Sept. 8, 1877. (VII.) Lillie Moyer (twin), bn. Sept. 8, 1877; died Apr. 25, 1878. (VII.) Granville Moyer, bn. Feb. 14, 1879. (VII.) Melvin Moyer, bn. Apr. 29, 1881; died May 10, 1881. (VII.) Isaiah Moyer, bn. June 6, 1882; died Nov. 25, 1892. (VII.) Alda Moyer, bn. Nov. 6, 1883.

VI. Rev. Franklin W. Moyer, bn. in Lincoln Co., Ont., Aug. 22, 1845. Mrd. Leah Houser, Oct. 15, 1867. P. O., Jordan, Ont. Minister of Mennonite Brethren in Christ. Children: (VII.) Morgan Moyer, bn. May 22, 1869; died July 27, 1881. (VII.) Charley Moyer, bn. Jan. 30, 1871. P. O., Fenwick, Ont. Clerk in store. (VII.) Rowley Moyer, bn. Apr. 15, 1874; died Apr. 12, 1884. (VII.) Nettie Moyer, bn. July 11, 1876; died May 7, 1878. (VII.) Hattie Moyer, bn. July 15, 1878; died Feb. 15, 1882. (VII.) Justus Moyer, bn. Feb. 22, 1883.

VI. William H. W. Moyer, bn. in Lincoln Co., Ont., Jan. 20, 1847. Mrd. Margaret M. Moyer, Feb. 4, 1868. P. O., Jordan, Ont. Farmer. Menn. Bre. in Christ. Children: Minerva, Irvin, Edwin, Sarah, Bosalpha, Herbert, Ellis.

VII. Minerva Moyer, bn. Mar. 15, 1869. Mrd. Byron Honsberger, —. P. O., Jordan Sta., Ont. One child: (VIII.) Flossy Honsberger.

VII. Irvin Moyer, bn. Feb. 11, 1871.
VII. Edwin Moyer, bn. May 17, 1873.
VII. Sarah Jane Moyer, bn. June 29, 1875.
VII. Bosalpha Moyer, bn. Mar. 5, 1878.
VII. Herbert Lorne Moyer, bn. Oct. 25, 1879.
VII. Ellis Moyer, bn. July 18, 1883.

VI. Solomon W. Moyer, bn. in Lincoln Co., Ont., Aug. 28, 1848. Mrd. Mary Jane Moyer, Oct. 10, 1872. P. O., Jordan, Ont. Farmer. Menn. Children: (VII.) Harper Moyer, bn. May 1, 1877. (VII.) Gordon Moyer, bn. Sept. 10, 1879. (VII.) Wayne Moyer, bn. Mar. 19, 1888.

VI. Margaret W. Moyer, bn. June 19, 1850. Mrd. William B. Rittenhouse, Mar. 17, 1874. P. O., Beamsville, Ont. Proprietor of "The Excelsior Fish Ponds," and fruit farm. Meth's. Children: **(VII.)** Nellie Rittenhouse, bn. Feb. 26, 1875. **(VII.)** Hilda Rittenhouse, bn. Sept. 28, 1877. **(VII.)** Howard Rittenhouse, bn. Apr. 29, 1883. **(VII.)** Bertha Rittenhouse, bn. Nov. 8, 1885. **(VII.)** Nelson Rittenhouse, bn. Apr. 22, 1887.

VI. Oliver W. Moyer, bn. Jan. 3, 1857. Mrd. Sarah B. Rittenhouse, P. O., Campden, Ont.

V. Catharine Wismer, bn. —; died young.

V. Henry Wismer, bn. June 29, 1821; died May 14, 1884. Mrd. Anna Kratz, in 1845. She was born June 25, 1821. No issue.

Mr. Wismer was one of the best known citizens in the county of Lincoln, Ont., having through official business and otherwise become known to a large number of persons. While young he enjoyed the few educational advantages which the county afforded. After marriage he engaged in farming in which he was very successful. In Jan. 1861, he offered himself for municipal honors, and by a majority of one vote, was elected a member of the township council, in what was undoubtedly the sharpest contested Municipal election ever held in the county of Lincoln. He was a member of the Twp., council for eight successive years. In 1870, he was elected Reeve of Louth Twp., which office he held for seven years. In 1875, he was elected Warden of Lincoln Co. He served as a member of the Louth Twp., council for 16 years. He lived on the shore of Lake Ontario, where he owned a farm of 80 acres which he sold for $12,000, and his estate at his death was worth $20,000. He was well known as a sterling and upright man, and a faithful worker for the best interest of the people, and enjoyed the high esteem of all who knew him.

V. Elizabeth Wismer, bn. May 16, 1823; died Aug. 4, 1879.

V. Veronica Wismer, bn. Apr. 2, 1828; died Jan. 23, 1884. Partially insane.

V. Solomon Wismer, (by second wife,) bn. June 13, 1837; died aged about one week.
IV. Barbara Wismer, bn. in Bucks Co., Pa., Apr. 15, 1785; died Apr. 17, 1851. Mrd. Henry Rickert, —. Children: Daniel, Isaac, Samuel, Catharine, Barbara, Frances, Henry, Jacob, Elizabeth.
V. Daniel Rickert, bn. —; died —. Mrd. —.
V. Isaac Rickert, bn. —; died —.
V. Samuel Rickert, bn. —; died —. Mrd. —.
V. Catharine Rickert, bn. —. Mrd. — Armatage.
V. Barbara Rickert. bn. —. Mrd. — Sherm.
V. Frances Rickert, bn. —. Mrd. — Delph, and — Hunsberger.
V. Henry Rickert, bn. —. Mrd. —. Have issue.
V. Jacob Rickert, bn. —; died —. Mrd. —. Had issue.
V. Elizabeth Rickert, bn. —. Mrd. — Berks —. Have issue.
IV. Catharine Wismer, bn. in Bucks Co., Pa., July 23, 1787; died in Canada. Aug. 4, 1858. Mrd. John High,* July 27. 1819. He was born in Bucks Co., Pa., July 27, 1770; died in Canada in 1833. Farmer and weaver. Menn. Children:
V. Anna High, bn. —; died 1838.
V. Abraham High, bn. —; died 1845.
V. Margaret High, bn. in Lincoln Co., Ont., Nov. 18, 1825; died Sept. 5, 1890. Mrd. Dilman Moyer, Sept. 5, 1843. He was bn. in Lincoln Co., Ont., Oct. 6. 1820; died Apr. 23, 1879. Farmer, real estate agent, and grain merchant. Menn. Children: Barbara, Catharine, John, Samuel, Annie, Lucinda, Susanna.
VI. Barbara Moyer, bn. in Lincoln Co., Ont., Oct. 29, 1844. Mrd. Charles Arrand, Nov. 14, 1867. P. O., Parkhill, Ont. Farmer. "Believer's ch." Children: (**VII.**) F. Tillman Arrand, bn. Apr. 28, 1872. (**VII.**) Eliza Arrand, bn. Jan. 11, 1874. (**VII.**) Mary Ann

---

* John Moyer of Wardsville, Ont., has coverlets made by him, also a copper kettle still in use brought from Philadelphia, and a brass clock Mr. High took with him to Canada made either by Henry or Abraham Wismer in Pennsylvania.

Arrand, bn. Mar. 5, 1875; died Mar. 14, 1875. (VII.)
Salena Arrand, born Mar. 8, 1876. (VII.) Oliver
Arrand, bn. Aug. 30, 1877. (VII.) Annie Melvina
Arrand, bn. Dec. 13, 1878. (VII.) Richard James
Arrand, bn. Apr. 29, 1880. (VII.) Norman Arrand,
bn. Oct. 25, 1886; died Apr. 25, 1887. (VII.) Ethel
May Arrand, bn. Dec. 24, 1888.
VI. Catharine Moyer, bn. Mar. 22, 1849. Mrd. Isaac
Saylor, May 2, 1871. P. O., Niagara Falls, N. Y.
Children: (VII.) Margaret Ann Saylor, bn. Aug. 30,
1872. (VII.) Eva Bell Saylor, bn. May 1, 1874. (VII.)
Flora Etta Saylor, bn. Oct. 1, 1876; died Nov. 11,
1876. (VII.) Catharine Saylor, bn. July 3, 1878.
(VII.) Hattie Saylor, bn. July 5, 1884; died Sept. 23,
1884.
VI. Anna Moyer, bn. 1850; died Sept. 21, 1881. S.
VI. John Moyer, bn. in Lincoln Co., Ont., June 7,
1853. Mrd. Esther Saylor, Dec. 21, 1876. She died
Mar. 5, 1883. P. O., Wardsville, Ont. Farmer.
Menn. Children: (VII.) Isaac Ervine Moyer, bn. Nov.
6, 1877; died Aug. 8, 1878. (VII.) Emma Grace Moy-
er. bn. June 14, 1880. (VII.) Mabel Bernice Moyer,
bn. June 12, 1879. (VII.) Cora Esther Moyer, bn.
Feb. 23, 1883. John mrd. second wife Margaret
Smith, Apr. 18, 1888. One child: (VII.) Rosinea Irene
Moyer, bn. Dec. 29, 1889.
VI. Samuel Moyer, bn. Dec. 26, 1855. P. O., Wards-
ville, Ont. S.
VI. Susanna Moyer, bn. Apr. 20, 1858. Mrd. Robert
Arrand, Dec. 20, 1877. P. O., Ferguson, Ontario.
Farmer. Ch. of God. Children: (VII.) Wilbert Ar-
rand, b. Oct. 22, 1878. (VII.) Mary Arrand, b. Mar. 19,
1881. (VII.) George Arrand, bn. Aug. 18, 1884.
(VII.) Margaret Arrand, bn. Oct. 9, 1886. (VII.)
Minnie Arrand, bn. Apr. 26, 1889.
VI. Lucinda Moyer, bn. Nov. 6, 1865; died Aug. 2,
1891. S.
IV. Veronica Wismer, bn. July 22, 1789; died in
infancy.
IV. Abraham Wismer, bn. in Bucks Co., Nov. 30,
1791; died June 25, 1859. Mrd. Elizabeth Leather-
man, Apr. 13, 1813. She was born Feb. 5, 1790; died

Apr. 15, 1845. Children: Samuel, Esther, Jacob, Catharine, Mary, Elizabeth, Abraham. For second wife Abraham mrd. Mary, daughter of Joseph Overholt, and widow of Abraham Bean, in 1847. She was born in 1804; died in Kent Co., Mich., in 1889. One child: Sarah.

He was the fourth owner and occupant of the Wismer homestead. During his early life he also distilled whiskey from apples on the farm. Thousands of bushels of apples were thus disposed of in the neighborhood. About 900 gallons of whiskey was the yield in a good season. This occupation so far carried on by every generation had its career ended by the subject of this sketch, who, from his earlier experience, and a full realization of the danger to, and demoralizing effects on the rising generation, could without the surrender of any convictions, abandon the heretofore popular "Still."

Mr. Wismer and wives were members of the Old Mennonite church at Deep Run, of which he was a deacon thirty years. During his term as deacon some stirring events took place ending in a division of the church. He was a popular man in the community, well read and posted in the ordinary business transactions of his day. Settling estates, clerking sales, writing wills and agreements, &c, occupied part of his time.

V. Samuel Wismer, bn. Nov. 14, 1814. Mrd. Elizabeth Kulp, —. She was born June 11, 1823. P. O., Plumsteadville, Pa. Farmer. Resides on a part of the old Wismer homestead. During his early life time he had two remarkable escapes. When a few years of age lightning struck his father's house. The electric bolt descended through the chimney, followed the pipe to the stove and went through the floor within a few feet of where he lay asleep in a little bed.

While yet a boy he and his brother Jacob were sent to cut up a tree top. Jacob, who was several years younger, seized the axe and slashed around among the limbs. The result was startling. Samuel was standing near by on the ground while Jacob was perched a little higher. The axe descended and made a clean cut through the hat to the skin of Samuel's forehead without drawing any blood or making a scratch. Mr. Wismer is a highly respected citizen, and he and wife are members of the Mennonite ch., Deep Run. Children: Eli, Anna, John, Mary, Elizabeth.

VI. Eli Wismer, bn. Jan. 25, 1844, on the southwestern part of the original tract, in Bedminster Twp., Bucks Co., Pa. He received a common school education in the district school at Deep Run, which was open four months and towards the close of his school days five months in a year. In 1865 he received a certificate from the Superintendent of Public Schools, to teach in the county. He taught four terms in his native township, and one at Plumsteadville.

He was appointed Assistant U. S. Marshall to take the ninth Census of Bedminster Township in 1870. In the same year he was married to Annie Myers, daughter of Joseph Myers, of Plumstead Township. She was born June 29, 1846. In 1871 he commenced farming on the farm on which he was born. At the organization of the Plumsteadville Dairy Men's Association in 1880 he was elected Secretary and soon after salesman for the association, which position he holds the twelfth consecutive year.

His father's teaching, in early life impressed on him the evils arising from the use of intoxicants, and during the Constitutional Amendment Campaign he was among the leading agitators in his community to prohibit the manufacture and sale thereof as a beverage. P. O., Plumsteadville, Pa. Farmer. Menn's. Children: **(VII.)** Harvey Wismer, bn. Sept. 4, 1873. **(VII.)** Clara Wismer, bn. Feb. 23, 1880; died Mar. 18, 1881.

VI. Anna Wismer, bn. Dec 6, 1847. Mrd. Cornelius Myers. (See Index of References No. 50.)

VI. John Wismer, bn. July 19, 1850; died Apr. 14, 1851.

VI. Mary Wismer, bn. Apr. 6, 1855. S.

VI. Elizabeth Wismer, bn. Sept. 19, 1862. S.

V. Esther Wismer, bn. Aug. 6, 1816. Mrd. David Newcomer. (See Index of References No. 51.)

V. Jacob Wismer, bn. Dec. 24, 1818; died Dec. 1890. Mrd. Sophia Loux, —. He was the fifth owner of the homestead reduced by his father to 70 acres.* Farmer. Menn. Children: Franklin, Levi.

VI. Franklin L. Wismer, bn. Aug. 11, 1848; died Oct. 18, 1888. Mrd. Magdalena Leatherman, —. She died Sept. 10, 1889. Children: **(VII.)** Emma Wismer, bn. Apr. 9, 1871. Mrd. John Rogerson, —. **(VII.)** Sallie Wismer, bn. —. S. **(VII.)** Henry L. Wismer, bn. Mar. 2, 1874. **(VII.)** Ervin Wismer, bn. June 28, 1880. **(VII.)** Alice Wismer, bn. Sept. 1887.

VI. Levi L. Wismer, bn. in New Britain, Bucks Co., Jan. 10, 1854. Mrd. Ida I. Holcombe, May 29, 1886. Res. 2617 Darien St., Philadelphia, Pa. Carpenter. No issue.

V. Catharine Wismer, bn. Oct. 18, 1821. Mrd. Rev. John Gross. (See Index of References No. 52.)

V. Mary Wismer, bn. Aug. 21, 1824; died Apr. 1, 1854. S.

V. Elizabeth Wismer, bn. Sept. 1, 1826; died Dec. 17, 1837.

V. Abraham Wismer born Oct. 14, 1829. Mrd. Catharine Bishop, —. She was born Feb. 24, 1830. Farmer. Owns the homestead with 72 acres. Menn's. Children: Henry, Mary, Jacob, Anna, Abraham, Enos, Lizzie, Emma.

VI. Henry Wismer, bn. Sept. 2, 1855. Mrd. Lydia Myers, Oct. 16, 1879. Farmer. Menn's. Children: **(VII.)** Kate Wismer, bn. Sept. 24, 1884. **(VII.)** Mary Emma Wismer, bn. June 4, 1887; died Feb. 5, 1888. **(VII.)** Ella Wismer, bn. Mar. 31, 1889.

VI. Mary Wismer, bn. Dec. 4, 1853; died July 5, 1891. Mrd. Abraham G. Overholt. (See Index of References No. 53.)

---

* Buildings were erected on the other 50 acres in 1843 and since occupied by Samuel Wismer. So far every transfer was made from father to son, either by private sale, will or agreement. Jacob willed the homestead to his son Levi, and a life-right to his widow. Levi refused to accept it under the provisions of his father's will, and this forced it to be offered at public sale in Feb. 1891, for the first time since it was occupied by the first ancestor Jacob Wismer about 165 years ago. The record of from father to son was also broken at this sale, the purchaser being a brother, and the occupant a nephew of the former owner.

VI. Jacob Wismer, bn. in 1857; died in 1858.
VI. Anna Wismer, bn. Apr. 28, 1859. Mrd. Ja.res
Bergey. (See Index of References No. 54.)
VI. Abraham B. Wismer, bn. Nov. 11, 1861. Mrd.
Ella Shelly, Jan. 29, 1885. Farmer. Menn. No is-
sue.
VI. Enos B. Wismer, bn. Jan. 9, 1868. Mrd. Mary
Overholt, —. P. O., Plumsteadville, Pa. Farmer.
Menn's. No issue.
VI. Lizzie Wismer, bn. Jan. 13, 1864. Mrd. William
B. Detweiler, Oct. 4, 1883. Farmer. Menn's. Chil-
dren: **(VII.)** Martha Detweiler, born Dec. 31, 1885.
(VII.) Abraham Detweiler, bn. Oct. 29, 1887. **(VII.)**
Bessie Detweiler, bn. July 30, 1889.
VI. Emma Wismer, bn. Apr. 18, 1871. Mrd. Abra-
ham Hiestand. (See Index of References No. 55.)
V. Sarah Wismer, bn. Mar. 15, 1849. Mrd. William
Overholt, Jr. (See Index of References No. 56.)
Sarah mrd. second husband Elias F. Hunsberger.
(See Index of References No. 57.)
IV. Elizabeth Wismer, born on the old Wismer
homestead in Plumstead Twp., Bucks Co., Pa., July
24, 1794; died Aug. 12, 1852, aged 58 years 18 days.
Mrd. Abraham Kratz —, and with him located in New
Britain Twp., Bucks Co., where she spent the whole
of her married life.

She was a woman of rare intelligence, and Christian virtue, making her home an ideal one, and is consequently held in fond remembrance by all who knew
her. She was the mother of eleven children, seven
sons and four daughters. She with her husband was a
member of the Mennonite church, and died in the
triumphs of a living faith, and are buried at Blooming
Glen church yard. Farmer. Children: Henry, Levi,
Frances, Barbara, Abraham, William, Valentine,
Catharine, Christian, Elizabeth, Reuben.
V. Henry Kratz, bn. Feb. 27, 1815; died Feb. 15,
1873. Mrd. Mary Jane Harris, —. She died —.
Children: **(VI.)** Josiah Kratz, bn. —; died young. **(VI.)**
John Kratz, bn. —; mysteriously disappeared.
V. Levi Kratz, bn. in Bucks Co., Pa., Feb. 28, 1817.
Mrd. Lydia A. Clark, Mar. 21, 1885. Farmer and

gardener in Clay Co., Ill. Mr. Kratz, Menn., Mrs. Kratz, Christian ch. No issue.

V. Frances Kratz, bn. Jan. 17, 1819. Mrd. William E. Fretz, about 1840. P. O., Lawndale, Pa. Farmer. Ev. Ass'n. Children: Samuel, Elizabeth, Reuben, Abraham, Mary.

VI. Samuel K. Fretz, bn. June 14, 1841. Mrd. Mary E. Boyer, Jan. 7, 1865. P.O., Clayton, Del. Farmer. Meth. Ep. Children: **(VII.)** Ervin B. Fretz, bn. June 20, 1866. **(VII.)** Abraham B. Fretz, bn. Oct. 25, 1867. **(VII.)** Hannah E. Fretz, bn. May 5, 1871; died in 1872. **(VII.)** Fannie B. Fretz, bn. Feb. 11, 1873. **(VII.)** Horace B. Fretz, bn. Oct. 19, 1876. **(VII.)** Peter B. Fretz, bn. Sept. 6, 1878. **(VII.)** William B. Fretz, bn. Sept. 9, 1880. **(VII.)** Emma B. Fretz, bn. Sept. 16, 1882.

VI. Elizabeth Fretz, bn. Dec. 27, 1843. Mrd. Charles George, —. Children: **(VII.)** William George, bn. —; died in infancy. **(VII.)** Jacob George, bn. Mar. 30, 1883.

VI. Reuben K. Fretz, bn. in Bucks Co., Dec. 2, 1846. Mrd. Mary R. Detweiler, Nov. 21, 1868. P. O., Lucon, Pa. Farmer. Menn's. Children: **(VII.)** Garret D. Fretz, bn. Sept. 28, 1869. **(VII.)** Fannie D. Fretz, bn. Dec. 8, 1871. **(VII.)** Annie D. Fretz, bn. Feb. 25, 1875. **(VII.)** William D. Fretz, bn. Mar. 13, 1877; died Oct. 11, 1879. **(VII.)** Henry D. Fretz, bn. July 21, 1879. **(VII.)** Wilson D. Fretz, bn. May 8, 1882. **(VII.)** Reuben D. Fretz, bn. Sept. 3, 1884. **(VII.)** Abraham D. Fretz, bn. Apr. 27, 1887.

VI. Abraham K. Fretz, bn. May 9, 1851. Mrd. Anna Amanda Hechler, Oct. 15, 1881. P. O., Hatfield, Pa. Ev. Ass'n. Children: **(VII.)** Mary Alice Fretz, bn. Sept. 3, 1882. **(VII.)** Aaron Melrose Fretz, bn. Feb. 15, 1887.

VI. Mary B. Fretz (twin), bn. May 9, 1851. S.

V. Barbara Kratz, bn. June 29, 1821; died Oct. 12, 1890. Mrd. Henry K. Myers in 1842. He was born in 1817. Farmer. Menn's. Children: **(VI.)** Levi Myers, bn. in 1843; died in 1887. S. **(VI.)** Huldah Myers, bn. in 1848. Mrd. Amos Myers. (See Index of

References No. 58.) **(VII.)** Elias Myers, bn. in 1854; died 1862.

V. Abraham Kratz, bn. Feb. 25, 1823. Mrd. Elizabeth Dateman, —. P. O., Dublin, Pa. Wagon-maker. Mr. K. Menn., Mrs. K. Luth. Children:
VI. Menan Kratz, bn. Oct. 11, 1850. Mrd. Catharine Aker. Dec. 22, 1875. She was bn. Nov. 5, 1851. Wheelwright. Mrs. K. Ger. Ref. One child: **(VII.)** Elva Kratz, bn. Oct. 5, 1887.

VI. Abraham D. Kratz, bn. Sept. 6, 1856. Mrd. Sarah Derstine, Feb. 19, 1881. She was bn. Apr. 3, 1860. P. O., Dublin, Pa. Farmer. Menn's. Children: **(VII.)** Lizzie Kratz, bn. Jan. 31, 1882. **(VII.)** Sallie Kratz, bn. Mar. 15, 1883. **(VII.)** Leidy Kratz, bn. Jan. 17, 1886. **(VII.)** A. Linford Kratz, bn. June 22, 1890.

VI. Amanda Kratz, bn. June 9, 1860. Mrd. Jeremiah W. Fillman, Oct. 12, 1880. P. O., Dublin, Pa. Farmer. Mrs. F. Menn. Children: **(VII.)** Ella Fillman, bn. Aug. 15, 1881. **(VII.)** Stella Fillman, bn. Aug. 5, 1884. **(VII.)** Ida May Fillman, bn. Feb. 27, 1887. **(VII.)** Lizzie Fillman bn. Nov. 22, 1889.

V. William Henry Kratz, bn. July 26, 1825; died May 7, 1871. Mrd. Martha I. Kennedy, Oct. 18, 1849. She was born Sept. 12, 1824; died Jan. 12, 1876. Farmer. Children: Emily, Joseph, William, Janet, Horace, James, Martha.

VI. Emily E. Kratz, bn. May 26, 1851; died Sept. 26, 1862.

VI. Joseph Kratz, bn. May 11, 1853; died Sept. 28, 1862.

VI. William Henry Kratz, bn. Sept. 21, 1855; died Sept. 24, 1862.

VI. Janet Ferris Kratz, bn. Mar. 19, 1857. Mrd. Mahlon Clymer Haldeman, July 11, 1878. P. O., Hamlin, Minn. Druggist. Baptists. Children: **(VII.)** Eva Ferris Haldeman, bn. July 14, 1879. **(VII.)** Grace Anna Haldeman, bn. Dec. 28, 1881. **(VII.)** Horace Kratz Haldeman, bn. May 27, 1886.

VI. Horace Greeley Kratz, bn. in Bucks Co., Aug. 4, 1859. Mrd. Anna Apel, Oct. 22, 1889. Milk dealer

in Philadelphia. Baptist, wife Ger. Ref. One child:
(VII.) Horace Harry Kratz, bn. Aug. 12, 1891.

VI. James Monroe Kratz, bn. Jan. 6, 1862; died Apr.
12, 1878.

VI. Martha Isabella Kratz, bn. July 13, 1865. Attends Presby. ch.

V. Valentine Kratz, bn. Feb. 24, 1828. Mrd. Sarah,
daughter of William and Mary Kratz, in 1852. Farmer. Menn's. Children: Mary, Allen, William, Abraham, Valentine, Tobias, Henry, Sarah, Emma, Laura.

VI. Mary Ann Kratz, bn. Nov. 23, 1853; died —.

VI. Allen Kratz, bn. June 28, 1855. S.

VI. William Kratz, bn. May 8, 1858; died aged 10
months.

VI. Abraham L. Kratz, bn. Dec. 24, 1859. Mrd.
Anna, dau. of Daniel Myers, Dec. 26, 1886.

VI. Valentine Kratz, bn. Mar. 31, 1862; died aged
2 years.

VI. Tobias Kratz, bn. June 13, 1864; died aged 2
years.

VI. H. Ervin Kratz, bn. in Bucks Co., Pa., Mar. 8,
1867. Attended public school from age of 6 until
11 years, when his mother died. He was then hired
to his Uncle Henry K. Myers, where he remained 3
years, then hired to William and Amos Myers for
two years, going to school in winter, after which he
returned to his Uncle Henry K. Myers, where he
remained four years. On Mar. 1, 1890, he arrived at
Pomona, Kans., where he has since been employed by
the month. S.

VI. Sarah Kratz, bn. Sept. 3, 1869; died 1891. Mrd.
Oliver J. Mills, of Tinicum, Oct. 5, 1889. P. O.,
Lansdale, Pa. One child: (VII.) Clara Mills, bn. Nov.
17, 1890.

VI. Emma E. Kratz, bn. June 8, 1871; died aged 9
months.

VI. Laura Kratz, bn. Feb. 1, 1875.

V. Catharine Ann Kratz, bn. in Bucks Co., Pa., Feb.
24, 1830; died Nov. 29, 1863. Mrd. Rev. Abraham
F. Detweiler, May 27, 1855. He was bn. Apr. 6,
1829. Moved to Illinois in 1856. Farmer and minis-

ter. P.O., Lewisville, Ill. Menn. Children: Roseana,
Catharine, Mary, Abraham.

VI. Roseana K. Detweiler, bn. Oct. 2, 1858. Mrd.
Frank Clark. No issue.

VI. Catharine Ann Detweiler, bn. Oct. 15, 1859.

VI. Mary Elizabeth Detweiler, bn. June 29, 1861.
Mrd. Charles Schroder, Oct. 20, 1885. Farmer. Chil-
dren: **(VII.)** Estella Catharine Schroder, bn. Oct. 8,
1886. **(VII.)** Caroline Schroder, bn. Feb. 2, 1887.
(VII.) William Augustus Schroder, bn. Dec. 8, 1889.
(VII.) Levi K. Schroder, bn. Apr. 5, 1892.

VI. Abraham Lincoln Detweiler, b. May 17, 1863. S.

V. Christian Kratz, bn. Mar. 22, 1832; died July 31,
1834.

V. Elizabeth Kratz, bn. May 24, 1835; died Sept. 15,
1840.

V. Reuben W. Kratz, bn. in New Britain, Bucks
Co., Pa., Feb. 23, 1838. In the fall of 1852 his father
and mother died in the space of five weeks. Left an
orphan at the early age of 14 years, he went to Plumstead, Pa., where he attended one winter term of
school. In the following spring he hired to H. K.
Myers for eight months at farm work. Then appren-
ticed to his brother Abraham at wagon-making, serving one year and nine months. In the spring of 1856,
he faced towards the West, believing there were
better things in store for the young than in the
densely inhabited East; went to Whiteside, Co., Ill.
and worked at wagon-making, breaking prairie with
an ox team, threshing, &c. In 1860 he married Emaline A. Swena, of Sterling, Ill. In the spring of 1863
they loaded their goods and effects in an old wagon
and started for Kansas. Their whole wealth consisted
of a team, wagon, bed, stove, a few minor articles of
household goods, and $21 in cash. They started for a
point in eastern Kansas to find a home for themselves,
and on May 10, 1863, located where they now reside,
in Appanoose Twp., Franklin Co., Kans. P. O.,
Michigan Valley, Kans. Here they lived in a log cabin
with puncheon floor and clapboard roof. In August
Mr. Kratz joined the state Militia, and served in
Kansas and Missouri 18 months. While on such duty

the family remained without a protector, and he had permission to go home at times and get supplies for their maintenance. The nearest mill was 20 miles away and run only one day in a week. The nearest trading store was at Lawrence, 32 miles distant. The Militia was disbanded in 1864, and from that time Mr. Kratz was able to be at home and care for his family. Neighbors were a long distance apart. No settlement except along the streams, and it was common to visit neighbors 10 or 12 miles distant. The Sac and Fox reserve was near by and Indians were plenty, but always peaceable and friendly. Mrs. Kratz was left alone one night, and sleeping with the doors open, several Indians entered to inquire for whiskey. She informed them the whiskey, if there was any, was at the wakeup, about three miles distant, and they retired.

In the winter of 1865, through the kindness of two of their old neighbors in Illinois, Messrs. C. C. Alexander, and John Benjamin, who advanced the money, they were able to buy a stock farm of 152 acres; 37 acres of this was afterwards sold to assist in paying for the balance. In 1878, Mr. Kratz purchased 240 acres, making a farm at this date of 355 acres. In the spring of 1866 he erected a log cabin 16x16 feet foundation. This the family occupied until the fall of 1873, when a more commodious house was built, but this the family soon outgrew, and in the spring of 1886 a house costing over $3,000 was erected. In an early day Mr. Kratz determined to give strict attention to raising stock, and he has never allowed himself to lose sight of this idea. He has at times 150 head of cattle, 40 head of horses, and 200 hogs feeding, making a specialty of fattening beef cattle. The business has not always been prosperous, owing to grasshoppers, chinch bugs and dry weather. School facilities have always been good—probably as good as many in the older states. Mr. Kratz has served on the School Board in his district 24 years. He and wife are members of the Congregational ch. Children: Frances, William, Horace, Lemuel, Amy, Harriet, Esther.

VI. Frances R. Kratz, bn. Dec. 26, 1860. Mrd.
Watson Beaman, Mar. 11, 1884. P. O., Coronado,
Kans. Children: **(VII.)** Chaney Ray Beaman,* bn.
Feb. 3, 1885; died Aug. 23, 1890. **(VII.)** Ava Charlottie
Beaman, bn. Apr. 29, 1886. **(VII.)** Infant son, bn.
Mar. 21, 1888; died Mar. 31, 1888. **(VII.)** Effie Cath-
arine Beaman, bn. July 8, 1889.

VI. William Henry Kratz, bn. June 26, 1867. S.

VI. Horace Clement Kratz, bn. Aug. 22, 1870. S.

VI. Lemuel Abraham Kratz, bn. Feb. 7, 1872.

VI. Amy Elizabeth Kratz, bn. Aug. 18, 1876.

VI. Harriet Emeline Kratz, bn. Mar. 29, 1878.

VI. Esther Amelia Kratz, bn. Nov. 23, 1882.

IV. Esther Wismer, bn. Feb. 8, 1797; died Feb. 5,
1877. Mrd. Jacob Bergey, July 15, 1814. Children:
Abraham, Susan, Jacob, John, Anna.

V. Abraham Bergey, bn. Aug. 30, 1815; died Nov.
8, 1888. Mrd. Anna Kile, —. She was born Aug. 30,
1817; died Mar. 19, 1860. Farmer. Menn's. Children:
Anna, Mary, Jacob, James, Oliver, Susanna, etc.
—Mrd. second wife, Mary Gross, —; she died —. No
issue.

VI. Anna Bergey, bn. Apr. 21, 1843; died June 16,
1891. Mrd. John Godshalk, —. Farmer. Menn's.
Children: **(VII.)** Samuel B. Godshalk, bn. Feb. 25,
1880; died Aug. 7, 1881. **(VII.)** Isaiah B. Godshalk,
bn. May 29, 1881; died June 9, 1882. **(VII.)** Isaac B.
Godshalk, bn. Oct. 23, 1882; died July 24, 1885.
(VII.) Jacob B. Godshalk, bn. Mar. 24, 1884; died
Aug. 16, 1886. **(VII.)** Daniel B. Godshalk, bn. Jan. 1,
1886. **(VII.)** Harvey B. Godshalk, bn. Sept. 19, 1887;
died Dec. 8, 1887.

VI. Mary Bergey, bn. —. Mrd. — Sampey. He
died —. Children all deceased. Mary mrd. second
husband, William J. Leatherman, —. P. O., Plumsteadville, Pa. Have issue.

* While out herding stock he rode his horse onto an old
well covered over with boards and dirt, and which breaking
through, precipitated him down 108 feet to the bottom and
the horse on top of him. His mother was the first to go down
into the well by a hastily improvised windlass and rope to
rescue the mangled remains of her first born.

VI. Jacob Bergey, bn. —. P. O., Fountainville, Pa.
VI. James Bergey, bn. Mar. 23, 1851. Mrd. Anna
Wismer, Nov. 7, 1878. P. O., Fountainville, Pa.
Farmer. Menn's. Children: **(VII.)** Noah Bergey, bn.
Dec. 26, 1880. **(VII.)** Hattie Bergey, bn. Aug. 14,
1882 **(VII.)** Infant son, bn. and died Sept. 8, 1888.
VI. Oliver Bergey (twin), bn. Mar. 23, 1851 Mrd.
Hettie Detweiler, Jan. 17, 1880. She was born May
24, 1862. P. O., Fountainville, Pa. Farmer. Menn's.
Children: **(VII.)** Lizzie Bergey, bn. Feb. 26, 1881.
(VII.) Mamie Bergey, bn. July 5, 1882. **(VII.)** Wilson
Bergey, bn. Oct. 9, 1883. **(VII.)** Pricilla Bergey, bn.
Nov. 19, 1885. **(VII.)** Anna Bergey, bn. Aug. 19,
1889.
VI. Susanna Bergey, bn. —; died small. Others
died single.
V. Susan Bergey, bn. Sept. 28, 1816; died Apr. 3,
1889. Mrd. Abraham Funk, Aug. 28, 1836. P. O.,
Levin, Pa. Farmer. Menn. About two years ago,
by the upsetting of a load of hay, he hurt his ankle in
such a manner that it was necessary to amputate the
foot. Children: Samuel, Jacob, Annie, Hester, Will-
iam, John, Matilda, Mary, Henry, Abraham, Sus-
anna, Elizabeth, Oliver.
VI. Samuel Funk, bn. —; died an infant.
VI. Jacob Funk, bn. —. Mrd. Margaret Albright,
—. Resides in Trenton, N. J. Children: **(VII.)** John
Funk. **(VII.)** Mahlon Funk. **(VII.)** Clinton Funk.
(VII.) Daniel Funk. **(VII.)** Annie Funk.
VI. Annie E. Funk, bn. Oct. 9, 1841. Mrd. Henry
D. Haldeman, Dec. 25, 1868. He died Dec. 4, 1888.
P. O., Levin, Pa. Farm laborer. Menn's. No issue.
VI. Hettie B. Funk, bn. —. Mrd. Daniel C. Kratz,
Feb. 14, 1862. P. O., Lucon, Pa. Farmer. Menn's.
Children: Anna, Abraham, Amanda, Maria, Esther,
Sylvanus, Araminda, Elizabeth, Emma, Harry.
VII. Anna F. Kratz, bn. Jan. 13, 1863. Mrd. Peter
Hunsberger, - . P. O., Lucon, Pa. Farmer. Chil-
dren: **(VIII.)** Elmer K. Hunsberger, bn. Mar. 23, 1889.
(VIII.) Edwin K. Hunsberger, bn. Aug. 16, 1890.
VII. Abraham F. Kratz, bn. Mar. 31, 1865; died Apr.
24, 1885.

Old Mennonite Church, Deep Run, Bucks Co., Pa.

VII. Amanda F. Kratz, bn. Nov. 20, 1866. Mrd. Abraham L. Alderfer, Jan. 5, 1889. P. O., Lucon, Pa. Laborer. One child: **(VIII.)** Bertha K. Alderfer, bn. Feb. 15, 1890.

VII. Mary F. Kratz, bn. Jan. 1, 1867. Mrd. Joseph L. Wismer. (See Index of References No. 59.)

VII. Esther F. Kratz, bn. June 27, 1871.

VII. Sylvanus F. Kratz, bn. Jan. 10, 1873.

VII. Mintie F. Kratz, bn. Nov. 19, 1874.

VII. Elizabeth F. Kratz, bn. Sept. 19, 1876; died Feb. 1877.

VII. Emma F. Kratz, bn. Dec. 24, 1877.

VII. Harry F. Kratz, bn. Mar. 13, 1880.

VI. William Funk, bn. —. Mrd. Susanna Gehman, —. P. O., Doylestown, Pa. Children: **(VII.)** Samuel. **(VII.)** Abraham. **(VII.)** Gerilla. **(VII.)** Mary. **(VII.)** John. —Mrd. second wife Mary Ann Kime, —. Children: **(VII.)** Jesse. **(VII.)** Oscar. **(VII.)** Willie, and one died.

VI. John B. Funk, bn. —. Mrd. Sallie Johnson, —. P. O., Fountainville, Pa. Children: **(VII.)** Ella. **(VII.)** Clayton. **(VII.)** Dora, and two died.

VI. Matilda Funk bn. —. Mrd. Charles Jones, —. P. O., Ambler, Pa. Children: **(VII.)** Mattie. **(VII.)** Infant died. **(VII.)** Laura. **(VII.)** Roy, (dec'd). **(VII.)** Mabel.

VI. Mary Funk, bn. —. Mrd. Abraham Kile, —. P. O., Levin, Pa. Blacksmith. Menn's. Children: **(VII.)** Addie. **(VII.)** Annie. **(VII.)** Mary. **(VII.)** John. **(VII.)** Emma. **(VII.)** Katie. **(VII.)** Abraham. **(VII.)** Oliver. **(VII.)** Daniel. **(VII.)** Lizzie.

VI. Henry Funk, bn. —. Mrd. Malinda Kayfoss, —. Resides in Maryland.

VI. Abraham Funk, bn. —. Mrd. Lizzie Wambold, —. P. O., Ambler, Pa.

VI. Susanna Funk, bn. in New Britain, Pa., Mar. 26, 1853. Mrd. William J. Fuss, Nov. 18, 1876. He was born in Worcester Twp., Montg. Co., Nov. 7, 1850. P. O., Skippack, Pa. Tinsmith. Farmer. Menn's. Children: **(VII.)** Harvey Fuss, bn. Sept. 28, 1877. **(VII.)** John Fuss, bn. Jan. 21, 1880. **(VII.)** Newton Fuss, bn. Feb. 26, 1881. **(VII.)** Lizzie Fuss, bn. Oct. 2, 1882. **(VII.)** Mary and Martha Fuss (twins), bn.

13

Mar. 15, 1884. (VII.) Annie Fuss, bn. Feb. 12, 1886.
(VII.) Emma and Ella Fuss (twins), bn. Apr. 17, 1890.
(VII.) Laura Fuss, bn. Oct. 24, 1891.
V. Jacob Bergey, bn. Aug. 31, 1818. Mrd. Susanna
Leatherman, —. Children: Catharine, Mary, Esther.
—Jacob mrd. second wife, widow — Nice, —. No
issue.
VI. Catharine Bergey, bn. —. Mrd. Isaac L. Kulp.
—. P. O., Danbora, Pa. Children: (VII.) Lizzie.
(VII.) Hettie. (VII.) Isaac. (VII.) Jacob (dec'd). (VII.)
Harvey (dec'd). (VII.) Sallie. (VII.) Katie, etc.
VI. Mary Ann Bergey, bn. —. Mrd. Abraham L.
Kulp, —. P. O., Danboro, Pa. Farmer. Menn. No
issue.
VI. Esther Bergey, bn.—. Mrd. Henry B. Detweiler,
—. P. O., Dublin, Pa. No issue.
V. John Bergey, bn. Feb. 21, 1823. Mrd. Susanna
Wismer, —. P. O., Graters Ford, Pa. No issue.
V. Anna Bergey, bn. July 11, 1830. Mrd. William
Garges, —. Farmer. Children: Amanda, Hettie,
Abraham, John, Henry.
VI. Amanda Garges, bn. —. Mrd. Christian K.
Meyer, —. P. O., Plumsteadville, Pa. Carpenter
and undertaker. Menn's. One child: (VII.) Edwin G.
Meyer, bn. in 1881.
VI. Hettie Garges, bn. May 10, 1857. Mrd. Benja-
min Wismer. (See Index of References No. 60.)
VI. Abraham Garges, bn. —. Mrd. Mary Ann
Swartley, —. P. O., Chalfont, Pa.
VI. John Garges, bn. —. Mrd. — Moyer.
VI. Henry Garges, bn. —. S.

III. Annie Wismer, bn. in Bucks Co., Pa., Aug. 27,
1759; died —. Mrd. Feltie Ruth, —. He died, —.
Children: (IV.) Henry. (IV.) Jacob. (Both went to
Canada.) Ann mrd. second husband Frank Albright,
of Hilltown, Pa., some time previous to 1788. They
moved to Monroe Co., N. Y. where they resided in
1824.

III. Mary Wismer, bn. in Bucks Co., Nov. 15, 1761;
died —. Mrd. Christian Knipe, in 1815. Resided in

Gwynedd, and ten years later in Montgomery Twp., Montg. Co. Children: (IV.) Joseph Knipe, (bachelor) and probably a son John.

III. Henry Wismer, bn. in Bucks Co., Feb. 15, 1764; died 1823. Mrd. Mary Freed, May 19, 1785. Lived in Montg. Co. Distiller. Menn's. Children: John, Barbara, Mary, Elizabeth, Nancy, Henry, Susan.

IV. John Wismer, bn. Oct. 2, 1786; died - . S.

IV. Barbara Wismer, bn. Sept. 28, 1788; died June 19, 1858. Mrd. Abraham Kolb, —. He was bn. Nov. 19, 1789; died Sept. 14, 1856. Farmer. Menn's. Children: John, Mary, Catharine, Henry, Ann.

V. John Kolb, bn. 1811; died 1832. S.

V. Mary Kolb, bn. Sept. 2, 1813; died Sept. 2, 1836. Mrd. William Fritzcharles, —. No issue.

V. Catharine Kolb, bn. Jan. 31, 1816; died —. Mrd. Andrew Gallagher —. Children: (VI.) John Henry Gallagher, bn. —. (VI.) Barbara Jane Gallagher, bn. —. Mrd. Michael Ham, —. (VI.) Mary Ann Gallagher, bn. —. Mrd. Ira Reifsnyder. P. O., Linfield, Pa. (VI.) Abraham James Gallagher, bn. —. Was killed in the Rebellion. Catharine mrd. second husband Adam Bry —.

V. Henry Wismer Kulp, bn. 1819; died —. Mrd. Susanna T., daughter of Rev. Geo. Hellerman, of Germantown, Pa., in 1844. Farmer. Menn's. Children: Sarah, Hetty, George, Winfield, Emma, Annie, Ellie, Mary.

VI. Sarah Frances Kulp, bn. in 1845. Mrd. Samuel A. Topham, —. Res. Philadelphia. Children: (VII.) Samuel A. Topham, bn. 1876. (VII.) Percival Topham, bn. 1877; died 1879.

VI. Hetty Kulp, bn 1847; died 1851.

VI. George A. Kulp, bn. 1849; died 1851.

VI. Winfield Scott Kulp, bn. 1851. Mrd. Bella Breinging, in 1872. Tailor in Phila. One child: (VII.) Frank Kulp.

VI. Emma Jane Kulp, bn. 1855; died 1857.

VI. Annie Kulp, bn. 1857; died in 1875. A lovely Christian, esteemed by all who knew her.

VI. Ellie V. Kulp, bn. 1860. Mrd. Jacob Hartman, —. Confectioner in Phila. No children.

VI. Mary Adelia Kulp, bn. 1867.

V. Ann Kolb, bn. Sept. 17, 1825. Mrd. William D. Hunsicker, Feb. 22, 1844. He died May 30, 1887. P. O., Norristown, Pa. Farmer. Ref. ch. Children: Mary, Abraham, William, Daniel, Joseph, Milton, Irvin, Annie, Lizzie, Emma.

VI. Mary Jane Hunsicker, bn. Feb. 4, 1847. Mrd. John S. Boyer, —. P. O., Norristown, Pa. Farmer. Ger. Ref. Children: (**VII.**) Howard T. Boyer, bn. May 19, 1868. (**VII.**) Ida May Boyer, bn. Apr. 20, 1876.

VI. Abraham K. Hunsicker, bn. Aug. 22, 1849. Mrd. Susan Tyson, —. P. O., Collegeville, Pa.

VI. William Henry Hunsicker, bn. Apr. 8, 1851: died Jan. 22, 1859.

VI. Daniel K. Hunsicker, bn. Aug. 27, 1853; died Aug. 24, 1855.

VI. Joseph C. Hunsicker, bn. Jan. 23, 1856. Mrd. Alice Rhoades. P. O., Iron Bridge, Pa. Farmer. Children: (**VII.**) Norman R. Hunsicker, bn. July 23, 1879. (**VII.**) Quintin LeRoy Hunsicker, bn. Jan. 29, 1881. (**VII.**) Bertha Isaphine Hunsicker, bn. May 29, 1883. (**VII.**) Mary Idella Hunsicker, bn. Apr. 23, 1886. (**VII.**) H. Earl Hunsicker, bn. Apr. 18, 1889. (**VII.**) J. Vernon Hunsicker, bn. Nov. 19, 1890; died July 14, 1892.

VI. Milton K. Hunsicker, bn. Apr. 1, 1858. Mrd. Rosa Smith, —. P. O., Iron Bridge, Pa.

VI. Irvin K. Hunsicker, bn. Feb. 18, 1860. Mrd. Anna Stearly, —. P. O., Limerick Square, Pa.

VI. Annie K. Hunsicker, bn. Sept. 12, 1862. Mrd. Addison Forker, —. P. O., Trappe, Pa.

VI. Lizzie Ella Hunsicker, bn. Aug. 25, 1864. Mrd. Willis Bosler, —.

VI. Emma K. Hunsicker, bn. Apr. 19, 1867.

IV. Mary Wismer, bn. in 1791; died July 31, 1884, aged 93,-3,-5. Mrd. David Levingood, —. Children:

(V.) David, &c.—Mary mrd. second husband James Preston, —.

IV. Elizabeth Wismer, bn. Apr. 7, 1793; died unmarried.

IV. Nancy Wismer, bn. Mar. 1, 1796; died June 22, 1863. Mrd. David Shutt, —. He died, —. Nancy mrd. second husband Jacob Shutt. —.

IV. Henry Wismer, bn. 1798; died —.

IV. Susan Wismer, bn. Aug. 2, 1800; died Aug. 2, 1882. Mrd. John Clemence, —.

III. Joseph Wismer, bn. in Bucks Co., Pa., Apr. 1, 1765; died in Waterloo Co., Ont., Nov. 29, 1834, aged 69 y., 7 m., 28 d. Mrd. Hannah Fried, —. She died June 6, 1830, aged 69 yrs., 7 mo., 6 da. They moved to Canada in 1800, and settled near Blair, Ont., where they lived until death. Mason, weaver, and farmer. Children: Elizabeth, Henry, Barbara, Catharine, Jacob, John, Hannah.

IV. Elizabeth Wismer, bn. in Bucks Co., Pa., —; died —. Mrd. — Dodge. (V.) Son Joseph Dodge. P. O., Plattsville, Ont.

IV. Henry Wismer, bn. in Bucks Co., Pa., Dec. 20, 1789; died in Waterloo Co., Ont., Feb. 15, 1854. Mrd. Hannah Schlichter, Apr. 23, 1818. She was bn. Dec. 18, 1798, in Franklin Co., Pa.; died in Waterloo Co., Ont., June 26, 1878. Farmer. Menn's. Children: Joseph, Mary, David, Susanna, Daniel, Anna, Moses, Lydia, Elizabeth, Isaac.

V. Joseph Wismer, bn. Jan. 25, 1819. A deaf-mute. Res. Caledonia, Mich

V. Mary Wismer, bn. June 21, 1821; died Feb. 25, 1875. Mrd. Amos M. Clemens. Children: Henry, Hannah, Abraham, Mary, Noah, Rachel, Lydia.

VI. Henry Clemens, bn. —. Mrd. Martha Yules.

VI. Hannah Clemens, bn. —; died —. Mrd. Wendell Bowman, —. Children: (VII.) Mary Bowman, bn. July 23, 1865. Mrd. Simon Pender, 1883. P. O., Freeport, Mich. (VII.) Elo Bowman, bn. June 13, 1867. P. O., Caledonia, Mich. (VII.) Luella Bowman, bn. Mar. 18, 1873. P. O., Caledonia, Mich.

VI. Abraham Clemens, bn. —; died —. Mrd. Salome Bowman. Issue: **(VII.)** Olive M. Clemens, bn. —. Mrd. Norman Eby. · P. O., Caledonia, Mich.

VI. Mary Clemens, bn. —. Mrd. Edward Williams. P. O., Petoskey, Mich.

VI. Noah Clemens, bn. — Mrd. Maggie Dodge, —. P. O., Grand Rapids, Mich.

VI. Rachel Clemens, bn. —. Mrd. Edward Clark. P. O., Caledonia, Mich.

VI. Lydia Clemens, bn. —. Mrd. Washington Bowman. P. O., Oakfield, Mich.

V. David S. Wismer, bn. in Waterloo Co., Ont., June 3, 1823; died Aug. 2. 1884. Mrd. Elizabeth Weaver, Sept. 5, 1843. Farmer. Menn's. Children: Mary, Lydia, Isaac, Benjamin, Joseph, Nancy, David.

VI. Mary Ann Wismer, bn. in 1844. Mrd. Isaac Overholtzer. P. O., Berlin, Ont.

VI. Lydia Ann Wismer, bn. in 1845. Mrd. James Wright. P. O., Molesworth, Ont.

VI. Isaac Henry Wismer, bn. in 1848. Mrd. Mary Burkholder. P. O., Preston, Ont.

VI. Benjamin Slichter Wismer, bn. in 1850. Mrd. Dianna Abra, —. P. O., Imlay City, Mich. Teamster. Meth. Children: **(VII.)** Nancy Hannah Wismer, bn. Sept. 7. 1873. **(VII.)** Elizabeth Wismer, bn. July 9. 1875. **(VII.)** William Wismer, bn. Nov. 8, 1879.

VI. Joseph Wismer bn. in 1856.

VI. Nancy Wismer, bn. in 1857. Mrd. John Sherk. P. O., Brown City. Mich.

VI. David Ezra Wismer, bn. in 1865. ⸱

V. Susanna Wismer, bn. Nov. 27, 1825; died Nov. 28, 1825.

V. Daniel Wismer, bn. Sept. 29, 1826; died Oct. 30, 1827.

V. Anna Wismer, bn. Apr. 6, 1829; died Jan. 11, 1872. Mrd. Benjamin Shupe, Oct. 17, 1847. He was bn. July 27, 1823. P. O., New Dundee, Ont. Farmer. Tunkers. Children: Isaac, Hannah, Elizabeth, George.

VI. Isaac Shupe, bn. —; died Sept. 9, 1849.

VI. Hannah Shupe, bn. Aug. 10, 1850. Mrd. Eri Srigley, Mar. 13, 1881. He was bn. Nov. 2, 1853. P. O., Kurtzville, Ont. Farmer. Tunkers. Children: (**VII.**) Elmina Srigley, bn. June 9, 1882. (**VII.**) Anna Melissa Srigley, bn. Aug. 18, 1884. (**VII.**) Melvin Srigley, bn. Apr. 11, 1887.

VI. Elizabeth Shupe, bn. Dec. 21, 1852. Mrd. George Eby, Apr. 9, 1878. P. O., Aden, Ont. Farmer. Mrs. Eby, Menn.

VI. George Shupe, bn. Apr. 6, 1855. Mrd. Elizabeth Becker, Apr. 9, 1878. P. O., New Dundee, Ont.. Farmer. Mrs. Shupe, Lutheran. Children: (**VII.**) Alvin Shupe, bn. May 8, 1879. (**VII.**) Hattie Shupe, bn. June 15, 1881. (**VII.**) Harvey Shupe, bn. Oct. 20, 1883. (**VII.**) Maurice Shupe, bn. Aug. 3, 1885.

V. Moses Wismer, bn. Sept. 15, 1831; died same day.

V. Lydia Wismer, bn. in Ont., May 2, 1833. Mrd. Joseph C. Bowman, Oct. 5, 1852. P. O., Caledonia, Mich. Farmer. Menn's. Children: Nancy, Hannah. Maria, Solon.

VI. Nancy Bowman, bn. July 15, 1854. Mrd. Elias Winter, —. P. O., Caledonia, Mich. Farmer. Evangelicals. Children: (**VII.**) Hannah Winter. (**VII.**) Orrin Winter. (**VII.**) Solon Winter.

VI. Hannah Bowman, bn. Sept. 25, 1856; died Feb. 23, 1872.

VI. Maria Bowman, bn. June 9, 1861. P. O., Caledonia, Mich. Dressmaker. U. Br. ch.

VI. Solon Bowman, bn. —. P. O., Caledonia, Mich. Farmer.

V. Elizabeth Wismer, bn. Apr. 11, 1835. Mrd. Solomon Albright, —. P. O., Jordan, Ont. Children: (**VI.**) Ezra Albright. Mrd. Margaret Moyer. P. O., Jordan, Ont. (**VI.**) Jacob Albright, bn. —. Mrd. —. P. O., Jordan, Ont.

V. Isaac Wismer, bn. Sept. 13, 1840; died Aug. 16, 1874. Mrd. Nancy Hilburn. Farmer. Menn. P. O., Galt, Ont. Children: (**VI.**) Cyrus Wismer. (**VI.**) John Wismer.

IV. Barbara Wismer, bn. in Chester Co., Pa., in 1792; died in Canada, Aug. 10, 1834, aged 42 years.

Mrd. Henry Schlichter, —. He died Aug. 11, 1834, aged 45 years. They were both victims of the cholera scourge which swept over Ontario in 1834. Had issue.

IV. Catharine Wismer, bn. in Chester Co., Pa., Apr. 11, 1794; died at Preston, Ont., Nov. 22, 1881. Mrd. Henry B. K. Bauman, May 4, 1813. He was bn. in Berks Co., Pa., Nov. 27, 1790; died at Preston, Ont., Feb. 12, 1858. Farmer. Menn. Children: Joseph, Henry, Hannah. Solomon, Peter, Elizabeth, Mary, Nancy. Abraham, Aaron.

V. Joseph K. Bauman, bn. in Pa., Apr. 10, 1814; died in Berlin, Mich., Jan. 15, 1890. Mrd. Susan Seehrist, Mar. 15, 1839. She died July 5, 1888. Farmer. Menn. Children: Catharine, Benuel. John, Henry, Joseph.

VI. Catharine Bauman, bn. Aug. 1, 1840. Mrd. Michael Millard,—. He died —. No issue. Catharine mrd. second husband William Holcomb, --. He died -- . No issue. Mrd. third husband Hiram Gross, . P. O., Tallmage, Mich. No issue.

VI. Benuel Bauman, bn. Dec. 23, 1843. Mrd. Mattie Cooper. P. O., Berlin, Mich. Children: (**VII.**) John Bauman, bn. . S. (**VII.**) William Bauman, bn. -- . S. (**VII.**) Minnie Bauman, bn. - . S. (**VII.**) Daisy Bauman, bn. . S. (**VII.**) Bessie Bauman, bn. -- . S.

VI. John Bauman, bn. June 24, 1846.

VI. Henry Bauman, bn. May 26, 1849.

VI. Joseph S. Bauman, bn. at Berlin, Mich., Dec. 3, 1863. Mrd. Mary Gardiner, Sept. 30, 1885. P. O., Berlin, Mich. Farmer. Children: (**VII.**) J. Earnest Bauman, bn. Sept. 14, 1888. (**VII.**) Charles H. Bauman, bn. May 20, 1891. (**VII.**) Katie E. Bauman, bn. May 30, 1892.

V. Henry Bauman, bn. Oct. 10, 1816; died Feb. 23, 1838.

V. Hannah Bauman, bn. Feb. 28, 1819; died —. Mrd. Noah Shantz. Issue five girls and five boys. (**VI.**) Aaron. (**VI.**) Emanuel, &c.

V. Solomon Bauman, bn. July 17, 1821; died Jan. 2, 1869. Mrd. Mary Stauffer, Mar. 7, 1843. Issue five boys and four girls. (**VI.**) Peter, &c.

V Peter Bauman, bn. at Preston, Ont., Aug. 26, 1825; died Mar. 19, 1884. Mrd. Catharine Bean, July 23, 1850. She was bn. Nov. 28, 1833; died Aug. 7. 1852. Millwright. Mr. B., Mennonite, Mrs. B., Evangelical. Children: Nancy, Catharine.

VI. Nancy Bauman, bn. May 15, 1851. Mrd. Benjamin B. Sherk. P. O., Breslau, Ont.

VI. Catharine Bauman, bn. in Ontario, Aug. 6, 1852. Mrd. David Groh, Apr. 13, 1879. P. O., Hespeler, Ont. Attend Evangelical ch. One child: **(VII.)** Flora May Groh, bn. Feb. 19, 1883.

V. Elizabeth Bauman, bn. July 7, 1828; died Feb. 23, 1890. Mrd. . No issue.

V. Mary Bauman, bn. Sept. 22, 1830. Mrd. Andrew Groff, May 30, 1868. P. O., Waterloo, Ont. Nine children.

V. Nancy Bauman, bn. Dec. 20, 1832. Mrd. William Lehman, Feb. 6, 1855. No issue.

V. Abraham Bauman, bn. at Preston, Ont., Nov. 30, 1834. Mrd. Mary Ann Allen, July 28, 1863. P. O., Doon, Ont. Carpenter. Menn. Children: Jane, Catharine, Henrietta, Wilhelmina.

VI. Jane Ann Bauman, bn. Jan. 22, 1865. Mrd. John H. Card, May 11, 1887. Children: **(VII.)** Clayton Card, bn. Feb. 29, 1888; died Feb. 14, 1889. **(VII.)** Eva J. Card, bn. Dec. 18, 1889. **(VII.)** Alberta B. Card, bn. Apr. 11, 1892.

VI. Catharine A. Bauman, bn. Apr. 6, 1867.

VI. Henrietta Bauman, bn. Jan. 23, 1870.

VI. Wilhelmina Bauman, bn. Sept. 8, 1872; died Aug. 21, 1873.

V. Aaron Bauman, bn. Mar. 20, 1837. Mrd. Mary Bitner, Aug. 11, 1863.

IV. Jacob Wismer, bn. in Pa., June 1797; died in Huron Co., Ont., Feb. 1875. Mrd. Susanna Detweiler, in 1825. She was bn. in Pa., June 22, 1810; died in Waterloo Co., Ont., July 2, 1874. He became a cripple, and made his living making ox yokes, rakes, axe handles and shingles. Menn. Children: Catharine, Levi, David.

V. Catharine Wismer, bn. in Waterloo Co., Ont., Jan. 5, 1839. Mrd. Henry Treffry, June 11, 1855.

P. O., Burnside Station. Manitoba. Meth. Children:
Susanna, Phebe, Mary, Robert, Jacob, William,
Margaret, Emma, Jacob, Catharine, Lydia, George.
VI. Susanna Treffry, bn. June 29, 1856. Mrd. Solo-
mon Beck, May 24, 1879. P. O., Burnside Station,
Man. Farmer. Ch. of England. Children: **(VII.)**
James Beck, bn. Apr. 27, 1882. **(VII.)** Emma Beck,
bn Oct. 21, 1887. **(VII.)** Eva Beck, bn. Sept. 6, 1889.
(VII.) Phebe Beck, bn. Sept. 5, 1892.
VI. Phebe Ann Treffry, bn. Jan. 16, 1858. Mrd.
Henry Voss, Jan. 17, 1876. P. O., Burnside Station,
Man. Farmer. Lutheran. Children: **(VII.)** Catharine
Voss, bn. Aug, 1878. **(VII.)** Henry Voss, bn. June
29, 1880. **(VII.)** Mary Voss, bn. Dec. 1, 1883. **(VII.)**
Violet Voss, bn. Sept. 6, 1885; died Nov. 6, 1885.
(VII.) Robert Voss, bn. Sept. 21, 1887. **(VII.)** Nor-
man Voss, bn. Oct. 24, 1888.
VI. Mary Ann Treffry, bn. Nov. 2, 1859. Mrd.
Thomas Beck, Aug. 17, 1882. P. O., Burnside Sta.,
Man. Ch. of England. Children: **(VII.)** William
Beck, bn. Sept. 20, 1883. **(VII.)** Charles Beck, bn.
May 6, 1887. **(VII.)** Eliza Beck, bn. Jan. 13, 1889.
VI. Robert John Treffry, bn. Dec. 25, 1861. Mrd.
Casiah Elizabeth Lee, Oct. 24, 1888. P. O., Burnside
Sta., Man. Meth's. Children: **(VII.)** Jorsa Treffry,
bn. Oct. 23, 1889. **(VII.)** Robert Leslie Treffry, bn.
June 6, 1892; died Mar. 30, 1893.
VI. Jacob Treffry. bn. Mar. 22, 1864; died Mar. 25,
1864.
VI. William Henry Treffry, bn. Apr. 12, 1865. Mrd.
Anna May Kizer. of Michigan, Jan. 27, 1892. P. O.,
Burnside Sta.. Man. Meth. One child: **(VII.)** Carrie
May Treffry, bn. Jan. 23, 1893.
VI. Margaret Treffry, bn. July 28, 1867. Mrd.
Frank E. Green, Dec. 25, 1889. Res. 90 Hallot St.,
Winnipeg, Man. Miller. Ch. of England. Children:
(VII.) Mabel Catharine Green, bn. June 23, 1892.
(VII.) Ivy Green, bn. Sept. 25, 1893.
VI. Emma Treffry, bn. Jan. 12, 1871. Mrd. James
Acheson, Feb. 9, 1888. P. O., Burnside, Man.
Children: **(VII.)** Arthur Acheson, bn. Mar. 9, 1889.
(VII.) Martha Mabel Acheson, bn. Mar. 17, 1890.

(VII.) Alislnese Acheson, bn. May 6, 1891. (VII.)
Florence Irena Acheson, bn. Sept. 9, 1893.
  VI. Jacob Treffry, bn. July 13, 1873. (Twin.)
  VI. Catharine Treffry, bn. July 13, 1873. Mrd.
Frederick W. Green, July 13, 1892. Res. 90 Hallot
St., Winnipeg, Man. Miller. Ch. of England. One
child: (VII.) Islay Catharine Green, bn. Aug. 7, 1893;
died Sept. 26, 1893.
  VI. Lydia Ann Treffry, bn. Apr. 30, 1876. Seamstress. Meth. S.
  VI. George Treffry, bn. Apr. 9, 1879.
  V. Levi Wismer, bn. in Waterloo Co., Ont. Aug.
10, 1840. Mrd. Mary Jane Broderick, —. P. O.,
Redman, Mich. Joiner and millwright. Has been
the owner of six patents, five in Canada, and
one in the United States, being an improvement on
bee hives. Mr. Wismer is not a member of any
denomination of Christians, but feeling that he is "a
chosen vessel of God, as one chosen from the depth
of poverty and ignorance," he has preached at times
for the last fifteen years. Children: (VI.) Mary Eliza-
beth Wismer, bn. Apr. 26, 1872. Mrd. John James
Cornish. P. O., Redman, Mich. Farmer. (VI.)
William Jacob Wismer, bn. Jan. 19, 1874. (VI.)
Emma Rilla Wismer, bn. Sept. 12, 1875. (VI.) Ella
Norah Wismer, bn. Aug. 30, 1877. (VI.) Shadrach
Meshach Abednego Wismer, bn. Aug. 29, 1879.
(VI.) Isaiah Wismer, bn. Feb. 9, 1882. (VI.) Infant,
stillborn Aug. 29, 1884. (VI.) Catharine Wismer, bn.
July 30, 1885. (Twin.) (VI.) Infant son, stillborn
July 30, 1885. (VI.) Levi Wismer, bn. May 2, 1892.
  V. David Wismer, bn. in 1842; died in 1844.
  IV. John Wismer, bn. in Chester Co., Pa., Apr. 2,
1799; died in Waterloo Co., Ont., July 23, 1890.
Mrd. Susannah Cressman, —. She was bn. in Pa.,
1801; and died Sept. 1838. Farmer. Menn's. Chil-
dren: Jacob, Hannah, Abraham, Joseph, Elizabeth,
Susan, John, Henry, Esther.
  V. Jacob Wismer, bn. in Waterloo Co., Ont., Feb.
23, 1823. Mrd. Leah Hamacher, July 11, 1855. P.
O., Garlington, Kans. Farmer. Evangelical. Chil-
dren: Nancy, Cyrus, Sarah, Aaron.

VI. Nancy Wismer, bn. July 13, 1856. Mrd. George
M. Beck, Nov. 15, 1876. P. O., Kill Creek, Kans.
Farmer. Evangelical. Children: (VII.) Sarah Ellen
Wismer, bn. Sept. 17, 1877. (VII.) Alice Wismer, bn.
Feb. 28, 1879; died Jan. 20, 1880. (VII.) David
Franklin Wismer, bn. May 31, 1880; died Mar. 11,
1887. (VII.) Sylvia Wismer, bn. Mar. 7, 1882. (VII.)
Amanda Wismer, bn. Sept. 28, 1884. (VII.) Aaron
Wismer, bn. Dec. 2. 1886. (VII.) Laura Wismer, bn.
Feb. 7. 1888. (VII.) Minnie Wismer, bn. Nov. 20,
1890. (VII.) George Garfield Wismer, bn. Mar. 9,
1893.
VI. Cyrus Wismer, bn. Feb. 3, 1859; died Sept. 30,
1861.
VI. Sarah Jane Wismer, bn. in Huron Co., Ont.,
Aug. 27. 1860. Mrd. John Schnellbacher, Nov. 27,
1879. He died —. One child: (VII.) Nola Aletta
Schnellbacher, bn. Sept. 3, 1881. Sarah mrd. for her
second husband Levi Andre, June 11. 1889. P. O.,
Princeton, Kans. Farmer. Evangelical ch. Children:
(VII.) Mary Ethel Andre, bn. July 3. 1890. (VII.)
Jacob Raymond Andre, bn. Nov. 20, 1891.
VI. Aaron Wismer, bn. in Huron Co., Ont., June
11, 1862. Mrd. Lillian Kallfleisch, in 1886. P. O.,
Garlington, Kans. Farmer. Evangelical. Children:
(VII.) Nettie May Wismer, bn. Dec. 2, 1888. (VII.)
Millie Wismer, bn. Dec. 28, 1890. (VII.) Alice Wis-
mer, bn. Dec. 12, 1892.
V. Hannah Wismer, bn. in Waterloo Co., Ont., May
23, 1825. Mrd. Jesse Penfold, —. P. O., Elora,
Ont. Mrs. P., Meth. Children: Susanna, David, Eli-
jah, James, Thomas. Elizabeth, John, Phoebe,
Harriet, Hannah, Jesse.
VI. Susanna Penfold, bn. in Waterloo, Ont., Aug.
18, 1841. Mrd. Thomas Batters, Feb. 27, 1861. P.
O., Neepawa, Man. Farmer. Children: Jesse, Catha-
rine, William, Eliza, Elizabeth, Mary, Phoebe, John,
Thomas, Harriett, James.
VII. Jesse Edward Batters, bn. Dec. 23, 1861. Mrd.
Charlotte Letitia Walker, June 19, 1885. P. O.,
Neepawa, Man. Farmer. Presby. One child: (VIII.)
Melvine Campbell Batters, bn. Aug. 13, 1888.

VII. Catharine Batters, bn. Oct. 28, 1863; died Jan. 29, 1864.

VII. Eliza Jane Batters, bn. Nov. 3, 1864; died June 10, 1867.

VII. William Batters, bn. Jan. 13, 1867. Mrd. Elizabeth McIntosh, July 16, 1892. P. O., Holland, Man. Stone mason and farmer. Presby.

VII. Elizabeth Batters, bn. Apr. 3, 1869. Mrd. Antonia Meachan, Jan. 4, 1887. P. O., E. Saginaw, Mich. Employed in the Round House, E. Saginaw, Mich. Presby. Children: **(VIII.)** Maggie Meachan, bn. Apr. 16, 1889. **(VIII.)** Airrell Meachan, bn. May 13, 1891.

VII. Mary Hannah Batters, bn. May 31, 1871. P. O., Gorrie, Ont. Tailoress. Presby. S.

VII. Phoebe Ann Batters, bn. Aug. 16, 1873. P. O., Neepawa, Man. Tailoress. Presby. S.

VII. John Henry Batters, bn. Sept. 7, 1875. Presby.

VII. Thomas Batters, bn. Jan. 1, 1878. Presby.

VII. Harriett Matilda Batters, bn. Mar. 7, 1880.

VII. James Wellington Batters, bn. Sept. 27, 1882.

VI. David Penfold, born Mar. 18, 1844; died Aug. 1849.

VI. Elijah Penfold, born Aug. 17, 1845; died May 1865.

VI. James Penfold, born Aug. 13, 1847; died Aug. 1848.

VI. Thomas Penfold, born in Waterloo Co., Ont., Apr. 4, 1849. Mrd. Margaret Annettie Harvey, Aug. 4, 1884. P. O., Prince Arthur's Landing, Ont. Governor of Port Arthur's Jail. Presby. Children: **(VII.)** Garnet Scully Penfold, bn. Nov. 20, 1886. **(VII.)** Harvey Stanley Penfold, bn. Feb. 25, 1893.

VI. Elizabeth Penfold, bn. Mar. 25, 1851. Mrd. J. B. Hewitt, Mar. 7, 1883. P. O., Hetland, South Dakota. Farmer. Four children.

VI. John Henry Penfold, bn. Nov. 18, 1853. Mrd. Emma Holzworth, Dec. 19, 1883. P. O., Elora, Ont. Farmer. Children: **(VII.)** Marvin Penfold, bn. Dec. 1, 1884; died July 30, 1885. **(VII.)** Russel Penfold, bn. Dec. 20, 1886. **(VII.)** Mary Hannah Penfold, bn.

Dec. 25. 1888. (VII.) Emma Pearl Penfold, bn. Apr. 22, 1890.

VI. Phœbe Ann Penfold, bn. June 1, 1856. Mrd. Robert Peel Winfield, Mar. 10, 1887. P. O., Elora, Ont. Farmer. No issue.

VI. Harriet Amanda Penfold, bn. Sept. 6, 1858; died June 1869.

VI. Hannah Penfold, bn. Dec. 25, 1860. P. O., Elora, Ont. S.

VI. Jesse Penfold, bn. June 19, 1866. P. O., Portage La Prairie, Man. S.

V. Abraham Wismer, bn. in Waterloo Co., Ont., Apr. 1827; died July 1861. Mrd. Susanna Mott. She was bn. in Oxford Co., Ont., Sept. 10, 1833. Children: Rachel, John, Stillman, Rebecca.

VI. Rachel Cornelia Wismer, bn. in Middlesex Co., Ont., Nov. 23, 1854. Mrd. Henry Nichols, June 19, 1877. He was bn. Mar. 29, 1842, in Middlesex Co., Ont. P. O., Glendale, Ont. Farmer. Baptists. Children: (VII.) Levert Judson Nichols, bn. Apr. 2, 1878. (VII.) Ida Alberta Nichols, bn. Dec. 24, 1879. (VII.) Henry Leroy Nichols, bn. Jan. 9, 1886

VI. John Louis Wismer. P. O., Doon, Ont.

VI. Stillman J. Wismer, bn. --. Mrd. Mary Musser. P. O., Blair, Ont.

VI. Rebecca Wismer, bn. —; died —.

V. Joseph Wismer, bn. near Roseville, Ont., Apr. 20, 1829. Mrd. Charlotte Hewitt, —. She was bn. July 1, 1836. P. O., Blair, Ont. Farmer. Children: Susanna, Mary, Benjamin, Adelina, Sarah, Hannah, Joseph, John, William.

VI. Susanna Wismer, born May 29, 1852. Married George Millard, Dec. 1, 1870. He died in Apr. 1879. Farmer. Children: (VII.) Elizabeth Millard, bn. Nov. 10, 1871. (VII.) John Millard, bn. July 12, 1873. (VII.) Benjamin Millard, bn. June 15, 1875. Susanna, mrd. second husband William Airess, Dec. 25, 1882. P. O., Winterbourne, Ont. Farmer. Children: (VII.) Hannah Airess, bn. Apr. 16, 1884. (VII.) William Airess, bn. Oct. 27, 1887. (VII.) Hugh Airess, bn. May 7, 1893.

VI. Mary Ann Wismer, bn. May 7, 1854: died Aug. 1856.

VI. Benjamin Wismer, bn. Mar. 14, 1856. Married Maggie Airess, Oct. 15, 1886. P. O., Ayr, Ont. Carpenter. Children; **(VII.)** Charlotte Wismer, bn. Feb. 15, 1888. **(VII.)** Maggie Wismer, bn. Aug. 1890. **(VII.)** Julia Wismer, bn. June 1891. **(VII.)** Benjamin Wismer, bn. May 18, 1893.

VI. Adelina Wismer, bn. Nov. 14, 1858. Mrd. William Short. —. P. O., Hespeler, Ont. Farmer. Children: **(VII.)** James Short, bn. Aug. 1, 1879. **(VII.)** Charlotte Short, bn. Dec. 17, 1882. **(VII.)** Joseph Leonard Short, bn. May 24, 1891.

VI. Sarah Jane Wismer, bn. Nov. 7, 1860. Mrd. Thomas Mighton, —. P. O., Almaville, Ontario. Farmer. Children: **(VII.)** Charlotte Paulina Mighton, born July 16, 1878. **(VII.)** Eva Matilda Mighton, bn. Oct. 22, 1879. **(VII.)** Harriet Jane Mighton, bn. June 7, 1893.

VI. Hannah Wismer, bn. Jan. 4, 1867. Mrd. George Gress, —. P. O., Ayr, Ont. Carpenter and builder. Children: **(VII.)** George Gress, bn. May 4, 1886. **(VII.)** Ethel Gress, bn. July 6, 1888. **(VII.)** Charlotte Gress, bn. July 9, 1890.

VI. Joseph Wismer, bn. July 14, 1869. Mrd. Elizabeth Caruthers in 1889. P. O., Blair, Ont. Children: **(VII.)** William John Wismer, bn. Feb. 28, 1890. **(VII.)** Sarah Jane Wismer, bn. Jan. 14, 1892.

VI. John Wismer, bn. Apr. 26, 1873. P. O., Blair. Ont. Blacksmith.

VI. William Wismer, bn. Nov. 28, 1874.

V. Elizabeth Wismer, bn. in Roseville, Ont., Mar. 13, 1831. Mrd. William Abra. Feb. 17, 1846. P. O., Blair, Ont. He was bn. in Snaffham, Eng., Nov. 6, 1815; died near Blair, Ont., July 20, 1889. Farmer. Baptists. Children: Deanna, Hannah, Joseph, Moses, Susanna, John, William, Elizabeth, Harry, Eliza, Julia, Jacob, Noah, Mary.

VI. Deanna Abra, bn. Jan. 10, 1847. Mrd. Benjamin Wismer, —. Residence, Imlay City, Mich. Teamster. Meth. Children: **(VII.)** Nancy Hannah Wismer, bn. Sept. 7, 1873. **(VII.)** Elizabeth Wismer, bn. July 9, 1875. **(VII.)** William Wismer, bn. Nov. 8, 1879.

VI. Hannah Abra, bn. May 12, 1848. P. O., Blair, Ont. Baptist. S.

VI. Joseph Abra, bn. Nov. 24, 1849. Mrd. Helen Wallace, —. P. O., Roseville, Ontario. Farmer. Attends Baptist church. Children: **(VII.)** Helen Abra, bn. Sept. 10, 1874. **(VII.)** John William Abra, bn. Mar. 29, 1879. **(VII.)** Elizabeth Abra, bn. Jan. 13, 1883. **(VII.)** Janet Abra, bn. Mar. 7, 1887.

VI. Moses Abra, bn. Sept. 6, 1851. Mrd. Maggie Little, Dec. 20, 1882. P. O., Doon, Ont. Farmer. Baptists. Children: **(VII.)** Susanna Abra, bn. Apr. 28, 1884. **(VII.)** Harry L. Abra, bn. June 1, 1887; died Aug. 27, 1888. **(VII.)** Caroline Abra, bn. Feb. 24, 1889.

VI. Susanna Abra, bn. Dec. 6, 1853; died Jan. 4, 1879. Mrd. John Marshall, Oct. 3, 1873. He died Dec. 15, 1881. Farmer. Presby. One child: **(VII.)** Elizabeth Marshall, bn. May 8, 1875.

VI. John Abra, bn. Feb. 20, 1856; died Dec. 5, 1858.

VI. William Abra, bn. Mar. 28, 1858. Mrd. Maggie W. Hall, Feb. 17, 1881. P. O. North Bay, Ont. Carpenter. Baptist. Children: **(VII.)** William James Abra, bn. Apr. 6, 1882. **(VII.)** Robert Hall Abra, bn. July 29, 1884; died Sept. 29, 1884.

VI. Elizabeth Abra, bn. Jan. 13, 1861; died June 3, 1861.

VI. Harry Y. Abra, bn. Mar. 31, 1862. Mrd. Aggie Murray, Sept. 5, 1893. P. O., Doon, Ont. Farmer.

VI. Eliza Young Abra, bn. Aug. 26, 1865. P. O., Blair, Ont. Baptist. S.

VI. Julia Ann Abra, bn. Mar. 26, 1867. P. O., Blair, Ont. Baptist.

VI. Jacob Finch Abra, bn. Mar. 10, 1870.

VI. Noah Abra, bn. July 7, 1872.

VI. Mary Ann Abra, bn. Jan. 20, 1874. Baptist.

V. Susan Wismer, bn. Aug. 1833. Mrd. William Pickett, —. P. O., Corinth, Mich. Children: Elizabeth, John, Esther, Joseph, Mary, Amos, George, Jesse.

VI. Elizabeth W. Pickett, bn. in Ont., Apr. 9, 1850. Married Cyrus Noggle, —. P. O., Shelbyville, Mich. Children: Ellen, Rose, Ruth, Clark, Anda, Blanche, Liva, Edith, Malinda, Jesse.

VII. Ellen Almira Noggle, bn. Mar. 13, 1873. Mrd. W. B. Manning, Aug. 2, 1890. P. O., Bradley, Mich. Children: (**VIII.**) Oscar Almon Manning, bn. June 20, 1892. (**VIII.**) Jessie Pearl Manning, bn. Mar. 10, 1893.

VII. Rose Etta Noggle, bn. Jan. 22, 1875. Mrd. G. E. Bush, Feb. 21, 1893. P. O., Shelbyville, Mich.

VII. Ruth E. Noggle, bn. June 15, 1878; died June 15, 1878.

VII. Clark Almon Noggle, bn. Apr. 30, 1880.

VII. Anda E. Noggle, bn. July 12, 1882; died June 8, 1884.

VII. Blanche Elma Noggle, bn. Mar. 4, 1884; died June 28, 1885.

VII. Liva Susanna Noggle, bn. Nov. 9, 1885.

VII. Edith May G. Noggle, bn. Oct. 27, 1887.

VII. Malinda Wilhelminia Noggle, bn. July 11, 1890.

VII. Jessie M. Noggle, bn. Dec. 28, 1893.

VI. John W. Pickett, bn. Oct. 6, 1851.

VI. Esther W. Pickett, bn. Sept. 17, 1853; died same day.

VI. Joseph W. Pickett, bn. Oct. 7, 1854.

VI. Mary W. Pickett, bn. July 15, 1856; died Jan. 1, 1888.

VI. Amos W. Pickett, bn. Oct. 4, 1860.

VI. George W. Pickett, bn. Oct. 28, 1862. Mrd. Stella Gill, May 27, 1885. P. O., Corinth, Mich. Farmer. Children: (**VII.**) Fernie E. Pickett, bn. Sept. 25, 1887. (**VII.**) R. Glen Pickett, bn. Oct. 28, 1890.

VI. Jesse W. Pickett, bn. Mar. 6, 1869. P. O., —, Mich. Farmer. S.

V. John Wismer, bn. Aug. 1835. Mrd. Nancy Snyder, Sept. 1856. P. O., Blair, Ont. Farmer. Menn. Children: Benjamin, John, David, Henry, Leah, Nancy, Isaiah.

VI. Benjamin Snyder Wismer, bn. June 10, 1857. Mrd. Catharine Kumpf, Feb. 10, 1879. P. O., Blair, Ont. Farmer. Menn. Children: (**VII.**) Nancy Wismer, bn. Jan. 20, 1880; died May 11, 1880. (**VII.**)

14

Sarah Wismer, bn. Sept. 12, 1881; died Jan. 27, 1891. (VII.) Leah Wismer, bn. Aug. 10, 1883; died Jan. 21, 1891. (VII.) Mary Wismer, bn. Nov. 22, 1885. (VII.) Catharine Wismer, bn. Dec. 28, 1888.

VI. John Wismer, bn. Apr. 1859. Mrd. Susanna Gehman. May 1885. Farmer. Menn.

VI. David Wismer, bn. June 12, 1861. Mrd. Esther Shantz. Oct. 1, 1889. P. O., Blair, Ont. Farmer. Menn. One child: (VII.) David Elton Wismer, bn. Aug. 11, 1890.

VI. Rev. Henry Wismer, bn. Mar. 23, 1863. Mrd. Lucinda Miller, Jan. 3, 1888. P. O., Wyandott, Ont. Minister. Engaged in farming until 1892, when he was appointed as minister to Maryboro Twp., Wellington Co., Ont., Mennonite Bre. in Christ. Children: (VII.) Harold Wismer, bn. May 27, 1891. (VII.) Russel Wismer, bn. Aug. 12, 1893.

VI. Leah Wismer, bn. Jan. 28, 1865. Mrd. John R. Naissmith, Apr. 21, 1891. P. O., Blair, Ont. Farmer. One child: (VII.) John Wismer Naismith, bn. Feb. 3, 1893.

VI. Nancy Wismer, bn. May 1867. Mrd. John Gehman, Oct. 1887. P. O., Freeport, Ont. Farmer. Menn.

VI. Isaiah Wismer, bn. Aug. 1870. Farmer. Menn. S.

V. Henry Wismer, bn. in Waterloo Co., Ont., July 10, 1837. Mrd. Margaret Smith, June 23, 1860. P. O., Amulree, Ont. Farmer. Menn's. Children: Elizabeth, Emma, Ellen, Annie, George, Susan, Henry.

VI. Elizabeth Wismer, bn. in Ont., Jan. 5, 1864. Mrd. George J. Stueck, Feb. 8, 1880. P. O., Hampstead, Ont. Post Master. Mrs. S., Lutheran. Children: (VII.)Maggie A. Stueck, bn. Jan. 21, 1881.(VII.) Albert J. Stueck, bn. Mar. 25, 1884. (VII.) Adeline H. Stueck, bn. Jan. 2, 1886.

VI. Emma Wismer, bn. Dec. 22, 1866. Mrd. Levi Cook, Mar. 2, 1885. P. O., Amulree, Ont. Farmer. Menn's. Children: (VII.) Margaret Ellen Cook, born Oct. 2, 1886; died next day. (VII.) Henry Edward Cook, bn. Dec. 21, 1887. (VII.) Phœbe Ann Cook, bn. Aug. 11, 1889. (VII.) William Cook, bn. May 3, 1890. (VII.) Maggie Cook, bn. Feb. 11, 1893.

VI. Ellen Wismer, bn. Nov. 2, 1869. Mrd. William Cook, Mar. 10, 1887. P. O., Amulree, Ont. Farmer. Lutherans. Children: **(VII.)** Ephraim Cook, bn. Oct. 2, 1888. **(VII.)** Robert Cook, bn. Aug. 15, 1890.

VI. Annie Wismer, bn. Mar. 13, 1873. Luth. S.

VI. George Wismer, bn. July 11, 1876.

VI. Susan Wismer, bn. Nov. 10, 1878; died Apr. 3, 1880.

VI. Henry Wismer, bn. Sept. 26, 1889.

V. Julia Esther Wismer, bn. in Waterloo Co., Ont. Mar. 18, 1840. Mrd. James Webster, Oct. 2, 1855. He was bn. in Renicnmir, Forpershire, Scotland. Miller. Baptists. Children: William, Georgiana, John.

VI. William Alexander Webster, bn. in Waterloo Co., Ont., Mar. 14, 1857. Mrd. Sheloa A. Slipp, Aug. 1879. Res. 111 Moody St., Waltham, Mass. Photographer. Baptists. One child: **(VII.)** William A. Webster, Jr. bn. Sept. 14, 1883.

VI. Georgiana Elizabeth Webster, bn. in Brattleboro, Vt., Oct. 19, 1860; died Mar. 28, 1863.

VI. John Thomas Webster, bn. at Brattleboro, Vt., Feb. 14, 1862. Mrd. Annie L. Francis, Sept. 28, 1888. P. O., Cambridgeport, Mass. Merchant. One child: **(VII.)** J. Russel Webster, bn. Apr. 12, 1891.

III. Barbara Wismer, bn. in Bucks Co., Pa., Mar. 9, 1766; died Jan. 28, 1861, aged 94 years, 10 months and 19 days. Mrd. Joseph Wismer of Hilltown, Pa. He was bn. July 23, 1753; died in Chester Co., Pa., Aug. 30, 1820, aged 67 years, 1 month and 7 days. Went to Canada in 1800. (See page 120.) Children: Elizabeth, Barbara, Catharine, Esther, Henry, Henry, Joseph, Jacob, Mary, Anna.

IV. Elizabeth Wismer, bn. in Bucks Co., Dec. 8, 1782. Mrd. Jacob Ruth. (See page 120.)

IV. Barbara Wismer, bn. in Bucks Co., June 13, 1785. Mrd. Mark Fretz. (See page 122.)

IV. Catharine Wismer, bn. in Bucks Co., Jan. 23, 1787; died Sept. 23, 1859. Mrd. John Althouse. (See page 123.)

IV. Esther Wismer, mrd. John Cressman. (See page 124.)

IV. Henry Wismer, bn. Mar. 11, 1792; died an infant. (See page 128.)

IV. Henry Wismer, bn. Mar. 10, 1794, in Bucks Co.; died in Waterloo Co., Ont., June 11, 1876, aged 82 years, 3 months and 1 day. Mrd. Mary Cressman, —. She was bn. in Montgomery Co., Pa., Aug. 17, 1792; died in Waterloo Co., Ont., July 12, 1872, aged 79 years, 10 months and 25 days. Came to Canada in 1806. Mr. Wismer went to Canada in 1815. Farmer. Menn's. Children: Barbara, Abraham, Daniel, Jacob, Elizabeth, Esther, Mary, Henry. (See page 128.)

V. Barbara Wismer, bn. Oct. 25, 1816; died —. Mrd. David Baer (See page 129.)

V. Abraham Wismer, bn. Sept. 2, 1818; died Sept. 7, 1823.

V. Rev. Daniel Wismer, bn. July 29, 1820. Mrd. Sallie Erb. (See page 128.) She was bn. in Waterloo Co., Ont., Apr. 4, 1823; died in Marion Co., Kans., Oct. 17, 1885. Farmer and minister. Menn's. Children: Noah, Moses, Isaac, Esther, Henry, Lydia, Daniel. — Daniel mrd. second wife widow Lydia Brubaker.

VI. Noah E. Wismer, bn. Dec. 29, 1844; died Apr. 9, 1867.

VI. Moses E. Wismer, bn. Apr. 9, 1846. Mrd. Lena Snider. P. O., Preston. Ont. (See page 128.)

VI. Isaac E. Wismer, bn. Sept. 15, 1847. Mrd. Susanna Snider. P. O., Elmira, Ont.

VI. Esther Wismer. Mrd. John B. Kraft. (See page 128).

VI. Henry E. Wismer, bn. Feb. 18, 1851; died in Marion Co., Kans., Aug. 8, 1887. Mrd. Mary Ann Martin.

VI. Lydia Wismer, bn. in Waterloo Co., Ont., July 14, 1853. Mrd. Samel S. Moyer. P. O., Berlin, Ont. School teacher, Ivory button maker, now bookkeeper. Menn. Bre. in Christ. Children: (VII.) Elmina Moyer, stillborn Feb. 19, 1875. (VII.) Amasa Moyer, bn. Mar. 1, 1876; died Sept. 9, 1877. (VII.) Alvin Moyer, bn. May 14, 1877. (VII.) Daniel Moyer, bn. Feb. 26, 1879. (VII.) Myron Moyer, bn. Apr. 30, 1881. (VII.) Sarah Ann Moyer, bn. Mar. 23, 1883; died —. (VII.) Cora Moyer, bn. Apr. 8, 1887. (VII.) Cella Moyer, bn. May 20, 1890.

VI. Daniel Wismer, bn. in Waterloo Co., Ont., Jan. 31, 1860. Mrd. Theresa Giekel. P. O., Berlin, Ont.

V. Jacob Wismer, bn. Jan. 9, 1822; died Sept. 9, 1823.

V. Elizabeth Wismer, mrd. Moses B. Snyder. (See page 130.)

V. Esther Wismer, mrd. Daniel Shantz. (See page 131.)

V. Mary Wismer, mrd. Abraham S. Cressman. (See page 132.)

V. Henry Wismer, bn. in Waterloo Co., Ont., Aug. 21, 1833; died in Texas, Mar. 15, 1885. Mrd. Hattie, daughter of John Bliehm.

III. Christian Wismer, bn. in Bucks Co., Dec. 17, 1767; died Oct. 11, 1852. Mrd. Mary Rosenberger, —. Farmer. Lived and died in Skippack Twp., Montg. Co. Menn's. Children: Jacob, Abraham, Barbara, Henry, David, Elizabeth, Ann, Mary, Hannah, Christian.

IV. Jacob Wismer, bn. June 10, 1795; died about 1852. Mrd. Mary Detweiler —. Farmer. Mr. W., Baptist, Mrs. W., Menn. Children: Jacob, Christian, Isaac, Henry.

V. Jacob D. Wismer, bn. in Montg. Co., Sept. 28, 1820. Mrd. Catharine Hunsberger, of Chester Co., Pa., Apr. 8, 1845. P. O., Parkers Ford, Pa. Farmer. Mr. W., Meth., Mrs. W., Menn. Children: Benjamin, Mary, Elizabeth, Winfield, Kate, Jacob, Joseph.

VI. Benjamin F. Wismer, bn. Feb. 15, 1846. Mrd. Kate R. Urner of Chester Co., Sept. 28, 1876. P. O., Battle Creek, Mich. Dairyman. Seventh Day Adventists. Children: (VII.) Maggie May Wismer, bn. July 3, 1877. (VII.) Irvin W. S. Wismer, bn. Aug. 18, 1879. (VII.) Ella Bertha Wismer, bn. Feb. 12, 1883; died June 26, 1883. (VII.) Bertha Wismer, died in infancy.

VI. Mary M. Wismer, bn. Feb. 3, 1848. Mrd. John Wagoner, —. P. O., Spring City, Pa. Farmer. Ger. Ref. One child: (**VII.**) Harry Levi Wagoner.

VI. Elizabeth H. Wismer, bn. Apr. 19, 1851. Mrd. William F. Latshaw, —. P. O., Spring City, Pa. Farmer. Menn's. Children: (**VII.**) Harry J. Latshaw. (**VII.**) Willis W. Latshaw. (**VII.**) J. Irvin Latshaw. (**VII.**) Mary Kate Latshaw.

VI. Winfield S. Wismer, bn. July 1, 1852. Mrd. Flora High of Chester Co., Pa., —. P. O., Parkers Ford, Pa. Ger. Bap. Children: (**VII.**) Edgar H. Wismer. (**VII.**) Charles J. Wismer.

VI. Kate R. Wismer, bn. Oct. 14, 1854. P. O., Parkers Ford, Pa. Ger. Bap. S.

VI. Jacob C. Wismer, bn. Dec. 8, 1857. Farmer. S.

VI. Joseph M. Wismer, bn. May 2, 1861. P. O., Parkers Ford, Pa. Farmer. Baptist. S.

V. Christian D. Wismer, bn. —. Mrd. —.

V. Isaac Wismer, bn. —; died —. S.

V. Henry Wismer, bn. —. Mrd. —.

IV. Rev. Abraham Wismer, bn. in Skippack, Montg. Co., Pa., Mar. 15, 1797; died Oct. 15, 1877. Mrd. Susanna Kolb —. She was bn. June 23, 1804; died Feb. 23, 1855. Farmer and minister. He was ordained to the ministry of the Mennonite church, which he served for 38 years, 24 of the 38 years as bishop. Children: Henry, Susanna, David, Abraham.

V. Rev. Henry K. Wismer, bn. Feb. 11, 1823. Mrd. Mary Cole, Oct. 13, 1850. She was bn. May 6, 1826. P. O., Creamery, Pa. Farmer and minister. He was ordained to the ministry of the Mennonite church, June 5, 1883. Children: Abraham, Susan, Catharine, Benjamin, Henry, Elizabeth.

VI. Abraham Wismer, bn. Jan. 20, 1852; died Feb. 28, 1853.

VI. Susan C. Wismer, bn. in Montg. Co., Mar. 28, 1853. Mrd. Joseph C. Gander, son of deacon Joseph Gander, Sept. 2, 1875. He died Oct. 24, 1880. Farmer. Menn's. One child: (**VII.**) Harry W. Gander, bn. Oct. 5, 1878. Susan, mrd. second husband Milton H. Walters, Nov. 11, 1882. P. O., Rudy, Pa. Miller, Justice of the Peace, dealer in real estate, farmer,

and at present time member of the Legislature of Pa.
Mr. W.. Luth., Mrs. W.. Menn. Children: (VII.)
Laura W. Walters, bn. Aug. 21, 1883. (VII.) Howard
W. Walters, bn. Feb. 2, 1885. (VII.) Emma Norman
W. Walters, bn. Oct. 17, 1889.

VI. Catharine Wismer, bn. Sept. 29, 1854; died Dec.
29, 1878.

VI. Benjamin Wismer, bn. Jan. 27, 1856. Mrd.
Hettie Garges, Dec. 11, 1880. P. O., Creamery, Pa.
Farmer. Menn's. Children: (VII.) Mary G. Wismer,
bn. Jan. 15, 1886; died next day. (VII.) Amanda G.
Wismer, bn. May 18, 1889.

VI. Henry Wismer, bn. Sept. 3, 1860; died Apr. 6,
1875.

VI. Elizabeth Wismer, bn. July 4, 1866; died Oct.
21, 1887.

V. Susanna Wismer, bn. —. Mrd. John Bergey.
No issue.

V. David K. Wismer, bn. Oct. 1, 1830. Mrd. Sarah
H. Bergey, Mar. 23, 1856. P. O., Creamery, Pa.
Farmer. Menn's. Children: Elizabeth, Susanna,
Abraham, Joseph, Mary, Sallie, Henry, David,
Jonas, Lydia, Annie, Louisa, Amanda.

VI. Elizabeth B. Wismer, bn. Mar. 1, 1857. Mrd.
Peter Conver. P. O., Elroy, Pa.

VI. Susan B. Wismer, bn. Sept. 15, 1858. Mrd. Samuel Alderfer. P. O., Iron Bridge, Pa.

VI. Abraham B. Wismer, bn. Apr. 10, 1860; died
Oct. 14, 1866.

VI. Joseph B. Wismer, bn. Feb. 9, 1863. Mrd.
Anna Diffenderfer. P. O., Franconia Square, Pa.

VI. Mary Wismer, bn. May 6, 1865; died Apr. 29,
1875.

VI. Sallie B. Wismer, bn. Aug. 18, 1867. Mrd.
Nelus K. Godshall, Dec. 27, 1884. P. O., Creamery,
Pa. Children: (VII.) Lizzie W. Godshall, bn. Dec.
4, 1885. (VII.) Henry W. Godshall, bn. Aug. 15,
1887. (VII.) Lovina W. Godshall, bn. Sept. 18, 1889.
(VII.) Joseph W. Godshall, bn. Feb. 20, 1891; died
Aug. 18, 1891. (VII.) David W. Godshall, bn. Apr.
18, 1892.

VI. Henry B. Wismer, bn. Nov. 9, 1869. Mrd. Lizzie Shatz. P. O., Harleysville, Pa.

VI. David B. Wismer, bn. Feb. 11, 1872. S.

VI. Jonas B. Wismer, bn. Nov. 4, 1873; died Aug. 24, 1874.

VI. Lydia B. Wismer, bn. June 29, 1875.

VI. Annie B. Wismer, bn. Mar. 15, 1877.

VI. Louisa B. Wismer, bn. Feb. 4, 1881.

VI. Amanda B. Wismer, bn. June 17, 1883.

V. Abraham K. Wismer, bn. Jan. 4, 1834. Mrd. Sophia Alleback, in 1855. She died in 1863. P. O., Graters Ford, Pa. Children: Christian, Susan, Abraham, John. —Abraham mrd. second wife Franey R. Landis, in 1866. Farmer. Ch. of God. Children: Mary, Franey, Sophia.

VI. Christian A. Wismer, bn. Nov. 6, 1856. Mrd. Emma E. Fry. daughter of Eli Fry. Dec. 20, 1879. P. O., Graters Ford, Pa. Farmer. Ref. ch. Children: (**VII.**) Eli F. Wismer, bn. July 6, 1885. (**VII.**) Charles' E. Wismer, bn. Dec. 10, 1887.

VI. Susan A. Wismer, bn. Nov. 19, 1858. Mrd. Abraham K. Landis, in 1882. P. O., Graters Ford, Pa. Farmer. River Brethren. Children: (**VII.**) Franie W. Landis, bn. Jan. 7, 1883. (**VII.**) Mary W. Landis, bn. Mar. 14, 1885. (**VII.**) Henry W. Landis, bn. Oct. 16, 1887.

VI. Abraham A. Wismer, bn. May 14, 1861. Mrd. Annie W. Kauffman. Jan. 1, 1885. P. O., Graters Ford, Pa. Farmer. Menn's. Children: (**VII.**) Christian K. Wismer, bn. Oct. 13, 1886. (**VII.**) Ezra K. Wismer, bn. Mar. 1, 1889.

VI. John A. Wismer, bn. Aug. 26, 1863; died in 1864.

VI. Mary L. Wismer, bn. Sept. 17, 1867; died in 1868.

VI. Franie L. Wismer, bn. Dec. 25, 1868.

VI. Sophia L. Wismer, bn. July 30, 1879.

IV. Barbara Wismer, bn. Aug. 12, 1798; died . Mrd. John Conner. —. Moved to Ohio, he died soon after moving there. No issue. Barbara mrd. second husband Abraham Bean . No issue.

IV. Henry Wismer, bn. Aug. 13, 1800; died May 26, 1884. Mrd. Hannah Bean, in 1821. She died Dec. 9, 1824. Children: John, Kate. — Henry mrd. second wife Catharine Detweiler, Oct. 18, 1825. Children: Samuel, Christian, Mary, Anna, Eliza, Barbara, Lydia.

V. John Wismer, bn. Mar. 24, 1822; died May 1, 1889. Mrd. Mary G. Bean, —. She died Nov. 14, 1888. Farmer. Menn. Children: Henry, John, Catharine, Lewis, Emanuel.

VI. Henry B. Wismer, bn. May 20, 1846. Mrd. Mary A. Wireman, Nov. 21, 1867. She was bn. Sept. 8, 1850. P. O., Schwenksville, Pa. Farmer. Mrs. W., Ref. ch. Children: (VII.) John W. Wismer, bn. Oct. 27, 1870. (VII.) Katie W. Wismer, bn. Apr. 21, 1872; died Aug. 4, 1873. (VII.) Lizzie W. Wismer, bn. Dec. 13, 1873. (VII.) Mary W. Wismer, bn. Sept. 3, 1875. (VII.) Harry W. Wismer, bn. Mar. 4, 1877. (VII.) Annie W. Wismer, bn. Aug. 4, 1878. (VII.) Alvin W. Wismer, bn. Jan. 4, 1880; died July 1, 1887. (VII.) Alma W. Wismer, bn. Nov. 19, 1881. (VII.) Jennie W. Wismer, bn. Mar. 19, 1883. (VII.) Flora W. Wismer, bn. Oct. 10, 1884. (VII.) Willie W. Wismer, bn. Jan. 30, 1885. (VII.) Alice W. Wismer, bn. Mar. 18, 1886; died Oct. 20, 1887. (VII.) Ella W. Wismer, bn. Sept. 1, 1889.

VI. John B. Wismer, born Feb. 1, 1849. Married Amanda B. Kratz, Mar. 2, 1876. She died Aug. 10, 1886. P. O., Linfield, Pa. Merchant miller. Menn. Children: (VII.) Irvin K. Wismer, bn. Oct. 19, 1877. (VII.) Warren K. Wismer, bn. June 12, 1879. (VII.) Hannah K. Wismer, bn. Jan. 6, 1882.

VI. Catharine B. Wismer, bn. Sept. 24, 1851. Mrd. James T. Grater, Jan. 11, 1873. He died June 20, 1883. P. O., Grater's Ford, Pa. Farmer. Menn. Children: (VII.) Mary W. Grater, bn. May 27, 1874. (VII.) Sarah W. Grater, bn. Apr. 3, 1876; died Mar. 14, 1878. (VII.) Sylvester W. Grater, bn. Aug. 3, 1878. (VII.) Catharine W. Grater, bn. Aug. 8, 1880. (VII.) James W. Grater, bn. Mar. 12, 1883; died Sept. 21, 1883.

VI. Lewis B. Wismer, bn. Nov. 9, 1853. Mrd. Alice E. Fry, Jan. 29, 1881. She was bn. May 18, 1859. P. O., Collegeville, Pa. Practical slater. Ref. ch. Children: **(VII.)** Ralph F. and Anna Wismer, (twins), bn. Nov. 29, 1881. **(VII.)** Mary F. Wismer, bn. Aug. 11, 1884. **(VII.)** Herbert F. Wismer, bn. Nov. 20, 1888; died Aug. 16, 1889. **(VII.)** Lillian F. Wismer, bn. Nov. 20, 1888; died Aug. 3, 1889.

V. Catharine Wismer, bn. Mar. 24, 1822; died Oct. 4, 1867. Mrd. John Gashow, Nov. 24, 1846. Children: Mary, Henry, Catharine, Sarah, John, Frances, Elizabeth, Samuel, Willie, Hannah.

VI. Mary Ann W. Gashow, bn. June 17, 1848; died Feb. 22, 1890. Mrd. Horace U. Rosenberger, July 24, 1869. He died Feb. 18, 1890. Children: **(VII.)** Harry G. Rosenberger, bn. July 24, 1870; died Sept. 29, 1870. **(VII.)** John G. Rosenberger, bn. Mar. 15, 1873. **(VII.)** Horace G. Rosenberger, bn. Feb. 18, 1875. **(VII.)** Franklin G. Rosenberger, bn. Apr. 15, 1882; died July 18, 1884. **(VII.)** William G. Rosenberger, bn. Feb. 11, 1886.

VI. Henry W. Gashow, bn. Dec. 16, 1850. Mrd. Catharine C. Rosenberger, Sept. 30, 1876. She was bn. June 10, 1854. Children: **(VII.)** Elizabeth R. Gashow, bn. Jan. 24, 1879. **(VII.)** Landes R. Gashow, bn. Feb. 27, 1881. **(VII.)** Mamie R. Gashow, bn. June 15, 1886.

VI. Catharine W. Gashow, bn. Feb. 12, 1852. Mrd. Robert Goodman. Children: **(VII.)** John G. Goodman, bn. Dec. 27, 1875. **(VII.)** Martha G. Goodman, bn. Jan. 14, 1877. **(VII.)** Annie G. Goodman, bn. Oct. 20, 1878. **(VII.)** Daniel G. Goodman, bn. Dec. 10, 1879. **(VII.)** Mary G. Goodman, bn. July 29, 1881; died Aug. 5, 1881. **(VII.)** Sallie G. Goodman, bn. Nov. 21, 1882. **(VII.)** Robert G. Goodman, bn. Nov. 2, 1884. **(VII.)** Susanna G. Goodman, bn. Nov. 1, 1886. **(VII.)** Harrison G. Goodman, bn. Nov. 4, 1888. **(VII.)** Clementine G. Goodman, bn. Aug. 30, 1890.

VI. Sarah W. Gashow, bn. Sept. 24, 1854. Mrd. Henry C. Moyer, Feb. 12, 1876. P. O., Sellersville, Pa. Children: **(VII.)** John G. Moyer, bn. Oct. 3, 1877. **(VII.)** Henry G. Moyer, bn. July 7, 1879. **(VII.)**

Ellen Norah Moyer, bn. July 29, 1881. **(VII.)** Leidy
G. Moyer, bn. Nov. 16, 1883. **(VII.)** Anna Mary
Moyer, bn. Oct. 30, 1885. **(VII.)** Franklin G. Moyer,
bn. Sept. 28, 1890.

VI. John W. Gashow, bn. June 6, 1856. Mrd. Kate
F. Nice, Nov. 12, 1881. Children: **(VII.)** Abraham N.
Gashow, bn. Oct. 24, 1882. **(VII.)** Henry N. Gashow,
bn. Dec. 2, 1885.

VI. Frances W. Gashow, bn. Dec. 16, 1857; died
Jan. 15, 1858.

VI. Elizabeth W. Gashow, bn. Sept. 3, 1859. Mrd.
Henry C. Godshall, Nov. 30, 1878. Children: **(VII.)**
Mary G. Godshall, bn. July 16, 1880. **(VII.)** Harry
G. Godshall, bn. July 7, 1882. **(VII.)** Abraham G.
Godshall, bn. July 14, 1887. **(VII.)** John G. Godshall,
bn. May 25, 1889.

VI. Samuel W. Gashow, bn. May 8, 1861. Mrd.
Carrie Shearer, Feb. 13, 1886. P. O., Perkasie, Pa.
Mr. G., Ref. Mrs. G., Luth. ch. One child: **(VII.)**
William Henry Gashow, bn. Sept. 22, 1890.

VI. Willie W. Gashow, bn. Feb. 14, 1863.

VI. Hannah W. Gashow, bn. Dec. 2, 1864. Mrd.
Alfred S. Moyer, Sept. 15, 1887. He died Nov. 6,
1889. One child: **(VII.)** Irvin Enos G. Moyer, bn.
Feb. 20, 1889. Hannah mrd. second husband Irving
H. Swink, Aug. 19, 1891.

V. Samuel Wismer, bn. July 16, 1826. Mrd. Sarah
Allebach, —. Children: Sarah, Kate.

VI. Sarah A. Wismer, bn. —. Mrd. Jacob Kistner.
P. O., Hatfield, Pa. Children: **(VII.)** Elizabeth W.
Kistner, bn. Apr. 27, 1872; died Nov. 5, 1873. **(VII.)**
Henry W. Kistner, bn. Feb. 8, 1874; died Nov. 2,
1875. **(VII.)** Catharine W. Kistner, bn. Sept. 11,
1875. **(VII.)** Isaac W. Kistner, bn. Apr. 10, 1878.
(VII.) Lydia W. Kistner, bn. Oct. 10, 1880. **(VII.)**
Samuel W. Kistner, bn. Oct. 16, 1887.

VI. Kate A. Wismer, bn. - ; died . S.

V. Christian Wismer, born Jan. 5, 1829. Mrd.
Sarah Cole, Dec. 25, 1852. She was bn. Apr. 11,
1832; died Mar. 9, 1881. P. O., Trappe, Pa. Farmer.
Lives on the homestead. Menn's. Children: Benjamin, Henry, Abraham, Catharine, Mary, Christian.

VI. Benjamin Wismer. bn. May 21, 1854; died Mar. 2, 1855.

VI. Henry Wismer, bn. Oct. 5, 1856. Mrd. Ella Grimley. P. O., Trappe, Pa. Farmer. Children: **(VII.)** Gideon Wismer, bn. Feb. 5, 1880 **(VII.)** Bertha Wismer, bn. Mar. 1, 1881. **(VII.)** Harry Wismer, bn. Mar. 3, 1882. **(VII.)** Christian Wismer, bn. Sept. 4, 1889.

VI. Abraham C. Wismer, bn. Nov. 25, 1858. Mrd. Harriet Kepler. —. P. O., Senatoga, Pa. Farmer. Luth. No issue.

VI. Catharine C. Wismer, bn. May 3, 1861. Mrd. Jacob Custer, —. P. O., Trappe. Farmer. Menn's. One child: **(VII.)** Royal Custer.

VI. Mary Ann Wismer, bn. Sept. 16, 1865. Mrd. Wayne S. Heebener, —. P. O., Norritonville, Pa. Farmer. Schwenkfelder. One child: **(VII.)** Grace Heebener.

VI. Christian C. Wismer, bn. Jan. 3, 1872.

V. Mary Wismer, bn. Sept. 22, 1830; died Mar. 13, 1882. Mrd. Henry B. Cassel, Nov. 25, 1849. Children: **(VI.)** Elizabeth Cassel, bn. Feb. 24, 1852. P. O., Creamery, Pa. S. **(VI.)** Catharine Cassel, bn. Mar. 4, 1857; died Aug. 9, 1857.

V. Anna Wismer, bn. Oct. 26, 1831. Mrd. Joseph R. Fry, Oct. 8, 1853. He died June 11, 1890. Moved to Ill., Apr. 1857. P. O., Sterling, Ill. Ch. of Christ. Children: John, Matilda, Emily, Martha, Josephine, Henry.

VI. John W. Fry, bn. Oct. 14, 1855. Mrd. Laura O'Hara, Aug. 11, 1886. Ch. of Christ. One child.

VI. Matilda W. Fry, bn. Nov. 24, 1856. Mrd. Orlando S. Bare, Nov. 26, 1874. Ch. of Christ. Children: **(VII.)** John Abram Bare, bn. Dec. 6, 1875. **(VII.)** Anna Mary Bare, bn. Apr. 29, 1877. **(VII.)** Verna Luella Bare, bn. Nov. 15, 1878. **(VII.)** Joseph O. Bare, bn. Mar. 12, 1880; died Apr. 17, 1880. **(VII.)** Agnes Evaline Bare, bn. Apr. 8, 1887. **(VII.)** Orlando Smith Bare, bn. Dec. 15, 1890.

VI. Emily W. Fry, bn. Dec. 7, 1858. Mrd. Elon G. Babcock, Sept. 1884. Ch. of Christ. Children: **(VII.)**

Clarence Lewis Babcock, bn. May 22, 1886. (VII.)
Mattie Celesta Babcock, bn. Aug. 9, 1887.

VI. Martha W. Fry, bn. Apr. 16, 1861. P. O., Sterling, Ill. Ch. of Christ. S.

VI. Josephine W. Fry, bn. Oct. 10, 1863; died May 22, 1864.

VI. Henry W. Fry, bn. June 22, 1866. Ch. of Christ. S.

V. Elizabeth Wismer, bn. Dec. 22, 1832; died —. Mrd. Jacob Detweiler, —. He died —. No issue.

V. Barbara Wismer, bn. Apr. 30, 1834. Mrd. Joseph B. Kreamer, Dec. 14, 1861. Children: Jacob, Catharine, Franklin, Mary, Ella, Anna, William, Elmer, Emma, Lizzie, Agnes.

VI. Jacob W. Kreamer, bn. Feb. 28, 1863. Mrd. Ellen F. Royer, Dec. 20, 1884. Children: (**VII.**) Harry R. Kreamer, bn. Dec. 5, 1885. (**VII.**) Elamina R. Kreamer, bn. Aug. 7, 1887. (**VII.**) Jeremiah R. Kreamer, bn. June 27, 1889. (**VII.**) Laura R. Kreamer, bn. May 23, 1891.

VI. Catharine W. Kreamer, bn. Dec. 26, 1864. Mrd. John N. Frey. Ref. ch. One child: (**VII.**) Frank Herman Frey, bn. Feb. 9, 1891.

VI. Franklin W. Kreamer, bn. Mar. 29, 1866; died Mar. 30, 1868.

VI. Ella Kreamer, bn. Oct. 16, 1867.

VI. Mary Kreamer, bn. Oct. 16, 1867; (twin) died next day.

VI. Anna W. Kreamer, bn. Apr. 14, 1869. Mrd. Adam S. Keonig. Children: (**VII.**) Martha May K. Keonig, bn. May 1, 1887. (**VII.**) John K. Keonig, bn. Apr. 3, 1889. (**VII.**) William Henry Keonig, bn. Apr. 30, 1870. (**VII.**) Elmer W. Keoning, born Sept. 3, 1871. (**VII.**) Emma W. Keonig, bn. May 11, 1873. (**VII**) Lizzie W. Keonig, bn. Feb. 16, 1875. (**VII.**) Agnes W. Keonig, bn. Mar. 16, 1876.

V. Lydia D. Wismer, bn. Oct. 17, 1835. Mrd. Isaac A. Landis, Oct. 17, 1863. He was bn. Dec. 20, 1838. P. O., Providence Square, Pa. Farmer. Children: (**VI.**) Kate W. Landis, bn. Sept. 5, 1864; died June 2, 1884. Mrd. John H. Zetty, Nov. 3, 1883. No issue. (**VI.**) Mary W. Landis, bn. Aug. 22, 1866. Mrd.

Wilson M. Underkoffler, Jan. 12, 1889. Machinist.
(VI.) Daniel W. Landis, bn. Mar. 5, 1869. Mrd.
Maggie Heck, July 25, 1891. (VI.) Lizzie W. Landis,
bn. Feb. 20, 1876.

V. Henry Wismer, bn. Feb. 17, 1838; died Aug. 29,
1838.

IV. David Wismer, bn. Apr. 5, 1802; died Sept.
1876. Mrd. Hannah Shutt. —. Farmer. River
Brethren. Children: Joseph, Maria, Sarah, Hannah.
Daniel, Hester.

V. Joseph S. Wismer, bn. —. Mrd. Mary Tyson.
P. O.. Creamery, Pa. Farmer. Children: Salome,
David, Joseph, Barbara, Amos.

VI. Salome Wismer, bn. —. S.

VI. David Wismer, bn. —. Mrd. Mary Kulp, —.
P. O., Norristown, Pa. One child: (VII.) Russel Wismer.

VI. Joseph T. Wismer, bn. —. Mrd. Mary F.
Kratz. —.

VI. Barbara Wismer, bn. —. S.

VI. Amos Wismer, bn. S.

V. Maria Wismer, bn. —; died —. Mrd. Jacob Ruth,
—. Children: (VI.) Malinda. (VI.) Ambrose. (VI.)
Michael.

V. Sarah Wismer, bn. —. S.

V. Hannah Wismer, bn. —. Mrd. David Lenhart,
—. Farmer. River Brethren. P. O.. Silver Spring,
Lancaster Co., Pa. Children: (VI.) Lizzie. S. (VI.)
Abraham. S.

V. Daniel Wismer, bn. —. Mrd. Augustine Humsberger, —. Shoemaker and groceryman. Children:
(VI.) Louisa. (VI.) Alice. (VI.) Willie. (VI.) Mary.

V. Hester Wismer, bn. —; died —. Mrd. Henry
FitzGerald, —. Six children, died young.

IV. Elizabeth Wismer, bn. Apr. 14. 1804; died, single, aged 80 years.

IV. Ann Wismer, bn. June 14, 1808; died —. Mrd.
Michael Bean, —. Farmer. Menn's. One child:

V. Henry Bean, bn. —. Mrd. Sarah Schantz, —.
P. O., Center Square, Pa. Farmer. Children: (VI.)
Annie. (VI.) George.

IV. Mary Wismer, bn. Apr. 21, 1810; died single.

IV. Hannah Wismer, bn. June 13, 1814; died small.
IV. Christian Wismer, bn. Apr. 13, 1817. Mrd.
Mary Cassel, Dec. 3, 1837. She was bn. Apr. 24,
1814. Retired farmer. Mr. Wismer is a man of venerable appearance, who with his wife have been faithful members of the River Brethren church at Lawndale, Pa., for many years. About 30 years ago he
was ordained deacon, and in the faithful discharge of
his religious duties it has been his chief joy to see his
beloved Zion prosper in the Lord, while his patriarchal appearance, and presence in Zion is a source
of inspiration to his fellow laborers in the Master's
cause. In old age he is still abundant in labors for
his Redeemer, and a crown awaits him beyond. "Let
me die the death of the righteous, and let my last end
be like his." Children: Susanna, Sarah, Elizabeth,
Jacob, Mary, Joel, David.
V. Susanna Wismer, bn. July 24, 1839. Mrd. David
Ruth, Nov. 1864. P. O., Lawndale, Pa. Mason. Ev.
Ass'n. Children: Christian, Mary, Sallie, Lizzie.
VI. Rev. Christian W. Ruth, bn. Sept. 1, 1865. Mrd.
Emma J. Springer, of Indianapolis, Ind., Sept. 19,
1885. Res. 305 S. Penna. St., Indianapolis, Ind.

Mr. Ruth lived with his grandfather, Christian
Wismer, on the farm for several years; he then went
to live with his uncle Jacob Wismer, who was a merchant and tailor, remaining until 1882, when he went
to learn the printing trade in the office of John G.
Stauffer, of Quakertown, Pa. After serving his apprenticeship, he was recommended as being competent
of taking charge of an office, and accordingly was
employed as foreman of a printing office in Indianapolis, Ind., Apr. 1, 1884.

In July 1884 at the age of 18 years he received local preacher's license, and began preaching. In the fall
of this year he resigned his position as foreman of the
printing office, and began to travel as an evangelist or revivalist on the interdenominational line, laboring in any
church where called. He is a member of the "Heavenly Recruit Association" church, for which denomination he has established some churches in Indiana.
He was ordained, and received Elder's license in July

1889, but by request continued as an evangelist. Up to date he has conducted revival services in thirteen states, and all through the Province of Ontario. Since 1884 he has traveled about 8,000 miles annually. In revival work he has been eminently successful. He has not attempted a revival at any place where he has continued a week or more, without some converts, and he has frequently conducted revivals where more than a hundred were converted in a few weeks. Children: (VII.) Emma Naomi Ruth, bn. Nov. 26, 1886. (VII.) George Christian Ruth, bn. Nov. 28, 1888. (VII.) Raymond Reber Ruth, bn. Jan. 1, 1891.

VI. Mary Ruth, bn. July 19, 1868. Mrd. Nathan Ivan Hunsberger. He was bn. May 15, 1868. P. O., Lawndale, Pa. Farmer. Ev. Ass'n. One child: (VII.) Walter R. Hunsberger, bn. June 7, 1890.

VI. Sallie Ruth, bn. May 1871. Mrd. Harvey K. Bishop, July, 1890. P. O., Benjamin, Pa., Ev. Ass'n.

VI. Lizzie Ruth, bn. Jan. 12, 1879. Ev. Ass'n. S.

V. Sarah Wismer, bn. June 25, 1841. River Brethren ch. S.

V. Elizabeth Wismer, bn. June 11, 1843. Mrd. Henry Allabough, Oct. 11, 1866. P. O., Lawndale, Pa. Laborer. Children: (VI.) David W. Allabough, bn. May 13, 1869. S. (VI.) William W. Allabough, bn. Feb. 25, 1871. S. (VI.) Mary W. Allabough, bn. July 14, 1873. S.

V. Jacob C. Wismer, bn. Aug. 11, 1848. Mrd. Catharine Stout, Oct. 30, 1873. P. O., Lawndale, Pa. Mr. Wismer was educated principally in the common schools, and attended Ursines College two terms. He resides at Lawndale, where he has an establishment manufacturing clothing doing a business of about $50,000 annually. Children: (VI.) Joel Wismer, bn. May 23, 1875; died Mar. 7, 1877. (VI.) Charles Wismer, bn. Jan. 6, 1878. (VI.) William Wismer, bn. May 28, 1879. (VI.) Catharine S. Wismer, bn. Sept. 9, 1892.

V. Mary Wismer, bn. Oct. 17, 1850; died Sept. 14, 1866.

V. Joel Wismer, bn. Jan. 7, 1853. Mrd. B. Shelly, Jan. 29, 1876. P. O., Lawndale, Pa. Farmer. River

Brethren. Children: (VI.) Jacob Wismer, bn. Jan. 9, 1877. (VI.) Sallie Wismer, bn. Oct. 10, 1879; died Jan. 20, 1883. (VI.) Matilda Wismer, bn. Dec. 7, 1883. (VI.) Christian Wismer, bn. Nov. 6, 1887; burned to death Oct. 29, 1888. (VI.) Anna Mary Wismer, bn. Mar. 17, 1889.

V. David C. Wismer, bn. Mar. 25, 1857. Mrd. Annie R. Roberts, Sept. 19, 1878. She was bn. Dec. 19, 1859. P. O., Quakertown, Pa. Machinist, dealer in machinery, and mechanical engineer. Atheist, Freethinker. Children: (VI.) Edwin R. Wismer, bn. July 10, 1879. (VI.) Joel R. Wismer, bn. Mar. 20, 1881. (VI.) Horace Darion R. Wismer, bn. May 20, 1884. (VI.) Leroy R. Wismer, bn. Sept. 30, 1887. (VI.) Walter R. Wismer, bn. Feb. 23, 1890. (VI.) Pearl Olivia R. Wismer, bn. Nov. 13, 1891.

III. Esther Wismer, bn. in Bucks Co., Oct. 19, 1771; died Apr. 22, 1852. Mrd. John Funk —, 1791. He was born about 1771; died in Hilltown Twp., in 1819, aged 48 years. Farmer. Menn's. Children: Michael, Samuel, Jacob, John, Abraham, Joseph, Mary, Barbara, Catharine, Elizabeth, Anna, and one drowned in a tanner's vat.

IV. Michael Funk, bn. July 1, 1793; died Feb. 22, 1878. Mrd. —, daughter of Abraham Hunsberger, —. She died —. Children: Abraham, Magdalena, Elizabeth, Catharine. — Michael mrd. second wife —, daughter of Lawrence Hipple, Sen. Weaver, farmer, sawyer, near Campden, Ont. Menn's.

V. Abraham Funk, bn. —; died in 1847. Mrd. Barbara Fretz in 1844. She was bn. in Lincoln Co., Ont., Jan. 15, 1824; died in 1847. Farmer. Menn's. Children: Mary, Jacob.

VI. Mary Funk, bn. Dec. 28, 1844. Mrd. Isaac G. Hunsberger, Apr. 14, 1863. He was bn. Sept. 13, 1841. P. O., South Cayuga, Ont. Farmer. Menn's. Children: Annie, Rosetta, Jacob, John.

VII. Annie Maria Hunsberger, bn. Nov. 6, 1864. Mrd. Henry Huber, Jan. 10, 1886. Farmer. Ev. Ass'n. Children: (VIII.) Burness Huber, bn. Mar. 10,

1887. (VIII.) Clara Elizabeth Huber, bn. Sept. 21, 1888.

VII. Rosetta Hunsberger, bn. Jan. 13, 1872; died May 13, 1877.

VII. Jacob Hunsberger, bn. Dec. 1, 1876. Ev. Ass'n.

VII. John Elmer Hunsberger, bn. Dec. 5, 1878.

VI. Jacob Funk, bn. Oct. 26, 1846; died Feb. 20, 1885. Mrd. Dinah Housberger, Nov. 26, 1867. Farmer. Menn's. Children: (VII.) William H. Funk. (VII.) Arthur James Funk. (VII.) Sarah Jane Funk. (VII.) Aggie Mabel Funk. (VII.) John Franklin Funk. (VII.) Mary Elizabeth Funk. (VII.) Joseph Funk, (dee'd).

V. Magdalena Funk, bn. —. Mrd. John Houser, —.

V. Elizabeth Funk, bn. —. Mrd. —.

V. Catharine Funk, bn. —. Mrd. Michael Morter.

IV. Samuel Funk, bn. Apr. 14, 1795; died Nov. 9, 1871. Mrd. Edith Benner, daughter of Sabastian Benner, of Franconia Twp., Pa., in 1824. She was bn. Dec. 13, 1786; died Mar. 25, 1860. Carpet and linen weaver. Lived near Blooming Glen, Pa. Menn's. One child:

V. John Funk, bn, Apr. 17, 1826. Mrd. Mary Fretz, daughter of Abraham Fretz, of Hilltown, Pa., Oct. 17, 1852. She was bn. Oct. 1, 1823. P. O., Telford, Pa. Farmer, tailor. Menn's. Children: (VI.) Susanna Funk, bn. Sept. 27, 1860; died same day. (VI.) Samuel F. Funk, bn. Dec. 11, 1861; died Jan. 24, 1881. Operator. Menn.

IV. Jacob Funk, bn. in Springfield Twp., Bucks Co., Dec. 16, 1796; died Sept. 4, 1875. Mrd. Margaret Haldeman. She died Aug. 17, 1829. Children: Mary, Catharine.—Jacob mrd. second wife, Susanna Fretz, daughter of Martin Fretz of Hilltown Twp., Dec. 9, 1830. She was bn. Mar. 23, 1802; died Feb. 4, 1890, aged 87 ys., 10 mos., 11 ds. Mason, bricklayer and farmer. Menn's. Children: Margaret, Esther, John, Sarah, Abraham, Jacob, Susan.

V. Mary Ann Funk, bn. in Hilltown Twp., Bucks Co., Oct. 5, 1821. Mrd. Jacob Beidler, Apr. 23, 1844. Residence Chicago, Ill. Presby. Children: Joseph,

Augustus, William, Francis, Emma. John, David, George.

VI. Joseph Beidler, bn. Sept. 12, 1845; died Oct. 22, 1845.

VI. Augustus F. Beidler, bn. Oct. 5, 1848. Mrd. Mary Louise Hannah, Oct. 16, 1890. Res. Hinsdale, Ill. Dealer in real estate in Chicago, Ill. Congregational. One child: **(VII.)** Augustus Hannah Beidler.

VI. William Henry Beidler, bn. Jan. 20, 1851. Mrd. Ada M. Gregory, July 5, 1877. Lumberman in Chicago, Ill. Episcopalian. Children: **(VII.)** William Henry Beidler, bn. Dec. 24, 1880; died Aug. 7, 1881. **(VII.)** Walter Gregory Beidler, bn. June 10, 1883; died Apr. 10, 1884.

VI. Francis Beidler, bn. Oct. 18, 1854. Mrd. Elizabeth M. Loose, Mar. 8, 1893. Lumber dealer in Chicago, Ill. Presby.

VI. Emma Beidler, bn. Feb. 28, 1857. Mrd. Arthur B. Camp, Oct. 5, 1887. Res. Chicago, Ill. Presby. Children: **(VII.)** Mary Beidler Camp. **(VII.)** Jay Beidler Camp.

VI. John Beidler, bn. Dec. 16, 1859; died July 22, 1881. Presby.

VI. David Beidler, bn. Apr. 13, 1862. Res. San Francisco, Cal. Collector.

VI. George Beidler, bn. Oct. 28, 1864. Real estate business, Chicago, Ill.

V. Catharine Funk, bn. in Bucks Co., Mar. 25, 1824. Mrd. George Swartley, Nov. 8, 1842. He was bn. in 1820. P. O., Colmar, Pa. Farmer. Menn's. Children: Oliver, Mary, Jacob.

VI. Oliver Swartley, bn. in 1845; died in 1853.

VI. Mary Swartley, bn. Feb. 24, 1852. Mrd. Francis P. Sheip, Oct. 21, 1873. P. O., Colmar, Pa. Farmer. Ger. Ref. Children· **(VII.)** Alma E. Sheip, bn. Mar. 29, 1875. **(VII.)** Arthur B. Sheip, bn. Dec. 22, 1876.

VI. Jacob F. Swartley, bn. 1855. Mrd. Sarah M. Geil, Nov. 6, 1888. She was bn. May 9, 1861. P. O., New Britain, Pa. Farmer. One child: **(VII.)** Catharine Swartley.

V. Margaret Funk, bn. Oct. 15, 1831; died Nov. 22, 1857. Mrd. Benjamin Frick, in 1853. Menn's. One child: **(VI.)** Samuel F. Frick, bn. July 27, 1856. Mrd. Lizzie Thierolf, June 13, 1891. P. O., Fricks, Penna.

V. Esther Funk, bn. July 1, 1833. Mrd. John L. Frick, in 1854. He died in 1880. Merchant and builder. Meth. Ep. Children: **(VI.)** Elizabeth, (deceased). **(VI.)** Jacob F., printer with Mennonite Publishing Co., Elkhart, Ind.; died at his home in Phila., Apr. 15, 1882. **(VI.)** Joel, printer in Philadelphia; died at his home July 6, 1881. **(VI.)** Edward, (dec'd). **(VI.)** Emma E. **(VI.)** Charles E.

V. John Fretz Funk, bn. in Hilltown Twp., Bucks Co., Pa., Apr. 6, 1835. He worked on the farm as soon as old enough, going to school in the winter season until he was in his nineteenth year (1854), when he commenced teaching in his native township, and taught during the winter for three successive winters. He also attended school at Freeland Seminary three months during the summer of 1855, and again in 1856. In the spring of 1857, after closing his school at Chestnut Ridge S. H., in Hilltown township, he went to Chicago, Ill., and engaged in the lumber business, in which he continued nine years. In the winter of 1859-60 he became a member of the Mennonite church at Line Lexington, Bucks Co., Pa. In January of 1864 he commenced the publication of the *Herald of Truth* and *Der Herold der Wahrheit*, and on the 19th of the same month was married to Salome Kratz, daughter of Jacob Kratz of Hilltown, Bucks Co., Penna. She was born on the 30th of August 1839. On the 28th of May 1865, he was ordained to the ministry in the Mennonite church near Gardner, Grundy Co., Ill. In April 1867 he removed to Elkhart, Ind., and established there the business house now known as the "Mennonite Publishing Company," first under his own name, and afterwards under the firm name of John F. Funk and Brother, after having associated with himself his brother Abraham K. Funk, and continued the business under this firm name until May 14, 1875, when the Mennonite Publishing Co., was organized. On the 6th of June 1892 he was chosen and ordained to the office of bishop

over six congregations including Elkhart, Yellow
Creek, Holdeman's, Olive, Salem and Nappanee dis-
tricts in Elkhart Co., Ind. Children: (VI.) Martha
Funk, bn. in Chicago, Ill. (VI.) Susan Mary, bn. and
died in Chicago, Ill. (VI.) Phœbe Funk, bn. in Elkhart,
Ind. Mrd. Abram B. Kolb, Jan. 3, 1893. He was
born near Berlin, Waterloo Co., Ont. Editor of
Herald of Truth and *Words of Cheer.* (VI.) Rebecca,
(dec'd). (VI.) Grace Anna, (dec'd). (VI.) John Edwin,
(dec'd).

V. Sarah Funk, bn. in Hilltown Twp., Bucks Co.,
Apr. 24, 1837; died Aug. 20, 1839.

V. Abraham Kratz Funk, bn. in Hilltown, Bucks
Co., Jan. 20, 1840. His early years were spent on his
father's farm. He attended school about four months
usually in the winter, and a month or two during the
summer. He commenced teaching in the public
schools of the county, at the age of 18, under the
county superintendency of Wm. H. Johnson. He attended school at Freeland Seminary, at Freeland, now
Collegeville, Montgomery Co., in 1859, and the Excelsior Normal Institute, at Carversville, Bucks Co.,
in 1861. After spending five years in farming during
the summer and teaching in winter, he went to Chicago, Ill., in the spring of 1863 and engaged in the
Lumber business. After a residence of five years in
Chicago, he went to Elkhart, and there entered into
a co-partnership with his brother, under the firm
name of John F. Funk and Brother, as publishers and
booksellers. They continued the publication of the
Herald of Truth and *Der Herold der Wahrheit,* and
also issued during the continuance of this co-partnership a number of religious works, the most important
of which was the great book of martyrs, in the German language, containing over 1100 quarto pages,
and the complete works of Menno Simon, which was
translated from the Holland and printed in English.
In 1875 he became one of the principal stockholders
in the Mennonite Publishing Co., which was then organized, and has since held the position of secretary
and treasurer of that institution. He married Annie

M. Landis, daughter of Joseph and Mary (Geil) Landis, of Greer's Corner, near Dublin, Bucks Co., Pa., Mar. 11, 1872. Mennonites. Children: (VI.) Mary Maude. (VI.) Edna Josephine. (VI.) Esther Winifred.

V. Jacob Silas Funk was bn. in Hilltown Twp., Bucks Co., Pa., Apr. 13, 1842. He spent his early days on his father's farm, and received, as was customary in those days, a fair, common school education. He afterwards, during the early part of 1862 and the summer of 1863, spent two terms at the Excelsior Normal Institute, at Carversville, Bucks Co. He taught in the schools of his native county, from 1862 to 1865. In the spring of 1865 he gave up that vocation and went to Chicago, Ill., and engaged in the lumber business. On the 28th of Sept., of the same year he purchased a scholarship in the Eastman Business College of that city, and took a commercial course, attending evenings only. After four years' residence in Chicago, he determined to engage in business for himself, and accordingly, in the spring of 1869, located at Chillicothe, Mo., where he opened a lumber yard and commenced business on his own account. On the 15th of January following (1870), he was married to Annie K. Stover, daughter of Jonas Stover, of E. Rockhill Twp., Bucks Co., Pa. He afterwards became connected with the North Western Lumber Co., who had their mills at Eau Claire, Wisconsin, and extensive yards at Hannibal, Mo ; and on the 20th of April 1880 moved with his family from Chillicothe to Hannibal. Afterwards when the duties of his position required him to be mostly in the neighborhood where the mills of the company were located, he found it more economical and convenient to have his family in that vicinity also, and accordingly, on the 20th of July 1885, he removed to Minneapolis, Minn. He continued with the above firm eleven years, during which time he gained with them the highest esteem and respect, both for his conscientious business integrity and his excellent qualifications for the work in which he was engaged. In the spring of 1890 he severed his relations with the N. W. Lumber

Co., but the warm feeling of esteem and respect which he had won for himself during these extended business relations continued to the end of his life.

He took an active part in the various civil, social and religious movements of the day, and was always ready and willing to assist in all enterprises of public interest, and held continuously positions of responsibility and honor. Soon after his removal to Chillicothe, in 1869, he was elected superintendent of the Sunday-school of the Presbyterian church of that city, which position he held until his removal to Hannibal in 1880. He was converted and united with the Third Presbyterian church of Chicago during the time of his residence there. In 1871 or 72 he was elected elder of the First Presbyterian church of Chillicothe. He was secretary of the school board of that city, and through his influence was built the beautiful new school building, costing from $45,000 to $50,000. In 1875 he was also member of the city council. During the last three years of his residence in Chillicothe he was correspondent of the *Globe Democrat*, a republican paper of St. Louis. During the summer of 1890, after severing his connection with the N. W. L. Co., he, with A. Fiero, was appointed, by the lumber manufacturers of the N. W., to inspect the system of grading employed by the leading manufacturers of the north-west, and their report was received with much favor and satisfaction. After the completion of this commission, he became connected with the T. B. Scott Lumber Co., of Merrill, Wis., and during a business trip through Illinois and Indiana, he was taken sick with a severe bilious attack, and after nearly a week of suffering in hotels, in Terre Haute, Ind., Chicago. Ill.. and on the road, he reached his home in Minneapolis. Minn.. on the 22d of September. The disease assumed a complicated form which resulted in blood poisoning, and after three weeks more of intense suffering, which he bore with patience, he died on the 15th of Oct. 1890, aged 48 y., 6 m., 2 d. Presbyterians. Children: **(VI.)** Emma Laura Funk, bn. Mar. 30, 1871; died Oct. 16, 1872. **(VI)** Frederick Stover Funk, bn. Jan. 26, 1873; died Mar. 20, 1877.

(VI.) Gertrude Elizabeth Funk, bn. Feb. 25, 1877.
(VI.) Susan Anna Funk, bn. Jan. 29, 1885.
V. Susan Elizabeth Funk, bn. May 4, 1846. Mrd.
Henry W. Gross, June 17, 1875, son of Joseph N.
Gross. Mr. Gross is a graduate of the Millersville,
Pa., State Normal school, having graduated in June
1873. At the time of his marriage he was principal of
the public schools at Etna, Allegheny Co., Pa. His
present occupation is farming and creamery business.
Members of the Presbyterian church of Doylestown,
Pa., of which he was ordained elder in Jan. 1890.
Children: (VI.) Sarah Ella Gross. (VI.) Emma Laura
Gross. (VI.) Esther Gross. (VI.) Walter Gross, bn.
in 1889; died Mar. 8, 1890.
IV. John Funk, bn. 1798; died 1834. Mrd. Fannie
Wismer. Clock and watch maker. Menn's. Children:
Sarah, Henry, Rachel, Michael.
V. Sarah Funk, bn. Jan. 1, 1822. Mrd. Jacob Shad-
dinger. —. Farmer. Menn's. One child:
VI. John F. Shaddinger, bn. in 1848. Mrd. Mina
Worman, Apr. 4, 1874. P. O., Gardenville, Pa. Jus-
tice of the Peace. Ger. Ref. Children: (VII.) Clara
Shaddinger, bn. June 3, 1876; died Sept. 3, 1877.
(VII.) Henry W. Shaddinger, bn. July 18, 1878; died
May 9, 1879. (VII.) Walter Shaddinger, bn. Feb. 26,
1880.
V. Henry W. Funk, bn. July 18, 1825. P. O., Gar-
denville, Pa. Farmer. Menn. S.
V. Rachel Funk, bn. Mar. 20, 1828; died Dec. 20,
1841.
V. Michael Funk, bn. Nov. 17, 1830; died Sept. 23,
1846.
IV. Abraham Funk, bn. —; died at Mauch Chunk,
Pa. Not known that he had any family.
IV. Joseph Funk, bn. in Hilltown Twp., Bucks Co.,
Oct. 30, 1800; died Jan. 21, 1882. Mrd. Sarah Cy-
pher, Nov. 10, 1829. In early life he learned the
milling trade, and worked as journeyman at Springtown. After marriage he purchased the old Landis
farm in Springfield Twp., where he lived until his
death. Mr. Funk's manners were bluff, speaking at
all times what he thought was right and just. He was

very fond of fishing and hunting, and in his 80th year would hunt for squirrels and rabbits, and fish with the fling net along the creek for sport.

In politics he was an ardent Republican, and a strong Anti-slavery man, and while doing all in his power to bring about the success of his principles, he never asked for any position or office. He was a member of the Lutheran church of Springfield of which he was an elder for a number of years. Children: William, Jonas, Joseph, John, Hester, David, Susanna, Tillman, Effie, Sarah.

V. William Funk, bn. —; died —. Mrd. Catharine Frankenfield, —. She died —. Children: Charles, —. (VI.) Charles Funk, bn. —. Mrd. — Frankenfield —. P. O., Hellertown, Pa. William mrd. second wife Elizabeth (Hess) Wierbach, —. One child: (VI.) —.

V. Jonas Funk, bn. —; died —. Mrd. Catharine Barron, —. One child: (VI.) Emma V. Funk, bn. —. Mrd. Henry Strunk, —. P. O., Springtown, Pa.

V. Joseph S. Funk, bn. Apr. 1, 1831. Mrd. Annie Fretz, Nov. 23, 1857. She was bn. Jan. 29, 1837. P. O., Ridge, Pa. Farmer. Mr. F., Luth., Mrs. F., Menn. Children: Adeline, Elmer.

VI. Adeline Funk, bn. Jan. 28, 1859. Mrd. Gideon Rosenberger, of Bedminster, Jan. 8, 1880. Farmer. Children: (VII.) Joseph Rosenberger. (VII.) Minnie Catharine Rosenberger.

VI. Elmer E. Funk, bn. Aug. 15, 1864. Mrd. Philena Zeigenfoss, June 12, 1884. Teacher. Children: (VII.) Mamie Nora Funk. (VII.) Elmer Mallard Funk. (VII.) Anna Ray Funk.

V. John Funk, bn. —. Mrd. Sue Richards —. Mr. Funk served in the war.

V. Esther Funk, bn. —. Mrd. Peter Hartman —. P. O., Quakertown, Pa. Farmer. Luth. Children: (VI.) Mary Hartman, bn. Jan. 31, 1861. Mrd. Samuel Hofford, —. P. O., Quakertown, Pa. (VI.) Clara Hartman, bn. July 21, 1862. Mrd. George Weitz —. P. O., Richland Centre, Pa. (VI.) Francis Hartman, bn. Feb. 26, 1863. (VI.) Joseph Hartman, bn. July 29, 1874.

V. David Funk, bn. —; died in the service of the U. S. in the Red River Expedition. S.

V. Susanna Funk, bn. —; died —. Mrd. Titus Richards —. P. O., Easton, Pa. One boy: (**VI.**) Clinton A. Richards.

V. Tillman S. Funk, bn. —. Mrd. Elizabeth Emma J. Stover, —. P. O.. Pleasant Valley, Pa. Laborer. Luth. One child: (**VI.**) David Funk.

V. Ellie Funk, bn. Jan. 16, 1847. Mrd. John L. Koch. P. O., Pleasant Valley, Pa. Farmer. Luth. Children: (**VI.**) Oscar D. Koch, bn. Feb. 5, 1868. (**VI.**) Laura O. Koch, bn. Jan. 15, 1870. (**VI.**) Cora C. Koch, bn. Jan. 9, 1872. (**VI.**) John S. Koch, bn. Mar. 5, 1874. (**VI.**) Ira E. Koch, bn. Mar. 26, 1876. (**VI.**) Kirby F. Koch, bn. Sept. 16, 1878; died Oct. 11, 1881. (**VI.**) Carrie S. Koch, bn. Sept. 15, 1880. (**VI.**) Harry A. Koch, bn. July 13, 1883. (**VI.**) Calvin R. Koch, bn. May 27, 1885. (**VI.**) Warren E. Koch, bn. Dec. 20, 1887.

V. Sarah Funk, bn. June 16, 1850. Mrd. Samuel S. Algert, June 4, 1869. P. O., Easton, Pa. Traveling salesman. Ref. ch. Children: (**VI.**) Irene Algert, bn. Oct. 18, 1870. Mrd. Horace Lehr, Feb. 22, 1892. P. O., Easton, Pa. Senior member of H. Lehr & Co. Organ manufacturers. (**VI.**) D. Stanley Algert, bn. Mar. 29, 1873. (**VI.**) Joseph F. Algert, bn. Feb. 25, 1875. (**VI.**) Carrie M. Algert, bn. Apr. 12, 1877. (**VI.**) Albert Austin Algert, bn. May 18, 1885; died Aug. 30, 1886.

IV. Polly Funk, bn. Feb. 13, 1802; died Oct. 16, 1880. Mrd. Jacob Swartley, Nov. 19, 1820. He was bn. Dec. 9, 1796; died July 6, 1881. Farmer. Menn's. Children: Infant, Sarah, Eliza, John, Mary, Jacob, Infant, Sophia, Infant, Susanna, Infant, Infant.

V. Daughter, bn. June 24, 1822; died in infancy.

V. Sarah Ann Swartley, bn. Apr. 3, 1823; died in infancy.

V. Eliza Swartley, bn. Mar. 3, 1824; died Jan. 19, 1890. Mrd. Jacob D. Rosenberger, Dec. 23, 1843. He was bn. Nov. 28, 1819. P. O., Souderton, Pa. Lived on and farmed the old Rosenberger farm near Reiff's Corners for 41 years. The farm is now in the possession of their youngest son Artemas. Dunkards. Children: Frank, Albert, Mary, William, Sarah, Hannah, Jacob, Ann. Isaiah, Alpheus, Amanda, Artemas, Susan.

VI. II. Frank Rosenberger, bn. Oct. 5, 1844. Mrd. Amanda E. Kline, of Upper Saucon, Sept. 5, 1869. P. O., Allentown, Pa. Early in life he embraced the profession of teaching, which he has followed for 29 years, and is one of the prominent teachers of Lehigh Co., Pa. One child: (VII. Robert Fulton Kline Rosenberger, bn. July 1, 1884.

VI. Albert Swartley Rosenberger, bn. —; died in infancy.

VI. Mary Matilda Rosenberger, bn. Feb. 6, 1847. Mrd. Jacob B. Snyder, of Hatfield, Pa., Mar. 1867. He died Nov. 10, 1868. One son: (VII.) Jacob R. Snyder. Mary mrd. second husband Jacob Tellman, of Rockhill, Pa. P. O., Hatfield, Pa. Farmer. Children: (VII) Carrie Ida Fellman, bn. —; died infant. (VII.) Kate R. Fellman. (VII.) Isaiah Fellman, bn. —; died —. (VII.) Frank Fellman, bn. —; died infant.

VI. William F. Johnston Rosenberger, bn. Nov. 29, 1848. Mrd. Wilhelmina Shellenberger, —. P. O., Souderton, Pa. Farmer. Children: (VII.) Milton Rosenberger, bn. —; died infant. (VII.) Hamilton Rosenberger, bn. —; died infant. (VII.) Harry Rosenberger. (VII.) Alvin Rosenberger.

VI. Sarah Jane Rosenberger, bn. Nov. 27, 1851. Mrd. John M. Kulp, of Hilltown, Pa. —. P. O., Dublin, Pa. Farmer. Children: (VII.) Leidy R. Kulp. (VII.) Mary Ellen Kulp.

VI. Hannah Etta Rosenberger, bn. Feb. 17, 1853. Mrd. Aaron H. Moyer, of Lower Salford, Pa., July 12, 1881. P. O., Harleysville, Pa. Farmer. Ger. Bap. Children: (VII.) Jacob Vincent Moyer, bn. Aug. 24, 1882; died May 6, 1886. (VII.) Eliza Ieedore Moyer. bn. Apr. 23, 1884; died May 6, 1886. (VII.) Hannah Ida Moyer, bn. Mar. 20, 1886. (VII.) Aaron Wilson Moyer, bn. Apr. 15, 1888. (VII.) Emma Miriam Moyer, bn. Feb. 27, 1890. (VII.) Ellen Rosa Moyer, bn. June 30, 1891.

VI. Jacob Rosenberger, bn. —; died in infancy.

VI. Ann Eliza Rosenberger, bn. Aug. 4, 1856. Mrd. Jacob S. Rosenberger, —. Own and occupy the Wireman farm near Chalfont, Pa. Children: (VII:) Paul Rosenberger, bn. —; died in infancy. (VII.) Elmer Wellington Rosenberger. (VII.) John Arthur Rosenberger. (VII.) Jacob Wilmer Rosenberger.

VI. Isaiah Rosenberger, bn. Apr. 11, 1858. Mrd. Jemima, daughter of David Rosenberger, of Hockertown, Pa. —. P. O., Harleysville, Pa. No issue.

VI. Alpheus Rosenberger, bn. —; died in infancy.

VI. Amanda Rosenberger, bn. —; died in infancy.

VI. Artemas Rosenberger, bn. May 10, 1863. Mrd. Mary Ann Hendricks, of Hilltown, Pa. —. P. O., Souderton, Pa. Owns old homestead near Reiff's Corners. Children: (VII.) Joseph Wesley Rosenberger. (VII.) Fanny Elizabeth Rosenberger. (VII.) Jacob Herman Rosenberger.

VI. Susan S. Rosenberger, bn. May 16, 1866. Mrd. William D. Kratz. He was bn. Nov. 29, 1859. P. O., Lawndale, Pa. Farmer. Ger. Bap. Children: (VII.) Lucretia R. Kratz, bn. May 29, 1882; died June 9, 1882. (VII.) Jacob R. Kratz, bn. Aug. 29, 1884. (VII.) Lavina R. Kratz, bn. Nov. 1, 1886. (VII.) Henry Clayton R. Kratz, bn. Nov. 28, 1888. (VII.) Artemas R. Kratz, bn. Dec. 16, 1890.

V. John F. Swartley was born in New Britain Twp., Bucks Co., Pa., July 29, 1826. He went west later in life and owned land and farmed near Rolling Prairie, in La Porte Co., Ind. For a number of years during the latter part of his life he traveled through various parts of the United States and Canada, visiting the large cities and places of interest and making it a point, on the last several presidential inaugurations, to be in Washington. With this purpose in view he went east to visit his relatives in the neighborhood of Line Lexington, the place of his nativity, during the month of Nov. 1892, and about the first of Jan. 1893 proceeded to Washington to spend the winter and remain until after the inauguration of President-elect Cleveland. On the 23d of January he was found dead in his room, at his hotel, having been asphyxiated by gas escaping from the burner, which by an accident had

been turned open. He was 66 years of age and a
bachelor. His remains were buried in the Line Lexington Mennonite grave yard. He was a member of
the Christian ch.

V. Mary Ann Swartley, bn. July 29, 1826; died —.
Mrd. Valentine Clymer —. He died —. Children:
Elmira, Sallie, Mary, Jacob, Emma.

VI. Elmira Clymer, bn. Dec. 5, 1849. Mrd. William
C. Knipe, Mar. 13, 1875. Res. 309 Center St. Beth-
lehem, Pa. Carpenter. Meth. Ep. Children: **(VII.)**
Walter W. Knipe, bn. Sept. 21, 1876. **(VII.)** Clara
M. M. Knipe, bn. Oct. 8, 1879.

VI. Sallie Clymer, bn. —. Mrd. William S. Kratz,
—. Res. Phila., Pa. Children: **(VII.)** Flora. **(VII.)**
Della. **(VII.)** Wellington, (dec'd). **(VII.)** Howard,
(dec'd). **(VII.)** Frank, (dec'd). **(VII.)** Raymond, (de-
ceased). **(VII.)** Irene, (dec'd). **(VII.)** George. **(VII.)**
Edwin and Abel, twins, (both dec'd).

VI. Mary Clymer, bn. —. Mrd. Aaron M. Kratz,
Jan. 8, 1878. P. O., Lansdale, Pa. Merchant. Ger.
Ref. One child: **(VII.)** A. Wesley Kratz, bn. May
16, 1880.

VI. Jacob Clymer, bn. —. Mrd. Emma Everhart
—. P. O., Norristown, Pa. One daughter: **(VII.)**
Birdie.

VI. Emma E. Clymer, bn. Apr. 7, 1859. Mrd. Wm.
G. Brand, May 5, 1884. P. O., Chalfont, Pa. Clerk.
Ref. ch. Children: **(VII.)** Infant, stillborn Dec. 29,
1885. **(VII.)** Infant, stillborn Oct. 23, 1888.

V. Jacob Swartley, bn. Dec. 14, 1828; died in infancy.

V. Sophia Swartley, bn. Feb. 7, 1832. Mrd. Henry
A. Price, Feb. 9, 1851. P. O., Harleysville, Pa.
Farmer. Ger. Bap. Ordained minister in 1867.
Children: Sarah and Mary (twins), John.

VI. Sarah Price, bn. Jan. 31, 1852. Mrd. Henry S.
Harr, Nov. 20, 1875. P. O., Telford, Pa. Miller and
farmer. Ger. Ref. No issue.

VI. Mary Price, bn. Jan. 31, 1852. Mrd. Wm. A.
Reed, Dec. 20, 1873. P. O., Kulpsville, Pa. Farmer.
Children: **(VII.)** Mary Reed, bn. Aug. 25, 1883. **(VII.)**
William Reed, bn. May 11, 1890.

VI. John Price, bn. June 6, 1854. Mrd. Mary Bradly, Apr. 1, 1876. Res. 1211 Somerset St., Philadelphia. Pa.

V. Son, bn. Sept. 16, 1834; died in infancy.

V. Susanna Swartley, bn. Nov. 7, 1835. Mrd. John L. Frick, —. He died Sept. 9, 1873. P. O., Fricks, Pa. Merchant. Menn's. Children: Isabella, Mary, Francis, Jacob, Sarah

VI. Isabella Frick, bn. Dec. 30, 1855. Mrd. James M. Hartzell, —. P. O., Chalfont, Pa. Miller. Children: **(VII.)** Laura. **(VII.)** Elsie. **(VII.)** Jennie. **(VII.)** Blanche.

VI. Mary Amanda Frick, bn. Dec. 30, 1855; died in infancy.

VI. Francis J. Frick, bn. Oct. 23, 1859. Mrd. Ida M. Barndt, —. P. O., Fricks, Pa. One child: **(VII.)** John Howard Frick.

VI. Jacob W. Frick, bn. Nov. 24, 1861. P. O., Fricks, Pa. S.

VI. Sarah Ellen Frick, bn. Sept. 19, 1865. Mrd. T. R. Hartzell, —. P. O., Colmar, Pa. Children: **(VII.)** Raymond Hartzell, died in infancy. **(VII.)** Lela Hartzell. **(VII.)** Pearl Hartzell.

V. Daughter, bn. July 9, 1841; died an infant.

V. Daughter, bn. June 9, 1843; died an infant.

IV. Barbara Funk, bn. Jan. 13, 1804, (still living Dec. 1893. Mrd. John Loux, Jan. 3, 1822. He was bn. Aug. 26, 1798; died Mar. 21, 1879. Carpenter. Ger. Ref. Children: Franklin, Elvey, William, Lewis, Mary, Levi, Reed, Eliza, John, Emeline.

V. Franklin Loux, bn. in Tinicum Twp., Feb. 17, 1823; died Apr. 6, 1861. Mrd. Catharine Zeigenfuss. She was bn. Jan. 11, 1825. Carpenter. Luth's. Children: Amanda, Elvey, Sarah, Mary, Emma, John.

VI. Amanda Loux, bn. Apr. 14, 1846. Mrd. Reed Fretz of Bedminster, Pa., Jan. 27, 1870. P. O., Bedminster, Pa. Farmer. Mrs. Fretz, Presby. Children: **(VII.)** Jacob Franklin Fretz, bn. Nov. 27, 1870. **(VII.)** Minerva Fretz, bn. July 21, 1872. **(VII.)** Anna Laura Fretz, bn. Aug. 18, 1873. **(VII.)** Nelson Oswald Fretz, bn. Nov. 3, 1875. **(VII.)** Mabel Celia

Fretz, bn. Nov. 3, 1877.   **(VII.)** Mary Matilda Fretz, bn. Dec. 31, 1879.

VI. Elvey Zachary Loux, bn Aug. 4, 1848; died 1852.

VI. Sarah Ann Loux, bn. July 13, 1850. Mrd. Jesse Walton, 1871. P. O., Hartsville, Pa.

VI. Mary Matilda Loux, bn. Oct. 16, 1852; died in 1878. Mrd. Levi Fluck in 1870. Children: **(VII.)** Elmer Fluck, (dec'd). **(VII.)** Jesse Fluck, (dec'd). **(VII.)** Lelah Fluck, (dec'd). **(VII.)** William Fluck.

VI. Emma Jane Loux. bn. June 13, 1855. Mrd. Levi Fluck, 1881. P. O., Doylestown, Pa. Child: **(VII.)** Lolla Fluck.

VI. John Loux, bn. Jan. 12, 1858. Mrd. Hannah Shaddinger, Jan. 7, 1882. P. O., Mechanic's Valley, Pa. Farmer. Menn's. Children: **(VII.)** Willa F. Loux, bn. Feb. 27, 1884. **(VII.)** John Franklin Loux, bn. Nov. 21, 1888.

V. Elvey Loux, bn. Feb. 12, 1825. Mrd. Magdalena Mill, Nov. 11, 1847. P. O., Allentown, Pa. In early life he was a shoemaker, then farmer and later merchant. Evangelical ch. Children: Titus, Edwin, Violetta, Clara, Wilson, Newton.

VI. Titus M. Loux, bn. Dec. 24, 1850.   Farmer in Dakota. S.

VI. Edwin M. Loux, bn. Oct. 26, 1852. Mrd. Rosa E. Fritz, Sept. 16, 1875. P. O., Allentown, Penna. Merchant. Attends Evangelical ch. Children: **(VII.)** Adina I. Loux. bn. Sept. 21, 1876. **(VII.)** Elvey E. Loux, bn. Dec. 4, 1877; died Aug. 18, 1878. **(VII.)** M. Mary Loux, bn. Sept. 25, 1880. (**VII.)** James F. Loux, bn. June 6, 1882. **(VII.)** Grace F. Loux, bn. Sept. 23, 1889.

VI. Violetta Loux, bn. Nov. 16, 1854.   Mrd. John S. Jacoby, Dec. 24, 1874. P. O., Allentown, Penna. Merchant. Evangelical ch. One child: **(VII.)** Edwin L. Jacoby. bn. Mar. 22, 1876.

VI. Clara Loux, bn. —. Mrd. Vabey Tice, —. P. O., Alburtis, Pa. Ev. Ass'n. Children: **(VII.)** Bertha Tice. **(VII.)** Edith Tice.

VI. Wilson Loux, bn. about 1870. P. O., Allentown, Pa. Merchant. Ev. Ass'n. S.

VI. Newton Loux, bn. —; died —, aged 4 years.

V. William Loux, bn. Jan. 20, 1827; died Dec. 5, 1843.

V. Lewis Loux, bn. in Tinicum Twp., Bucks Co., Feb. 19, 1829. Mrd. Eliza Hartman, daughter of Henry and Susanna Hartman, Aug. 6, 1854. P. O., Easton, Pa. Carpenter. Ger. Ref. Children: Annie, Ellen, Elizabeth.

VI. Annie Loux, bn. May 8, 1855. S.

VI. Ellen J. Loux, bn. July 14, 1858; died Apr. 12, 1861.

VI. Elizabeth Loux, bn. Jan. 26, 1864. Mrd. Edward Schnabel, Oct. 27, 1887. P. O., Bethlehem, Pa. Shoe store. One child: (VII.) Florence Elizabeth Schnabel, bn. Dec. 29, 1889.

VI. Mary Ann Loux, bn. July 4, 1831; died June 11, 1850. Mrd. John G. Mill, —. No issue.

V. Levi F. Loux, bn. Feb. 6, 1834. Mrd. Rachel Frier, Aug. 15, 1865. She died —. Levi mrd. second wife Fannie A. Carper, Sept. 12, 1878. P. O., Bedminster, Pa. Blacksmith. One child: (VII.) —.

V. Reed F. Loux, bn. July 27, 1836. Mrd. Lydia Jane Cooper, Dec. 21, 1861. P. O., Pipersville, Pa. Creameryman. Reformed ch. Children: (VI.) Sheridan Loux. (VI.) Laura Loux.

V. Eliza Loux, bn. Apr. 14, 1839; died July 21, 1872. Mrd. Isaac Crouthamel, Jan. 17. 1863. P. O., Line Lexington, Pa. Cabinet maker and undertaker. Ref. ch. Children: Elvy, Irwin, Emma, John.

VI. Elvy Crouthamel, bn. Nov. 10, 1863. Mrd. Maria Filman. P. O., Chalfont. Pa. Children: (VII.) Etta Crouthamel, bn. Aug. 21, 1885. (VII.) Zrma Crouthamel, bn. Aug. 18, 1888.

VI. Irwin Crouthamel, bn. Dec. 17, 1865. Mrd. Laura Wireback, Oct. 1, 1887. P. O., Lansdale, Pa. Children: (VII.) Arthur Crouthamel, bn. Nov. 6, 1888. (VII.) Russel Crouthamel, bn. Nov. 7, 1889.

VI. Emma Crouthamel, bn. May 13, 1868. 1010 Green St., Phila., Pa. S.

VI. John T. Crouthamel, bn. Oct. 27, 1870. S.

V. John Loux, bn. May 12, 1842; died Oct. 15, 1850.

V. Emeline Loux, bn. about 1847. Mrd. William Stehle, bn. in Germany; died May 1, 1891, aged 48 yrs. Res. Philadelphia, Pa. Children: (VI.) Laura. (VI.) William. (VI.) Herman, died in 1881. (VI.) Edward. (VI.) Annie. (VI.) Charles. (VI.) Sheriden. (VI.) Warren.

IV. Catharine Funk, bn. in Bucks Co., Pa., Oct. 9, 1805; died Sept. 20, 1889. Mrd. Moses Grobb, —, He was bn. Nov. 16, 1806; died May 2, 1877. Catharine went to Canada with her sister Elizabeth. Farmer and weaver. Menn's. Children: Esther, Jonas, Lydia, Mary. Elizabeth, Sarah, Franklin, Sophia.

V. Esther Grobb, bn. in Lincoln Co., Ont., Mar. 21, 1830. Mrd. Solomon Moyer, Feb. 4, 1851. Farmer. Menn's. Children: William, Ephraim, Isaac.

VI. William G. Moyer, bn. Mar. 8, 1852. Mrd. Susan Culp, Apr. 9, 1876. Farmer. Menn's. Children: (VII.) Norman C. Moyer, bn. Feb. 7, 1878. (VII.) Milton C. Moyer, bn. May 15, 1881. (VII.) Solomon C. Moyer, bn. Mar. 23, 1883. (VII.) Isaac C. Moyer, bn. Sept. 27, 1884. (VII.) Alberta C. Moyer, bn. Aug. 26, 1885. (VII.) Orpha C. Moyer, bn. Mar. 1, 1888.

VI. Ephraim Moyer, bn. Jan. 19, 1855. Mrd. Ella Smith, Oct. 23, 1889.

VI. Isaac Moyer, bn. July 30, 1863.

V. Jonas Grobb, bn. in Lincoln Co., Ont., Oct. 31, 1831. Mrd. Sarah Moyer, May 29, 1860. Farmer. Meth. Children: Valeria, Rowland, Alberta, Eva.

VI. Valeria Grobb, bn. May 24, 1861. Mrd. Thomas R. Gilmore, Oct. 11, 1887. Farmer. Meth. One child: (VII.) Leslie G. Gilmore, bn. June 20, 1892.

VI. Rowland Grobb, bn. Jan. 31, 1864; died Oct. 20, 1872.

VI. Alberta Grobb, bn. Jan. 10, 1876; died Aug. 3, 1878.

VI. Eva Elma Grobb, bn. Mar. 5, 1878; died Aug. 3, 1878.

V. Lydia Grobb, bn. Oct. 28, 1832; died May 16, 1891. Mrd. Joseph Houser, Jan. 23, 1854. Farmer. Meth. Children: Sarah, Mary, Franklin, Lucinda, Levi, Ida, Allen, Sophia, Amanda.

VI. Sarah Catharine Houser, bn. Nov. 4, 1854. Mrd. Solomon Smith, Dec. 24, 1873. P. O., South Cayuga, Ont. Farmer. Meth. Children: **(VII.)** Wilber M. Smith, bn. Dec. 11, 1875. **(VII.)** Loren E. Smith, bn. Dec. 19, 1882.

VI. Mary Jane Houser, bn. Mar. 12, 1858; died Feb. 18, 1865.

VI. Franklin Houser, bn. Dec. 2, 1860; died Feb. 14, 1865.

VI. Lucinda Houser, bn. May 28, 1863.

VI. Levi Houser, bn. Aug. 11, 1865. Mrd. Georgiana Hunsman, —. P. O., Beamsville, Ont. One child: **(VII.)** Mina Lorind Houser, bn. Apr. 3, 1892.

VI. Ida Houser, bn. June 18, 1868.

VI. Allen Houser, bn. Aug. 26, 1869.

VI. Sophia Houser, bn. Sept. 24, 1871.

VI. Amanda Houser, bn. May 21, 1874.

V. Mary Ann Grobb, bn. June 5, 1834. Mrd. William Tallman. Farmer and brickmaker. Meth. Children: James, Walter, Emma, Orpha, Clara, Sarah.

VI. James Harvey Tallman, bn. Jan. 3, 1855. Mrd. Anna Russ, Nov. 15, 1877. Farmer and sawyer. Meth. Children: **(VII.)** Clara Tallman, bn. Aug. 14, 1879. **(VII.)** James Wallace Tallman, bn. Oct. 17, 1883.

VI. Walter F. Tallman, bn. Dec. 29, 1856. Mrd. Eliza A. Beemer, of Clinton, Ont., Feb. 20, 1884. Farmer and brickmaker. Meth. Children: **(VII.)** Forence Helena Tallman, bn. Jan. 1, 1889. **(VII.)** Mary Elizabeth Tallman, bn. Dec. 26, 1891.

VI. Emma Tallman, bn. Mar. 8, 1861; died Dec. 29, 1863.

VI. Orpha Tallman, bn. Feb. 2, 1865.

VI. Clara Ann Tallman, bn. Apr. 29, 1867; died June 29, 1873.

VI. Sarah Tallman, bn. July 4, 1869; died Aug. 6, 1870.

V. Elizabeth Grobb, bn. in Lincoln Co., Ont., Nov. 3, 1835; died Sept. 8, 1876. Mrd. Thomas Brigham, in 1859. Laborer. Meth's. Children: Isaac, Kate, William, Mary.

VI. Isaac N. Brigham, bn. Jan. 26, 1861. Mrd. Isabelle Wilson, of Brantford, Ont., Sept. 14, 1887. P. O., Welland, Ont. Mechanical engineer. Baptists. Children: **(VII.)** Franklin Wilson Brigham, bn. June 20, 1889. **(VII.)** Nettie Elizabeth Brigham, bn. Nov. 7, 1891.

VI. Kate Sophia Brigham, bn. Dec. 9, 1862; died in 1865.

VI. William E. Brigham, bn. July 22, 1864; died in 1866.

VI. Mary Ann Brigham, bn. Apr. 19, 1866. Mrd. Gideon Burton, of Alpena, Mich., June 10, 1891. P. O., Alpena, Mich. Liveryman. Menn. "Trinity" ch., Alpena. One child: **(VII.)** Charles Wellington Burton, bn. Mar. 19, 1893.

V. Sarah Grobb, bn. in Lincoln Co., Ont., Aug. 23, 1838. Mrd. Wilson Nickerson, —. Farmer. Meth's. Children: John, Mary, Alice, Lillie, Anna, Nellie.

VI. John F. Nickerson, bn. Feb. 5, 1863. Mrd. Ellen Parnell. P. O., St. Catharines, Ont.

VI. Mary E. Nickerson, bn. Mar. 8, 1864. Mrd. John Currie, —. Farmer. Children: **(VII.)** Ethel Currie, bn. Oct. 1, 1885. **(VII.)** William Currie, bn. Oct. 26, 1886.

VI. Alice E. Nickerson, bn. Mar. 1, 1868. Mrd. Norris W. Stevens, Aug. 4, 1888. P. O., St. Catharines, Ont. Gardener. Meth's.

VI. Lillie C. Nickerson, bn. Apr. 8, 1873. Mrd. John W. Hack, Jan. 11, 1893. P. O., Jordan, Ont. Farmer. Meth.

VI. Anna S. Nickerson, bn. July 16, 1878.

VI. Nellie V. Nickerson, bn. Dec. 18, 1881.

V. Franklin Grobb, bn. in Clinton Twp., Lincoln Co., Ont., Nov. 29, 1843. Mrd. Martha Ismond, Nov. 6, 1872. P. O., Brantford, Ont. Manufacturer, occupying the position of Mechanical Supt., in the Brantford factory of the Massey-Harris Co. Ltd. Baptists. Children: **(VI.)** Charles Hillyard Grobb, bn. Oct. 7, 1873. **(VI.)** Frederick Ismond Grobb, bn. July 9, 1877. **(VI.)** Jessie Eveline Grobb, bn. July 14, 1883. **(VI.)** Robert Gordon Grobb, bn. Sept. 20, 1885.

V. Sophia Grobb, bn. Aug. 5, 1845.

IV. Elizabeth Funk, bn. in Bucks Co., Pa., Aug. 20, 1807; died Nov. 3, 1887. Elizabeth, in company with her sister Catharine Funk, went to Canada to visit friends, and while there Elizabeth mrd. John Rittenhouse, and they took their wedding trip to Bucks Co., Pa., horseback. They were married in 1826. Children: Michael, Andrew, Mary, Barbara, Jacob, John, Catharine, Abraham, George, Moses, Dinah, William.

V. Michael Rittenhouse, bn. Jan. 10, 1829; died Sept. 1856. Unmrd.

V. Andrew Rittenhouse, bn. —; died in infancy.

V. Mary Rittenhouse, bn. —; died in infancy.

V. Barbara Rittenhouse, bn. Apr. 19, 1833; died Oct. 4, 1871. Mrd. Henry Albright, Jan. 23, 1855. Farmer. Menn's. Children: **(VI.)** John Albright, bn. in Haldimand Co., Ont., Jan. 4, 1856. Farmer. **(VI.)** Abraham Albright, bn. Dec. 21, 1859. Mrd. Miss Price, Nov. 17, 1886. Button manufacturer at Berlin, Ont. Methodists. No issue. **(VI.)** Israel Albright, bn. Apr. 26, 1862. Mrd. Ella Tufford, Dec. 16, 1885. Laborer. Meth. No issue. **(VI.)** Ruby Albright, bn. Nov. 29, 1868. S.

V. Jacob F. Rittenhouse, bn. in Lincoln Co., Ont., Oct. 24, 1834. Mrd. Agnes Wismer, Feb. 1, 1859. She died Mar. 25, 1865. P. O., Campden, Ont. Children: Anna, Elizabeth, Martha.—Jacob mrd. second wife Barbara Kratz, Nov. 30, 1865. Farmer. Menn's. Children: Frank, Martin, Mary.

VI. Anna Rittenhouse, bn. in Lincoln Co., Ont., May 10, 1860. Mrd. Rev. Allen M. Fretz, of Bedminster, Bucks Co., Pa., Mar. 5, 1884, (his second wife). He was bn. in Tinicum Twp., Bucks Co., Dec. 12, 1853. P. O., Bedminster, Pa. Farmer, and resides on the homestead of his grandfather, Christian Fretz, now owned by his father Ely. When 17 years old he was sent by his parents to the Mennonite Seminary at Wadsworth, Ohio. He subsequently attended one term at the Excelsior Normal Institute at Carversville, Pa., after which he taught school eleven terms, working on his father's farm during the summer months.

In the fall af 1882 he accepted the nomination of the Republican party as a candidate to the state legislature, which was tendered him; his party being in the minority in that year's campaign, he was, with the rest of the ticket defeated. In 1883 the second Mennonite church at Deep Run called him to the pastorate of that church, and he was accordingly ordained to the ministry by Bishop Moses Gottshall, Oct. 13, 1883, and installed pastor of the same. Feeling the pressing need of an English paper in the interest of his branch of the Mennonite church, he, with the aid of Rev. N. B. Grubb, pastor of the church in Philadelphia, succeeded in getting out the prospectus of "*The Mennonite*," which was laid before the conference and accepted as one of the periodicals of the church. He is still one of the editors of the paper, which has since been enlarged and improved, and has steadily increased in popularity and circulation since it was started. On Nov. 24, 1893 he was ordained bishop by Rev. Wm. S. Godshall, assisted by Rev. J. S. Moyer, at Deep Run, Pa., and has the spiritual oversight as bishop of the Deep Run and Souderton churches. At the latter place a neat and substantial church edifice has recently been finished, of which he was elected pastor in full charge Feb. 9, 1893. Children: (**VII.**) Jacob Rittenhouse Fretz, bn. July 22, 1886. (**VII.**) Eli R. Fretz, bn. Nov. 27, 1888. (**VII.**) Viola Fretz, bn. Mar. 22, 1891.

VI. Elizabeth Rittenhouse, bn. in Lincoln Co., Ont., Jan. 7, 1862. S.

VI. Martha Rittenhouse, bn. Aug. 9, 1863; died Mar. 25, 1875.

VI. Frank K. Rittenhouse, bn. Sept. 24, 1866. Stationary engineer in Chicago, Ill. Mrd. Molly Kelly. Children: (**VII.**) Mary. (**VII.**) Frank.

VI. Martin K. Rittenhouse, bn. July 8, 1869. Res. Chicago, Ill.

VI. Mary K. Rittenhouse, bn. June 2, 1872.

V. John F. Rittenhouse, bn. in Lincoln Co., Ont., Feb. 13, 1836. Mrd. Elizabeth Honsberger, Nov. 23,

1858. P. O., Jordan, Ont. Farmer. He was ordained deacon of the Mennonite church in 1885, and ordained minister in the spring of 1889 at Moyer's church. Children: Infant, Solomon, Anna, Ettie, Enoch, Infant, Cinderella, Infant, Edith, Alberta, Valeria, Jonathan, David.

VI. Infant son, bn. Jan. 29; died Jan. 30, 1860.

VI. Solomon Rittenhouse, bn. July 4, 1861. Mrd. Mattie Moore, Dec. 1885. Meth's. Children: **(VII.)** Arthur Rittenhouse, bn. June 2, 1887. **(VII.)** Edith Rittenhouse, bn. Dec. 10, 1888.

VI. Anna Rittenhouse, bn. in Lincoln Co., Ont., Mar. 18, 1863. Mrd. Joseph Wismer. (See Index of References No. 62.)

VI. Ettie Rittenhouse, bn. Nov. 5, 1864. Mrd. Robert Martin, July 1, 1886. School teacher. Menn's. One child: **(VII.)** Leo Martin, bn. July 5, 1887.

VI. Enoch Rittenhouse, bn. Apr. 11, 1866; died Sept. 10, 1877.

VI. Infant son, bn. Nov. 3; died Nov. 5, 1868.

VI. Cinderella Rittenhouse, bn. Sept. 29, 1869. Mrd. Edward Wilson Fry. (See Index of References No. 75.)

VI. Infant son, bn. July 1; died Sept. 15, 1871.

VI. Edith Rittenhouse, bn. Sept. 11, 1872; died Sept. 18, 1880.

VI. Alberta Rittenhouse, bn. Oct. 8, 1874.

VI. Valeria Rittenhouse, bn. Oct. 24, 1875.

VI. Jonathan Rittenhouse, bn. Feb. 9, 1877.

VI. David Rittenhouse, bn. Aug 5, 1878; died Sept. 13, 1878.

V. Catharine Rittenhouse, bn. Jan. 1838; died Dec. 1872. Mrd. Jacob Swartz —. No issue.

V. Abraham Rittenhouse, bn. in Lincoln Co., Ont., Oct. 24, 1840. Mrd. Christena Kienzle, Feb. 10, 1863. P. O., Jordan, Ont. Farmer and minister. He was ordained to the ministry of the Mennonite church, at Moyer's church, Lincoln Co., Ont., Oct. 22, 1871. Children: Emma, Barbara, Sophia, Tobias, Naomi, Abraham, Jacob, Mary, John, William, Aaron, Moses, Margaret.

VI. Emma Alice Rittenhouse, bn. Jan. 9, 1864. Mrd. Isaac Reesor, of Cedar Grove, Ont., Dec. 16, 1890.

VI. Barbara Elizabeth Rittenhouse, bn. July 24, 1865. Mrd. Albert B. Reesor, of Cedar Grove, Ont., Jan. 13, 1891. One child: (**VII.**) Emma Reesor, bn. Jan. 2, 1893.

VI. Sophia Rittenhouse, bn. July 16, 1867. Mrd. David N. Reesor, Jan. 17, 1893.

VI. Tobias Rittenhouse, bn. Feb. 5, 1869.

VI. Naomi Rittenhouse, bn. Aug. 3, 1870.

VI. Abraham Rittenhouse, Jr., bn. July 28, 1872.

VI. Jacob Rittenhouse, bn. Aug. 28, 1874.

VI. Mary Rittenhouse, bn. July 29, 1876.

VI. John Rittenhouse, bn. Mar. 4, 1879.

VI. William Rittenhouse, bn. Apr. 6, 1881.

VI. Aaron Rittenhouse and Moses Rittenhouse, (twins,) bn. May 12, 1884.

VI. Margaret Rittenhouse, born and died Apr. 29, 1887.

V. George Rittenhouse, bn. in Lincoln Co., Ont., Sept. 12, 1843. Mrd. Mary Honsberger, Dec. 26, 1865. P. O., South Cayuga, Ont. Farmer. Menn's. Children: (**VI.**) John Emerson Rittenhouse, bn. June 11, 1867. Farmer. (**VI.**) Franklin Rittenhouse, bn. Jan. 13, 1869. Farmer. (**VI.**) Allen Rittenhouse, bn. Jan. 29, 1872. (**VI.**) Elizabeth Rittenhouse, bn. Mar. 4, 1874. (**VI.**) Sarah Rittenhouse, bn. Mar. 18, 1875. (**VI.**) Rosetta Rittenhouse, bn. June 22, 1879.

V. Moses F. Rittenhouse, bn. in Lincoln Co., Ont., Aug. 12, 1846. Mrd. Emma Stover, of Bucks Co., Pa., Dec. 1871. Lumber merchant in Chicago, Ill. Presbyterians. Children: (**VI.**) Edward F. Rittenhouse, bn. Nov. 3, 1872. (**VI.**) Charles J. Rittenhouse, bn. Nov. 13, 1874. (**VI.**) Walter Rittenhouse, bn. Mar. 31, 1879.

V. Dinah Rittenhouse, bn. May 23, 1848; died May 19, 1883. Mrd. Allen Moyer, Feb. 9, 1871. Nurseryman. Mrs. Moyer, Menn. Children: (**VI.**) Milton Moyer, bn. Feb. 22, 1872; died Oct. 30, 1875. (**VI.**) Ada Moyer, bn. Aug. 8, 1875. (**VI.**) Laura Moyer, bn. Oct. 10, 1877. (VI.) Lottie May Moyer, bn. Oct. 16, 1881.

V. William Rittenhouse, M. D , bn. in Lincoln Co., Ont., Sept. 5, 1852. Mrd. Mary, daughter of Wm. W. Moyer, of Campden, Ont., Apr. 2, 1874. Mr. Rittenhouse received a common school education, attending school in the winter months, and soon as he was old enough worked on his father's farm in the summer. Before he was quite seventeen, he obtained a certificate to teach, and on Jan. 1, 1870, took charge of his first school. For over thirteen years he labored in the school room, till failing in health he was compelled to seek other occupation. At the age of 22 while teaching a country school, at the modest sum of $400 a year, he was married. Three years later, he secured an appointment to a position in the Central school of St. Catharines, Ont. After four years of hard work, he was promoted to headmastership of the school. But the unceasing labor, the close confinement, and the loss of two of his children so wore upon his health, that in 1883 he resigned his position to seek some more active out door life. During the same year he began the study of medicine, and the next year he removed to Chicago; where in 1886 he received his degree at the College of Physicians and Surgeons, and at once settled down in the same city to engage in the practice of his profession. Children: (VI.) Ernest Rittenhouse, bn. May 1, 1876. (VI.) Jane Rittenhouse, bn. Apr. 12, 1881; died Aug. 25, 1882. (VI.) Henry Rittenhouse, bn. Aug. 3, 1883; died Oct. 23, 1883.

IV. Anna Funk, bn. in Bucks Co., Pa., —. Mrd. Jacob Geil, —. He was bn. in Bucks Co., Feb. 3, 1803. P. O., Chalfont, Pa. Farmer. Menn's. Children: John, Enos, Samuel.

V. John F. Geil, bn. in Bucks Co., Pa., Mar. 30, 1831. Mrd. Sarah A. Schofield, Apr. 5, 1860, in Livingston Co., Mich. She was bn. in Steuben Co., N. Y., Mar. 22, 1834. P. O., Williamsport, N. Dak. In early life Mr. Geil taught school for about ten years, and for twelve years was employed in making surveys for making and publishing county maps, mostly in Michigan. He later moved to Emmons Co.,

North Dakota, where he has been engaged for some years in farming.

In July 1889, he was appointed Deputy Clerk of the District court, for the reason that he understood the German language. His part of the work was to do business with the Russian German people that reside in Emmons Co., N. D. and which business consisted mainly of taking final proofs and filings for land. The Russian Germans greatly appreciated the favor of having in the office at the county seat, one who could converse and do business with them in their own language, and interpret and answer in German their German letters for them, and they soon came to the conclusion to do what they could to keep Mr. Geil in office at the county seat, and they soon had an opportunity of acting upon their conclusion. In Sept. 1890, Mr. Geil was nominated by a vote of 45 to 16 by the Republican county convention as a candidate for Register of Deeds, and in November of same year was elected to that office by a majority of 140, having received all the (150) Russian German votes, although said Russian Germans were nearly all Democrats.

In January 1892 John F. Geil was appointed a Notary Public in and for Emmons, N. D. by the Governor of the state. In the same year (1892) Mr. Geil was nominated by acclamation as a candidate for Register of Deeds, for another term, by both Republican and Democratic county conventions, and at the election of November 8th of same year was elected to that office unanimously,—receiving all the votes cast.

In addition to the duties performed as Register of Deeds, Mr. Geil does conveyancing, Notarial business, interpreting, and sundry clerical work. Since filling these offices his residence has been at Williamsport, the county seat. Meth. Ep. Children: Anna, Lincoln, Frederick.

VI. Anna E. Geil, bn. at Ann Arbor, Mich., Jan. 4, 1864, was engaged for a number of years in teaching public schools in Michigan, and North Dakota, in which she was very successful. She also taught vocal and instrumental music. She was married to Rev.

Charles S. Lane, Aug. 15, 1889. He was bn. in England, and his father was an Episcopal Clergyman. Rev. Mr. Lane was formerly a member of the North Dakota Methodist Episcopal Conference, and was stationed at Mandan, N. D., on the west side of the Missouri river. He was next assigned to Ardoch, and afterwards to Walhalla, both flourishing towns in the Red River Valley, N. D. In 1892, he was transferred to the Wisconsin conference and stationed at North Greenfield in that state, within the suburbs of Milwaukee. Mr. and Mrs. Lane, had previous to the meeting of conference in Wisconsin, in 1892, attended the Moody training school in Chicago.

Rev. Charles S. Lane, is an eloquent and effective preacher, and an energetic worker in the "Vineyard of the Lord," and in Mrs. Lane, he has an able assistant. She had taken an active part in Sundayschool and other religious work previous to her marriage, and that work has since increased in activity and extent, according to the opportunities and demands of her position.

VI. Lincoln Geil, bn. at Ann Arbor, Mich., Dec. 26, 1865. Mrd. Etta Miles of Detroit, Mich., Sept. 21, 1889. She was bn. in Michigan, Dec. 6, 1870. At the time of his marriage he kept a General Store at Winchester, Emmons Co., N. Dak. Early in 1890 they moved to Pierre, South Dak., where they remained only a few months, and then moved to Detroit, Mich., where he was conductor on the Street Cars until the fall of 1891, when he removed to North Dakota, where he took up a homestead in Logan township, 6 miles south-east of Williamsport. He is now Deputy Clerk of the District Court of Emmons Co., N. D. Children: (**VII.**) Anna Geil, bn. in Detroit, Mich., July 2, 1890. (**VII.**) William Geil, bn. May 23, 1892; died Sept. 16, 1892.

VI. Frederick Augustus Geil, bn. Sept. 13, 1870.

V. Enos F. Geil, bn. in Bucks Co., Pa., Apr. 27, 1836; died Mar. 17, 1891. Mrd. Mary Means, Feb. 10, 1859. P. O., Levin, Pa. Farmer. Menn's. Children: Amanda, Sarah, Anna.

VI. Amanda M. Geil, bn. Nov. 13, 1859. Mrd. Jonas M. Moyer, Jan. 15, 1880. Farmer. Menn's. Children: **(VII.)** Anna Laura Moyer, bn. May 29, 1881. **(VII.)** Mary G. Moyer, bn. Aug. 9, 1883. **(VII.)** Alice Moyer, bn. Sept. 3, 1885. **(VII.)** Sylvanus Moyer, bn. Feb. 4, 1888. **(VII.)** Mabel Moyer, bn. Dec. 10, 1892.
VI. Sarah M. Geil, bn. May 9, 1861. Mrd. Jacob F. Swartley, Nov. 6, 1888. Farmer. One child: **(VII.)** Catharine Swartley.
VI. Anna M. Geil, bn. May 14, 1865. Mrd. Oliver Keller —. Farmer. Luth's. Children: **(VII.)** Laura G. Keller, bn. Sept. 18, 1884. **(VII.)** Howard G. Keller, bn. May 28, 1887. **(VII.)** Walter M. Keller, bn. Nov. 22, 1888.
V. Samuel F. Geil, bn. in Bucks Co., Pa., Sept. 28, 1841. Mr. Geil received a good academic education in his native county. In 1859 he removed to Cleveland, O., where he began the study of law. After passing through the usual studies he was admitted to practice in the Supreme Court of the state of Ohio, Sept. 26, 1862. Having read law with Herrick and Barlow, he attended the Ohio State and Union Law College, at Cleveland, from which he graduated May 26, 1862. At the breaking out of the war in 1861, he was among the first to enter the volunteer service, and was appointed 1st Lieutenant of the 2d Regt. O. Cavalry, and remained until Dec. 11, 1861, when he resigned. In Nov. 1862 he removed to California, and took up his residence in Monterey Co., where he has been actively engaged in the practice of law. He served two terms as district Attorney of Monterey Co., and during his incumbency conducted many cases of great importance and public interest, in a highly satisfactory and successful manner. He has had a large and profitable practice for the last fifteen years. He is at the present time Attorney for the Southern Pacific Railroad Company and other corporations. For the last ten years there has not been a case in the county in which he resides, of any importance, either civil or criminal, that he has not been engaged in. Immediately after his arrival in California, he was admitted to practice in the Supreme Court

of the state of California, and all the Federal courts.
On Feb. 2, 1866 he married Josefa Sanchez, who
with the two living children are members of the
Roman Catholic church. Mrs. Geil descends from an
old and prominent Spanish family of the region of
country in which she lives. Her grandparents on her
mother's side were native Californians. Her father,
Don. Rafael Sanchez was private Secretary to Gov-
erner and General Micheltorena under Mexican rule.
Children: (VI.) Samuel Geil, bn. Mar. 8, 1867; died
Nov. 10, 1868. (VI.) Samuel Geil, bn. Nov. 1869;
died, aged 7 days. (VI.) Anna Geil, bn. in Monterey
Co., Cal., Feb. 13, 1870. Mrd. John J. Wyatt, Dec.
27, 1892. P. O., Salinas City, Cal. Lawyer. He,
Protestant. She, Catholic. (VI.) Lydia Geil, bn. Oct.
17, 1874; died June 15, 1885. (VI.) Herlind Geil, bn.
May 19, 1876.

III. John Wismer, bn. Mar. 10, 1774; died about
1840. Mrd. Esther Fry. —. Farmer and weaver.
Emigrated to Canada in 1800. They lived for a time
in Lincoln Co., then moved to Elgin Co., where he
died, aged 64 years. Children: Henry, Elizabeth,
Mary, Jacob, Barbara, John, Nancy, Margaret.

IV. Henry Wismer bn. in Bucks Co., Pa., Apr. 3,
1795; died Oct. 24, 1859. Mrd Nancy Moyer, Feb.
11, 1817. She died —. Farmer. Menn's. Children:
Barbara, John, Dilman, Jacob, Isaac, Esther, Andrew, Abraham, Henry, Samuel, Joseph, Catharine,
Daniel.

V. Barbara Wismer, bn. Dec. 17, 1817; died July
23, 1863. Mrd. David Hoover. Children: Christopher, Henry, John, Isaac, Mary.

VI. Christopher Hoover, bn. —. Mrd. Magdalena
Houser, Nov. 3, 1863. P. O., South Cayuga, Ont.
Farmer. Menn's. Children: (VII.) Nancy Hoover, bn.
—. Menn. S. (VII.) Mary Hoover, bn. —. Menn.
S. (VII.) Barbara Hoover, bn. —. Menn. S.

VI. Henry W. Hoover, bn. —. Mrd. Lydia Sherk.
P. O., Selkirk, Ont.

VI. Rev. John W. Hoover, bn. in York Co., Ont.,
Oct. 11, 1845. Mrd. Harriet Bristol, Dec. 25, 1867.

P. O., South Cayuga, Ont. Minister. Mrs. Hoover, cancer doctor. Brethren in Christ (Tunkards). Children: (VII.) Jennie Hoover, bn. Dec. 19, 1868. Dressmaker. (VII.) Omar Hoover, bn. July 14, 1871. Mrd. Mary A. Buckman, Oct. 4, 1893. P. O., South Cayuga, Ont. Farmer. (VII.) Bertha Olevia Hoover, bn. Jan. 6, 1879; died in 1888, aged 9 years, 4 months and 28 days.

VI. Isaac Hoover, bn. in York Co., Ont., Aug. 9, 1848. Mrd. Mary Nash, Mar. 27, 1878. P. O., Rodney, Ont. Farmer. Meth. Children· (VII.) Lorne Hoover, bn. Nov. 27, 1879. (VII.) Fannie Hoover, bn. May 20, 1881. (VII.) Pelma Hoover, bn. Apr. 6, 1885.

VI. Mary Ann Hoover, bn. —. Mrd. George Alair. P. O., Kippen. Ont.

V. John Wismer, bn. Feb. 9, 1819; died Oct. 25, 1858. Mrd. Elizabeth Moyer, —. She died —. One child: Jacob.—John mrd. second wife Anna Moyer, Apr. 11, 1852. Farmer. Ev. Ass'n. Children: Mary, Martha, Sophia, Solomon, John.

VI. Jacob Wismer, bn. —. P. O., Olympia, Wash.

VI. Mary Wismer, bn. in South Cayuga, Ont., Feb. 5, 1853. S.

VI. Martha Jane Wismer, bn. Sept. 5, 1854; died Sept. 22, 1854.

VI. Sophia Wismer, bn. in South Cayuga, Ont., Oct. 9, 1855. Mrd. John P. Eiler, Dec. 19, 1889. P. O., Cedar Falls, Iowa. Farmer. Meth's. One child: (VII.) Burness Wismer Eiler, bn. Apr. 1, 1891.

VI. Solomon G. Wismer, bn. in South Cayuga, Ont., Sept. 25, 1857. P. O., Cedar Falls, Iowa. Farmer. Ev. Ass'n. S.

VI. John E. Wismer, bn. Mar. 26, 1859. Mrd. Pricilla Moyer, Dec. 31, 1887. P. O., Brantford, Ont. Wagon maker. Meth. Children: (VII.) Howard Wesley Wismer, bn. Aug. 28, 1889. (VII.) Harvey Raymond Wismer, bn. Sept. 11, 1891.

V. Dilman Wismer, bn. June 23, 1820; died infant.
V. Jacob Wismer, bn. Jan. 9, 1822; died infant.
V. Isaac M. Wismer, bn. Nov. 23, 1823. Mrd. Elizabeth Fry, Mar. 23, 1848. P. O., South Cayuga, Ont.

Farmer. Ev. Ass'n. Children: Lavina, Menno, John, Anna, James, Melinda, Louisa, Alfred, Martha.

VI. Lavina Wismer, bn. Apr. 9, 1849; died Apr. 6, 1850.

VI. Menno Simon Wismer, bn. Aug. 9, 1850. P. O., South Cayuga, Ont. -

VI. John H. Wismer, bn. in South Cayuga, May 3, 1852. Mrd. Lydia E. Trafelet, Sept. 30, 1879. P. O., Port Elgin, Ont. Nurseryman. United Brethren ch. Children: (VII.) Winnie Laurel Wismer, bn. Sept. 29, 1880. (VII.) Pearl Eby Wismer, bn. May 13, 1886, (twin). (VII.) Emery Fry Wismer, bn. May 13, 1886.

VI. Annie E. Wismer, bn. Aug. 28, 1853; died Aug. 13, 1880.

VI. James Albert Wismer, bn. Nov. 14, 1855; died next day.

VI. Melinda Catharine Wismer, bn. Aug. 18, 1857.

VI. Louisa Ann Wismer, bn. Nov. 15, 1859; died same day.

VI. Alfred Isaac Wismer, bn. Nov. 6, 1862; died Feb. 1, 1869.

VI. Martha Emma Wismer, bn. Nov. 8, 1868.

V. Esther Wismer, bn. Sept. 1, 1825. Mrd. David High, Jan. 25, 1853. P. O., South Cayuga, Ont. Farmer. Menn's. Children: Magdalena, Henry, Catharine, Anna, Isaac, Jacob.

VI. Magdalena High, bn. Nov. 1, 1853. Mrd. Solomon Honsberger, Nov. 30, 1875. He died —. Magdalena mrd. second husband Solomon Houser, Mar. 22, 1881. P. O., Rainham, Ont. Farmer. Menn's. Children: (VII.) Aaron Houser, bn. Jan. 14, 1882; died Mar. 10, 1889. (VII.) Sarah Houser, bn. Mar. 12, 1884. (VII.) Ezra Houser, bn. July 6, 1886.

VI. Henry High, bn. Dec. 31, 1854. Mrd Catharine Honsberger. P. O., South Cayuga, Ont. Farmer. Menn's. Children: (VII.) Courtlin High, bn. Jan. 20, 1879; died July, 1880. (VII.) Samantha High, bn. May 25, 1881. (VII.) Emerson High bn. Nov. 14, 1886.

VI. Catharine High, bn. Apr. 30, 1857. Mrd. Samuel Eyman, May 23, 1879. P. O., North Pelham, Ont. Farmer. Children: (VII.) Esther Ann Eyman, bn. Dec. 7, 1880; died same day. (VII.) Melvin Eyman, bn. May 26, 1882. (VII.) Luetta Eyman, bn. July 1, 1883. (VII.) Luella Eyman, bn. Apr. 11, 1884; died Oct. 11, 1885. (VII.) William Eyman, bn. Aug. 27, 1886; died Nov. 29, 1886. (VII.) Christian Eyman, (twin) bn. Aug. 13, 1887; died Aug. 20, 1887. (VII.) Christopher Eyman, bn. Aug. 13, 1887; died Oct. 5, 1887. (VII.) Elsina Eyman, bn. June 26, 1889. (VII.) Alice Eyman, bn. June 20, 1892.

VI. Anna High (twin to Catharine), bn. Apr. 30, 1857. Mrd. Ephraim Sloat, July 5, 1885. P. O., Jordan Station, Ont. Laborer. Children: (VII.) Jacob Lamon Sloat, bn. Oct. 3, 1886. (VII.) Samuel Amon Sloat, bn. May 1888. (VII.) David Albon Sloat, bn. Apr. 21, 1889. (VII.) Avalene Sloat, bn. June 24, 1890; died Oct. 3, 1890. (VII.) Emmaretta Sloat, bn. Feb. 18, 1891.

VI. Isaac High, bn. Dec. 11, 1861. Mrd. Minnie Ann Fry, July 1888. P. O., 123, Bond St., Toronto. Carpenter and joiner. One child: (VII.) Evelyn Mary High, bn. Aug. 6, 1889; died Dec. 25, 1891.

VI. Jacob High, bn. Jan. 24, 1865. P.O., 139 Gelston St., Buffalo, N. Y. Carpenter and joiner. Ev. Ass'n.

V. Andrew Wismer, bn. Aug. 31, 1827. Married Catharine Swartz. She died —. Andrew mrd. second wife Sophia Stengle. P. O., Campden, Ont.

V. Abraham Wismer, bn. Dec. 6, 1829. Mrd. Mary Everts, —. P. O., South Cayuga, Ont. Children: (VI.) Gleason Wismer, bn. Sept. 18, 1875; died Jan. 24, 1876. (VI.) Catharine Wismer, bn. July 24, 1878.

V. Henry Wismer, bn. Jan. 22, 1832; died Feb. 1834.

V. Samuel Wismer, bn. July 12, 1834; died Sept. 29, 1858. Mrd. Sarah Fretz, daughter of David Fretz, Jan. 13, 1855. She was bn. Feb. 27, 1836; died June 15, 1857. Children: Elizabeth, Henry.—Samuel mrd. second wife Anna Hoover, —. Farmer. Menn's.

VI. Elizabeth Wismer, bn. in 1855. Mrd. Gleason E. Thoman, June 22, 1875. Farmer. Menn's. Children: (VII.) Isaiah Thoman, bn. May 20, 1876. (VII.) David Thoman, bn. Mar. 4, 1878. (VII.) Harvey

Thoman, bn. Mar. 10, 1880. (VII.) Manasseh Thoman, bn. Jan. 25, 1882. (VII.) Russel Thoman, bn. Oct. 30, 1883. (VII.) Mary Anna Thoman, bn. Mar. 28, 1886. (VII.) Sarah Elizabeth Thoman, bn. July 21, 1888.

VI. Henry F. Wismer, bn. June 5, 1857. Mrd. Annie May Reesor, Aug. 17, 1880. P. O., Whitevale, Ont. Farmer. Children: (VII.) Franklin Russel Wismer, bn. Aug. 20, 1881; died Dec. 21, 1881. (VII.) Mary Loranne Wismer, bn. Sept. 28, 1884.

V. Joseph Wismer, bn. Sept. 16, 1836; died Feb. 28, 1837.

V. Catharine Wismer, bn. Dec. 19, 1837. Mrd. Abraham Moyer. P. O., Jordan, Ont.

V. Daniel Wismer, bn. in Lincoln Co., Ont., Dec. 29, 1839. Mrd. Elizabeth Cober, Sept. 10, 1867. P. O., Rodney, Ont. Farmer. Mrs. Wismer, Tunkard. Children: Jacob, Matilda, Nancy, Mary, Hannah, Rebecca, Abraham.

VI. Jacob Wismer, bn. July 26, 1868.

VI. Matilda Wismer, bn. Apr. 13, 1870.

VI. Nancy Wismer, bn. Apr. 11, 1872. Mrd. Fred Schmiedendorf, Dec. 25, 1890. P. O., Preston, Ont. Carpenter. One child: (VII.) Menno Schmiedendorf, bn. Oct. 2, 1891.

VI. Mary Wismer, born Mar. 9, 1874.

VI. Hannah Wismer, bn. Nov. 15, 1876.

VI. Rebecca Wismer, bn. Jan. 25, 1879.

VI. Abraham Wismer, bn. Aug. 31, 1883.

IV. Elizabeth Wismer, bn. in Bucks Co., Pa., Oct. 3, 1796; died Nov. 26, 1881. Mrd. Samuel S. Moyer. He was born Oct. 16, 1794; died June 1871. He was familiarly known as "Fly Sam," from living on Fly Creek. Farmer. Menn's. Children: Barbara, John, William, Catharine, Elizabeth, Henry, Tilman, Esther, Israel, Moses, Aaron, Anna.

V. Barbara Moyer, bn, July 23, 1819; died May 28, 1864. Mrd. Samuel M. Moyer, —. He was bn. 1818; died July 6, 1883. Farmer. Evangelical ch. Children: William, Sarah, Jacob, Albert.

VI. William Moyer, bn. 1847; died an infant.

VI. Sarah Moyer, bn. 1857. Mrd. James Reece. P. O., Tintern, Ont. Children: (VII.) Annie Reece,

bn. in 1874. (VII.) Infant son, bn. 1882; died infant.
(VII.) Ethel Reece, bn. 1886. (VII.) Lauren Stanley
Reece, bn. 1889.
VI. Jacob M. Moyer, bn. in Lincoln Co., Ont., 1857.
Mrd. Sarah Lodema McCurdy, Feb. 12, 1879. P. O.,
Campden, Ont. Merchant. Evangelical ch. No issue.
VI. Albert M. Moyer, bn. Feb. 24, 1861. Mrd.
Jennie Smith, Sept. 15, 1886. P. O., Brantford, Ont.
Confectioner. Attends Presby. ch. Children: (VII.)
Percival Moyer, bn. Apr. 12, 1888; died May 16,
1888. (VII.) Charles Wesley Moyer, bn. Aug. 20,
1889; died Oct. 26, 1889. (VII.) Maggie May Moyer,
bn. May 31, 1890; died Nov. 20, 1890.
V. John W. Moyer, bn. Mar. 28, 1821; died May 27,
1891. Mrd. Mary Honsberger, Dec. 17, 1845. She
died Mar. 26, 1863. Children: Amanda, Freeman,
Emma, Agnes, Sarah, Rhoda, Melvin, Daniel, Mary.
--John mrd. second wife, Sarah Fretz, Nov. 29, 1868.
No issue. Farmer. Menn's.
VI. Amanda Moyer, bn. Sept. 27, 1846. Mrd. Benjamin
Comfort, Mar. 8, 1870. P. O., Tintern, Ont. Meth's.
Children: (VII.) John Herbert Comfort, bn. Jan. 4,
1871. (VII.) Agnes Arminta Comfort, bn. June 9,
1873. (VII.) William Hilton Comfort, bn. Dec. 30,
1876.
VI. Freeman H. Moyer, bn. Mar. 8, 1848. Mrd.
Annie Honsberger, Dec. 25, 1879. P. O., Campden,
Ont. Meth's. Children: (VII.) Mary Elsie Moyer, bn.
Feb. 12, 1881. (VII.) Hugh Ellis Moyer, bn. Feb. 8,
1883. (VII.) Fred Clare Moyer, bn. Nov. 6, 1887.
(VII.) John Wray Moyer, bn. Nov. 4, 1889.
VI. Emma Moyer, bn. Oct. 26, 1849. Mrd. Benoni
Crumb in 1877. No issue.
VI. Agnes Moyer, bn. Sept. 27, 1851. Mrd. Joseph
Gerber, March 6, 1870. P. O., Fremont, Michigan.
Tanner. Congregationalists. Children: (VII.) Theron
D. Gerber, bn. Feb. 13, 1871; died Sept. 16, 1881.
(VII.) Frank Gerber, bn. Jan. 12, 1873. (VII.) Mary
Gerber, bn. Dec. 10, 1875; died Sept. 2, 1876. (VII.)
Harry Gerber, bn. Dec. 6, 1879. (VII.) Ethel Gerber,
bn. Mar. 16, 1884. (VII.) Joseph Gerber, Jr., bn.
June 22, 1885.

17

VI. Sarah E. Moyer, bn. Oct. 26, 1853. Mrd. Josiah D. Albright, Dec. 31, 1879. Meth's. Children: **(VII.)** William Donald Albright, bn. Aug. 15, 1881. **(VII.)** Frederick Stanley Albright, bn. Mar. 23, 1883. **(VII.)** Margaret Albright, bn. Nov. 29, 1886. **(VII.)** Charles Raymond Albright, bn. Mar. 25, 1888.

VI. Rhoda Moyer, bn. Dec. 1, 1855. Mrd. Simeon N. Moyer. (See Index of References No. 63.)

VI. Melvin Moyer, bn. Mar. 21, 1858. P. O., St. Catharines, Ont. Meth.

VI. Daniel H. Moyer, bn. Feb. 28, 1860. P. O., Campden, Ont. Meth.

VI. Mary Jane Moyer, bn. Apr. 2, 1862. Mrd. Eli Oates Lane, —. P. O., Tintern, Ont. Meth. One child: **(VII.)** Flossey Lane.

V. William W. Moyer, bn. Mar. 23, 1823; died May 1, 1891. Mrd. Barbara Albright, —. She died —. Children: Sarah, Salome, Mary, Lena, Mahlon, William, Margaret, Aaron, Ezra.—William mrd. second wife, Anna Moyer, Nov. 19, 1865. Fruit grower and evaporator. Children: Curtis, Gilbert, Edward, Ella, Burness.

VI. Sarah Moyer, bn. —. Mrd. Samuel S. Nash. (See Index of References No. 64.)

VI. Salome Moyer, bn. —. Mrd. Jacob H. Eckhardt, —. P. O., 31 Sumner St., Hartford, Conn.

VI. Mary Moyer, bn. near Campden, Ont., Apr. 26, 1852. Mrd. Wm. F. Rittenhouse, M. D. (See Index of References No. 65.)

VI. Magdalena A. Moyer, bn. in Lincoln Co., Ont., Feb. 10, 1856. Mrd. Wm. H. Hipple, July 12, 1881. P. O., 27 William St., Hartford, Conn. Meth. Ep. No issue.

VI. Mahlon H. Moyer, bn. in Lincoln Co., Ont., Jan. 19, 1858. Mrd. Margaret C. Zimmerman, July 27, 1881. Res. 49 Oak St., Hartford, Conn. Stenographer. Meth. Ep. Children: **(VII.)** Ruth Moyer, bn. July 29, 1889. **(VII.)** Pauline Moyer, bn. June 16, 1892.

VI. William Henry Moyer, bn. - . S.

VI. Margaret Moyer, bn. --; died —.

VI. Aaron Moyer, bn. —; died —.

VI. Ezra Moyer, bn. — ; died —.

VI. Curtis Moyer, bn. Aug. 14, 1866. Res. Hartford, Conn. Book-keeper. Attends Cong'l ch. S.

VI. Gilbert L. Moyer, bn. Nov. 15, 1867. Res. Pittsburgh, Pa. Electrician. Ev. Ass'n. S.

VI. Edward A. Moyer, bn. Nov. 18, 1869. Res. Hartford, Conn. Machinist. Meth. Ep. S.

VI. Ella Moyer, bn. Dec. 31, 1871. P. O., Campden, Ont.

VI. Burness Moyer, bn. July 29, 1875.

V. Catharine Moyer, bn. in Lincoln Co., Ont., Jan. 17, 1825; died May 3, 1891. Mrd. Christian H. Honsberger, Mar. 19, 1848. He was bn. June 28, 1825. Farmer. Menn. ch. Children: Malinda, Elizabeth, Alfred, Samuel, Mary, Amanda, Aaron, Curtis.

VI. Malinda Honsberger, bn. in Lincoln Co., Ont., Dec. 25, 1848. Mrd. Jacob G. Culp, Mar. 2, 1871. P. O., St. Catharines, Ont. Farmer. Meth. Children: (**VII.**) Charles Ellston Culp, bn. Feb. 14, 1881. (**VII.**) Elsie Maud Culp, bn. Feb. 28, 1883.

VI. Elizabeth Honsberger, bn. Apr. 16, 1850; died May 30, 1851.

VI. Alfred Honsberger, bn. Aug. 17, 1853. Mrd. Eliza Ryckman, Apr. 2, 1879. P. O., St. Catharines, Ont. Farmer. Meth. Children: (**VII.**) Chester Franklin Honsberger, bn. Dec. 15, 1880; died Feb. 14, 1887. (**VII.**) Bessie Pearl Honsberger, bn. Jan. 14, 1888.

VI. Samuel Honsberger bn. in Lincoln Co., Ont., July 3, 1857. P. O., Jordan Sta., Ont. Mrd. Alberta Wismer, daughter of Tobias Wismer, Dec. 21, 1887. Farmer. Meth's. One child: (**VII.**) Ina May Honsberger, bn. Mar. 24, 1891.

VI. Mary Honsberger, bn. July 3, 1860. P. O., Jordan Sta., Ont. Meth. S.

VI. Amanda Honsberger, bn. Mar. 22, 1863. P. O., Jordan Sta., Ont. Music teacher. Meth. S.

VI. Aaron Honsberger, bn. Mar. 12, 1866. P O., Jordan Sta., Ont. Farmer. Meth. S.

VI. Curtis Honsberger, bn. June 23, 1872; died Nov. 24, 1872.

V. Elizabeth Moyer, bn. Feb. 17, 1827. Mrd. Jacob Albright, Feb. 17, 1846. P. O., Merritton, Ont.

Meth's. Children: Alma. Annie, Noah, Moses, Jacob, Barbara, Jesse, Lizzie.

VI. Alma Albright, bn. Dec. 19, 1847. P. O., Merritton, Ont. Seamstress. Meth. S.

VI. Annie Albright, bn. May 2, 1849. Mrd. William Greenwood, May 28, 1874. P. O., Merritton, Ont. Meth's. Children: (**VII.**) Samuel Herbert Greenwood. (**VII.**) Grace Greenwood. (**VII.**) William Fielding Greenwood. (**VII.**) Elizabeth Greenwood.

VI. Noah Albright, bn. May 16, 1851; died July 25, 1862.

VI. Moses Albright, bn. Oct. 13, 1853. Mrd. Eliza Rice, Oct. 26, 1882. P. O., Merritton, Ont. Boss weaver. Meth's. Children: (**VII.**) Ethel Gertrude Albright, bn. June 9, 1885. (**VII.**) Mabel Irene Albright, bn. Nov. 14, 1891.

VI. Jacob Albright, bn. Sept. 22, 1856. P. O., 122 High St., West Detroit, Mich. Meth. S.

VI. Barbara E. Albright, bn. Mar. 13, 1860. Mrd. George W. Pilling, June 24, 1884. P. O., Humberstone, Ont. Machinist. Mrs. Pilling was a music teacher before marriage. Meth. One child: (**VII.**) Elizabeth Pilling, bn. May 28, 1885.

VI. Jesse Albright, bn. Jan. 3, 1863. P. O., Merritton, Ont. Book-keeper. Meth. S.

VI. Lizzie Albright. bn. Aug. 13, 1866. P. O., Merritton, Ont. Meth. S.

V. Henry W. Moyer, bn. Apr. 6, 1828. Mrd. Nancy Ann House, daughter of Lewis House, Aug. 30, 1851. She was bn. Feb. 5, 1831; died June 12, 1875. Children: Lewis, Anna, Marietta.—Henry mrd. second wife Mary N. Fry, Dec. 19, 1876. P. O., Campden, Ont. Tinsmith. Ev. Ass'n. Children: Emery, Sidney.

VI. Lewis Allen Moyer, bn. Aug. 23, 1853. Mrd. Mary Margaret Albright, daughter of Daniel Albright, Aug. 23, 1874. She was born Nov. 24, 1855. Res. North Hamilton, Ont. Book-keeper for the Bell Organ and Piano Co., of Hamilton, Ont. Children: (**VII.**) Clayton Henry Moyer, bn. Dec. 27, 1874; died Aug. 11, 1893. (**VII.**) Gertrude Moyer, bn. Mar. 24, 1880. (**VII.**) Thomas Moyer, bn. Apr. 11, 1885. (**VII.**) Winifred Moyer, bn. Mar. 28, 1888.

VI. Anna Jane Moyer, bn. Sept. 27, 1856. S.
VI. Marietta Moyer, bn. June 12, 1865; died Mar. 9,
1880.
VI. Emery Fry Moyer, bn. May 8, 1881.
VI. Sidney Fry Moyer, bn. Dec. 9, 1884.
V. Tilman W. Moyer, bn. Feb. 10, 1831. Mrd.
Polly Hunsberger, Jan. 1854. She died Dec. 18,
1859. Children: Madilla, Samuel. —Tilman mrd.
second wife, Agnes Hunsberger, Feb. 1861. P. O.,
Campden, Ont. Furniture dealer, and undertaker.
Menn's. Children: Harvey, Pricilla, Orpha.
VI. Madilla Moyer, bn. May 16, 1856. Mrd. Levi
Fretz, Oct. 11, 1880. P. O., Campden, Ont. Fruit
grower. Meth's. Children: (VII.) Beatrice Fretz, bn.
Jan. 7, 1884. (VII.) Cora Fretz, bn. Aug. 21, 1888.
VI. Samuel Moyer, bn. Mar. 30, 1858; died Mar. 8,
1860.
VI. Rev. Harvey Moyer, bn. July 23, 1862. Mrd.
Kate Duncan, —. P. O., Walters Falls, Ont. Minis-
ter of Methodist ch. One child: (VII.) Beata Moyer.
VI. Pricilla Moyer, bn. May 4, 1867. Mrd. John E.
Wismer. (See Index of References No. 66.)
VI. Orpha Moyer, bn. Nov. 17, 1871; died May 5,
1885.
V. Esther Moyer, bn. in Lincoln Co., Ont., Mar. 16,
1833; died Sept. 1, 1881. Mrd. Jonas Moyer, Oct. 5,
1856. Farmer. Attended Menn. ch., Mrs. Moyer,
Ev. Ass'n. Children: Menno, Sylvester, Elizabeth,
Morgan, Simeon, Jonas, Annie, Alice.
VI. Menno Moyer, bn. Sept. 1, 1857. Mrd. Magda-
lena Louisa Hesse, —. P. O., Bloomingdale, Ont.
Farm laborer. Lutheran. Children: (VII.) Annie
Margaret Moyer. (VII.) William Angus Moyer. (VII.)
Sylvester Edward Moyer. (VII.) Bertha Elizabeth
Moyer. (VII.) Amelia Jane Moyer.
VI. Sylvester Moyer, D. D. S., bn. near Beamsville,
Lincoln Co., Ont., Feb. 20, 1859, on the homestead
of his grandfather where he spent the first 14 years
of his life, and where he learned to prattle the
"Pennsylvania Dutch," which has been of such ines-
timable benefit to him in his business life. When 14
years of age he with the family left the old home-

stead, and for nearly a year thereafter he tended bar
in a hotel. During the winter months of the four following years he attended a country school, working
for his board among the farmers. During the summer months he was variously employed in a Flax
mill, team driver, and "hired man," and thus managed to give his parents considerable assistance, and
pay the expenses of his education. When 18 years of
age he passed a teachers' examination, and at once
began to "train the young idea how to shoot." This
he continued to do for ten consecutive years. But the
confinement of the school room and too close attention to his studies in preparation for higher examinations somewhat overtaxed his physical powers.
This coupled with a strong desire to cross the "Her-
ring Pond" induced him to take a hurried trip to England during the summer of 1886. Before returning
he spent a week in the "Land o'cakes" and took a
short tramp among the farmers in the North of Ireland. The return trip from Glasgow to New York was
the roughest of the season. For six days as deep called
unto deep he was obliged to heave about everything
except the anchor. However the trip proved highly
beneficial to his health. Although fond of teaching,
but from the fact that teachers are poorly rewarded,
and stimulated also by mercenary motives and ex-
pectations, he directed his attention to the professions. He was then principal of the largest public
school in Waterloo Co., and in receipt of the largest
salary paid to a public school teacher in the county.
But he felt that he had reached the meridian of his
success, so he laid down the "ferrule" and took up
the forceps. In due time he received the degree of L.
D. S., and soon after the degree of D. D. S. from the
University of Toronto. Before the last candidate had
handed his papers to the examiners, he was "enroute"
to Galt, where he had bought an established practice,
and by the time that the result of his examination
reached him, he was in his office ready for business
and "thirsting for gore." His first patient was a
charity negro. Ominous he thought. But the cloud
had no "silver lining." Brighter days soon followed;

and now at the age of 33 after two years in his own dental office, he can only say that he is not sorry that he chose this as his profession. He was mrd. to Jennie Hunter, Oct. 12, 1886. P. O., Galt, Ont. Dentist. Presbyterian. Children: (VII.) Leslie Clare Moyer. (VII.) Alice Maud Moyer.

VI. Elizabeth Moyer, bn. Feb. 22, 1861. Mrd. Levi H. Stauffer, —. P. O., Breslau, Ont. Farmer. "Cosmopolitan" ch. No issue.

VI. Morgan Moyer, bn. in Lincoln Co., Ont., Nov. 16, 1863. Mrd. Marguerite Florence Bain, daughter of Frank Bain, Feb. 1, 1888. P. O., Montreal Junction, Ont. Real estate, and dealer in suburban city property. Attends Meth. ch. Children: (VII.) Hazel Estella Moyer, bn. Nov. 29, 1888. (VII.) Marguerite Olive Moyer, bn. Dec. 10, 1891.

VI. Simon Moyer, bn. in Lincoln Co., Ont., Feb. 20, 1866. Killed by lightning Aug. 11, 1892. He and his brother-in-law, Mr. Allan Eby, were plowing in a field when a storm came up suddenly. They took shelter under a tree, when they were struck by lightning, and both instantly killed. Their wives running out to see if any barns were struck, saw the horses running around the field, and went to learn the cause. They soon noticed a tree smoking, went to it and saw their husbands lying on each side of it with their feet nearly touching each other. One child: (VII.) Elva Moyer, bn. —; died —.

VI. Jonas A. Moyer, born May 30, 1869. Mrd. Charlotte McGiwinn, —. P. O., St. Thomas, Ont. Baggage and expressman on Ingersoll branch of Canadian Pacific Railway. Attends Meth. ch.; wife brought up a Roman Catholic. No issue.

VI. Anna Moyer, bn. Aug. 8, 1873. P. O., Galt, Ont. Baptist.

VI. Alice Moyer, bn. Aug. 5, 1876; died Feb. 28, 1881.

V. Rev. Israel W. Moyer, bn. in Lincoln Co., Ont., Apr. 16, 1835. Mrd Caroline Alberta House of Clinton Twp., Ont., June 4, 1861. P. O., Campden, Ont. House painter and minister. Mr. Moyer was converted in 1862. United with the Wesleyan Methodist

church of Smithville circuit, and was licensed as an
exhorter the same year, by the Quarterly Conference,
and placed on the circuit plan, with an appointment
for every two weeks, which he filled for two years.
In 1865 he was granted local preacher's license by
the Beamsville Quarterly Conference, and preached
every Sabbath for ten years. In 1875 he connected
himself with the Evangelical Association, under the
superintendency of Rev. S. N. Moyer, and preached
one year on the Campden and Gainsboro circuit,
traveling about thirty miles to his appointments, and
preaching twice every Sabbath. On account of the
German work, he not being able to preach in the
German language, the following year he returned to
the Wesleyan Methodist church as local preacher on
Beamsville circuit, preaching at Beamsville and
other points every Sabbath until 1882, when a change
was made in the circuit, after which he traveled about
twenty miles every Sabbath preaching twice, for two
years, Rev. J. Rowe, preacher in charge. Since 1885
he has preached every Sabbath morning at Jordan
Station, at which place he has preached for twenty-
five years. Children: Sarah, Alberta, James.

VI. Sarah Catharine Moyer, bn. Sept. 7, 1863;
died Apr. 14, 1865.

VI. Alberta Moyer, bn. Aug. 10, 1866. Mrd. Nelson
E. Honsberger, Dec. 23, 1884. P. O., Campden, Ont.
Ev. Ass'n. Children: (VII.) Charles Clarence Hons-
berger, bn. June 1, 1886; died May 2, 1891. (VII.)
Ethel Maud Honsberger, bn. May 13, 1888. (VII.)
Lucy Maria Honsberger, bn. Sept. 22, 1890. (VII.)
Hazel May Honsberger, bn. Sept. 19, 1892.

VI. James Arthur Moyer, bn. Apr. 7, 1870. P. O.,
Campden, Ont. Attends Methodist ch. S.

V. Moses W. Moyer, bn. in Lincoln Co., Ont., Sept.
17, 1837; died Apr. 26, 1890. Mrd. Catharine S.
High, Jan. 23, 1865. Carriage painter. Wesleyan
Meth. Children: (VI.) Owen Moyer, bn. in Cayuga,
Ont., Apr. 9, 1866. Freight clerk, and telegraph
operator, employed by the Grand Trunk Ry. Meth.
Ep. P. O., Jackson, Mich. S. (VI.) Malinda Moyer,
bn. Aug. 30, 1868. Res. 206 Dewitt St., Buffalo. S.

(VI.) William Moyer, bn. May 17, 1871. Res. 206 Dewitt St., Buffalo. S. **(VI.)** Tacy Moyer, bn. June 10, 1874. S. **(VI.)** Nellie Moyer, bn. Feb. 10, 1876; died Aug. 27, 1876. **(VI.)** Mabel Moyer, bn. Nov. 4, 1881.

V. Aaron W. Moyer, bn. in Lincoln Co., Ont., Feb. 25, 1840. Mrd. Catharine Honsberger, – –. She was bn. in Haldimand Co., Ont. in 1844. P. O., Campden, Ont. Farmer. Menn's. Children: **(VI)** Alpheus Moyer, bn. in 1872. **(VI.)** Sylvester Moyer, bn. in 1878. Ev. Ass'n ch.

V. Anna Moyer, bn. May 13, 1842. Mrd. Joseph M. Moyer, —. P. O., Campden, Ont. Farmer. One child: **(VI.)** Maud Moyer.

IV. Mary Wismer, bn. Jan. 5, 1800; died Dec. 22, 1880. Mrd. David Caughell. He died in 1848. Farmer in Elgin Co., Ont. Mr. C., mem. Ch. of England. Mrs. C., Disciple. Children: Maria, John, Alma, James, Henry, Edward.

V. Maria L. Caughell, bn. in Elgin Co., Ont., Mar. 11, 1821. Mrd. David M. Smith, – –. He died Nov. 23, 1853. Farmer. Ch. of England. Children: Alma, William, Mary, Malcolm.—Maria mrd. second husband, Abraham Grobb, Jan. 27, 1857. P. O., Portage La Prairie, Manitoba. Farmer. Children: Martha, Charles. (See Index of References No. 68.)

VI. Alma Smith, bn. June 3, 1845. Mrd. John McFadyen, —. Res. Victoria Road, Ont. Shoemaker. Meth's. Children: **(VII.)** Benjamin. **(VII.)** Jennie. **(VII.)** Martha.

VI. William Henry Smith, bn. Jan. 16, 1847. Mrd. Allie Parker, —. P. O., Treherne, Manitoba. Post master. Ch. of England. One child: **(VII.)** Reita Smith.

VI. Mary Jane Smith, bn. Nov. 8, 1848. Mrd. James A. Rose, Dec. 20, 1883. Miller. Ch. of England. P. O., Hargrove, Manitoba. No issue.

VI. Malcomb Smith, bn. Apr. 26, 1851; died Aug. 8, 1853.

V. John Caughell, bn. —. Mrd. Martha Green, —.

V. Alma Caughell, bn. —; died aged 19 years.

V. James Caughell, bn. —. Mrd. Rucena Bailey, —. P. O., St. Thomas, Ont.

V. Henry Caughell, bn. at Yarmouth Centre, Ont., Sept. 15, 1829. Mrd. Susan Thayer in 1851. She died —. Children: Maria, George, Arthur, Alma, Eve. — Henry mrd. second wife, Susan Wismer, daughter of Jacob Wismer, July 21, 1869. P. O., New Sarum, Ont. Farmer. Children: David, Annie, Martha, Mary.

VI. Maria Caughell, bn. Sept. 2, 1852. Mrd. James Chambers, Mar. 8, 1876. No issue.

VI. George Caughell, bn. May 6, 1854. Mrd. Frances Boughner, —. P. O., Aylmer, Ont. Nurseryman. Meth's. Children: (**VII.**) Ernest Caughell. (**VII.**) Cecil Caughell.

VI. Arthur Caughell, bn. Dec. 12, 1858. Mrd. Mary Brower, —. Railroad contractor. No children.

VI. Alma Caughell, bn. Nov. 15, 1861. Mrd. John D. Sinclair, —. P. O., Guilds, Ont. Farmer. Disciples. Children: (**VII.**) Henry Neil Sinclair, bn. — ; died —. (**VII.**) Flora Myrtle Sinclair, bn. —.

VI. Eve Caughell, bn. Oct. 5, 1865. Mrd. Daniel McLennan, —. P. O., Mt. Salem, Ont. Farmer. Children: (**VII.**) Edna Pearl McLennan, bn. May 28, 1886; died Sept. 25, 1886. (**VII.**) Lorne McLennan, bn. Oct. 30, 1887. (**VII.**) Grace McLennan, bn. Jan. 14, 1890; died Jan. 21, 1890.

VI. David J. Caughell, bn. Sept. 6, 1871. S.

VI. Annie L. Caughell, bn. May 23, 1874.

VI. Martha B. Caughell, bn. Jan. 26, 1876.

VI. Mary E. Caughell, bn. Mar. 28, 1882.

V. Edward Caughell, bn. —; died a young man. S.

IV. Jacob Wismer, bn. near Niagara, July 15, 1802; died Mar. 30, 1872. Mrd. Annie Wilcox, daughter of Wm. and Susan Wilcox, —. She was born Dec. 7, 1810; died Oct. 29, 1849. Mr. Wismer was a tall man, and stood 6 ft. 2 in. and weighed 300 pounds when at his best.

It is related that on a wager, he carried 12 bushels of oats in a bed-tick up an outside stairs. He afterwards said he could carry the oats easy enough, but the tick being so large rubbed against

the weather boards, and he had to steady himself
with one hand, and pull the tick along. Children:
Barbara, David, John, Henry, Elizabeth, Abraham,
Jacob, Susan.

V. Barbara Wismer, bn. Mar. 30, 1832. Mrd. John
Dicknison. P. O., Orvill, Ont. Farmer.

V. David Wismer, bn. in Yarmouth Twp., Ont.,
Aug. 10, 1834. Mrd. Sarah Hoskins, Dec. 6, 1860.
She was bn. Aug. 22, 1839. P. O., Rodney, Ont.
At the age of 20 years he purchased a farm of 150 acres
in Aldborough Twp., Ont., upon which he still resides.
During his early life game was very plentiful in his
section of the country, and on one occasion he killed
two deer at one shot, and four turkeys all in less than
an hour. Farmer. Disciples. Children: **(VI.)** Carrie
Wismer, bn. Oct. 21, 1864. Mrd. Duncan McNicol,
Nov. 14, 1889. P. O., St. Thomas, Ont. Drover.
(VI.) Alonzo Wismer, bn. Aug. 24, 1867. Mrd. Bessie
Leitch, Oct. 28, 1891. P. O., West Lorne, Ont.
Farmer. Disciples. **(VI.)** Henry Wismer, bn. Sept.
2, 1868. P. O., Rodney, Ont. S. **(VI.)** Mary Wis-
mer, bn. Mar. 12, 1870. S. **(VI.)** Edith Wismer, bn.
July 13, 1881.

V. John Wismer, bn. — ; died when 5 years old.

V. Henry Wismer, bn. — ; died when 9 years old.

V. Elizabeth Wismer, bn. in Elgin Co., Ont., Jan.
12, 1843. Mrd. William Trott, Dec. 29, 1863. P. O.,
Mount Brydges, Ont. Farmer. Ev. ch. Children:
Elizabeth, James, Mary, Grace.

VI. Elizabeth Ann Trott, bn. Aug. 17, 1867. S.

VI. James Strond Trott, bn. Mar. 27, 1870. S.

VI. Mary Trott, bn. Apr. 25, 1872. Mrd. James
Small, —. P.O., Mt. Brydges, Ont. Farmer. Presby's.
One child: **(VII.)** Russel Strond Small.

VI. Grace Trott, bn. Apr 21, 1874; died May 12,
1874.

V. Abraham Wismer, bn. in 1841. P. O., Rodney,
Ont. Farmer and cattle dealer. S.

V. Jacob Wismer, bn. Oct. 21, 1843; died Dec. 23,
1880. Mrd. Louisa Chatterson, —. Children: **(VI.)**
Clara Wismer, bn. —; died —. **(VI.)** Kenneth Wis-

mer, bn. —. 13 years old. (VI.) Susie Wismer, bn. —. 11 years old.

V. Susan Wismer, bn. in Elgin Co., Ont., May 25, 1845. Mrd. Henry Caughell. (See Index of References No. 67.)

IV. Barbara Wismer, bn. —; died —. Mrd. Abraham Grobb, son of Abraham and Elizabeth (Fretz) Grobb, Apr. 13, 1824. He was bn. in Lincoln Co., Ont., Feb. 19, 1803 (living 1889). Farmer. Menn's. Children: Elizabeth, John, Mary, Abraham, Margaret, Sarah, Moses, Ephraim, William.

V. Elizabeth Grobb, bn. Jan. 20, 1825; died Sept. 28, 1825.

V. John W. Grobb, bn. in Lincoln Co., Ont., Mar. 19, 1826. Mrd. Catharine Tallman, daughter of Oliver and Ann Tallman, Feb. 13, 1850. She was bn. Feb. 10, 1833; died —, 1855. Children: (VI.) Joshua Grobb, bn. Oct. 2, 1852.; died Nov. 19, 1869. (VI.) Barbara Ann Grobb, bn. Mar. 27, 1855; died Aug. 1855. — John mrd. second wife Frances, daughter of David and Susanna Honsberger, of South Cayuga, Oct. 7, 1856. She was bn. Nov. 4, 1835. Resides in Manitoba. Children: Walter, Maggie, Sylvester, Eli, Ettie, Annie, Jennie, Abraham.

VI. Walter Grobb, bn. Dec. 3, 1858. Mrd. Euretta Jane Lee, Oct. 29, 1884. Blacksmith. Resides in Manitoba. Children: (VII.) Loella May Grobb, bn. Oct. 10, 1885. (VII.) Alberta Larien Grobb, bn. Jan. 3, 1889.

VI. Maggie Grobb, bn. July 21, 1857. Mrd. Daniel Dashwood, Sept. 22, 1881. Blacksmith at South Cayuga, Ont. Children: (VII.) Charles Dashwood, bn. July 10, 1882. (VII.) William Arthur Dashwood, bn. May 11, 1884. (VII.) John Francis Dashwood, bn. Dec. 14, 1885. (VII.) Annie Mabel Dashwood, bn. May 22, 1889.

VI. Sylvester Grobb, bn. in South Cayuga, Ont., Sept. 29, 1860. Mrd. Jennie Trimble, Jan. 11, 1888. She was bn. in Huron Co., Manitoba, Feb. 9, 1868. Farmer in Manitoba. One child: (VII.) Maggie Ettie Grobb.

VI. Eli Grobb, bn. May 19, 1865. Res. Manitoba. S.

VI. Ettie Grobb, bn. Feb. 4, 1871.

VI. Annie Grobb, bn. Aug. 29, 1876.

VI. Abraham Arthur Grobb, bn. Oct. 17, 1878.

V. Mary Grobb, bn. Oct. 18, 1827; died Apr. 10, 1831.

V. Abraham Grobb, bn. in Elgin Co., Ont., Sept. 30, 1829. Mrd. widow Smith (Nee Maria L. Caughell), of Elgin Co., Ont. P. O., Portage La Prairie, Manitoba. Farmer. Children: Martha, Charles.

VI. Martha Grobb, bn. in Elgin Co., Ont., Oct. 2, 1857. Mrd. Henry Ogletree, May 2, 1883. Res. Manitoba. Children: **(VII.)** Roy Loran. **(VII.)** Charles Archibald.

VI. Charles E. Grobb, bn. in Lincoln Co., Ont., Oct. 22, 1859. Mrd. Margaret Ann Caruthers, Mar. 26, 1884. Res. Manitoba. Children: **(VII.)** Mabel Laura. **(VII.)** Hazel.

V. Margaret Grobb, bn. in Lincoln Co., Ont., June 18, 1831. S.

V. Sarah Grobb, bn. in Lincoln Co., Ont., Mar. 8, 1833. Mrd. William C. Smith, —. He died Apr., 1885. Hotel keeper. Mrs. Smith, Meth.

V. Moses W. Grobb, bn. in Lincoln Co., Ont., June 22, 1835. Mrd. Sarah Elizabeth Durham, Feb. 1863. She died Mar. 5, 1885. Children: **(VI.)** Adelaide Arminta Grobb, bn. Aug. 2, 1868. **(VI.)** Mary Martha Grobb, bn. July 31, 1872. **(VI.)** Joshua Charles Grobb, bn. Aug. 18, 1874. **(VI.)** Elmer Murry Grobb, bn. June 9, 1881.—Moses mrd. second wife Adelaide Eliza Durham, Jan. 1887. Builder. Presby.

V. Ephraim W. Grobb, bn. in Lincoln Co., Ont., July 8, 1837; died Aug. 14, 1885. Mrd. Susanna Wismer, Feb. 10, 1869. Farmer, also Township Assessor and Collector for 14 years. Presby. Children: **(VI.)** Millie Ann Grobb, bn. Mar. 16, 1871. **(VI.)** Hattie Jane Grobb, bn. June 4, 1879.

V. William H. Grobb, bn. in Lincoln Co., Ont., Mar. 27, 1843. Mrd. Elizabeth Ann James, —.

IV. John Wismer, bn. in Lincoln Co., Ont., Oct. 5, 1804; died Jan. 30, 1888. Mrd. Mary Crane, June 11, 1828. Farmer. Mrs. Wismer, Disciple. Children:

Elizabeth, Nancy, Henry, Amanda, John, Orlando, Alma, Mary, George, Stephen, Andrew, David.

V. Elizabeth Wismer, bn. Oct. 3, 1829. Mrd. Thomas McGregor. P. O., Belmont. Ont.

V. Nancy Wismer, bn. Sept. 9, 1831. Mrd. Jonathan W. Brooks, Aug. 17, 1851. P. O., Brush Creek, Ia. Farmer. Disciples. Children: Saphronia, Orlando, Mary, Stephen, Amanda, Frank, Etta.

VI. Saphronia Brooks, bn. Feb. 16, 1853. Mrd. Miles Charlton, —. P. O., Mapleton, Ont. Farmer. Disciples. Children: **(VII.)** Olive Charlton. **(VII.)** Coral Charlton. **(VII.)** Eva Charlton. **(VII.)** Orlando Charlton. **(VII.)** Ora Charlton.

VI. Orlando Brooks, bn. May 31, 1857. Mrd. Mary Beman, —. P. O., Eaton Rapids, Mich. School teacher. Disciples. Children: **(VII.)** Olive Brooks. **(VII.)** Mabel Veneta Brooks.

VI. Mary Elizabeth Brooks, bn. Dec. 21, 1858. Mrd. George H. Eckhart, —. P. O., Brush Creek, Iowa. Farmer. Later Day Saints. Children: **(VII.)** Edna Violet Eckhart. **(VII.)** Cecil May Eckhart.

VI. Stephen Ora Brooks, bn. July 19, 1863; died Sept. 29, 1887. School teacher. Disciple.

VI. Amanda Brooks, bn. Oct. 17, 1864. Mrd. John Jones, —. P. O., Fayette, Iowa. Carpenter. Disciple. One child: **(VII.)** Harold Carlyle Jones.

VI. Frank Brooks, bn. Apr. 5, 1868. Mrd. Lillian Marian Boots, —. P. O. Brush Creek, Ia. Farmer.

VI. Etta Brooks, bn. Dec. 5, 1872. Mrd. Fred Old Father, —. Carpenter. Disciple. One child: **(VII.)** Harry Lee Old Father.

V. Henry Wismer, bn. Oct. 26, 1833; died June 27, 1865. Mrd. Mary Taylor, —. She died —.

V. Amanda Wismer, bn. Oct. 19, 1835. Mrd. Jesse Hoover, —. P. O., Aylmer, Ont.

V. John Franklin Wismer, bn. Jan. 19, 1838. Mrd. Emeline Burns, — . P. O., Kingsville, Ont.

V. Orlando Wismer, bn. Dec. 27, 1839; died Oct. 5, 1863. Mrd. Clarinda Caughell, —. No issue.

V. Alma Wismer, bn. Dec. 16, 1841. Mrd. Robert Putnam, —. P. O., St. Thomas, Ont.

V. Mary Wismer, bn. Feb. 8, 1844. Mrd. Nicholas
Pero, —. P. O., St. Thomas, Ont.

V. George W. Wismer, bn. Apr. 29, 1846. Mrd.
Lavina Bishop, —. P. O., Flint, Mich.

V. Stephen Wismer, bn. May 28, 1848. Mrd. Carrie
Burns, —. P. O., Staples, Ont.

V. Andrew Wismer, bn. Mar. 28, 1850. Mrd. Carrie
Butchart. P. O., Mapleton, Ont. Farmer. Ch. of
Christ. Children: (VI.) Henry Franklin Wismer, bn.
Mar. 7, 1877. (VI.) Arthur Gavin Wismer, bn. July
7, 1878. (VI.) Mary Evelyn Wismer, bn. May 13,
1882.

V. David Wismer, bn. Oct. 10, 1852. Mrd. —. P. O.,
Groton Park.

IV. Nancy Wismer, bn. Feb. 12, 1807. Mrd. Samuel
Houser, — Farmer. Menn's. Children: Barbara,
Margaret, Abraham, Magdalena.

V. Barbara Houser, bn. —. Mrd. David Fretz, Aug.
30, 1859. He was bn. Mar. 5, 1838; died Mar. 28,
1878. Farmer. Menn's. Children: William, Franklin, Elizabeth, Nancy, David, Sophia, Lavina. — Barbara mrd. second husband, Andrew Kratz, Feb. 14,
1884. P. O., Jordan, Ont.

VI. William Fretz, bn. Sept. 2, 1860. Mrd. Maggie
Troup, Sept. 22, 1881. P. O., Jordan, Ont. Farmer.
Children: (VII.) Myrtle Fretz, bn. July 17, 1885.
(VII.) Lillian Fretz, bn. Nov. 18, 1888.

VI. Franklin Fretz, bn. Nov. 3, 1861. Mrd. Catharine, daughter of Rev. Daniel Honsberger, Oct. 3,
1888. P. O., Jordan Sta., Ont. Meth. One child:
(VII.) Clarence Elton Fretz, bn. Jan. 26, 1890.

VI. Elizabeth Fretz, bn. Dec. 11, 1862. Mrd. James
Troup, Oct. 5, 1882. Farmer. Meth's. Children:
(VII.) Franklin Troup. (VII.) David Troup. (VII.)
Mildred Troup.

VI. Nancy Fretz, bn. July 9, 1864. Mrd. Alexander
Troup, Jan. 3, 1882. Track foreman on G. T. R. R.
Meth's. Children: (VII.) Arthur Troup, bn. Apr. 8,
1884. (VII.) William Troup, bn. June 26, 1886. (VII.)
Roy Troup, bn. Mar. 11, 1889.

VI. David Fretz, bn. in Lincoln Co., Ont., Mar. 5, 1866. Mrd. Minnie Troup, Jan. 1890. Carpenter. Meth's.

VI. Sophia Fretz, bn. Dec. 25, 1867. Mrd. Martin L. Ressor, Feb. 15, 1888. Farmer. Meth's. One child: **(VII.)** Edna May Ressor, bn. Dec. 18, 1889.

VI. Lavina Fretz, bn. Feb. 7, 1869. Meth.

V. Margaret Houser, bn. July 30, 1836. Mrd. Samuel J. Fretz, Apr. 15, 1856. He was bn. May 1, 1834. P. O., Jordan, Ont. Farmer. Menn's. Children: Anna, John, Mary, Sarah, Catharine, Barbara, Jacob, Margaret, Sylvester, Albert, Emanuel, Emerson.

VI. Anna E. Fretz, bn. Feb. 4, 1857; died Dec. 18, 1887. Mrd. Solomon H. Moyer. Farmer. Menn's. Children: **(VII.)** Ervin Moyer, bn. June 27, 1879; died May 25, 1880. **(VII.)** Maggie Moyer, bn. Dec. 26, 1880. **(VII.)** Sylvester Moyer, bn. Oct. 5, 1882. **(VII.)** Clayton Moyer bn. May 5, 1885.

VI. John Franklin Fretz, bn. Dec. 30, 1858; died Oct. 20, 1859.

VI. Mary Fretz, bn. Apr. 20, 1860.

VI. Sarah Fretz, bn. July 25, 1861. Mrd. Solomon H. Eckhardt, Mar. 25, 1888. Laborer. Menn. Br. in Christ.

VI. Catharine Fretz, bn. Mar. 14, 1863. Mrd. Joshua Atyeo, Nov. 25, 1884. Farmer. Children: **(VII.)** William Edward Atyeo, bn. Sept. 12, 1885. **(VII.)** Samuel Delos Atyeo, bn. Jan. 17, 1887.

VI. Barbara Fretz, bn. Nov. 30, 1864. Mem. Menn. Br. in Christ. S.

VI. Jacob H. Fretz, bn. Oct. 17, 1866. Mem. Menn. Br. in Christ. S.

VI. Margaret Fretz, bn. May 29, 1869; died Nov. 1, 1869.

VI. Sylvester Fretz, bn. Oct. 2, 1870.

VI. Albert Fretz, bn. Jan. 27, 1874; died May 12, 1880.

VI. Emanuel Fretz, bn. Jan. 17, 1877.

VI. Emerson Fretz, bn. July 5, 1879; died Nov. 16, 1880.

V. Magdalena Houser, bn. July 9, 1842. Mrd. Christopher Hoover. (See Index of References No. 84.)

V. Abraham Houser, bn. in Haldimand Co., Ont., June 9, 1849. Mrd. Fidelia Gayman, Apr. 29, 1875. P. O., Dunnville, Ont. Fruit grower. Menn's. Children: **(VI.)** William Housser, bn. Dec. 16, 1877. **(VI.)** Isaac Housser, bn. Jan. 9, 1880; died Jan. 23, 1880.

IV. Margaret Wismer, bn. Dec. 30, 1809; died May 30, 1877. Mrd. Stephen Wilcox, about 1829. He died Oct. 19, 1888. Farmer. Baptists. Children: Esther, Susan, Henry, George, Mary.

V. Esther Wilcox, bn. at New Sarum, Ont., Sept. 29, 1830. P. O., Orwell, Ont. Baptist. S.

V. Susan Wilcox, bn. in Dorchester Twp., Ont., Sept. 19, 1832. Mrd. Albert Secord, —. P. O., St. Thomas, Ont. One child: **(VI.)** Ida Secord, bn. —; died —.

V. Henry Wilcox, bn. Dec. 16, 1835; died Apr. 3, 1880. Mrd. Naomi Stehes.

V. George M. Wilcox, bn. in Yarmouth Twp., Ont., Jan. 25, 1838. Mrd. Margaret Elliott, Nov. 10, 1864. P. O., St. Thomas, Ont. Machinist. Disciples' ch. No children.

V. Mary E. Wilcox, bn. Jan. 17, 1841; died Aug. 1, 1854.

III. Elizabeth Wismer, bn. in Bucks Co., Pa., Apr. 3, 1776; died —. Mrd. Jacob Fry in 1794. He was bn. Jan. 27, 1768; died—. Emigrated to Canada in 1800. Children: Mary, Henry, Barbara, Jacob, John, Amos, Elizabeth, Samuel, Dilman, Joseph, Isaac, Catharine.

IV. Mary Fry, bn. in Bucks Co., Pa., July 3, 1795; died May 30, 1876. Mrd. Moses Couse, June 22, 1824. Farmer. Presby's. Children: Elizabeth, Barbara, Anna, Mary, Margaret, Catharine.

V. Elizabeth Couse, bn. Apr. 9, 1825; died Oct. 18, 1883. Mrd. James S. Henry, —. He died Apr. 17, 1882.

V. Barbara Couse, bn. Oct. 5, 1826. Mrd. Joseph Snyder, —. P. O., Toronto, Ont.

18

V. Anna Couse, bn. Oct. 24, 1828. Mrd. Niel Mac Gregor, —. He died —. P. O., St. Catharines, Ont.

V. Mary Couse, bn. June 16, 1830. Mrd. Jacob Oldham, —. He died —. P. O., Beamsville, Ont. Merchant. Presby's. Children: Jeanie, James, Minnie, Alexander, Jessie, John.

VI. Jeanie Oldham, bn. Dec. 8, 1855. Mrd. Thomas Kemp, —. P. O., Seaforth, Ont. Miller. Children: (**VII.**) May. (**VII.**) Robert. (**VII.**) Kenneth. (**VII.**) Beverly.

VI. James Oldham, bn. July 18, 1857. Mrd. — Wismer. P. O., Brantford, Ont.

VI. Minnie Oldham, bn. June 21, 1859. Presby.

VI. Alexander Oldham, bn. May 8, 1865. Presby.

VI. Jessie Oldham, bn. Dec. 17, 1866. Presby.

VI. John Oldham, bn. Nov. 16, 1869. Presby.

V. Margaret Couse, bn. Mar. 9, 1832. Mrd. Charles Hunter. He died —. P. O., Windson, Ont. Merchant.

V. Catharine Couse, bn. June 27, 1839. Mrd. Dr. — McClean, —. He died —. Mrd. second husband John Longuin, —. Res. Brooklyn, N. Y.

IV. Henry Fry, bn. in Bucks Co., Pa., Mar. 27, 1797; died July 30, 1887. Mrd. Anna High, Apr. 3, 1823. Farmer. Menn's. Children: Elizabeth, Catharine, Catharine, Barbara, Anna, Mary John, Henry, Jacob, William, Martha.

V. Elizabeth Fry, bn. Mar. 14, 1824. Mrd. Isaac Wismer. (See Index of References No. 69.)

V. Catharine Fry, bn. Aug. 18, 1825; died Nov. 21, 1825.

V. Catharine Fry, bn. June 12, 1827. Mrd. Valentine Honsberger, Nov. 26, 1851. P. O., South Cayuga, Ont. Farmer. Ev. Ass'n. Children: Solomon, Annie, Henry, Jerome, Isaac, Samuel, Oscar, Edward, Martha, George, Elsie.

VI. Solomon Honsberger, bn. in 1853; died in 1853.

VI. Annie Honsberger, bn. in 1854. Mrd. Freeman H. Moyer. (See Index of References No. 70.)

VI. Henry F. Honsberger, bn. in 1857.

VI. Jerome F. Honsberger, M. D., bn. in Haldimand Co., Ont., Oct. 6, 1859. Mrd. Alberta C. Stoddard,

of Delhi, Ont., Oct. 14, 1890. P. O., Delhi, Ont.
Methodists. Dr. Honsberger received his early education in the district schools, going to school during
the winter months, and during the summer assisted
on his father's farm. But his ambitious young mind
soon made him dissatisfied with his limited education,
and the small opportunities which a farm life afforded
for advancement. Accordingly at the age of 17, he,
with his brother, began to prepare himself for the 3d
class teachers' examination, and with the help of the
lady teacher who boarded in their home, by improv-
ing every spare moment often studying till midnight
after a hard day's work on the farm, they passed the
examination successfully. In the fall succeeding the
examination he attended the Model School, in Caledonia, obtained his certificate, and at the beginning
of the New Year, began teaching. After teaching for
3 years, he spent a term at the Collegiate Institute,
Brantford, and in July 1880, passed the 2d class
teachers' examination there, carrying off a scholarship given by that Institution for proficiency. He
next attended the Normal School at Toronto, obtained his Professional 2d class certificate, and taught
for two years more. But as is often the case he was
only using the profession of teaching as a stepping-
stone to something higher. Ever since his boyhood
he had made up his mind to be a doctor, and now he
was about to enter upon the fulfillment of that dream.
In the fall of 1882, he began his medical course at
Trinity Medical College, Toronto, passed his examinations successfully at the end of each year, and
graduated in March 1886, both from Trinity Medical
College and Trinity University, standing at the head
of his class at the University. A few weeks later he
sailed for England, where he spent six months con-
tinuing his studies in the largest hospital, and under
the most distinguished physicians of London. Here
he passed another examination, taking the degree of
Licentiate of the Royal College of Physicians, of
England. He returned in November, and in the following spring located in Delhi, a thriving little town
in Norfolk Co., Ont., where he has worked a large

and lucrative practice. Though he has been less than six years in actual practice, Dr. Honsberger is already widely known throughout that district as a clever young physician, whose ability is sure to gain for him a leading place in his profession.

VI. Isaac Honsberger, bn. and died in 1861.
VI. Samuel Honsberger, bn. and died in 1863.
VI. J. Oscar Honsberger, bn. in 1864.
VI. Edward Honsberger, bn. in 1866; died in 1871.
VI. Martha Honsberger, bn. in 1869; died in 1869.
VI. George H. Honsberger, bn. in 1871.
VI. Elsie Honsberger, bn. and died in 1873.

V. Barbara Fry, born Oct. 7, 1829. Mrd. John Houser, Oct. 7, 1864. P. O., Campden, Ont.

V. Anna Fry, bn. Feb. 7, 1831; died Jan. 31, 1859. Mrd. Jacob Hipple, Jan. 23, 1855. Children: William, Frank.

VI. William H. Hipple, bn. Nov. 28, 1855. Mrd. Magdalena A. Moyer, July 12, 1881. P. O., Hartford, Conn. Stenographer. No issue.

VI. Frank Hipple, bn. in Lincoln Co., Ont., Jan. 9, 1858. Mrd. Anna, daughter of Judge H. B. Whitbeck, of New York City, Apr. 18, 1888. Mr. Hipple attended the public schools until 16, then went to the Grammar school at Beamsville, Ont. one year. He next attended the Collegiate Institute in St. Catharines for one year. He then taught school in Niagara Twp., Lincoln Co. for two years, after which he went to the McGill University, Montreal, where he remained two years. He then came to New York, and studied one year in the law department of the University of New York, after which he was admitted to the New York Bar. In 1884 he went abroad and remained in England two years for the benefit of his health, and recreation. On his return he located in New York where he has been since engaged in the practice of law. Democrat. Episcopalian.

V. Mary Fry, bn. Mar. 21, 1834. Mrd. Jacob Hipple, Feb. 19, 1861. P. O., Campden, Ont. School teacher and farmer. Ev. Ass'n. Children: (**VI.**) Arminta Hipple, bn. Dec. 11, 1863; died Feb. 21, 1864. (**VI.**) Alpheus H. Hipple, bn. Feb. 25, 1865.

Dentist at Stratford, Ont. (VI.) Clara Hipple, bn. Mar. 5, 1867. (VI.) Lillie M. Hipple, bn. May 17, 1875.

V. John Fry, M. D., bn. Apr. 30, 1836. Mrd. Caroline Overholt, Sept. 28, 1864. P. O., Selkirk, Ont. Physician. Ch. of Christ. Children: (VI.) Charles Vernon Fry, bn. Aug. 29, 1866. Wholesale drygoods in Detroit, Mich. Ch. of Christ. S. (VI.) Frank DeWitt Fry, bn. July 15, 1868. Law student in Toronto University. Ch. of Christ. S. (VI.) Lillie M. Fry, bn. Sept. 17, 1870. School teacher. S. (VI.) Minnie N. Fry, bn. Sept. 17, 1870. S.

V. Henry Fry, bn. Sept. 17, 1838; died Feb. 8, 1863.

V. Jacob Fry, bn. in Lincoln Co., Ont., Mar. 3, 1841. Mrd. Samantha Ann Reece, Nov. 17, 1863. P. O., Jordan, Ont. Farmer. Meth's. Children: (VI.) Bertha Fry, bn. Nov. 22, 1866; died Nov. 26, 1868. (VI.) Loyell Judson Fry, bn. Jan. 13, 1868. Mrd. Addie Jane Simmerman, Feb. 17, 1891. P. O., Jordan, Ont. Farmer. Meth's. (VI.) Melvin Ollie Fry, bn. Dec. 2, 1871. P. O., Jordan, Ont. Bookkeeper, and stenographer. Meth.

V. William Fry, bn. Sept. 24, 1843. Mrd. Lydia Hayney, Aug. 30, 1871. P. O., Fenwick, Ont.

V. Martha Fry, bn. Nov. 24, 1846. Mrd. Benjamin Moot, Feb. 25, 1868. P. O., Pelham, Ont.

IV. Barbara Fry, bn. Dec. 25, 1802; died March 5, 1886. Mrd. Jacob Overholt, Aug. 6, 1833. Carpenter and farmer. Menn's in early life, later joined Ev. Ass'n. Children: Samuel, Isaac, Mary, Elizabeth, Sophia, Sarah, Israel.

V. Samuel Overholt, bn. May 25, 1834; died Oct. 25, 1857. S.

V. Isaac Overholt, bn. Dec. 10, 1835. Mrd. Matilda Hoover, Nov. 11, 1850. P. O., South Cayuga, Ont. In early life taught school, now farmer. Meth's. Children: Mary, Hervey, Emma, Ella, Percey.

VI. Mary Catharine Overholt, bn. Dec. 7, 1859. Mrd. Rev. H. C. Dunsmore, —. Minister of Congregational ch. Children: (VII.) Harry Coyne Duns-

more, bn. —; died —. **(VII.)** Percey Robert Dunsmore, bn. —; died —.

VI. Hervey Overholt, bn. Aug. 5, 1861. Meth. S.

VI. Emma R. Overholt, bn. Feb. 27, 1870. P. O.,
South Cayuga, Ont. School teacher. Meth. S.

VI. Ella R. Overholt, bn. Feb. 27, 1870, (twin). P.
O., South Cayuga, Ont. School teacher. Meth. S.

VI. Percey Overholt, bn. Apr. 5, 1879.

V. Mary Overholt, bn. Apr. 11, 1837. Mrd. Samuel
M. Moyer, —. He died —. P. O., Campden, Ont.

V. Elizabeth Overholt, bn. June 12, 1838. Mrd.
Joseph Sherk, Aug. 28, 1873. P. O., Selkirk, Ont.
Farmer. Disciples. One child: **(VI.)** Joseph Melvin .
Sherk, bn. June 30, 1874. Attending high school at
Dunnville, Ont.

V. Sophia Overholt, bn. Apr. 12, 1840. Mrd. Val-
entine Stengel. He died —. P. O., Campden, Ont.
Sophia mrd. second husband, Andrew Wismer. (See
Index of References No. 71.)

V. Sarah Overholt, bn. in Lincoln Co., Ont., Apr.
22, 1841. Mrd. Peter E. Culp, Sept. 24, 1861. P.O.,
Beamsville, Ont. Farmer. Meth's. Children: Mary,
Matilda, James, Emma, Israel, Lettie.

VI. Mary Jane Culp, bn. Jan. 20, 1863; died Aug. 5,
1865.

VI. Matilda Ann Culp, bn. Aug. 3, 1864. P. O.,
Beamsville, Ont. Menn.

VI. James Henry Culp, bn. Aug. 28, 1866. P. O.,
Beamsville, Ont. Farmer.

VI. Emma Elizabeth Culp, bn. Apr. 8, 1869. Mrd.
Jerome Tufford, Sept. 14, 1886. P. O., Beamsville,
Ont. Farmer. One child: **(VII.)** Arthur Jerome
Tufford, bn. Aug. 5, 1887.

VI. Israel Judson Culp, bn. Nov. 12, 1871. Mrd.
Bertha Goudie, Dec. 22, 1892. P. O., Tonawanda,
N. Y. Street paver.

VI. Lettie Bell Culp, bn. Oct. 13, 1874. Mrd. Charles
D. Barber, Sept. 16, 1890. P. O., Beamsville, Ont.
Public laborer. One child: **(VII.)** Charles Lloyd Bar-
ber, bn. Oct. 28, 1892.

V. Israel Overholt, bn. Mar. 22, 1843. Mrd. Caroline Beck, Mar. 21, 1865. P. O., South Cayuga, Ont.

Retired farmer, now engaged in bee keeping. Ev.
Ass'n. One child: **(VI.)** Lilly Idora Overholt, bn.
Nov. 25, 1868. Mrd. Isaac W. High, Dec. 15, 1886.
Farmer. No issue.
IV. Jacob Fry, bn. in Lincoln Co., Ont., Sept. 15,
1804; died May 7, 1845. Mrd. Elizabeth Nash, Mar.
2, 1830. Farmer. Mr. Fry, Mennonite; after his
death Mrs. Fry joined Ev. Ass'n ch. Children: Mary,
Joseph, Abraham, Elizabeth, Anna, Salome.
V. Mary Fry, bn. Nov. 30, 1830. Mrd. Henry
Honsberger, Oct. 29, 1851. He was bn. Oct. 21,
1822. Farmer. Ev. Ass'n. Children: Mary, Jacob,
Salome, William.
VI. Mary Honsberger, bn. Sept. 6, 1852. Mrd.
Freeman M. Moyer, Dec. 4, 1875. He died Nov. 22,
1887. Children: **(VII.)** Milton Leslie Moyer, bn. Jan.
29, 1879. **(VII.)** William Arden Moyer, bn. Sept. 4,
1887.
VI. Jacob Honsberger, bn. July 25, 1855; died Aug.
28, 1884. Mrd. Saphrona C. Culp, Feb. 18, 1880.
One child: **(VII.)** Eva Dell Honsberger, bn. Dec. 9,
1882.
VI. Salome Honsberger, bn. Apr. 14, 1859; died
June 28, 1890. Mrd. William H. Crowe, Dec. 21,
1887. Children: **(VII.)** Effie Crowe, bn. Dec. 16, 1888.
(VII.) Ethel Crowe, bn. Dec. 24, 1889.
VI. William Honsberger, bn. Jan. 30, 1862. Mrd.
Minnie A. Haist, Jan. 25, 1888. P. O., Jordan, Ont.
Farmer. Ev. Ass'n.
V. Joseph N. Fry, bn. Nov. 27, 1832. Mrd. Nancy
Albright, Dec. 3, 1861. P. O., Campden, Ont.
Farmer. Ev. Ass'n. Children: **(VI.)** John E. Fry,
bn. Sept. 15, 1862. P. O., Oaklawn, Ill. Carpenter.
Attends Meth. ch. S. **(VI.)** Daniel W. Fry, bn.
June 2, 1865. Mrd. Margaret Hedden, Sept. 1886.
Res. 113 Emily St., Buffalo, N. Y. Stenographer and
type writer. Meth's. No issue. **(VI.)** Jacob O Fry,
bn. July 1, 1867; died Sept. 3, 1869. **(VI.)** Henry
Edgar Fry, bn. Mar. 5, 1871. Res. 41 India St., Bos-
ton, Mass. Stenographer. Congregational ch.
V. Abraham Fry, bn. Aug. 10, 1835. Mrd. Martha
Jane Pysher, Jan. 30, 1861. P. O., Jordan, Ont.

Farmer. Ev. Ass'n. Children: Wilford, Edward, David, Sylvester, Abraham.

VI. Wilford Kirby Fry, bn. Oct. 29, 1862. Mrd. Jessie Olway Zimmerman, Dec. 17, 1890. P. O., Jordan, Ont.

VI. Edward Wilson Fry, bn. Aug. 5, 1864. Mrd. Cinderella Rittenhouse, Jan. 14, 1890. P. O., Jordan, Ontario.

VI. David Pysher Fry, bn. Feb. 23, 1866. Mrd. Caroline Dohn, Sept. 29, 1886. P. O., Tintern, Ont. One child: (VII.) Abram Delbert Fry.

VI. Sylvester Melvin Fry, bn. Apr. 25, 1871. Res. Chicago, Ill. S.

VI. Abraham Delbert Fry, bn. June 5, 1872; died Sept. 19, 1872.

V. Elizabeth Fry, bn. Nov. 3, 1837. Mrd. Rev. Robert A. Clark, May 18, 1871. At the time of their marriage Mr. Clark was an itinerant minister of the United Brethren ch. and continued to preach until 1882, when they settled on a farm, where they remained until the spring of 1890, and then he resumed preaching again. He was bn. in Cumberland, England. Children: (VI.) John Benson Clark, bn. Feb. 23, 1872. (VI.) Alberta Viola Clark, bn. Feb. 16, 1874. (VI.) Annie Mary Clark, bn. Apr. 20, 1878. (VI.) Robert Fry Clark, bn. Feb. 10, 1880.

V. Anna Fry, bn. Apr. 8, 1840. Mrd. Andrew Bilger, Feb. 8, 1870. P. O., South Cayuga, Ont. Shoemaker and shoe merchant. Ev. Ass'n. Children: (VI.) William Fry Bilger, bn. Dec. 6, 1870. (VI.) John Edward Bilger, bn. June 9, 1872. (VI.) Jacob Alborn Bilger, bn. Jan. 11, 1874. (VI.) Charles Ruby Bilger, bn. July 12, 1876. (VI.) Gertie Bilger, bn. Nov. 4, 1880. (VI.) Anna Lavilla Bilger, bn. Dec. 19, 1882; died Dec. 28, 1884.

V. Salome Fry, bn. Aug. 16, 1842. Mrd. William H. Michener, Dec. 27, 1864. P. O., Dunnville, Ont. Carriage maker. Meth's. Children: (VI.) Alberta Michener, bn. May 18, 1868. Mrd. John Dohn, Jan. 15, 1889. P. O., Buffalo, N. Y. (VI.) Jennie Ann Michener, bn. Jan. 5, 1872. (VI.) Harold Herbert

Michener, bn. May 6, 1878. (VI.) Ethel Winifred Michener, bn. June 10, 1883.

IV. John Fry, bn. Aug. 7, 1806; died Jan. 23, 1884. Mrd. Anna Moyer, Mar. 24, 1829. She was bn. Oct. 30, 1806; died Oct. 7, 1851. Blacksmith. In early life belonged to Mennonite ch., later he joined the Evangelists, and finally became a Universalist. Children: Jacob, David, Dilman, Henry, John, Samuel, Anna, Elizabeth, Catharine, Joseph. — John mrd. second wife, Magdalena (Honsberger) High, Dec. 21, 1852. Children: Mary, Barbara.

V. Jacob Fry, bn. in Lincoln Co., Ont., Dec. 31, 1829. Mrd. Mary Ann Cowlthorp, Oct. 1, 1850. She died Oct. 12, 1879. P. O., Cottam, Ont. Farmer. Meth's. Children: John, Ellen, Rosetta, Rozaltha, James, Susan, Eusebia, Clara, Jacob.

VI. John Harlen Fry, bn. Jan. 27, 1852. Mrd. Lauretta Wigle, May 5, 1880. She died Jan. 3, 1885. Res. Chicago, Ill. Carpenter. Meth's. One child: (VII.) Asa Harlen Fry, bn. Mar. 9, 1882; died Sept. 6, 1882.

VI. Ellen Delena Fry, bn. Oct. 5, 1853. Mrd. Charles Totten, Feb. 4, 1892. P. O., Essex, Ont.

VI. Rosetta Catharine Fry, bn. May 24, 1855. Mrd. John Vickers, Feb. 26, 1879. He died Sept. 7, 1880. Farmer. Meth's. One child: (VII.) Earle Ranson David Vickers.

VI. Rozaltha Fry, bn. May 24, 1855 (twin); died June 12, 1855.

VI. James Richard Fry, bn. July 26, 1859. Mrd. Effie May Janson Leamington, Dec. 17, 1890. Res. Buffalo, N. Y. Meth's.

VI. Susan Elizabeth Fry, bn. Sept. 22, 1861; died May 1, 1864.

VI. Eusebia Ann Fry, bn. June 9, 1864. Mrd. Alfred Gascoyne. P. O., Essex, Ont. Farmer. Meth's. Children: (VII.) Orpha Viola Gascoyne, bn. Sept. 6, 1886. (VII.) Raymond Aurillan Gascoyne, bn. Jan. 10, 1888; died Sept. 11, 1888. (VII.) Peray Harlan Gascoyne, bn. Apr. 19, 1891.

VI. Clara Leslie Fry, bn. Nov. 4, 1866. S.

VI. Jacob M. Fry, bn. Jan. 27, 1869. S.

V. David Fry, bn. Dec. 28, 1831. P. O., Dunnville,
Ont. S.

V. Dilman Fry, bn. May 30, 1833. Mrd. Louisa
Jones, —. P. O., South Cayuga, Ont. Carpenter
and farmer. Children: Sarah, John, Wellette, Janette,
David, Rosa, Mary, George, Orpha, Eva.

VI. Sarah Elizabeth Fry, bn. Dec. 18, 1861. P. O.,
31 Sackville, Toronto, Ont. Baptist. S.

VI. John Malcolm Fry, bn. Sept. 2, 1863. Mrd.
Jessie Deamude. P. O., South Cayuga, Ont. Mrs.
Fry, Baptist. Children: (VII.) Della Fry, bn. Jan. 16,
1886. (VII.) Donald Blane Fry, bn. Nov. 15, 1887. (VII.)
Helena Fry, bn. Jan. 21, 1890; died Feb. 15, 1891.
(VII.) Mildred Fry, bn. July 11, 1892.

VI. Wellette Fry, bn. Sept. 8, 1865. Mrd. John A.
Housberger, Jan. 7, 1885. P. O., Dunnville, Ont.
Painter. Mrs. Fry, Baptist. Children: (VII.) Muriel
Constance Housberger. (VII.) Harold Housberger.
(VII.) Murry Housberger. (VII.) Estella Housberger.

VI. Janette Fry, bn. Aug. 8, 1867. Mrd. Erie L.
Crumb, Feb. 23, 1886. P. O., Dunnville, Ont.
Painter. Children: (VII.) William Benonni Crumb.
(VII.) Robert Victor Crumb. (VII.) Edward Frederick
Crumb.

VI. David Allen Fry, bn. Mar. 27, 1871. P. O.,
South Cayuga, Ont. S.

VI. Rosa Bell Fry, bn. June 11, 1872. P. O., South
Cayuga, Ont. Teacher. S.

VI. Mary Emma Fry, bn. Aug. 11, 1874. P. O.,
South Cayuga, Ont. Evangelical ch. S.

VI. George Edward Fry, bn. Sept. 12, 1876.

VI. Orpha Estella Fry, bn. Aug. 22, 1879; died Jan.
22, 1880.

VI. Eva May Fry, bn. May 26, 1881. Ev. Ass'n ch.

V. Henry Fry, bn. Nov. 17, 1834; died Jan. 1, 1835.

V. John Fry, bn. Apr. 12, 1836; died Feb. 19,
1841.

V. Samuel J. Fry, bn. Dec. 24, 1838. Mrd. Magda-
lena Houser, Sept. 27, 1864. P. O., Dunnville, Ont.
Baker. Inclines to Universalist ch. Children: John,
Naomi, Jason, Agnes, Magdalena, Annie, Samuel.

VI. John Sylva Fry, bn. July 14, 1865. Mrd. Maggie Sullivan, Oct. 27, 1886. P. O., 252 Ohio St., Buffalo, N. Y. Baker. Mrs. F., Catholic. Children: **(VII.)** Nellie Lauretta Fry, bn. July 22, 1887; died Dec. 30, 1891. **(VII.)** Maggie Leland Fry, bn. Dec. 2, 1889. **(VII.)** Katie Fry, bn. Nov. 12, 1891.

VI. Naomi Fry, bn. Feb. 24, 1867. P. O., Buffalo, N. Y. Single.

VI. Jason Fry, bn. June 23, 1868; died Mar. 25, 1869.

VI. Agnes Fry, bn. Oct. 2, 1869.

VI. Magdalena Ophelia Fry, bn. Nov. 15, 1870.

VI. Annie Laurie Fry, bn. Aug. 12, 1872. Res. Newark, Del.

VI. Samuel Iva Fry, bn. Feb. 19, 1874.

V. Anna Fry, bn. Feb. 15, 1841; died Mar. 7, 1867. Single.

V. Elizabeth Fry, bn. Aug. 19, 1843. P. O., South Cayuga, Ont. S.

V. Catharine Fry, bn. Aug. 14, 1846. Mrd. Abram W. Dickhout, in 1867. P.O., Dunnville, Ont. Farmer. Children: **(VI.)** Meta Annetta Dickhout, bn. Aug. 22, 1870. Mrd. Bert Elderidge, of Buffalo, N. Y., May 28, 1891. Commissioner of the fruit market. **(VI.)** Edith Luella Dickhout, bn. June 12, 1872. **(VI.)** Earle L. Elmore Dickhout, bn. Aug. 4, 1874. **(VI.)** Mary Maud Dickhout, bn. Apr. 15, 1877. **(VI.)** Genevieve Somerville Dickhout, bn. Apr. 11, 1879. **(VI.)** Robbie Roy Dickhout, stillborn Nov. 29, 1881. **(VI.)** Percival Lorne Dickhout, bn. July 27, 1886.

V. Joseph Fry, bn. Nov. 23, 1848; died Dec. 29, 1848.

V. Mary Fry, bn. Aug. 25, 1855; died 1882. Mrd. Emerson High, Feb. 1882. P.O., South Cayuga, Ont. Farmer. Mennonites. One child: **(VI.)** Orpha Jane High, bn. Dec. 1882.

V. Barbara Fry, bn. Feb. 25, 1858; died Mar. 27, 1858.

IV. Amos Fry, bn. June 29, 1808; died Oct. 26, 1827. S.

IV. Elizabeth Fry, bn. May 4, 1810; died Mar. 25, 1839. Mrd. David Grobb, Sept. 23, 1828. He was bn. Dec. 9, 1804; died Mar. 3, 1890. Blacksmith, wagon-maker and farmer. Menn's. Children: Elizabeth, Joshua, Barbara, Jacob, Anna.

V. Elizabeth Grobb, bn. in Lincoln Co., Ont., June 26, 1829; died Oct. 2, 1887. Mrd. David E. Culp, Nov. 12, 1850. Farmer. Meth's. Children: **(VI.)** David H. Culp, bn. Oct. 9, 1851; died Sept. 3, 1879. S. **(VI.)** Mary Ursula Culp, bn. June 25, 1853; died Feb. 11, 1872. S. **(VI.)** Dudley Jonas Culp, bn. Apr. 30, 1855. **(VI.)** Joshua F. Culp, bn. July 28, 1859. **(VI.)** Martha C. Culp, bn. Dec. 25, 1861. **(VI.)** Elizabeth Susan Etta Culp, bn. June 5, 1864. **(VI.)** Ella Amelia Culp, bn. July 28, 1867. **(VI.)** Evelyn Louisa Culp, bn. Aug. 12, 1869. **(VI.)** Silas Wright Culp, bn. Apr. 9, 1872.

V. Joshua Grobb, bn. Jan. 18, 1831; died Oct. 15, 1858. S.

V. Barbara Grobb, bn. in Lincoln Co., Ont., Mar. 3, 1833; died Nov. 7, 1890. Mrd. James E. Nelles, Jan. 5, 1855. Farmer and pump-maker. Meth's. Children: Emerson, Ella, Anna, James, David, Barbara, Rowland.

VI. Emerson W. Nelles, bn. Jan. 28, 1856.

VI. Ella A. Nelles, bn. Mar. 17, 1857. Mrd. George H. Horning, Dec. 26, 1883. Farmer. Meth's. Children: **(VII.)** Roy Nelles Horning, bn. Aug. 22, 1886. **(VII.)** Lloyd Harris Horning, bn. Nov. 3, 1888.

VI. Anna E. Nelles, bn. Jan. 10, 1861.

VI. James Edgar Nelles, bn. July 22, 1864.

VI. David Henry Nelles, bn. Mar. 21, 1867.

VI. Barbara Maud Nelles, bn. Oct. 17, 1872.

VI. Rowland C. Nelles, bn. Mar. 29, 1876.

V. Jacob Fry Grobb, bn. in Lincoln Co., Ont., June 17, 1835. Mrd. Mary Matilda Depew, Feb. 25, 1863. Wheelwright and farmer. Attends Meth. ch. Children: **(VI.)** Clara A. Grobb, bn. Jan. 23, 1864; died Nov. 14, 1879. **(VI.)** Ida Elizabeth Grobb, bn. Sept. 26, 1865. Mrd. Jacob Albright, Dec. 19, 1889. Farmer. Meth's. **(VI.)** Arletta May Grobb, bn. July 19, 1868.

V. Anna Grobb, bn. in Lincoln Co., Ont., May 7, 1838. Mrd. Ira F. Culp, Nov. 5, 1862. Farmer.

Meth's. Children: (VI.) Joshua G. Culp, bn. Oct. 11,
1863; died Aug. 31, 1865. (VI.) Lillie Jane Culp, bn.
Aug. 25, 1866; died Mar. 12, 1880. (VI.) William D.
Culp, bn. Oct. 4, 1868. (VI.) Martha Barbara Culp,
bn. Dec. 23, 1870; died Aug. 10, 1871. (VI.) Rosabelle
Culp, bn. June 15, 1873. (VI.) Anna Culp, bn. Nov.
1, 1874. (VI.) Fred Nelles, and Frank Depew Culp,
bn. July 24, 1883.

IV. Samuel Fry, bn. in Lincoln Co., Ont., May 15,
1812; died Nov. 28, 1881. Mrd. Anna Nash, Jan. 2,
1838. Farmer. Ev. Ass'n. Children: Jacob, Elias,
Samuel, Mary, Sarah, Anna.

V. Jacob N. Fry, bn. June 10, 1839; died Aug. 26,
1850.

V. Elias N. Fry, bn. Nov. 1, 1841. Mrd. Catharine
Houser, Sept. 25, 1866. P. O., Campden, Ont.
Wheelwright. Ev. Ass'n. Children: (VI.) Alberta
Fry, bn. Aug. 21, 1869. (VI.) Rosa Fry, bn. Aug. 4,
1872. (VI.) Sanford Fry, bn. Nov. 3, 1874. (VI.)
Charles Fry, bn. Oct. 15, 1876. (VI.) Edith Fry, bn.
Mar. 6, 1878; died 1880. (VI.) Willie Fry, bn. June
22, 1882. (VI.) Lottie Fry, bn. Feb. 16, 1885.

V. Samuel N. Fry, bn. Nov. 19, 1843. Mrd. Sarah
C. Grobb, Oct. 1, 1872. P. O., Jordan, Ont. Farmer.
Ev. Ass'n. Children: (VI.) Annie Rosetta Fry, bn.
May 29, 1876. (VI.) Alpheus Leland Fry, bn. Mar.
22, 1883.

V. Mary Fry, bn. Feb. 1, 1846. Mrd. Henry W.
Moyer. (See Index of References No. 72.)

V. Sarah Fry, bn. Aug. 12, 1848; died Sept. 15,
1886.

V. Anna Fry, bn. Oct. 30, 1850; died Jan. 30, 1876.
Mrd. Samuel M. Houser, Oct. 31, 1872. P. O.,
Campden, Ont. Farmer. Ev. Ass'n. Children: (VI.)
Nellie Belle Houser, bn. Oct. 8, 1873. (VI.) Sarah
Dell Houser, bn. Nov. 14, 1875.

IV. Dilman Fry, bn. Feb. 15, 1815; died Jan. 8,
1883. Mrd. Eve Werner, Jan. 4, 1838. Blacksmith.
Disciples. Children: Catharine, William, Jacob,
Caroline, Julian.

V. Catharine Fry, bn. in Haldimand Co., Ont., Dec.
5, 1838. Mrd. James Edgar Ellsworth, Apr. 30, 1856.

P. O., Hamilton, Ont. Unitarians. Children: **(VI.)**
Ideuma E. Ellsworth, bn. in Walpole, Ont., July 25,
1857. Dressmaker. Unitarian. **(VI.)** Emily H. Ellsworth, bn. in Walpole, Ont., Nov. 4, 1859. Unitarian.
(VI.) Jacob Fry Ellsworth, bn. in Walpole, Ont.,
Nov. 9, 1862. Mrd. Hattie Davis, of Albion, N. Y.,
Nov. 28, 1887. P. O., Hamilton, Ont. Clerk. **(VI.)**
Alexander W. Ellsworth, bn. in Rainham, Ont., Nov.
25, 1864. Clerk. **(VI.)** Edgar L. Ellsworth, bn. Sept.
24, 1866. Clerk. **(VI.)** Eve E. Ellsworth, bn. Oct. 13,
1869. Unitarian. **(VI.)** Rodney O. Ellsworth, bn. Mar.
12, 1872. Clerk. **(VI.)** Charles W. Ellsworth, bn.
June 9, 1874. Printer. **(VI.)** Kanneth J. Ellsworth,
bn. Nov. 4, 1876. **(VI.)** Richard S. Ellsworth, bn.
May 8, 1879.

V. William Fry, M. D., bn. Aug. 20, 1840; died
Mar. 29, 1876. Mrd. Mary E. Nevens, —. Physician.
No issue.

V. Jacob Fry, bn. Sept. 30, 1842. Mrd. Elizabeth
Honsberger. P. O., Wellington, Ont. Veterinary
surgeon, graduate of the Toronto Veterinary College.
Children: **(VI.)** Harry W. Fry, bn. Jan. 5, 1868. Mrd.
Frances, daughter of Dr. Joseph Michener, May 23,
1889. P. O., Dunnville, Ont. Veterinary surgeon.
Meth's. No issue. **(VI.)** William A. Fry, bn. Sept. 7,
1872. P. O., Ingersoll, Ont. Printer. **(VI.)** Myrtle E.
Fry, bn. May 30, 1879.

V. Caroline Fry, bn. Aug. 2, 1844. Mrd. William G.
Scott. P. O., Dunnville, Ont.

V. Julian Fry, bn. June 1, 1846. Mrd. R. H. Mc
Kenna. V. S. P. O., Picton, Ont.

IV. Joseph Fry, bn. Oct. 6, 1817; died Sept. 22,
1855. S.

IV. Isaac Fry, bn. in Lincoln Co., Ont., Aug. 17,
1819; died Apr. 16, 1892. Mrd. Mary Albright, Dec.
12, 1841. She was bn. Apr. 21, 1823; died Apr. 15,
1892. In early life Mr. Fry followed carpentering in
in the neighborhood of the "Twenty" in Ont. In 1852
he moved to South Cayuga, Ont., where for about a
year he managed a general store for James Henry of
Beamsville. In 1853 he purchased the stock and good
will from Mr. Henry, and secured the appointment

of Post Master, when the office was first established
in the same year, and carried on the business (general
store and post office) successfully for over 30 years.
Having provided a comfortable home for his wife and
twelve children he retired from business about 1886,
with an income sufficient for all family needs and
comforts. He for many years also held the office of
Clerk and Treasurer of the township, and for over
thirty years discharged the duties of local preacher of
the Evangelical Association ch., in a very acceptable
manner. He was very enthusiastic in all church and
Sunday school work. Children: Matilda, Maria,
Menno, Pricilla, Isaac, John, Mary, Solomon, Ellen,
Allen, Emily, Martha.

V. Matilda Fry, bn. —. S.

V. Maria Fry, bn. in Lincoln Co., Ont., Mar. 25,
1844. Mrd. Nelson Drake. P. O., Cayuga, Ont.
Merchant. Meth's. Children: **(VI.)** Francis Alpheus
Drake, M. D., bn. Feb. 23, 1863. Mrd. — Eggman.
Res. 409 Connecticut St., Buffalo, N. Y. Physician.
Meth. **(VI.)** Florence M. Drake, bn. July 26, 1865.
S. **(VI.)** Chester A. Drake, bn. Feb. 14, 1867. S.
(VI.) Daisy E. Drake, bn. Nov. 23, 1872. S.

V. Menno S. Fry, bn. in Lincoln Co., Ont., Dec. 16,
1845. Mrd. Margaret Pennington. She died about
1876. P. O., Chicago, Ill. Bookkeeper. Meth.
Children: **(VI.)** George Fry. **(VI.)** Constance Fry.
Menno mrd. second wife —.

V. Pricilla Fry, bn. in Lincoln Co., Ont., Jan. 11,
1848. Mrd. D. B. Phillips. P. O., Woodstock, Ont.
Druggist. Meth's. Children: **(VI.)** Wesley Tennyson
Phillips, bn. Jan. 1875; died July 1881. **(VI.)** Mary
Winnfred Phillips, bn. June 1877.

V. Isaac Fry, bn. in Lincoln Co., Ont., Dec. 9,
1849; died Sept. 27, 1873. School teacher. Meth.

V. John Henry Fry, bn. Nov. 3, 1851; died Jan. 16,
1871. School teacher. Methodist.

V. Mary Jane Fry, bn. in Haldimand Co., Ont., Feb.
3, 1854. Mrd. Albion Wardell. P. O., Hamilton,
Ont. Unitarian. One child: **(VI.)** Bud Hope Wardell.

V. Solomon Milton Fry, bn. in Haldimand Co., Ont.,
Mar. 1, 1856. Mrd. Bina Ethel Maxim, Sept. 1,

1879. P. O., Brantford, Ont. Merchant. Unitarian. One child: **(VI.)** Roy Jay Fry.

V. Ellen Fry, bn. in Haldimand Co., Ont., June 15, 1858. Mrd. Rev. Robert H. Balmer, Aug. 21, 1879. He was bn. in Kingston, Ont. Sept. 2, 1853. He was educated in Hamilton, Toronto, and Montreal, Canada, completing his theological studies in the Wesleyan Theological Seminary of Montreal. He was ordained to the ministry of the Methodist church of Canada June 1879. At the time of the union of the Methodist bodies in Canada he removed to the United States and connected himself with the Detroit Conference of the Methodist Episcopal church Sept. 1884 in which he had been offered an excellent appointment. During 1888, he was invited unanimously to the pastorate of the Methodist Episcopal church at Weston, Ohio, where he has remained 3 years having more than ordinary success in revivals and building. At the meeting of the Central Ohio Conference at Toledo Sept. 1891, he was stationed at Napoleon, the county seat of Henry Co., Ohio, where he is still (1892) serving. Mrs. Balmer has proved an excellent partner for her husband in his ministerial work, assisting him in his work, winning and maintaining a high degree of respect on every charge where they have unitedly labored. Children: **(VI.)** John Ernest Balmer, bn. May 6, 1883. **(VI.)** Robert Wesley Balmer, bn. Sept. 3, 1886. **(VI.)** Grace Margurite Balmer, bn. Mar. 17, 1891.

V. Rev. Allen Burness Fry, bn. in Haldimand Co., Ont., Oct. 14, 1861. Mrd. Mary E. Jordan, of Port Robinson, June 17, 1891. P. O., Dublin, Ind. Mr. Fry received a common school education, and at the age of 18 years began teaching school in his native province and which he followed for seven years. In January 1889 he came to the United States, and in April of the same year he entered the ministry of the Methodist Episcopal church. One child: **(VI.)** Naomi Livingstone Fry, bn. Sept. 6, 1892.

V. Emily Fry, bn. in Haldimand Co., Ont., Oct. 4, 1863. P. O., South Cayuga, Ont. Meth.

V. Martha Fry, bn. in Haldimand Co., Ont., July 3, 1866. P. O., Toronto, Ont. Stenographer. Meth.
IV. Catharine Fry, bn. Nov. 27, 1821; died May 17, 1889. Mrd. — Albright. Son: Jacob. P. O., South Cayuga.

III. Samuel Wismer, bn. in Bucks Co., Pa., Jan. 2, 1778; died in Elgin Co., Ont., Mar. 31, 1868. Mrd. Fannie Crammer, May 11, 1811. She was born Feb. 11, 1783; died Mar. 23, 1844. Emigrated to Canada. Children: Abraham, Jacob, Elizabeth, John, Samuel, Fannie, Nancy.
IV. Abraham Wismer, bn. —; died —. Mrd. Isabella Lincoln, —. Children: (V.) James Henry. (V.) Abraham. (V.) John. (V.) Emily. (V.) Samantha. (V.) Almira.
IV. Jacob Wismer, bn. Jan. 5, 1814; died in Bayham, Ont., Sept. 18, 1884. Mrd. Almira Pace, May 29, 1851. She was bn. Oct. 18, 1834. Farmer. Meth's. Children: Perlina, William, Wesley, Albert.
V. Perlina Wismer, bn. May 29, 1854. Mrd. George Tribe, Oct. 5, 1879. P. O., Straffordville, Ont. Farmer. United Brethren. Children: (VI.) Emma Tribe, bn. Feb. 19, 1881. (VI.) Mary Tribe, bn. July 21, 1884. (VI.) Murtie Tribe, bn. May 15, 1886. (VI.) Nora Tribe, bn. Sept. 29, 1891.
V. William Wismer, bn. in Elgin Co., Ont., June 24, 1858. Mrd. Annie Williams, about 1879. P. O., Burlington, Iowa. Foreman in wheel factory. One child: (VI.) Carl Wismer, bn. Oct. 29, 1884.
V. Wesley Wismer, bn. June 16, 1860; died June 25, 1877.
V. Albert E. Wismer, bn. Nov. 5, 1865. P. O., Burlington, Iowa. Mechanic. S.
IV. Elizabeth Wismer, bn. in Lincoln Co., Ont., Jan. 5, 1814. (twin); died Feb. 10, 1887. Mrd. Jacob Bently, May 28, 1832. Farmer in Bayham Twp., Ont. Mr. B., Mem. ch. of England; Mrs. B., Meth. Children: Fannie, Elizabeth, Samuel, Tamar.
V. Fannie Bently, bn. in Grimsby, Ont., May 2, 1833. Mrd. Edwin Faris Johnson, Apr. 1, 1856. Children: Eleanor, Elizabeth.—Fannie mrd. second

husband William Thomas in 1885. P. O., Vienna, Ont.

VI. Eleanor Frances Johnson, bn. Nov. 24, 1858. Mrd. Henry Wm. Alteman, Apr. 5, 1875. Children: **(VII.)** Peter Wesley Alteman, bn. Feb. 9, 1876. **(VII.)** Charles Ernest Alteman, bn. July 31, 1878. **(VII.)** Eleanor Caroline Alteman, bn. Dec. 5, 1880. **(VII.)** Henry Wm. Alteman, bn. Nov. 26, 1884; died in 1891.

VI. Elizabeth Elsie Johnson, bn. Dec. 9, 1865; died Oct. 2, 1868.

V. Elizabeth Bently, bn. in Bayham, Ont., Sept. 26, 1835. Mrd. Henry Paulding Marlatt, Mar. 14, 1861. He died Feb. 2, 1892. Children: **(VI.)** Jacob Marlatt, bn. Dec. 11, 1861; died July 17, 1881. **(VI.)** William Marlatt, bn. Sept. 24, 1863; died Sept. 27, 1879. **(VI.)** John F. Marlatt, bn. Oct. 27, 1865. **(VI.)** Alexander J. Marlatt, bn. Sept. 19, 1867. **(VI.)** Sarah Jane Marlatt (twin), bn. May 28, 1870. **(VI.)** Elizabeth Ann Marlatt, bn. May 28, 1870. **(VI.)** Joseph Marlatt, bn. Feb. 1, 1873. **(VI.)** Cecil Marlatt, bn. June 26, 1876.

V. Samuel Bently, bn. in Bayham Twp., Ont., Nov. 25, 1840. S.

V. Tamar Lucinda Bently, bn. Dec. 4, 1845. Mrd. William Martin Tribe, Dec. 12, 1863. Children: Jane, Elizabeth, Jacob, Ambrose, Emeline, Adeline, Amy, Susanna, Joseph.

VI. Jane Tribe, bn. May 5, 1865. Mrd. James Acker, Mar. 5, 1887. One child: **(VII.)** May Acker, bn. Feb. 15, 1889.

VI. Elizabeth Tribe, bn. Feb. 19, 1871. Mrd. —. One child: **(VII.)** —.

VI. Jacob Tribe, bn. June 7, 1872.

VI. Ambrose Tribe, bn. May 2, 1874.

VI. Emeline Tribe, bn. Mar. 9, 1877.

VI. Adeline Tribe, bn. Feb. 10, 1882.

VI. Amy Tribe, bn. June 7, 1884.

VI. Susanna Tribe, bn. Apr. 23, 1886.

VI. Joseph Tribe, bn. Jan. 23, 1890.

IV. John Wismer, bn. May 4, 1816.

IV. Samuel Wismer, bn. Feb. 13, 1820; died about 1851. Unmrd.
IV. Fannie Wismer, bn. Oct. 13, 1823.
IV. Nancy Wismer, bn. Apr. 22, 1825; died about 1850. Mrd. Isaac Ryckman, -. Children: **(V.)** Mary Ann Ryckman, bn. —; died young. **(V.)** Nancy Ryckman, bn. —; died young.

DANIEL WISMER, SON OF JACOB WISMER.

II. Daniel Wismer, bn. —; died —. He was sickly, and was provided for by his brother Abraham, until his (Daniel's) death. His portion of his father's estate he willed to his brother Abraham, on condition that he provide for and take care of him during his life time, which on falling due was paid to Abraham early in 1795.

JOHN WISMER, SON OF JACOB WISMER.

II. John Wismer, bn. —; died in 1794. He lived with Jacob Angeny, Jr., where he died. From Feb. 1784, until his death he was looked after by his brother Henry who furnished his wearing apparel, &c. paying for same out of his own (John Wismer's) estate. The £3. 6s. willed by Jacob Souder, and paid into the hands of his brother Henry, and his portion of his father's estate, also in Henry's care, the remainder of which after his (John Wismer's) death was paid in 1795 to his remaining brothers and sisters, is conclusive evidence that he had no issue. Among the items of sickness and funeral expenses paid to Jacob Angeny, Jr., by Henry Wismer, in accordance with the custom of the times, was "2 gallons and 3 quarts of whiskey for John's burying 10 shillings 2 pence.

DESCENDANTS OF MARK WISMER, SON OF JACOB WISMER.

II. Mark Wismer, bn. in Bucks Co., Pa., in 1737; died in 1831, aged 94 years and 22 days, buried at Deep Run. Mrd. —. Weaver by trade. The house in which he lived during his last years, and in which he died is an old log cabin still standing near the old Wismer homestead. In style and appearance it is a curiosity. A representation of it is given on another page. Children: Henry, Susan, David, Mark, Catharine, Daniel, Barbara, Elizabeth, Anna.

III. Henry Wismer, bn. in Bucks Co., Pa., Feb. 2, 1766; died Sept. 17, 1844. Mrd. Susanna —.* For his second wife he married Kate Crout. No issue. He was known as "Whig Henry." Farmer. Children all by first wife: David, Moses, Solomon, Mary, Elizabeth, Emanuel, Aaron, Anna.

IV. David Wismer, bn. Sept. 6, 1798; died —. Mrd. Mary Stover, daughter of Daniel Stover, —. Mason. Christian ch. Children: Aaron, Henry, Levi, John, Mary, Josiah, Jonas, Samuel, Catharine.

V. Aaron S. Wismer, bn. Feb. 15, 1824. Mrd. Anna Andrews, Jan. 10, 1850. P. O., Upper Blacks Eddy, Pa. Children: Rachel, Joseph, Mary, William, John, Anna, George, Aaron, William, Margaret, Dennis, David, Samuel.

VI. Rachel Wismer, bn. Feb. 28, 1851.

VI. Joseph Wismer, bn. Apr. 11, 1852. Mrd. Margaret Milker, —. P. O., Phillipsburg, N. J. Children: **(VII.)** Anna Wismer. **(VII.)** Raymond Wismer.

---

* "She is supposed to have been a half-bred Indian of English descent, and a most noble and beautiful woman."

VI. Mary C. Wismer, bn. Sept. 18, 1853.

VI. William Henry Wismer, bn. Sept. 8, 1855; died Sept. 17, 1857.

VI. John S. Wismer, bn. Aug. 14, 1857. Mrd. Lydia Gilmer, —. P. O., Milford, N. Y. Children: **(VII.)** Anna Wismer. **(VII.)** John Wismer. **(VII.)** Samuel Wismer. **(VII.)** Maggie Wismer. **(VII.)** George Wismer. **(VII.)** Nellie Wismer, (dec'd).

VI. Anna Elizabeth Wismer, born Feb. 29, 1859; died Apr. 11, 1891. Mrd. Jacob Ulmer, —. One child: **(VII.)** Ida May Ulmer, died aged 14 days.

VI. George Wismer, born Sept. 16, 1860. Mrd. Emma Sheetz, —. P. O., Phillipsburg, N. J. Children: **(VII.)** Lulu Wismer. **(VII.)** Harvey Wismer.

VI. Aaron S. Wismer, Jr., bn. Apr. 26, 1862.

VI. William D. Wismer, bn. July 26, 1864.

VI. Margaret Wismer, bn. Sept. 14, 1866. Mrd. Ray Balliet, —. One child: **(VII.)** May Balliet.

VI. Dennis Wismer, bn. Aug. 6, 1868.

VI. David Wismer, bn. July 16, 1870.

VI. Samuel Wismer, bn. Sept. 23, 1873.

V. Henry Wismer, bn. —; died —. S.

V. Levi Wismer, bn. —; died —. Mrd. Mary Ann Wismer, —. Children: Emma, William, Hugh, Henry.

V. John Wismer, bn. —. Mrd. — Heaney.

V. Mary Wismer, bn. —; died —. Mrd. Dennis O. Daniel, —. Children: Laura, Albert (dec'd), Clinton.

V. Josiah Wismer, bn. —; died —. S.

V. Jonas Wismer, bn. —; died —.

V. Samuel Wismer, bn. —; died —.

V. Catharine Wismer, bn. —; died —.

IV. Moses Wismer, bn. Nov. 18, 1800; died Oct. 21, 1874. Mrd. Mary Slifer, daughter of Henry and Elizabeth Slifer, —. She died —. Children: Samuel, Elizabeth, William, Aaron, Mary, Delilah, Rebecca, Henry, Lydia, Charles, John.—Moses mrd. second wife, Barbara, widow of Daniel Fretz (maiden name Hockman), Oct. 28, 1847. Farmer, weaver, Menn's. Children: Israel, Eliza.

V. Samuel Wismer, bn. —. Mrd. —. P. O., Neshaminy, Pa. Children: **(VI.)** Susanna. **(VI.)** Samuel. **(VI.)** Henry. **(VI.)** Barbara. **(VI.)** Elizabeth.

V. Elizabeth Wismer, bn. —; died in infancy.

V. William S. Wismer, bn. July 31, 1828. Mrd. Mary Landis, Dec. 16, 1849. P. O., Bedminster, Pa. In early life shoemaker, now farmer. Mr. Wismer enlisted July 12, 1863, in the 90th Regt., Pa. Vols., served all through Wilderness campaign of battles, and Todd's tavern, where he was wounded in the right arm between the wrist and elbow. While in front of Petersburgh he had a severe attack of rheumatism lasting nearly four weeks, and was unable to be on duty. Was in the engagement at North Ann river, and at the battle of the Welden and Petersburgh R. R.. Aug. 19, 1864, he was taken prisoner, and confined in the famous Libby prison two days, Belle Isle seven weeks and three days, and in Salsburry, N. C., a little over four months; altogether a prisoner of war for six months and twelve days. Luth's. Children: Jacob, Moses, William, Joseph, Mary, Hannah, Marcellina, Susanna, Francis, Infant.

VI. Jacob L. Wismer, bn. Jan. 31, 1851; died May 22, 1855.

VI. Moses L. Wismer, bn. Apr. 3, 1853. Mrd. Elizabeth Steer, —. She was bn. Apr. 15, 1856. P. O., Bedminster, Pa. Carpenter, farmer. Deacon, Lutheran ch., Dublin. Children· **(VII.)** William Henry S. Wismer, bn. Sept. 1, 1877. **(VII.)** Andrew S. Wismer, bn. Mar. 7, 1882. **(VII.)** Noah S. Wismer, bn. Jan. 6, 1884.

VI. William L. Wismer, bn. July 6, 1855. Mrd. Caroline Popp, Dec. 15, 1877. She was bn. in Wertemburgh, Germany, Mar. 2, 1855; died Oct. 31, 1887. Children: **(VII.)** Violetta P. Wismer, bn. Sept. 26, 1879. **(VII.)** Isaac P. Wismer, bn. Mar. 12, 1882. —William mrd. second wife, Mrs. Lucinda Miller, daughter of John C. Crouthamel, Jan. 4, 1890. She was bn. Nov. 29, 1857. P. O., Dublin, Pa. Saddler. Mr. W., Lutheran. Mrs. W., Ger. Ref.

VI. Joseph L. Wismer, bn. Oct. 10, 1857. Mrd.

Martha J. Burrows (Nee Hopkins). --. Grocery merchant in Philadelphia.

VI. Mary Elizabeth Wismer, bn. June 25, 1859. Mrd. Milton Strawn. He was bn. Apr. 27, 1858. P. O., Dublin, Pa. Farmer. Luth's. Children: **(VII.)** Irwin W. Strawn. bn. Aug. 29, 1881. **(VII.)** Howard W. Strawn. bn. Sept. 13, 1883. **(VII.)** Warren W. Strawn. bn. Oct. 24, 1885. **(VII.)** Martha Jane Strawn, bn. Oct. 8, 1887. **(VII.)** Bertha W. Strawn, bn. Aug. 17, 1889.

VI. Hannah Wismer, bn. July 31, 1861; died Apr. 9, 1862.

VI. Marcellina L. Wismer, bn. June 2, 1864. Mrd. John H. McCrork, -. He was bn. May 14, 1860. P. O., Blake, Ohio. Ditcher. Luth's. Children: **(VII.)** Mary Ellen W. McCrork, bn. Sept. 22, 1889. **(VII.)** Flossy W. McCrork. bn. Mar. 13, 1891.

VI. Susanna L. Wismer, bn. May 2, 1866; died Feb. 2, 1875.

VI. Francis Henry Wismer, bn. July 23, 1868. P.O., Olympia, Washington. S.

VI. Infant son, stillborn, Feb. 20, 1863.

V. Aaron Wismer, bn. —; died young.

V. Mary Ann Wismer, bn. —. Mrd. Levi Wismer. (See Index of References No. 74.)

V. Delilah Wismer, bn. —. Mrd. John Rensheimer, --. He died —. Children: **(VI.)** Lydia Alice Rensheimer. **(VI.)** — Rensheimer. (dec'd).—Delilah mrd. second husband, Henry Lehr. —. Children: **(VI.)** Hattie Lehr. **(VI.)** — Lehr.

V. Rebecca Wismer, bn. —. Mrd. Reuben Gruver. —. Children: **(VI.)** — Gruver. **(VI.)** Mary Gruver.

V. Henry S. Wismer, bn. Mar. 23, 1838. When 18 years old he went to Ohio (1856). Mrd. Maggie A. Rice, July 9, 1861. She was bn. Feb. 25, 1841. Moved to Huntington, Ind., in Mar. 1870. Farmer. Lutherans. No issue.

V. Lydia Wismer, bn. in Bucks Co., Pa., May 26, 1841. Mrd. Joseph S. Long, Apr. 12, 1864. P. O., Wadsworth, Ohio. Farmer. Ref. ch. Children: Clara, Sarah, David.

VI. Clara Ellen Long, bn. June 9, 1865; died Nov. 3, 1887.

VI. Sarah May Long. bn. Oct. 1, 1867. Mrd. Peter E. Keller, March 13, 1888. P. O., Wadsworth, Ohio. Laborer. Ref. ch. Children: **(VII.)** Olie Janetta Keller, bn. Dec. 22, 1889. **(VII.)** Joseph Ervin Keller, bn. Apr 20, 1891.

VI. David E. Long, bn. Sept. 13, 1872.

V. Charles Wismer, bn. —: died small.

V. John Wismer, bn. —; died small.

V. Israel H. Wismer, bn. in Bucks Co., Pa., July 10, 1848. Mrd. Mary E. Smith, Nov. 4, 1871. P. O., Wismer, Pa. Carpenter and farmer. Luth's. Children: **(VI.)** Willie S. Wismer. **(VI.)** Steward S. Wismer. **(VI.)** Horace S. Wismer. **(VI.)** Amos S. Wismer.

V. Eliza Ann Wismer, bn. June 30, 1850. Mrd. Henry W. Wismer. (See Index of References No. 76.)

IV. Solomon Wismer, bn. in Bucks Co., Nov. 5, 1802; died May 13, 1857. Mrd. Catharine Kile. She was bn. Feb. 8, 1814. Farmer and carpenter. Luth's. Children: Edmund, Mary, Abraham, Infant. Hartman, Catharine. Susanna, Enos, Elizabeth, Aaron, Oliver, Martha, Isaac.

V. Edmund K. Wismer, bn. in Bucks Co., Pa., June 13, 1834. Mrd. Susan Lear, Sept. 19, 1857. Res. 916 Kurtz St., Philadelphia, Pa. Harness maker. Luth's. Children: Ella, Harvey.

VI. Ella Minta Wismer, bn. Sept. 19, 1859. Mrd. Otto Schmolze, Sept. 29, 1881. Children: **(VII.)** Edna Lillian Schmolze. **(VII.)** Anna Estella Schmolze. **(VII.)** Emma Dune Schmolze. **(VII.)** Emily Oterson Schmolze.

VI. Harvey W. Wismer, bn. July 20, 1861. Mrd. Annie Dengler, Oct. 10, 1887. Res. 918 Kurtz St., Philadelphia, Pa. Harness maker. Children: **(VII.)** Carl Edmund Wismer, bn. Jan. 13, 1890. **(VII.)** John Millard Wismer, bn. May 14, 1892.

V. Mary Wismer, bn. Oct. 7, 1835. Mrd. Joseph L. Wismer. (See Index of References No. 77.)

V. Abraham K. Wismer, bn. June 21, 1838. Mrd. Hannah Bergstresser, Nov. 24, 1860. Shoemaker.

Luth. He enlisted Aug. 23, 1862, in Company H, 138th Reg't., Penna. Vols., was in several engagements, and was taken prisoner in the battle of Frederick Junction, July 9, 1864, and was confined in the famous Libby prison. After his release he arrived at Annapolis, Md., Sept. 26, and died Sept. 30, 1864. No issue.

V. Infant bn. and died June 22, 1839.

V. Hartman K. Wismer, bn. June 19, 1840. Mrd. Harriet Van Horn, —. Res. 927 Master St., Philadelphia, Pa., Children: (VI.) Robert Lane Wismer, bn. near Flemington, N. J., June 13, 1865. (VI.) Laura Wismer, bn. in Bucks Co., Pa., Dec. 19, 1867; died Jan. 3, 1873. (VI.) Deborah Gross Wismer, bn. in Bucks Co., Jan. 10, 1870; died Dec. 26, 1889. She was the pet of the family, and a great favorite among her Wismer relatives, and a noble, kind-hearted and loving Christian lady. She was engaged to be married on the day she was buried. Lutheran. (VI.) Howard Wismer, bn. in Bucks Co., May 17, 1872. (VI.) Isaac Gross Wismer, bn. Apr. 7, 1874. (VI.) Mary Wismer, bn. Mar. 7, 1876; died Oct. 16, 1876. (VI.) Catharine Wismer, bn. May 29, 1878. (VI.) Eolah J. Wismer, bn. Jan. 21, 1881. (VI.) Eugene Wismer, bn. Aug. 22, 1883; died Mar. 4, 1884. (VI.) Pamella Wismer, bn. Jan. 4, 1885. (VI.) Walter Van Horn Wismer, bn. Aug. 24, 1887. (VI.) Harriet Wismer, bn. Mar. 28, 1890. (VI.) Anna Wismer, bn. Sept. 25, 1892.

V. Catharine K. Wismer, bn. in Bucks Co., Pa., May 12, 1842. Mrd. Rev. Louis Trautman, Apr. 9, 1862. He was bn. in Montpellier, France, emigrated to this country in early childhood with his parents, and settled in Allegheny City, Pa. At about the age of 16 years he entered a course of studies preparatory to the ministry at the Academy at Zellienople, Butler Co., Pa , and completing his studies at the Pennsylvania College, at Gettysburg, and the Theological Seminary of the same place. He was ordained to the ministry of the Lutheran church in 1861, and the same year took charge of the Lutheran church at Ostand, Washington Co., Ohio, preaching in both the English and German languages. He later moved to

Canton, Ohio and took charge of a congregation near
that place, together with another congregation near
Massillon, Ohio where he served until within a few
weeks of his death which occurred on March 22, 1865
in Canton, O., where he is buried. Children: (VI.)
Martha Florine Trautman, bn. July 27, 1863; died
Aug. 1863. (VI.) Alexander L. Trautman, bn. Feb.
17, 1865. Mrd. Emma May Reep, of Erwinna, Pa.,
Nov. 24, 1892. Res. 2629 Penn Ave., Pittsburgh, Pa.
Clerk. (VI.) Leander A. Trautman, bn. Feb. 17,
1865. (Twin.) Res. 2629 Penn Ave., Pittsburgh, Pa.
Finished his course as law student, and was admitted
to the Allegheny county bar, on Saturday, March 18,
1893, having passed with the highest honors. S.—
Catharine mrd. second husband, Josiah B. Nobbs.
He died Feb. 13, 1893, in the 66th year of his age.
He was a well known resident of the Twelfth ward,
Pittsburgh, Pa., and no other man in the ward has
been more thoroughly identified with its interests
than Mr. Nobbs, and his death will be universally re-
gretted. Mr. Nobbs was born in London, England,
Nov. 2, 1827, and came to America when quite young.
For over half a century he has been a resident of the
Twelfth ward. For a number of years he was superintendent of the metal working department of the
Pennsylvania railroad shop, and has been engaged in
his present business, that of tinsmith, since before
the war. He has always been an ardent Republican
and prominently identified with the interests of the
community, business and political. Several times he
has been elected to councils, to the school board and
to the office of alderman, and at the time of his death
was the treasurer of the O'Hara school board, and
one of the warmest friends and supporters of that institution. He was president of the Acme Building &
Loan Association, member of the Knights of the
Mystic Chain, of the American Legion of Honor,
Royal Arcanum, Equitable Aid Union and United
Workmen. His life has been one of uprightness and
integrity. Lutheran's. Children: (VI.) Edmund Stan-
ton Nobbs, bn. Sept. 22, 1871; died May 30, 1872. (VI.)
Lillian Mabel Nobbs, bn. Apr. 7, 1873. Student. (VI.)

Rella Gertrude Nobbs, bn. Oct. 18, 1875; died Sept. 6, 1876. (VII.) Villa Eugenia Nobbs, bn. Nov. 26, 1877; died Mar. 1878. (VI.) Myra Olevia Nobbs, bn. Dec. 23, 1878. (VI.) John Roney Nobbs, bn. Aug. 21, 1885; died Aug. 11, 1888. (VI.) Joseph Harvey Nobbs, bn. Feb. 27, 1887; died June 24, 1887.

V. Susanna Wismer, bn. in Bucks Co., Pa., Mar. 6, 1844. Mrd. Joseph I. Anderson, June 8, 1865. Children: (VI.) Charles Herbert Anderson, bn. July 20, 1866. (VI.) Mary Ann Anderson, bn. May 5, 1868; died July 29, 1868.--Susanna mrd. second husband, Thos. A. Hoffman, Oct. 20, 1881. P. O., Box 1072 Salt Lake City, Utah. Mrs. H., Lutheran.

V. Enos Wismer, bn. Nov. 1845; died May 1847.

V. Elizabeth Wismer, bn. Feb. 20, 184—. Mrd. Anthony Hoffman, —. Res. 704 Wallace St., Phila. One child: (VI.) Lillie Bertha Hoffman, bn. Sept. 3, 1874.

V. Aaron K. Wismer, bn. Oct. 12, 1848. Mrd. Elmira Rice, in 1871. Res. 1213 N. 12th St., Phila. Harness maker. Luth. Children: (VI.) Winfield Wismer, bn. 1873; died 1874. (VI.) Minnie Estella Wismer, bn. 1875. (VI.) Frank Raymond Wismer, bn. 1881. (VI.) Blanch Estella Wismer, bn. 1887.

V. Oliver K. Wismer, bn. in Bucks Co., May 19, 1850. Mrd. Matilda Kemery, June 4, 1873. She died —. Res. 201 Tremont St., Boston, Mass. Carpenter. Baptist. Children: (VI.) Anna May Wismer, bn. June 4, 1874. (VI.) Martha L. Wismer, bn. June 25, 1876.

V. Martha Wismer, bn. May 22, 1852. Mrd. George W. Lynch, —. He was bn. Jan. 28, 1848. Res. 44th and North Sts., Pittsburgh, Pa. Children: (VI.) Harry Lynch, bn. Jan. 14, 1873. Mrd. Ella Hogue, Sept. 15, 1892. Res. Lawrenceville, Pittsburgh, Pa. (VI.) Hannah Catharine Lynch, bn. May 23, 1876. (VI.) Mary Virginia Lynch, bn. Aug. 26, 1879. (VI.) Frank Benjamin Lynch, bn. Mar. 9, 1882.

V. Rev. Isaac K. Wismer, bn. in Bucks Co., Pa., Sept. 24, 1853. Mrd. Mary Louisa Kirkbride, July 1, 1885. P. O., Latrobe, Pa. When Mr. Wismer was 3½ years of age his father died, and a year later his

mother took the two youngest of the family (Martha
and himself), and moved to Carversville, Pa., where
they lived four years, and where he attended the village school, and laid the foundation of his education.
When ten years old he went to live near the old homestead, with Aaron S. Meyers, a farmer, with whom he
remained four years, after which he lived with his
brother, Hartman K. Wismer, near Plumsteadville for
four years, attending school in the winter season.
When 18 years old he hired to Isaac Gross, a neigh-
boring farmer. In the spring of 1872, he went to
Philadelphia, and engaged in the harness making
trade with his brother Edmund K. Wismer. After
several years, he felt moved to prepare himself for
the ministry, and accordingly entered a "select"
school for young men and boys, George Eastburn,
M. A., Principal, from which he graduated in June
1878, and was at once examined to enter the University of Pennsylvania, and having received a free
scholarship entered that institution in Sept. 1878
from which he graduated in June 1882. In Sept. of
the same year he entered the Lutheran Theological
Seminary, Phila., from which he graduated in May
1885, and was ordained to the ministry at the meeting of the Ministerium of Pennsylvania June 2, 1885.
He was called to, and accepted the pastorate of the
Lutheran church at Du Bois, Clearfield Co., Pa., Oct.
1, 1885, and after a pastorate of six years and eight
months, he resigned and accepted a call to the pastorate of the Lutheran church of Latrobe, Westmoreland Co., Pa., June 1, 1892. Children: (**VI.**) Ida May
Wismer, bn. June 26, 1886. (**VI.**) Martha Florine
Wismer, bn. Dec. 9, 1888.

IV. Mary Wismer, bn. June 17, 1804; died July 21,
1875. Mrd. Josiah Walton, —. He was born Dec.
15, 1782; died Dec. 28, 1855. Farmer. Quakers.
Children: Benjamin, Edmund, Margaret, Uree,
Martha, Susan.

V. Benjamin Walton, bn. Nov. 15, 1829; died Aug.
3, 1850.

V. Edmund Walton, bn. Feb. 11, 1832. Res. 819
Spring Garden St., Phila., Pa.

V. Margaret Walton, bn. June 9, 1834. Mrd. Edwin Tomlinson, Dec. 22, 1853. P. O., Byberry, Pa. Farmer and auctioneer. Children: Benjamin, Ella, Walter, Clara, Anna, Bertha, Bessie, Edwin, Raymond.

VI. Benjamin W. Tomlinson, bn. Dec. 25, 1854. Mrd. Amy C. Osmond, Dec. 25, 1879. P. O., Morrisville, Pa. Farmer. Auctioneer. Children: **(VII.)** Ellie M. Tomlinson, bn. Nov. 10, 1880; died Nov. 12, 1880. **(VII.)** Emily A. Tomlinson, bn. Oct. 25, 1881. **(VII.)** Charles R. Tomlinson, bn. Mar. 30, 1885; died Apr. 13, 1885. **(VII.)** Alethia M. Tomlinson, bn. Mar. 8, 1888; died Sept. 16, 1888. **(VII.)** Esther M. Tomlinson, bn. Mar. 29, 1890. **(VII.)** Edwin Earl Tomlinson, bn. Sept. 15, 1892.

VI. Ella Tomlinson, bn. Nov. 8, 1857. Mrd. Harry Jenkins, Dec. 19, 1878. Res. 553 Bailey St., Camden, N. J. Children: **(VII.)** M. Edna Jenkins, bn. Dec. 20, 1879. **(VII.)** Frances H. Jenkins, bn. Oct. 18, 1887.

VI. Walter Tomlinson, bn. Dec. 5, 1860. Mrd. Anna L. Knight, Dec. 24, 1883. P. O., Byberry, Phila., Pa.

VI. Clara Tomlinson, bn. July 31, 1862. Mrd. J. Lincoln Knight, Oct. 11, 1882. P. O., Wilburtha, N. J. Farmer. Presby. Children: (triplets), Linda, Lizzie, Maggie, all bn. Jan. 24, 1887. **(VII.)** Lizzie and Maggie, died soon after birth. **(VII.)** Linda Knight, died Aug. 7, 1887.

VI. Anna Mary Tomlinson, bn. Sept. 7, 1864. Mrd. Howard Watson, Oct. 17, 1888. P. O., Byberry, Phila., Pa. Carpenter. Children: **(VII.)** Harry Lewis Watson, bn. May 12, 1890. **(VII.)** Howard Chester Watson, bn. Nov. 1, 1892.

VI. Bertha Tomlinson, bn. Mar. 12, 1874; died Jan. 6, 1876.

VI. Bessie Edna Tomlinson, bn. Dec. 11, 1874.

VI. Edwin C. Tomlinson, bn. Aug. 3, 1876.

VI. J. Raymond Tomlinson, bn. Sept. 2, 1880.

V. Uree Anna Walton, bn. Aug. 7, 1836. Mrd. John P. Headley. P. O., Horsham, Pa.

V. Martha Walton, bn. Nov. 15, 1838. Mrd. Joseph B. Shropshire, —. He died —.

V. Susan Walton, bn. June 3, 1841; died Sept. 12, 1871. S

V. Israel Walton, bn. Oct. 16, 1843; died Mar. 9, 1844.

V. Mary Walton, bn. Apr. 1, 1846; died Apr. 16, 1883. S.

IV. Elizabeth Wismer, bn. June 5, 1806; died June 15, 1875. Mrd Elias Wis.ner. (See Index of References No. 78.)

IV. Emanuel Wismer, bn. July 16, 1809; died Aug. 29, 1885. Mrd. Elizabeth Angeny, —. She died fall of 1892. Carpenter. Menn's. Children: Samuel, William, Abraham, Katy, Salome, Henry, John, Alfred, Hannah.

V. Samuel A. Wismer, bn. —. Mrd. Mary Ann Snyder, —. She died Feb. 2, 1865. One child: Mary. —Samuel mrd. second wife, Christiana Mast, —. Children: Catharine, Amanda, Lizzie, Sarah, Martha, Ella.

VI. Mary Wismer, bn. Jan. 31, 1865. Mrd. William H. Esser, —. Children: **(VII.)** Zenas Esser, bn. May 12, 1888. **(VII.)** Elizabeth Esser, bn. July 24, 1891; died Sept. 11, 1891.

VI. Catharine Wismer, bn. Mar. 7, 1866. Mrd. Wilson Huber, —.

VI. Amanda Wismer, bn. Dec. 10, 1867. Teacher. Single.

VI. Lizzie Wismer bn. Feb. 1870.

VI. Sarah Wismer, bn. —.

VI. Martha Wismer, bn. —.

VI. Ella Wismer, bn. —.

V. William A. Wismer, bn. —. Killed at the battle of Antietam.

V. Abraham A. Wismer, bn. —. Mrd. Martha Bisset, —. Children: William, Mary.

V. Katy Ann Wismer, bn. —. Mrd. Edward Trauger, —. He died Oct. 5, 1891. Children: Rosella, Joseph, Lincoln, Robert.

VI. Rosella Trauger, bn. July 31, 1864; died Nov. 16, 1866.

VI. Joseph Trauger, bn. —.

VI. Lincoln Trauger, bn. —.

VI. Robert Trauger, bn. —. Mrd. Susan Landis, —. She died —. One child: **(VII.)** Lydia Trauger.

V. Salome Wismer, bn. June 18, 1845; died Nov. 30, 1866. S.

V. Henry Wismer, died young.

V. John Wismer, died young.

V. Alfred Wismer, died young.

V. Hannah Wismer, died young.

IV. Aaron Wismer, bn. Jan. 13, 1812; died June 13, 1822.

IV. Ann Wismer, bn. Dec. 12, 1814. Mrd. George Michener, Sept. 28, 1837. He died —. Farmer. Meth's. Children: Amos, Seth, Alfred, Charles, Mary. Ann mrd. second husband, George Border, Oct. 1, 1860. No issue.

V. Amos R. Michener, bn. July 7, 1838; died Sept. 2, 1868. Mrd. Amanda Burroughs, Feb. 14, 1865. Blacksmith. Mrs. M., Meth. Children: Lincoln, George. Mr. Michener enlisted at the breaking out of the Rebellion, and served three years in company D., 5th Reg't. Penna. Cavalry Vol. and received an honorable discharge.

VI. A. Lincoln Michener, bn. Dec. 2, 1865. Mrd. Emma K. Martindale, Mar. 7, 1888. P. O., Camden, N. J. Salesman, wholesale dry goods. Episcopalian. One child: **(VII.)** Maria B. Michener, bn. Dec. 4, 1890.

VI. George P. Michener, bn. July 14, 1867. Mrd. Edith Moore, Jan. 30, 1889. P. O., Camden, N. J. Sash and blind maker. Attends Meth. ch. One child: **(VII.)** Leon B. Michener, bn. Dec. 21, 1890.

V. Seth Michener, bn. Dec. 3, 1839. Mrd. Harriet R. Boilean, of Bustleton, Pa., Mar. 23, 1864. P. O., Watsontown, Pa. Butcher. Children: **(VI.)** Infant, died aged 3 days. **(VI.)** William B. Michener, bn. Mar. 16, 1866; died Mar. 23, 1875. **(VI.)** Anna M. Michener, bn. Jan. 23, 1868. S. **(VI.)** Jennie P. Michener, bn. Dec. 10, 1869; died Apr. 25, 1888. **(VI.)** Hattie Michener, bn. Feb. 28, 1873. **(VI.)** Seth K. Michener, bn. Mar. 23, 1875. **(VI.)** Cora M. Michener, bn. Jan. 6, 1877; died Sept. 27, 1890. **(VI.)** Maud E.

Michener, bn. June 4, 1878. (VI.) Charles T. Michener, bn. Nov. 21, 1879. (VI.) Lulu E. Michener, bn. Aug. 21, 1881. (VI.) Infant boy, bn. Nov. 12, 1882; died Dec. 20, 1882. (VI.) Bertha A. Michener, bn. May 26, 1884. (VI.) George A. Michener, bn. Nov. 23, 1886.

V. Alfred Michener, bn. Nov. 22, 1842; died July 1890. Enlisted in the 5th Reg't, Penna. Cavalry Vol., in Sept. 1864. Served one year, and was honorably discharged at the close of the war.

V. Charles T. Michener, bn. July 20, 1845. Mrd. Ellen Laura Keller, Mar. 5, 1872. She died Apr. 1874. One child: (VI.) Vernie Michener, bn. Jan. 10, 1873; died Apr. 1873.—Charles mrd. second wife, Martha C. Nicely. Sept. 27, 1883. Post Master and merchant at Dewart, Pa. Presbyterians. One child: (VI.) Charles Vincent Michener, bn. Sept. 11, 1885.

V. Mary E. Michener, bn. Mar. 30, 1849; died aged 3 months.

III. Susan Wismer, bn. —; died —. Single.

III. David Wismer, bn. in Bucks Co., Pa., —; died —. Mrd. Lydia Everett, —. Farmer. Menn's. Emigrated from Bucks Co., to Canada in 1806. Settled in Markham Twp., Ont., where he purchased a tract of 500 acres of land. Children: Moses, Asa, Jacob, Henry, Nancy, Lydia, David, Samuel.

IV. Moses Wismer, bn. Feb. 27, 1794; died —. Mrd. Eunice Noble, —. Farmer. Christian ch.

IV. Asa Wismer, bn. in Bucks Co., Pa., Mar 14, 1795; died Sept. 30, 1869. Mrd. Elizabeth Lighte. She died Nov. 12, 1860. Farmer. Menn's. Children: Catharine, Jacob, David, Artemas, Elizabeth, Henry, Regina, Asa.

V. Catharine Wismer, bn. Aug. 6, 1818; died June 3, 1827.

V. Jacob Wismer, bn. Nov. 13, 1819. Mrd. Anna Heighes, May 4, 1856. P. O., Forestville, Mich. Farmer. Christian ch. Children: Elizabeth, Hannah, Alpha, James, Ella, George.

VI. Elizabeth A. Wismer, bn. Nov. 21, 1858. Mrd. Osro E. Van Wormer, Apr. 23, 1877. P. O., Sand Beach, Mich. Miller. One child: **(VII.)** Myrtle A. Van Wormer, bn. Jan. 27, 1878.

VI. Hannah K. Wismer, bn. Nov. 25, 1860. Mrd. James M. Smiley, June 3, 1890. P. O., Sigel, Mich. Farmer. Latter Day Saint ch. Children: **(VII.)** Marshall J. Smiley, bn. Apr. 26, 1891. **(VII.)** Frances E. Smiley, bn. Aug. 21, 1892.

VI. Alpha W. Wismer, bn. Apr. 27, 1861. Mrd. Kate E. Oughton, Oct. 4, 1886. P. O., Forestville, Mich. Farmer. One child: **(VII.)** Alphoretta May Wismer, bn. Dec. 3, 1889.

VI. James H. Wismer, bn. June 10, 1863. S.

VI. Ella P. Wismer, bn. —. Mrd. Isaac Pipher, Dec. 3, 1890. P. O., Jeddo, Mich. Farmer. Latter Day Saints.

VI. George T. Wismer, bn. Nov. 21, 1874.

V. David Lighte·Wismer, Jr., bn. Jan. 27, 1822. Mrd. Catharine Anderson, Mar. 10, 1846. She died June 19, 1871. P. O., New Market, Ont. Retired farmer. Methodists. Children: John, Marshall, Wellington, Albert. — Mr. Wismer mrd. second wife, Elizabeth Eves, Mar. 6, 1873. One child: Walter.

VI. John A. Wismer, M. A., bn. Nov. 29, 1846. Mrd. Julia S. Webster, Aug. 28, 1870. Is a graduate with honors of Trinity University in Toronto, Ont., and for the past ten years has been a Master in one of the leading educational institutions there. Children: **(VII.)** Ernest. **(VII.)** Floyd. **(VII.)** Karl. **(VII.)** Winifred.

VI. Marshall Hamilton Wismer, bn. May 23, 1849; died Dec. 1, 1881. Teacher. Unmarried.

VI. Wellington Howard D. Wismer, bn. Oct. 15, 1853. Mrd. Catharine Bamer. Teacher. Children: **(VII.)** Hamilton David Wismer, bn. Apr. 20, 1874. In mail and printing office. Toronto, Ont. **(VII.)** Edith Wismer. **(VII.)** Alice Mabel Wismer. **(VII.)** Wilford J. Wismer. **(VII.)** Maud Elizabeth Wismer. **(VII.)** Gordon S. Wismer. **(VII.)** Arthur Horace Wismer, (dec'd).

VI. Albert Edwin C. F. Wismer, bn. May 16, 1862. Mrd. — O'Neil. P. O., Grand Rapids, Mich. Painter in Harrison wagon works.

VI. Walter Ives Wismer, bn. May 15, 1874.

V. Artemus Wismer bn. Dec. 23, 1824; died Jan. 23, 1825.

V. Elizabeth Wismer, bn. Jan. 12, 1826; died Apr. 16, 1827.

V. Henry H. Wismer, bn. in Markham, Ont., Aug. 9, 1829; died Mar. 20, 1881. Mrd. Anna E. Miller. She was bn. Oct. 4, 1828; died Apr. 10, 1871. Farmer. Methodists. Children: George, Isaac, Fidelia, Clarissa.

VI. George M. Wismer, bn. Apr. 14, 1856. Mrd. Anna E. Hunter, Dec. 6, 1884. P.O., Corunna, Mich. Merchant. Meth. Ep. No issue.

VI. Isaac Wismer, bn. —; died - .

VI. Fidelia Wismer, bn. June 18, 1859. Mrd. Philip Badgers, Sept. 28, 1886. P. O., Ballantrae, Ont. Farmer. Christian ch. No issue.

VI. Clarissa Jane Wismer, bn. in Markham, Ont., June 10, 1863. Mrd. Elias Degeer, Dec. 13, 1881. P. O., Ballantrae, Ont. Farmer. Christian ch. Children: **(VII.)** George Malcolm Degeer, bn. 1882. **(VII.)** Annie Degeer, bn. 1883. **(VII.)** Zella Degeer, bn. 1885. **(VII.)** Earnest Hillard Degeer, bn. 1889.

V. Regina Wismer, bn. in Markham, Ont., July 26, 1831. Mrd. George Morrison. He was bn. in Ireland in 1831. P. O., Nottawa, Ont. Farmer. Meth's. Children: Elizabeth, Annie, David, Mary, Thomas, Scotburn.

VI. Elizabeth Morrison, bn. June 20, 1856. S.

VI. Annie Morrison, bn. June 20, 1856. (Twin.) Mrd. John P. Baker, Dec. 3, 1890. P. O., Nottawa, Ont. Farmer. Meth's.

VI. David Morrison, bn. July 1, 1858.

VI. Mary Morrison, bn. Sept. 19, 1860. Mrd. Thomas Jackson, Mar. 2, 1887. P. O., Nottawa, Ont. Miller. Meth's. One child: **(VII.)** Lillian May Jackson, bn. July 27, 1888.

VI. Thomas Henry Morrison, bn. Mar. 19, 1864. S.

VI. Scotburn Buist Morrison, bn. Oct. 10, 1867. S.

V. Asa Wismer, bn. Aug. 9, 1834; died Dec. 6, 1881.
IV. Jacob Wismer, bn. in Bucks Co., Pa., Nov. 9,
1798. Mrd. Elizabeth Wurts, Feb. 3, 1823. She was
bn. Sept. 27, 1801; died in fall of 1850. Farmer.
Children: Delilah, Emeline, Anna, Enos, Maria,
Jacob, Abraham, Lewis, Abraham.—Jacob mrd. sec-
ond wife, Julia Curtis, Dec. 2, 1852.
V. Delilah Wismer, bn. in York Co., Ont., Aug. 31,
1824. Mrd. Henry Jackson, Jan. 29, 1850. He died
Sept. 26, 1892. P. O., Nanticoke, Ont. Farmer.
Episcopalians. Children: Wellington, Elizabeth,
Edith, William.
VI. Wellington Jackson, bn. Dec. 7, 1850. Mrd.
Esther Bangfield, —. Res. 93 Emily St., Buffalo, N.
Y. House carpenter. Episcopalian. One child: **(VII.)**
Sybilla Jackson.
VI. Elizabeth Jackson, bn. Sept. 12, 1854. Mrd.
James Johnson, —. P. O., Nanticoke, Ont. Farmer.
Meth. Children: **(VII.)** William Henry Johnson.
(VII.) Edith Delilah Johnson. **(VII.)** Annie Mabel
Johnson. **(VII.)** James Arthur Johnson.
VI. Edith Jackson, bn. Jan. 7, 1857. Mrd. George
Albert Evans, —. P. O., Cheapside, Ont. Farmer.
Episcopalians. Children: **(VII.)** Ainsley Romain
Evans. **(VII.)** Ida Edith Evans. **(VII.)** Margaret Deli-
lah Evans. **(VII.)** William Henry Evans, (dec'd).
(VII.) Albert Edward Evans. **(VII.)** Lizzie Mabel
Evans. **(VII.)** Julia Maud Evans.
VI. William Frederick Jackson, bn. Feb. 20, 1859.
Mrd. Annie Ross, —. P. O., Nanticoke, Ont. Farm-
er. Episcopalian. Children: **(VII.)** Warren Jackson.
(VII.) Lillian Delilah Jackson.
V. Emeline Wismer, bn. Aug. 13, 1826. Mrd. Ana-
nias Turner. P. O., Toronto, Ont.
V. Anna Wismer, bn. Jan. 15, 1829; died 1842.
V. Enos Wismer, bn. Jan. 14, 1831; died 1842.
V. Maria Wismer, bn. Jan. 28, 1833; died 1842.
V. Jacob Everett Wismer, bn. July 9, 1835. Mrd.
Sarah Adaline Morrison, of Painesville, Ohio, Oct.
20, 1857. She died Mar. 4, 1874. P. O., Markham,
Ont. Children: Laura, John, George, Ada.—Mr.
Wismer mrd. second wife, Mary Coleman, Oct. 3,

1876. She died Feb. 12, 1890. One child: Lizzie.
Mr. Wismer left home in 1852, went to Ohio, where
he remained until 1857, when he removed to Nanticoke, Ont. In 1861, he returned to Painesville, Ohio,
and later, went south and worked in the Government
Navy yard as ship carpenter. In the winter of 1870
he moved to Allegan, Mich., and engaged in farming.
He has also been occupied as merchant and fruit
grower. He has also traveled quite extensively, having traveled from the C. P. R. limits to the southern
boundaries of the U. S. and from the Atlantic to the
Pacific coasts. He is also a fisherman of note, having
made excursions among the lakes of Canada, and
taken many of the speckled beauties, and other vari-
eties, and aside from his other duties he has also con-
tributed articles to the press.

VI. Laura Janette Wismer, bn. at Nanticoke, Ont.,
Aug. 17, 1858. Mrd. Perley E. Lonsbury, Jan. 16,
1879. P. O., Kellogg, Mich. Farmer. One child: **(VII.)**
Beatrice M. Lonsbury, bn. June 3, 1880.

VI. John Everett Wismer, bn. at Port Dover, Ont.,
Nov. 24, 1861. General salesman in Chicago, Ill. S.

VI. George Clark Wismer, bn. at Painesville, Ohio,
Apr. 12, 1863. Druggist at Hinsdale, Ill.

VI. Ada May Wismer, bn. at Port Burwell, Ont.,
July 18, 1866. Mrd. Reuben W. Hamlin, in Santa
Barbara, California, Jan. 12, 1887. P. O., St. Catha-
rines, Ont. Ch. of England. Children: **(VII.)** Ada
Corinne Hamlin, bn. Dec. 9, 1889. **(VII.)** Cyrene
Hamlin, bn. Feb. 2, 1890. **(VII.)** Reuben Floyd Ham-
lin, bn. Oct. 10, 1891.

VI. Lizzie Jane Wismer, bn. Sept. 5, 1877.

V. Abraham Wismer, bn. Sept. 30, 1838; died 1842.

V. Lewis Levi Wismer, bn. Mar. 24, 1841; died
1842.

V. Abraham L. Wismer, bn. July 5, 1844. Mrd.
Fannie Andrews, —. P. O., 62 North Cotton, Toronto, Ont.

IV. Henry Wismer, bn. Dec. 31, 1800; died —.
Mrd. Barbara, daughter of Jacob and Anna (Wismer)
Angeny, —. "Pow Wow" doctor. Resided in Can-
ada. No issue.

IV. Nancy Wismer, bn. May 25, 1802; died Nov. 20, 1887. Mrd. Daniel Moore in 1819. He was bn. 1797; died 1855. Millwright. Christian church. Children: Henry, Lydia, Abraham, Mary, Julia, Daniel.

V. Henry Moore, bn. June 7, 1820; died Oct. 1842.

V. Lydia Moore, bn. Feb. 9, 1822. Mrd. Galon O. Gilbert, June 21, 1838. He died May 18, 1878. P. O., Cresswell, Ont. No issue.

V. Abraham Moore, bn. in Markham Twp., Ont., Feb. 6, 1824. Mrd. Zilpa Ann White, May 16, 1848. P. O., Faribault, Minn. In 1846 he moved to Oxford Co., Ont., and engaged in the saw mill business, and farming. In 1868 he moved to Minnesota where he has since been engaged in the foundry and machine business. Baptists. Children: Daughter, David, Charlotte, Lydia, Jeremiah, Sanford, Mary, Anna, Frederick, Archy.

VI. Daughter, bn. Feb. 26, 1849; died Mar. 28, 1851.

VI. David Martin Moore, bn. Dec. 18, 1850; died Oct. 22, 1851.

VI. Charlotte Moore, bn. Aug. 9, 1852. Mrd. Servetus W. Clark, July 4, 1874. P. O., Duluth, Minn. Laundry. Cong. Children: **(VII.)** Lillian W. Clark, bn. June 7, 1877. **(VII.)** Judson Smith Clark, bn. Apr. 19, 1884.

VI. Lydia Alfretta Moore, bn. Aug. 11, 1855. Mrd. F. Munroe, Oct. 25, 1876. P. O., Faribault, Minn. Cutter. Cong. ch. Children: **(VII.)** Archibald John Munroe, bn. Sept. 10, 1879. **(VII.)** Gordon Moore Munroe, bn. Nov. 1, 1885. **(VII.)** Charlotte Jean Munroe, bn. May 9, 1888.

VI. Jeremiah White Moore, bn. July 14, 1857. P. O., Denver, Col. S.

VI. Sanford A. Moore, bn. Apr. 26, 1859; died May 20, 1863.

VI. Mary Elizabeth Moore, bn. Nov. 17, 1862; died Nov. 28, 1862.

VI. Anna Adelaid Moore, bn. June 22, 1864. Mrd. Thomas B. Alcirk, Jan. 1, 1884. P. O., Duluth, Minn. Laundry. Methodists. Children: **(VII.)** Herbie Gordon Alkirk, bn. Sept. 8, 1884. **(VII.)** Edith May Alkirk, bn. June 30, 1886.

VI. Frederick Abraham Moore, bn. Mar. 18, 1867. P. O., West Superior, Wis. S.

VI. Archy Herbert Moore, bn. Apr. 11, 1870. Was drowned in Cannon river, June 26, 1886.

V. Mary Moore, bn. Mar. 15, 1826; died Mar. 5, 1840.

V. Julia Ann Moore, bn. Mar. 1, 1828. Mrd. Hezekiah Noble, Jan. 25, 1848. He was bn. Sept. 5, 1822. P. O., Little Britain, Ont. Farmer. Christian ch. Children: Eli, Alzinah, Thomas, Lydia, Nancy, Hezekiah, Alfaretta, Abraham.

VI. Eli Daniel Noble, bn. Feb. 3, 1849; died July 25, 1849.

VI. Alzinah Noble, bn. Feb. 25, 1850. Mrd. David Culbert, Dec. 25, 1870. P. O., Little Britain, Ont. Farmer. Children: (**VII.**) Evylena Culbert, bn. Apr. 16, 1872. (**VII.**) John Hezekiah Culbert, bn. Feb. 22, 1874. (**VII.**) Howard Noble Culbert, bn. July 18, 1875. (**VII.**) Maurice Lincoln Culbert, bn. June 18, 1880.

VI. Thomas Henry Noble, bn. Feb. 28, 1853. Mrd. Hannah E. Ramsey, Dec. 25, 1875. P. O., Cresswell, Ont. Farmer. Children. (**VII.**) Elizabeth Henrietta Noble, bn. Feb. 2, 1877; died Feb. 24, 1877. (**VII.**) Ethel May Noble, bn. July 8, 1878. (**VII.**) Vida Petala Noble, bn. Nov. 30, 1880. (**VII.**) Millie Alberta Noble, bn. May 2, 1883. (**VII.**) Julia Labella Noble, bn. Nov. 13, 1885. (**VII.**) Nancy Ann Noble, bn. Aug. 30, 1890; died same day.

VI. Lydia Ann Noble, bn. June 2, 1857. Mrd. Thomas Reazin, in 1879. P. O., Cresswell, Ont. Farmer. Children: (**VII.**) Florence Reazin, bn. Mar. 21, 1880. (**VII.**) Hezekiah Reazin, bn. Mar. 21, 1882. (**VII.**) Sarah Reazin, bn. Dec. 25, 1884.

VI. Nancy Noble, bn. July 20, 1858; died Aug. 15, 1883. Mrd. Charles Dann, Sept. 25, 1881. No issue.

VI. Hezekiah J. Noble, bn. Apr. 29, 1861; died Apr. 30, 1862.

VI. Alfaretta Noble, bn. Mar. 11, 1865. Mrd. Charles Dann, Jan. 27, 1892.

VI. Abraham Hezekiah Noble, bn. —.

V. Daniel J. Moore, bn. Mar. 13, 1830; died June 9, 1862.

IV. Lydia Wismer, bn. in 1805. Mrd. William Witter.

IV. David Wismer, bn. in Markham Twp., Ont., Dec. 22, 1807; died Sept. 8, 1890. Mrd. Mary Toman, Oct. 15, 1826. She was bn. Aug. 13, 1810; died July 16, 1883. They began married life with very little of this world's goods, but by industry and frugality they became the possessors of some property. They settled on Lot 17, Con. 7, in Markham Twp., Ont., which they cleared, and on which they resided until they died. They were members of the Christian church, of which he was a Deacon for many years, and to which in early life they walked and carried the baby, the distance being six miles. They lived together 57 years, and celebrated their golden wedding on Monday, Oct. 16, 1876. (The wedding day falling on Sunday.)

The family consisted of 14 children, of whom 11 were living. Of the 65 living descendants, including husbands and wives, 43 were present at the golden wedding. Twenty-two were prevented from attending on account of sickness, and otherwise. The table was elaborately spread, in the center of which stood a six story cake with flags rising from the center, on which the words "Welcome Home" were beautifully laid in gold leaf. Immediately before eating, the children sang the well known hymn, "Welcome Home," after which David Wismer and wife, their children with their husbands and wives, partook of the refreshments, and the grandchildren finishing the repast.

The artist, Mr. Tomlinson, of Stouffville, being present, a picture of the family group was admirably taken, after which the various golden, and other presents, were placed on platters, and the company gathered in the parlor to witness the presentation of the gifts, and to listen to an address by John Milne, one of the sons-in-law, which was as follows:

Dear Parents:—It is with mingled feelings of regret and pleasure that we are here assembled together to commemorate the fiftieth anniversary of your wedding day. With feelings of regret that on account of sickness and other unavoidable causes there are some of our children deprived of the privilege of meeting with us to-day and partaking alike of the pleasant associations and remembrances that this meeting will afford to us all; and also with regret that in the course of nature there is no human probability or liklihood that so many of this family will ever be permitted to meet you again on this side of eternity. But still we meet with united feelings of pleasure to know that God in His divine providence has graciously permitted you and us to enjoy a meeting of this kind, one which is granted to but few in this world. When we, your children, cast our minds back through our younger years we cannot but admire and derive great pleasure in contemplating the care and diligence you manifested in raising so large a family in such a manner as would enable them all to become honest, industrious and useful members of society and we trust in this respect your efforts have not been altogether in vain. We cannot but call to mind that in all your teachings you did not forget to continually draw our attention to the all important fact that there was an All-wise Providence to whom we should always look for guidance and support through our walks in this life. We must now congratulate you that God has so far blessed you with health, strength of mind and body, and prosperity in the things of this world far above the average of those of your ages, and now, dear parents, as we are met together on an occasion never to be forgotten, and one that will never occur again during our lives and in token of our love for you, and as remembrances to be cherished by you, dear father, we present you with these few small gifts, and to you dear mother we also present a few tokens of our love and esteem. These gifts, though small in themselves and representing but little in value, still they are rich in the love and esteem which we have towards you. Our united prayer is that God in His goodness may see fit to bless you both with many years of happy and peaceful companionship together, and when you are done with all the troubles and trials of this earthly career, you may have a seat in that eternal home promised to those who remain faithful to the end; and also when we, your children, and our families, have done with the things of this life, our humble prayer is that we may be permitted to meet with you there and be as one happy family united in Heaven. In conclusion we all say for once more, God bless you and all your posterity. Amen.

After the address the hymn "Shall we gather at the River," was heartily and feelingly sung by all.

Mrs. Wismer responded in a few words, by thanking her children and grandchildren for the love and esteem shown by them, and for the harmony exhibited towards each other, and presented each with a piece of the wedding cake.

Mr. Wismer also responded in a very interesting manner, referring back to the time when his father and mother with their six children, in the year 1805, moved from Bucks Co., Pa., to Markham, Ont., and described many of the trials the pioneers encountered, the implements used by them, and his wedding trip 50 years ago, when he and his wife went on horseback to get married. He then closed by thanking, in a very impressive manner, his children and grandchildren for the presents made to him and their mother, urging them to diligence and honest dealings in their duties of this life. Children: Nancy, Levi, Eli, Salome, Joseph, Philemon, Sarah, Lydia, Barbara, Enos, Albertina, Elijah, Catharine, Nellie.

V. Nancy Wismer, bn. in Markham Twp., Ont., in 1827. Mrd. Augustus von Buseck*, Jan. 1, 1845. P. O., Stouffville, Ont. Saddler. Luth's. Children: Charles, Theodore, Amelia, Arnetta, Eli, Mary.

VI. Charles William von Busick, bn. Nov. 22, 1846; died Aug. 31, 1849.

VI. Theodore Alexander von Busick, bn. July 14, 1849. Mrd. Elmira Huber, Aug. 9, 1870. She was bn. May 5, 1852. P. O., Stouffville, Ont. Saddler. Cong. ch. Children: (**VII.**) Arnette Constance Cecelia von Busick, bn. Sept. 12, 1871. (**VII.**) Rudolph Alexander von Busick, bn. Mar. 6, 1874. (**VII.**) Albert Edwin von Busick, bn. Aug. 24, 1884. (**VII.**) Leo Ottomer von Busick, bn. Feb. 11, 1887.

VI. Amelia Jane von Busick, bn. Oct. 6, 1851. Mrd. Ottomar Parecki, June 7, 1882. He was bn. Aug. 22, 1850. P. O., Erie, Pa. Jeweler. Luth's. No issue.

VI. Arnette Cecelia von Buseck, bn. Oct. 22, 1853; died Apr. 26, 1856.

VI. Eli Albert von Buseck, bn. Nov. 26, 1856. Mrd. Mary Keener, June 2, 1885. She was bn. June 20, 1857. P. O., Sunderland, Ont. Saddler. Luth's. No issue.

---

* Mr. von Buseck is a descendant of one of the oldest titled families in Germany.

VI. Mary Albertina von Buseck, bn. Nov. 6, 1860. Mrd. Archibald S. Leaney, Sept. 1, 1881. He was bn. May 2, 1856. P. O., Stouffville, Ont. Merchant. Luth's. One child: **(VII.)** Jesse Aileen Leaney, bn. Mar. 24, 1886.

V. Levi Wismer, bn. in York Co., Ont., Dec. 7, 1828. Mrd. Lucinda Osborne, Nov. 27, 1853. P. O., Ringwood, Ont. Farmer. Christian ch. Children: Levi, Emma, Ida, Effie, Rosa.

VI. Levi Franklin Wismer, bn. Apr. 25, 1859. Mrd. Elizabeth Cruickshank, Dec. 15, 1886. P.O., Au Sable, Mich. Millwright. Baptists. Children: **(VII.)** Ida Wismer, bn. Sept. 9, 1888. **(VII.)** Otto Wismer, bn. Mar. 10, 1891.

VI. Emma Floren Wismer, bn. Oct. 23, 1860. Mrd. Boyd Burk, Oct. 20, 1886. P. O., Brougham, Ont. Farmer. Church of England.

VI. Ida Wismer, bn. Apr. 18, 1868; died July 25, 1888.

VI. Effie Violette Wismer, bn. June 25, 1871. Baptist.

VI. Rosa Nell Wismer, bn. July 21, 1875. Baptist.

V. Eli Wismer, bn. Apr. 13, 1831; died May 7, 1871. Mrd. Matilda Kamphousen, Mar. 8, 1859. Children: **(VI.)** Edward. **(VI.)** Charles. **(VI.)** Arthur.

V. Salome Wismer, bn. Apr. 15, 1833; died Aug. 8, 1833.

V. Joseph Hume Wismer, bn. June 5, 1834; died May 20, 1854.

V. Philemon Wismer, bn. May 31, 1836; died Feb. 5, 1883. Mrd. Mary Ann Miller, July 7, 1857. P.O., Gore Bay, Manitolian Islands. Farmer. Christian ch. Children: Henrietta, Joseph, Jacob, Ida, Mary, Martha, Ethelda.

VI. Henrietta Louisa Wismer, bn. Apr. 25, 1858. Mrd. Bassil C. Cannuff, Sept. 15, 1879. P. O., Norwich, Ont. No issue.

VI. Joseph Lewis Wismer, bn. Dec. 30, 1860. Mrd. Lizzie Monzzeth, —. P. O., Gore Bay, Ont. Baker. Children: **(VII.)** Olive Monzzeth Wismer, bn. Apr. 20, 1886. **(VII.)** Effie Wismer, bn. May 17, 1887; died Apr. 3, 1889. **(VII.)** Harold S. Wismer, bn. Dec.

25, 1888. (VII.) Elfleda Isabella Wismer, bn. May 17, 1891.

VI. Jacob David Wismer, bn. June 15, 1864. P. O., Gore Bay, Ont. Presby. S.

VI. Ida Jane Wismer, bn. Mar. 1, 1868. Mrd. George A. Morris. P. O., Thornburg, Ont. Merchant. Children: (VII.) Gertrude Morris, bn. Sept. 26, 1889. (VII.) Ernest Russell Morris, bn. May 18, 1891.

VI. Mary Hannah Wismer, bn. Mar. 28, 1871.

VI. Martha Helena Wismer, bn. Mar. 2, 1873.

VI. Ethelda Albertina Wismer, bn. May 31, 1878.

V. Sarah Jane Wismer, bn. in York Co., Ont., Apr. 13, 1838. Mrd. John Balthurst Burk, Oct. 23, 1853. P. O., Brougham, Ont. Formerly blacksmith, now farmer. Ch. of England. Children: (VI.) Eleanor Burk, bn. Aug. 23, 1854; died Oct. 13, 1854. (VI.) Mary Magdalena Burk, bn. Oct. 10, 1855; died Aug. 25, 1859. (VI.) Eli Albert Augustus Burk, bn. Mar. 30, 1858; died Aug. 14, 1861.

V. Lydia Helen Wismer, bn. Feb. 29, 1840. Mrd. Henry Peard Hand, Sept. 14, 1862. P. O., Daytona, Fla.

V. Barbara Ann Wismer, bn. Feb. 1, 1842. Mrd. John Milne, Nov. 28, 1860, P.O., Essex Centre, Ont. In early life Mr. Milne taught school, since then has been largely in the manufacturing business, and is at present engaged in private banking and real estate. Meth's. Children: Florence, Arthur, Ariadne, John.

VI. Florence Milne, bn. Nov. 27, 1861. Mrd. Frank Leute, of Duluth, July 26, 1892. Railway despatcher.

VI. Arthur E. Milne, bn. Feb. 6, 1864. Mrd. Celinda Robinson, Sept. 28, 1887. Children: (VII.) Addie L. Milne, bn. July 1889. (VII.) Carlisle Milne, bn. Sept. 1891.

VI. Ariadne Milne, bn. Sept. 23, 1866. Mrd. Orlando C. Barrie, Feb. 22, 1886. Manufacturer of paints. Children: (VII.) Earl Barrie, bn. Nov. 26, 1888. (VII.) Millie Barrie, bn. Aug. 1890. (VII.) Leland Barrie, bn. Dec. 1891.

VI. John H. Milne, bn. Sept. 28, 1878.

V. Enos Everett Wismer, bn. Feb. 11, 1844. Mrd. Jemima Young, Mar. 20, 1864. She died Mar. 1880. P. O., Essex Centre, Ont. Farmer, carpenter, stonemason. Children: Albert, Joseph, Elijah, Theodore, Susan, Alice, Clarence.— Enos mrd. second wife, Robena McConnochie, Sept. 14, 188-. Presby's. One child: Archie.

VI. Albert Everett Wismer, bn. Dec. 5, 1866. Mrd. Elizabeth Kendrick, in 1888. P. O., Essex, Ont. Farmer. Meth's. Children: **(VII.)** Lulu Wismer. **(VII.)** Ethel Wismer.

VI. Joseph Wismer, bn. Dec. 7, 1867. Mrd. Mrs. Sicksmith, in 1890. Tin smith in Toronto, Ont.

VI. Elijah Wismer, bn. Dec. 7, 1867 (twin). Mrd. — Styler, in 1889. P. O., Essex, Ont. Sawyer. One child: **(VII.)** Jemima Wismer.

VI. Theodore Augustus Wismer, bn. Nov. 27, 1868. Mrd. — Copeland, in 1888. P. O., Essex, Ont. Mechanic. Meth's. Children: **(VII.)** Enos Wismer. **(VII.)** Alice Wismer.

VI. Susan Wismer, bn. June 8, 1870; died Apr. 25, 1871.

VI. Alice Alberta Wismer, bn. Feb. 25, 1873. Mrd. George Loucks, in 1890. P. O., Detroit. Machinist. Meth's. One child: **(VII.)** Bella Loucks.

VI. Clarence Eugene Wismer, bn. Feb. 25, 1880.

VI. Archie M. Wismer, bn. Dec. 15, 1885; died Feb. 4, 1888.

V. Albertina Wismer, bn. in Markham Twp., Ont., Feb. 12, 1846. Mrd. James Logie, Nov. 9, 1862. He was born on a Mill farm in Morayshire, Scotland, Apr. 3, 1838. His mother died while he was an infant At 17 years of age he was compelled to seek on this side of the Atlantic a home which unhappily Scotia denies to so many of her sons. Chopping and clearing land occupied the first five years of his experience in Canada, when he was appointed teacher in the school in Feversham, county of Grey, with no other qualification than youth, energy, and the limited education acquired at the Parochial school in his native parish. After three years service as teacher, he engaged in business in Feversham, at which he continued with varied success in several towns in Canada, when, in 1885, he moved to Michigan with his family and engaged in business in Ithea, Gratiot county. During 1887 he was appointed Steward of Alma College, an institution chartered by the state, and under the care of the Presbyterian Synod of Michigan, where he and wife now reside. Presbyterians. Children: Charlotte, Mary, William, Eva.

VI. Charlotte Louisa Logie, bn. June 11, 1864. Mrd. James A. Ovas, of Rapid City, Manitoba, — Millowner. Presby. Children: **(VII.)** Charlotte Albertina Ovas. **(VII.)** James McDonald Ovas. **(VII.)** Colin Alexander Ovas. **(VII.)** Kathleen Ovas.

VI. Mary Albertina Logie, bn. May 10, 1867. Mrd. Robert T. Butchart, —. Railway Agt. Mrs. B., Presby. Mr. B., Meth. P. O., Rapid City, Manitoba. No issue.

VI. William James Logie, bn. Jan. 3, 1870. P. O., Rapid City, Manitoba. Miller. Presby. S.

VI. Eva Anne Laing Logie, bn. Mar. 21, 1872. Mrd. Fred A. Rundle, —. P. O., Detroit, Mich. Pattern maker. Mrs. R., Presby. Mr. R., Meth. No issue.

V. Elijah Wismer, bn. Apr. 7, 1848. Mrd. Susannah, daughter of Daniel Strickler, Esq., Sept. 18, 1871. P. O., Markham, Ont. Farmer, owns the old homestead in Markham Twp., known as the Willowdale farm. In 1890 he purchased 55 acres of the Hunter estate known as Apple Grove Cottage, and moved thereon. His wife inherited 20 acres, so they own in all 120 acres. Christian ch. Children: **(VI.)** Charles Walter Wismer, bn. Sept. 5, 1872. **(VI.)** Ella Elizabeth Wismer, bn. Dec. 22, 1875. **(VI.)** Ina Augusta Wismer, bn. Apr. 26, 1880. **(VI.)** Edith Mary Wismer, bn. Jan. 24, 1884.

V. Catharine Caroline Wismer, bn. in York Co., Ont., July 8, 1850. Mrd. Francis Coleman, Feb. 10, 1869. P. O., Oshawa, Ont. Farmer. Children: **(VI.)** Mary Elizabeth Coleman, bn. in 1871. **(VI.)** Arnetta Jane Coleman, bn. in 1873.

V. Nellie Wismer, bn. Apr. 5, 1852. Mrd. Hugh Wilson Barrie, Sept. 19, 1871. P. O., 70 Baltimore

Ave., Detroit, Mich. Commercial traveler. Cong. Children: Minnie, Malcom.

VI. Minnie Augusta Barrie, bn. Oct. 1872. Mrd. Fred H. Wilson, in 1890. One child: **(VII.)** Crida Gertrude Wilson, bn. in 1891.

VI. Malcom Herbert Barrie, bn. in 1879,

IV. Samuel Wismer, bn. Mar. 7, 1811; died Dec. 16, 1884. Mrd. Anna Urmy, Mar. 15, 1831. She died May 7, 1882. Farmer. Menn's. Children: Frances, Dorothy, Judith, Lucy.

V. Frances Wismer, bn. May 18, 1833; died —. Mrd. Michael Honsberger, —. He died —. Frances mrd. second husband, John Baker, —. He died —.

V. Dorothy Wismer, bn. Aug. 27, 1834. Mrd. John Pipher in 1851. P. O., Stouffville, Ont.

V. Judith Wismer, bn. Mar. 28, 1836. Mrd. Aretus Urmy, Apr. 9, 1857. P. O., Markham, Ont. Farmer. Children: **(VI.)** Emily Jane Urmy, bn. Jan. 21, 1858. **(VI.)** Albert Walter Urmy, bn. Nov. 4, 1865. **(VI.)** Ed Stanley Urmy, bn. Aug. 18, 1870.

V. Lucy Wismer, bn. Oct. 3, 1841; died Aug. 15, 1844.

III. Mark Wismer, bn. in Bucks Co., Feb. 12, 1775; died Feb. 16, 1858. Mrd. Mary Elizabeth Nunnamaker. —. She died Feb. 12, 1853. Mason. Luth's. Children: John, Catharine, Maria, Jonas, Samuel, Nancy, Mark, Jacob.

IV. John Wismer, bn. —; died —. Mrd. Catharine Krout, —. She died —. Son: Joseph.—John mrd. second wife, Catharine Roofner,—. Daughter: Mary.

V. Joseph Wismer, bn. —. Mrd. Catharine Shoup, —. Children: **(VI.)** Lincoln (dec'd). **(VI.)** Amanda (dec'd). **(VI.)** Catharine. **(VI.)** Monroe.

V. Mary Wismer, bn. —.

IV. Catharine Wismer, bn. July 24, 1802; died Oct. 4, 1844. Mrd. Jacob Landis. (See Index of References No. 79.)

IV. Maria Wismer, bn. —. Mrd. Samuel Worthington, —. Children: **(V.)** Mary Worthington, bn. —. Mrd. Phineas Gilbert, —. **(V.)** Mark Worthington, bn. —. Mrd. Mary Renner, —.

IV. Jonas Wismer, bn. — ; died —. Mrd. — Benner. Children: (V.) Anna Wismer, bn. —. P. O., Plumsteadville, Pa. (V.) Tomacilla Wismer, bn. --. Mrd. Thomas White, —. P. O., Point Pleasant, Pa.

IV. Samuel Wismer, bn. Oct. 20, 1808. Mrd. Mary Ann Roofner, Dec. 23, 1838. P. O., Pipersville, Pa. Miller. Luth. Children: Elizabeth, Anna, Samuel.

V. Elizabeth Wismer, bn. Mar. 7, 1841. Mrd. Edward Updegraff. P. O., Pipersville, Pa. Farmer. (VI.) Edgar, (deceased). (VI.) Ervin.

V. Anna C. Wismer, bn June 10, 1842. Mrd. Henry G. Gilmore. P. O., Erwinna, Pa. Stone mason. Mrs. G., Catholic. Children: Samuel, Laura, Martha, Henry, William, Anna, Bertha.

VI. Samuel Gilmore, bn. June 11, 1866.

VI. Laura Jennetta Gilmore, bn. May 31, 1868. Mrd. James W. Johnson. P. O., Barberstown, N. J. Children (VII.) Walter Johnson. (VII.) Estella Johnson. (VII.) Samuel Johnson.

VI. Martha Jane Gilmore, bn. Sept. 8, 1870.

VI. Henry Forest Gilmore, born March 9, 1872. (Twin.)

VI. William Edwin Gilmore, bn. Mar. 9, 1872.

VI. Anna Catharine Gilmore, bn. Oct. 15, 1876.

VI. Bertha May Gilmore, bn. July 12, 1883; died Sept. 11, 1884.

V. Samuel Wismer, bn. Aug. 1, 1848; died Aug. 12, 1874. Catholic. S.

IV. Nancy Wismer, bn. Mar. 7, 1813; died —. Mrd. Michael Shoup, —. He was bn. Feb. 10, 1819; died Oct. 14, 1889. Laborer. Children: Mary, Mark, Katie.

V. Mary Ann Shoup, bn. in Bucks Co., Pa., —. Mrd. John Miller. P. O., Plumsteadville, Pa. Shoemaker. Children: (VI.) Theodore Miller. (VI.) Matilda May Miller, (deceased). (VI.) Augustine Miller, (deceased). (VI.) Shady Miller, (deceased). (VI.) Eleanore Miller.

V. Mark Shoup, bn. —. P. O., Norristown, Pa.

V. Katie Ann Shoup, bn. —.

IV. Mark Wismer, bn. Aug. 27, 1812; died Aug. 30, 1886. Mrd. Deborah Johnson Strawn, Dec. 1834.

Farmer. Baptists. Children: Hettie, Mary, Thomas, Edward, Joseph.

V. Hettie A. Wismer, bn. May 18, 1836. Mrd. Thomas A. Darrah, Dec. 3, 1857. He died Aug. 27, 1890. P. O., Doylestown, Pa. Farmer. Baptists. Children: Charles, William.

VI. Charles W. Darrah, bn. Aug. 4, 1859; died May 2, 1892. Mrd. Katie Conlan, Apr. 17, 1881. Florist. Children: (**VII.**) T. Armstrong Darrah, bn. Feb. 21, 1883. (**VII.**) Maggie H. Darrah, bn. Nov. 15, 1886.

VI. Wm. T. H. Darrah, bn. Feb. 23, 1863. P. O., Doylestown, Pa. Has a country seat, and lives retired. Attends Presbyterian ch. S.

V. Mary Etta Wismer, bn. June 19, 1839. Mrd. Owen Craven, Jan. 1, 1867. Res. 622 W. Cumberland St., Phila., Pa. Real estate Agt. Baptists. Children: (**VI.**) Emma J. Craven, bn. Dec. 17, 1871. S. (**VI.**) Horace B. Craven, bn. July 29, 1873; died July 29, 1874. (**VI.**) Howard B. Craven, bn. Aug. 11, 1884; died Dec. 11, 1884.

V. Thomas Watson Wismer, bn. Mar. 18, 1845. Mrd. Mary Anna Kaisinger, Oct. 20, 1868. P. O., Mechanics Valley, Pa. Farmer. Children: (**VI.**) George W. Wismer, bn. Aug. 29, 1869. (**VI.**) Nellie W. Wismer, bn. May 30, 1874. (**VI.**) May S. Wismer, bn. Nov. 29, 1875.

V. Edward E. Wismer bn. Feb. 26, 1848; died Mar. 2, 1848.

V. Joseph Fell Wismer, bn. Sept. 11, 1851. Mrd. Josephine C. Wiley, Dec. 30, 1874. P. O., Buckmansville, Pa. Farmer. Children: (**VI.**) Carrie J. Wismer, bn. Dec. 28, 1875. (**VI.**) Edward E. Wismer, bn. Aug. 15, 1878. (**VI.**) Lizzie K. Wismer, bn. Oct. 29, 1881. (**VI.**) Newlin W. Wismer, bn. Nov. 7, 1887.

IV. Jacob N. Wismer, bn. Mar. 29, 1815; died June 16, 1890. Mrd. Sarah Afflerback, Aug. 5, 1848. She was bn. July 4, 1829; died Sept. 11, 1885. Miller. Christian ch. Children: Samuel, Aaron, Maria, Mary, Sarah, Jacob, Jonathan, Susanna.

V. Samuel A. Wismer, bn. Aug. 21, 1850. Mrd. Amy M. Hall, June 19, 1880. Blacksmith. Christian ch. No children.

V. Aaron A. Wismer, bn. May 4, 1853. Mrd. Matilda Cooper, Oct. 14, 1878. P. O , Lumberville, Pa. Stone mason. Christian ch. No children.

V. Maria E. Wismer, bn. Mar. 29, 1856. Mrd. J. Albert Hall, Dec. 23, 1880. Blacksmith in Phila., Pa. Christian ch. No children.

V. Mary C. Wismer, born Feb. 15, 1859. Mrd. Charles Eckhart, July 29, 1880. Christian ch. Children: **(VI.)**

V. Sarah Jane Wismer, bn. Nov. 29, 1861. Mrd. Philetus R. Pittman, Mar. 4. 1880. Christian ch. One child. **(VI.)** —.

V. Jacob A. Wismer, born Sept. 4, 1864. Mrd. Annie Raith, June 16, 1891. Christian ch.

V. Jonathan Francis Wismer, bn. Mar. 14, 1869. Christian ch.

V. Susanna Matilda Wismer, born Sept. 11, 1872. Christian ch.

III. Catharine Wismer, born —; died --. Mrd. Joseph Black, —. Menn's. One child: Zenas.— Joseph left home when his son Zenas was six weeks old, and was never heard from since.

IV. Zenas W. Black, bn. Oct. 22, 1800; died Dec. 1889. Mrd. Susanna, daughter of Capt. Emanuel Solliday, of the war of 1812. She was born Aug. 5, 1805; died —. Baptists. Children: William, Wilhelmina, Jeremiah, Mary, Emanuel, Cyrus, Hannah, Morris, Zenas, John.

V. William S. Black, bn. in Tinicum township, Bucks Co., Apr. 24, 1823. Mrd. Lydia Ann Gilbert, Feb. 22, 1849. She died Feb. 5, 1855. **(VI.)** Two children, (stillborn).—William mrd. second wife, Margery Anna Lindsay, Dec. 22, 1857. P. O., Harrisburg, Pa. Children: William, Charles, Franklin, Helen, William, Richard, Caroline.

Mr. Black, when a boy about two years old, was taken by his grandmother Catharine Black, (Nee Wismer), with whom he lived until she died when he

21

was about ten years old. During the time he lived
with his grandmother he attended school very regularly winter and summer; but at that time the country school was only an apology for a school, as many
of the teachers were very indifferent, in fact, some of
the pupils were better qualified to teach than the
teacher. After his grandmother's death he went home
to his father and mother for a short time, and then
was placed with a farmer in Bedminster Twp., to do
the chores in and around the house and barn and go
to school, which was a very advantageous change to
him so far as the school was concerned. He attended
Deep Run school during those two years most of the
time, winter and summer. An excellent teacher had
charge of the school who took great pride in seeing
his pupils learn.

At the close of his farm life Mr. Black began to
look around for something to do whereby he could
realize money for his labor. The best paying offer
was that of "tow boy" on the canal, which his mother
opposed very much, and also gave him some advice
which he has never forgotten, and which no doubt
has kept him out of many difficulties. The people, at
least some of them, at that day thought the occupation of a boatman was degrading. But notwithstand-
ing some "tow boys" have risen to exalted stations —
one to the Presidency of the United States, and another to the Attorney Generalship of the commonwealth of Pennsylvania. In the fall of 1839, Mr.
Black hung up the tow line for good and cast his eye
in another direction. In December 1839 his father
bound him an apprentice, to learn the art and mystery
of the printing business, to Gen. John S. Bryan,
then the publisher of the *Doylestown Democrat*, and
the printing office was the college from which he
graduated in 1844. His master was always kind to
him and trusted him implicitly with much of the
financial matters in the establishment. In those days a
boy learning the printing business in a country office
had three days in the office, and three days out carrying the mail and newspapers. That system has long
since been abolished.

Being free in 1844 he made a pilgrimage to Philadelphia in search of employment, which he soon secured, and where he worked for twenty years, ten of these years he was foreman of the establishment at a good salary for those days. In March 1865 he moved to New Castle, Pa., where he published the *New Castle Gazette and Lawrence County Democrat* for some fourteen or fifteen years, but did not get rich, being more anxious to help others than himself. In 1872 he was elected Mayor of the City of New Castle, Pa., as a Democrat, over his Republican opponent, his majority being 149 votes. The usual Republican majority in the city was from six to eight hundred.

On the first day of January 1879 he was appointed to a clerkship in the Auditor General's Department of the commonwealth of Pennsylvania. In May 1881 the administration changed and consequently the clerks changed. He then went to Watsontown, Northumberland county, and conducted a newspaper establishment for some time, when he was persuaded to take a clerkship in a bank—the hardest work he ever did—the business was entirely new to him, having no experience at all in that line of business. After four years he relinquished his position in the bank and went back to the printing business, at which he was working when elected Alderman of the Sixth Ward of the City of Harrisburg.

VI. William Henry Black, bn. May 21, 1859; died Jan. 11, 1865.

VI. Charles John Black, bn. May 14, 1862; died Oct. 5, 1877.

VI. Franklin Jackson Black, bn. in Phila., Pa., Dec. 13, 1864. Mrd. Nettie May Fox, of Rochester, Pa., —. P. O., Mechanicsburg, Pa. Presby's. No children.

VI. Helen Louisa Black, bn. at New Castle, Pa., Mar. 11, 1867. School teacher. Presby. S.

VI. William Smith Black, bn. at New Castle, Pa., Oct. 8, 1869. P. O., Harrisburg, Penna. Printer. Presby.

VI. Richard Vaux Black, bn. Mar. 13, 1872; died July 27, 1872.

VI. Caroline Hulda Black, bn. in New Castle, Pa., Apr. 15. 1873. Graduate of the Normal school at Bloomsburg, Pa. Presby.

V. Wilhelmina Chapman Black, bn. in Bucks Co., Oct. 28. 1825. Mrd. James Clark, of Manchester, England, July 14, 1844. He is supposed to have been lost at sea. Machine printer. Children: Susanna, Hannah, William, Emily.—Wilhelmina mrd. second husband, Joseph H. Allen, Sept. 19, 1861. He was bn. Oct. 4, 1834; died Oct. 26, 1875. Boatman. Meth's. Children: Wilhelmina, Josephine, Annie.

VI. Susanna B. Clark, bn. Feb. 26, 1846. Mrd. Henry Umstead, Nov. 25, 1865. Res. 45 Tyrell Av., Trenton, N. J. Sawyer. Baptist. Children: Frank, Charles, Jonah, Albert, Harry.

VII. Frank W. Umstead, bn. Oct. 18, 1866. Mrd. Effie T. Siefert, —. P. O., Trenton, N. J. Children: **(VIII.)** James Umstead. **(VIII.)** William Umstead.

VII. Charles O. Umstead, bn. Apr. 16, 1873.

VII. Jonah Umstead, bn. June 25, 1875.

VII. Albert Umstead, bn. Nov. 29, 1877.

VII. Harry Umstead, bn. Nov. 14. 1885.

VI. Hannah Mary Clark, bn. in Providence, R. I., Dec. 22, 1850. Mrd. Alonzo P. Geddes. He died Sept. 1, 1890. Res. Phila., Pa. Keep boarding house. Meth. Children: Joseph, Alfred, Franklin, Everett, Martha, Emily.

VII. Joseph Henry Geddes, bn. Feb. 8, 1870. Mrd. Mary Armstrong. Res. 35 Wister St., Phila., Pa. Driver. One child: **(VIII.)** Infant son, bn. July 22, 1891; died Oct. 15, 1891.

VII. Alfred Cooper Geddes, bn. June 5, 1875.

VII. Franklin W. C. Geddes, bn. Feb. 24, 1878.

VII. Everett P. Geddes, bn. Nov. 13, 1882.

VII. Martha Emma Geddes, bn. Sept. 10, 1886.

VII. Emily Myers Geddes, bn. Aug. 14, 1890.

VI. William H. Clark, bn. Feb. 24, 1853. Mrd. Mary Fields, —. Resides in Phila., Pa. Children: **(VII.)** Annie Clark, bn. —; died —. **(VII.)** Ellen

Clark, bn. —; died —. (VII.) Wilhelmina Clark, bn. —.

VI. Emily E. Clark, bn. Mar. 1, 1855; died Sept. 27, 1892. Mrd. Samuel M. Myers, Dec. 22, 1880. Res. 79 Klagg Ave., Trenton, N. J. Policeman. Meth's. No issue.

VI. Wilhelmina Solliday Allen, bn. Sept. 23, 1862. Mrd. Horace J. Geddes, Dec. 21, 1881. P. O., Uhlerstown, Pa. Lock-tender. Baptists. Children: (VII.) Douglass Geddes, bn. Oct. 31, 1882. (VII.) Horace J. Geddes, bn. June 29, 1884. (VII.) Allen H. Geddes, bn. Apr. 12, 1886; died Apr. 17, 1886. (VII.) Elizabeth C. Geddes, bn. June 20, 1887. (VII.) W. Clark Geddes, bn. Dec. 29, 1889. (VII.) James Geddes, bn. Feb. 12, 1892; died Feb. 14, 1892.

VI. Josephine H. Allen, bn. Oct. 26, 1864. Mrd. Joseph F. Tighe, Apr. 28, 1886. Res. Pittsville, Phila., Pa. Paperhanger. Catholics. Children: (VII.) Wilhelmina Tighe, bn. Mar. 1, 1887. (VII.) Sylvester Tighe, bn. Nov. 30, 1889. (VII.) Agnes Tighe, bn. Apr. 1, 1892.

VI. Annie H. Allen, bn. Nov. 3, 1867. Mrd. Abram Martin Porter, Dec. 29, 1884. Res. 151 E. Duval St., Phila., Pa. Police officer. Baptist. Children: (VII.) Marion Helen Porter, bn. Sept. 20, 1886. (VII.) Maggie Grace Porter, bn. July 23, 1889.

V. Jeremiah S. Black, bn. Nov. 24, 1828; died Nov. 1, 1860. Mrd. Delilah Holcomb, Feb. 25, 1855. Boatman. Attended Meth's and Bap. ch's. Children: Edwin, Wilmer, Eugene.

VI. Edwin Forest Black, bn. Oct. 4, 1856; died May 3, 1860.

VI. Wilmer Davis Black, bn. Jan. 8, 1858. Mrd. Mary Frankenhouse, Dec. 24, 1879. Res. 1113 Poplar St., Phila., Pa. Milk dealer. Children: (VII.) Wilmer Morris Black, bn. Oct. 2, 1880. (VII.) Delilah Holcomb Black, bn. Mar. 6, 1882. (VII.) Harvey Summers Black, born Dec. 8, 1883. (VII.) Mary Frankenhouse Black, bn. Oct. 14, 1885. (VII.) Bertha Black, bn. June 28, 1888. (VII.) Elsie Laurie Black, bn. Sept. 5, 1890.

VI. Eugene Leslie Black, bn. Aug. 28, 1859; died Dec. 2, 1862.

V. Mary Black, bn. in 1831; died —.

V. Emanuel S. Black, bn. in Plumstead, Pa., Oct. 23, 1833. Mrd. Hannah Holford, Feb. 22, 1870. Res. 1113 Poplar St., Phila., Pa. Brick-layer, and stationary engineer. Attends Baptist ch. Children: **(VI.)** Ellen Frances Black, bn. Nov. 28, 1870. **(VI.)** William Wallace Black, bn. Dec. 21, 1871.

V. Cyrus S. Black, bn. Feb. 10, 1836. Mrd. Maria Shaddinger, daughter of Joseph and Ann Shaddinger, Nov. 1, 1878. She was bn. Apr. 3, 1842. Blacksmith. Baptist. No issue.

V. Hannah Black, bn. in 1838; died in 1839.

V. Morris Black, bn. Nov. 19, 1840. P. O., Point Pleasant, Pa.

V. Zenas W. Black, bn. Nov. —, 1844. P. O., Point Pleasant, Pa.

V. John W. Black, bn. —, 1846; died 1847.

III. Daniel Wismer, bn. in Bucks Co., Pa., Sept. 2, 1780; died in 1854. Mrd. — Ott. No issue.—Mrd. second wife, — Ruth, —. Children: Delila, Henry, John.—Daniel mrd. third wife, Elizabeth Lott, —. Laborer. Attended Mennonite ch. Children: Epernetus, Josiah, Joseph, George, Elizabeth, Zenas, Catharine.

IV. Delila Wismer, bn. —; died —.

IV. Henry Wismer, bn. —; died in 1853. Mrd. Susanna Ott, —. Farmer. Ger. Ref. Children: Levi, Henry, Mary, Joseph, Elizabeth, Francis.

V. Levi Wismer, bn. —; died about 1884. Mrd. Lydia Nichols, —. Children: **(VI.)** Lizzie Wismer. **(VI.)** Susan Wismer.

V. Henry Wismer, bn. in Bedminster, Pa., Oct. 29, 1843. Mrd. Mary Louisa Wentz. P. O., Doylestown, Pa. Farmer. Baptists. Children: **(VI.)** Laura A. Wismer, bn. Apr. 19, 1870. Mrd. Wm. Carr, Dec. 25, 1891. Res. 19 Thompson St., Philadelphia, Pa. Weaver. Ref. ch. No children. **(VI.)** Emma V. Wismer, bn. Aug. 29, 1874.

V. Mary Wismer, bn. Aug. 15, 1845. Mrd. Jonh McNeal, Dec. 25, 1872. P. O., Carversville, Pa. Farmer. Attends Christian ch. One child: **(VI.)** Robert McNeal, bn. Sept. 16, 1875.

V. Joseph Wismer, bn. Sept. 16, 1847. Mrd. Janetta B. Green, of Quakertown, Pa., Feb. 13, 1873. P. O., Solebury, Pa. After his father's death he was taken by a family of Friends by name of Armitage, with whom he found a good home. Farmer. Meth. Children: **(VI.)** Charles A. Wismer, bn. and died Jan. 13, 1877. **(VI.)** Hannah M. Wismer, bn. Aug. 16, 1879.

V. Elizabeth Wismer, bn. Aug. 24, 1851. Mrd. John Lightcap, Jan. 1, 1874. P. O., Tradesville, Penna. Butcher. Attends Meth. ch. Children: **(VI.)** Laura May Lightcap, bn. May 24, 1876. **(VI.)** Evan Lightcap, bn. Dec. 9, 1877. **(VI.)** Walter Jacob Lightcap, bn. May 29, 1888.

V. Francis Wismer, bn. —; died —.

IV. John Wismer, bn. —; died —.

IV. Epernetus Wismer, bn. —. Mrd. —. P. O., Wismer, Pa. In early life taught school. No issue.

IV. Josiah L. Wismer, bn. July 29, 1818; died Jan. 30, 1893, highly respected and esteemed by all his acquaintances. Mrd. Achsah J. Hall, - . She was bn. Feb. 29, 1826. P. O., Plumsteadville, Pa. Farmer. Attended Menn. ch. Children: Charles, Sarah, Mary, Elias, Catharine, Henry, Joseph, Jacob, Jesse, Lydia, Wilson, Eperneatus.

V. Charles H. Wismer, bn. at Southampton, Pa., Aug. 22, 1842. Mrd. Kate Kratz, —. P. O., Plumsteadville, Pa. Laborer. Children: **(VI.)** Lydia Wismer. **(VI.)** Mary Wismer. **(VI.)** Emma Wismer.

V. Sarah Wismer, bn. in Plumstead Twp., Feb. 24, 1843. Mrd. Samuel Murray, —. He died —. One child: **(VI.)** Maggie Murray.—Sarah mrd. second husband, John McStay, —. P. O., Wismer, Pa. One child: **(VI.)** Josiah McStay.

V. Mary J. Wismer, bn. Sept. 6, 1845. Mrd Jacob Shadinger. (See Index of References No. 80.)

V. Elias Wismer, bn. June 6, 1847. Mrd. Barbara Swartz, —. P. O., Plumsteadville, Pa. Mason. Children: **(VI.)** Oscar Wismer. **(VI.)** Jesse Wismer. **(VI.)**

Rosie Wismer. (**VI.**) Minnie Wismer. (**VI.**) Bertie
Wismer. (**VI.**) Lilie Wismer.

V. Catharine A. Wismer, bn. Apr. 17, 1849. Mrd.
Thomas Wonders, P. O.. Doylestown, Pa. Children:
(**VI.**) Launie Wonders. (**VI.**) Debbie Wonders.

V. Henry Wismer (twin), bn. Apr. 17, 1849; died
Feb. 4, 1864.

V. Joseph L. Wismer, bn. Jan. 17, 1852. Mrd. Emeline Sims, —. Children: (**VI.**) Josie Wismer. (**VI.**)
Willie Wismer.

V. Jacob H. Wismer, bn. Oct. 22, 1853. Mrd. Sarah
Ann Kratz, Jan. 29, 1876. P. O., Plumsteadville,
Pa. Carpenter. Mrs. W., Ger. Bap. Children: (**VI.**)
Rosella Wismer, bn. Nov. 17, 1876. (**VI.**) Elizabeth
Wismer, bn. June 23, 1878. (**VI.**) Franklin K. Wis-
mer, bn. May 25, 1880. (**VI.**) Wilson K. Wismer, bn.
June 5, 1882. (**VI.**) Samuel K. Wismer, bn. Sept. 22,
1885. (**VI.**) Bertha May Wismer, bn. Dec. 7, 1887.
(**VI.**) Sarah Wismer, bn. June 4, 1890.

V. Jesse Wismer, bn. Sept. 6, 1856; died Jan. 29,
1863.

V. Lydia A. Wismer, bn. Sept. 6, 1859. Mrd. Frank
Trumbour, —. Children: (**VI.**) Willie Trumbour.
(**VI.**) Clara Trumbour.

V. Wilson J. Wismer, bn. Sept. 6, 1861.

V. Eperneatus Wismer, bn. Aug. 6, 1864; died Nov.
1885.

IV. Joseph L. Wismer, bn. Dec. 27, 1823. Mrd.
Rebecca W. Algard. —. She died Dec. 4, 1853. One
child: Lucetta.—Joseph mrd. second wife, Mary
Wismer, —. P. O., Plumsteadville, Pa. Farmer.
Children: Edward, Brock, David, Rebecca, Emma,
Joseph, Hartman, Ada, Michael.

V. Lucetta A. Wismer, bn. Oct. 21, 1853. Mrd.
William J. Kepler, Dec. 11, 1875. P. O., Carvers-
ville, Pa. Blacksmith. Mrs. K., Presby. One child:
(**VI.**) Lizzie Dora Kepler, bn. Mar. 5, 1879.

V. Edward Wismer, bn. Feb. 28, 1855; died Sept.
13, 1855.

V. Brock Wismer, bn. Mar. 9, 1856. Mrd. Ella
Cooney, Feb. 16, 1882. P. O., 1114 Water St., War-

ren, Pa. Children: (VI.) Mary. (VI.) Gertrude. (VI.)
Frank. (VI.) Anna.

V. David S. Wismer, bn. Mar. 11, 1858. Mrd. Ella
Amey, Dec. 17, 1887. P. O., Richlandtown, Pa. One
child. (VI.) Charles Wismer.

V. Rebecca Wismer, bn. Mar. 14, 1860. Mrd. Harvey Fretz, Sept. 19, 1891. He was bn. Jan. 30, 1864.
P. O., Gardenville, Pa.

V. Emma Wismer, bn. Aug. 23, 1861; died Feb. 24,
1880.

V. Joseph G. Wismer, bn. June 12, 1863; died Feb.
14, 1864.

V. Hartman Wismer, bn. Nov. 24, 1864; died Sept.
1, 1865.

V. Ada Wismer, bn. Jan. 14, 1866; died Nov. 6,
1866.

V. Michael W. Wismer, bn. Sept. 29, 1870.

IV. George Wismer, bn. —. Mrd. Barbara Fretz,
—. Res. Philadelphia. Children: (V.) John. (V.)
Reuben. (V.) Daughter, mrd. Reuben Krout. All in
Philadelphia.

IV. Zenas Wismer, bn. in Bucks Co., Oct. 26, 1821.
Mrd. Ann Sophia Umstead, in 1844. She died —.
Children: Caroline, Emma, Jenks, Rocilla. – Zenas
mrd. second wife, Rebecca L. Smith, in 1863. P. O.,
Carversville, Pa. Farmer. Children: Mary, Sarah.

V. Caroline Wismer, bn. July 2, 1847; died in 1853.

V. Emeline Wismer, bn. Sept. 2, 1848. Dressmaker
at Doylestown, Pa. Lutheran. S.

V. Jenks Wismer, bn. Jan. 13, 1851. Mrd. Amanda
Huber, Oct. 10, 1874. P. O., Plover, Pa. Carpenter.
Ger. Ref. One child: (VI.) Sallie Wismer, bn. June 1,
1879.

V. Rocilla Wismer, bn. Nov. 14, 1852. Mrd. Albert
B. Barnes, Nov. 8, 1877. P. O., Doylestown, Pa.
Farmer. Mrs. B., Presby. One child: (VI.) Frank Z.
Barnes, bn. Dec. 25, 1880.

V. Mary Elizabeth Wismer, bn. Aug. 28, 1865. S.

V. Sarah Annie Wismer, bn. Apr. 26, 1870. S.

IV. Elizabeth Wismer, bn. Nov. 5, 1825. Mrd. Peter
Beeler, —. He was bn. July 2, 1820; died Jan. 19,
1858. Children: Mary, Hannah, Peter, John, Sallie,

Lizzie.—Elizabeth mrd. second husband, Andrew S. Michener, —. No issue. Mrs. Michener, Ger. Ref.

V. Mary Beeler, bn. Oct. 3, 1847. Mrd. Edward Heath, —. P. O., Lambertville, N. J. No issue.

V. Hannah Beeler, bn. Jan. 23, 1849; died Apr. 14, 1858.

V. Peter Beeler, bn. Mar. 5, 1853. Mrd. Lizzie Myers, Oct. 20, 1877. P. O., Wismer, Pa. Carpenter and undertaker. Ger. Ref. Children: (**VI.**) Alice Beeler, bn. Nov. 27, 1883. (**VI.**) Horace Beeler, bn. Dec. 11, 1886.

V. John Beeler, bn. Feb. 25, 1856; died Mar. 14, 1856.

V. Sallie Beeler, bn. Feb. 25, 1856 (twin). Mrd. Harry Gaugel, Nov. 9, 1878. P. O., Gardenville, Pa. Farmer. Ger. Ref. No issue.

V. Lizzie Beeler, bn. Sept. 24, 1859. Mrd. Daniel Michener. Children: (**VI.**) Rose Rell Michener, bn. Nov. 6, 1876. (**VI.**) Elmer Michener, bn. Mar. 2, 1880.

IV. Catharine Wismer, bn. Sept. 22, 1828. Mrd. Isaac Maust. P. O., Locktown, N. J. Mason. Children: Mary, Lizzie, Sarah.

V. Mary Maust, bn. Jan. 11, 1849. Mrd. Peter King. P. O., Pipersville, Pa.

V. Lizzie Maust, bn. Aug. 15, 1851. Mrd. Newberry Hager. P. O., Idell, N. J.

V. Sarah Maust, bn. July 30, 1858. Mrd. George R. Sherman, Sept. 8, 1877. P. O., Locktown, N. J. Farmer. Mrs. S., mem. Christian ch. One child: (**VI.**) Katie Sherman, bn. Sept. 23, 1887.

CHRISTIAN WISMER, SON OF JACOB WISMER.

II. Christian Wismer, bn. —; died Feb. 20, 1795. At the close of his life he resided with Jacob Angeny, Jr. His share of his father's estate, and a small legacy from Jacob Sowder, was held in trust by Henry Wismer. In 1796 all that remained of Christian's estate was divided among his remaining brothers and sisters. The above division of his estate is also conclusive evidence that he had no issue. A prominent item among his funeral expenses is 2 gallons and 2 quarts of whiskey.

"In drawing conclusions from Henry Wismer's *Day Book*, we are led to believe that John and Christian were the most prominent of the three wild sons of Jacob Wismer the first."

NANCY WISMER, DAUGHTER OF JACOB WISMER.

II. Nancy Wismer, bn. —; died —. Mrd. Henry Kephart, —. Moved to Virginia, where descendants still reside. Children: Stophel, Henry, etc.

III. Stophel Kephart, bn. —.

III. Henry Kephart, bn. —; died —. Mrd. —. Children: Polly, Anna, Elizabeth, Nancy, Henry, John, Margaret, Catharine.
IV. Polly Kephart, bn. Feb. 3, 1799. Mrd. David Ray, —. Children: Joseph, Frank, Lindy, Nelly, Josiphene, John, James.
IV. Anna Kephart, bn. Nov. 29, 1800; probably died small.
IV. Elizabeth Kephart, bn. Feb. 3, 1802.
IV. Nancy Kephart, bn. June 24, 1805.
IV. Henry Kephart, bn. in Va., Sept. 23, 1807. Mrd. Mary Cole, May 21, 1834. P. O., Lilly, Va. Farmer and weaver. Methodist. Children: Maria, John.
V. Maria Kephart, bn. in 1837. Mrd. John Gilmer, —. He died —. Children: (VI.) George D. Gilmer, bn. 1859. (VI.) Nelly Gilmer, bn. 1863. (VI.) — Gilmer, bn. dead. - Maria mrd. second husband, Frank Klinesorgh, —. He died May 20, 1885.
V. John Kephart, bn. May 29, 1839. Mrd. Mary Allen, May 1864. P. O., Lilly, Va. Farmer. Menn's. Children: William, Charles, B—, Mary, John, Martha.

VI. William Henry Kephart, bn. May 25, 1865. Mrd. Elizabeth Gilmer. P. O., Mount Sidney, Va. Farmer. Children: **(VII.)** Welden Kephart. **(VII.)** — Kephart.

VI. Charles O. Kephart, bn. Sept. 7, 1866. S.

VI. B. Kephart, bn. Oct. 15, 1868.

VI. Mary Kephart, bn. Aug. 29, 1870.

VI. John T. Kephart, bn. Feb. 9, 1874.

VI. Martha Kephart, bn. Aug. 29, 1876.

IV. John Kephart, bn. Jan. 3, 1810.

IV. Margaret Kephart, bn. Feb. 7, 1812. Mrd. — Owens. Children: Harriet, Sarah, Thomas, Elizabeth, Mary, Dorcas.

IV. Catharine Kephart, bn. Feb. 1, 1814. Mrd. William Lash, —. Children: Maria, Joseph, Mary, Maggie.

DESCENDANTS OF ABRAHAM WISMER,
SON OF JACOB WISMER.

II. Abraham Wismer, bn. in Bucks Co., Pa., Feb. 20, 1743; died Apr. 27, 1828. Mrd. Anna —. She was born July 21, 1746; died Nov. 20, 1823. Weaver Children: Jacob, Elizabeth, Anna, Mary.

III. Jacob Wismer, bn. Dec. 1, 1769; died Nov. 15, 1842. Lived and died near Pipersville, Pa., and was miller at Esquire Loux's mill. Unmrd.

III. Elizabeth Wismer, bn. Oct. 24, 1771; died —. Mrd. Abraham Tinsman, —. Moved to Westmoreland Co., Pa.

III. Anna Wismer, bn. Oct. 19, 1784; died Mar. 6, 1860. Mrd. —. One child.
IV. Elias Wismer, bn. Feb. 28, 1803; died Oct. 10, 1870. Married Elizabeth Wismer, —. Carpenter. Children: Henry, Mary, Catharine, Lewis, Amos.
V. Henry W. Wismer, bn. in Bucks Co., Pa., Mar. 7, 1832. Mrd. Eliza Ann Wismer, Jan. 29, 1870. P. O. Wismer, Pa.

Mr. Wismer was educated in the common schools. Early in life he engaged in the mercantile business in partnership with his father for several years, and afterwards on his own account. After the death of his father, he went into partnership with his brother-in-law Joseph R. Lear. He still continues in the business at the old stand. He has been the Postmaster at Wismer ever since it was founded in 1872. He has been Auditor of the township for 9 years, and has been Judge, Clerk, and Inspector of election for a number of times. He was a Director of the Point Pleasant Bridge Co., and was made President of the company, which position he still holds. He is also Treasurer of the Bucks Co., Mutual Fire Insurance Co., and is Manager and Treasurer of the Union Dairyman's Association, and Director of Danboro and Point Pleasant turnpike. In politics he is a Republican. Mrs. Wismer, Baptist. Children: (VI.) A daughter, stillborn. (VI.) Harmon Wismer, bn. Aug. 28, 1873; died Mar. 3, 1875. (VI.) Preston Wismer, bn. Oct. 25, 1875; died —, 1875. (VI.) Maynard Wismer, bn. May 31, 1877. (VI.) Ella Wismer, bn. Apr. 2, 1881. (VI.) Mary Wismer, bn. Oct. 29, 1886.

V. Mary Ann Wismer, bn. Feb. 22, 1834. Mrd. Joseph R. Lear. (See Index of References No. 81.)

V. Catharine Wismer, bn. Apr. 22, 1836. Mrd. Jacob W. Sterner, June 28, 1855. P. O., Trevose Sta., Pa. Miller. Children: Alaminda, Emma, Grant, Mary, Edward.

VI. Alaminda Sterner, bn. in Sussex Co., N. J., Feb. 20, 1857. Mrd. George Ridge, Feb. 12, 1880. P. O., Churchville, Pa. Farmer. Children: (VII.) Clara Ridge, bn. Oct. 15, 1881. (VII.) Alvin Ridge, bn. Nov. 19, 1888.

VI. Emma Sterner, bn. in Bucks Co., Pa., Feb. 3, 1860. Mrd. Thomas La Rue, Feb. 22, 1882. P. O., Trevose, Pa. Farmer. Children: (VII.) Cora La Rue, bn. Apr. 9, 1883. (VII.) Bessie La Rue, bn. July 26, 1885.

VI. Grant Sterner, bn. Nov. 20, 1866.

VI. Mary Sterner, bn. Jan. 21, 1869.

VI. Edward Sterner, bn. May 29, 1874.

V. Lewis Wismer, bn. Oct. 10, 1839. Mrd. Annie Shaddinger. Res. Phila., Penna. Mason. Baptist. Children: (VI.) Lottie Wismer, S. (VI.) Emma Wismer, S.

V. Amos Wismer, bn. Aug. 16, 1845; died Feb. 18, 1876. Mrd. Amanda Shaddinger, —. Mrs. W., Baptist. Children: (VI.) Laura M. Wismer, bn. Oct. 3, 1867. Baptist. (VI.) Mary E. Wismer, bn. Feb.

1870. Presby. (VI.) Benjamin Wismer, bn. Apr. 17, 1874; died Mar. 20, 1888.

III. Mary Wismer, bn. Apr. 22, 1778; died Oct. 26, 1868. Mrd. John Engert, —. Blacksmith. Children: Abraham, Annie.
IV. Abraham Engert, bn.—; died —. S.
IV. Annie Engert, bn. —. Mrd. John Kratz, —. Farmer. Children: Mary, Isaac.
V. Mary Kratz, bn. —. Mrd. John Crouthamel, —. P. O., Bedminster, Pa. Blacksmith. Children: (VI.) Mary Ann Crouthamel. (VI.) — Crouthamel.
V. Isaac Kratz, bn. —. S.

DESCENDANTS OF FELIX WISMER OF WYTIKON, SWITZERLAND.

I. — Wismer, the earliest ancestor of this branch of whom we have any information, was a farmer and lived in the village of Wytikon, Canton Zurich, Switzerland. The village of Wytikon is situated three miles from Zurich, and at one time consisted of 34 families, 15 families bearing the name of Wismer. He is supposed to have belonged to the Reformed church.* He had but one child, a son:

II. Felix Wismer, born in Wytikon, Switzerland, and lived on the old homestead. Is also supposed to have belonged to the Reformed church. And also had but one child, a son:

III. John Wismer, born in Wytikon, Canton Zurich, Switzerland, in Oct. 1778; died in 1849. He was a farmer, and inherited the old homestead from his father. In early life he married, but his wife died soon after, leaving no issue. In 1829 he married a widow Regula Glættly, (Nee Muller). After the death of her husband she emigrated to the United States with her sons, and died in 1877 aged 79 years. Members of the Reformed church of Switzerland. Children: John, Henry, Elizabeth, Jacob, Solomon.

IV. John Wismer, bn. in Wytikon, Canton Zurich, Switzerland, in 1830. Emigrated to the United States in 1850. P. O., Olney, Oregon. No family.

---

* The Reformed church was the state church, and was closely guarded by the government. In former years it suppressed every other religious organization.

22

IV. Henry Wismer, bn. in Wyticon, Canton Zurich, Switzerland, Apr. 28, 1832. Emigrated to the United States in 1855. After landing he at once set out for Dubuque, Iowa, where he arrived Mar. 12th. In this city he resided until 1863. In the spring of this year he moved with his mother to Dayton Twp., Bremer Co., Iowa, where he purchased 80 acres of land, to which he soon added 40 acres more. At this time Dayton Twp. had but few settlers, and his nearest neighbors lived a mile distant. On Sept. 16, 1865, he was married to Rosina Messerly. In the fall of 1890 he sold his farm in Dayton Twp., and purchased ten acres in Sumner, Iowa. On the 3d of Oct., 1890, while he and wife were driving through a part of Sumner on the way to their purchase on which they were building a new house, the horse took fright as they turned a corner, the wagon was upset and they were hurled to the ground. Mr. Wismer was slightly injured, but Mrs. Wismer died Oct. 14, 1890 from the effects of injuries received by the accident. P. O., Sumner, Iowa. Presbyterians. Children: Bennie, A —, Edward, Leila, Martha.

V. Bennie H. Wismer, bn. July 16, 1866; died Feb. 8, 1868.

V. A. J. Wismer, bn. in Bremer Co., Iowa, Feb. 20, 1868. He remained at home on the farm until he was 21 years of age, and attended the district school during the winter. He is now engaged in the restaurant business in Sumner, Iowa.

V. Edward A. Wismer, bn. in Bremer Co., Iowa, Mar. 15, 1870. Was brought up on his father's farm, and received his education in the public school. Tonsorial artist in Sumner, Iowa. Presbyterian.

V. Leila E. Wismer, bn. in Bremer Co., Iowa, Dec. 31, 1872. Mrd. F. M. Lyon, in 1890. P. O., Sumner, Iowa. Presbyterian. One child: **(VI.)** Edna Lucile Lyon, bn. Jan. 31, 1892.

V. Martha M. Wismer, bn in Bremer Co., Iowa, Apr. 29, 1874. She attended the district schools until she was 14 years of age, when she was sent to school at Cedar Falls, Iowa. P. O., Sumner, Iowa. Presbyterian.

IV. Elizabeth Wismer, bn. in Wytikon, Canton Zurich, Switzerland, in 1834. Still resides in Switzerland. Mrd. Jacob Fries, —. He died,—. One child: **(V.)** — Fries. She mrd. second husband Jacob Diggleman, —.

IV. Jacob Wismer, bn. in Wytikon, Canton Zurich, Switzerland, May 26, 1836. Emigrated to the United States in 1855. Mrd. Frederica Hickethier, in 1859. P. O., Bethany, Oregon. Farmer. Presby's. Children: Emma, Bertha, Louisa, Walter, Otto, John, Ida, Carl, Solomon, Frederica.

V. Emma Wismer, bn. May 29, 1860. Mrd. Henry Hamel. P. O., Bethany, Oregon. Farmer. Presby's. Children: **(VI.)** Bertha Hamel. **(VI.)** Ida Hamel. **(VI.)** Willie Hamel. **(VI.)** Otto Hamel. **(VI.)** Emma Hamel. **(VI.)** Alfred Hamel.

V. Bertha Amelia Wismer, bn. Nov. 23, 1862; died Aug. 1, 1863.

V. Louisa Mary Wismer, bn. May 22, 1864. Mrd. J. F. Dysle. P. O., Bethany, Oregon. Blacksmith. Presby's. Children: **(VI.)** Hedwig Dysle, **(VI.)** Walter Dysle, **(VI.)** Ida Dysle.

V. Walter Jacob Wismer, bn. June 30, 1866.

V. Otto John Wismer, bn. May 4, 1868.

V. John Jacob Wismer, bn. Oct. 20, 1870.

V. Ida Julia Wismer, bn. Feb. 8, 1873.

V. Carl Enoch Wismer, bn. May 23, 1875.

V. Solomon Henry Wismer, bn. Apr. 4, 1878.

V. Frederica Hortensias Wismer, bn. Apr. 22, 1880.

IV. Solomon Wismer, bn. in Wytikon, Canton Zurich, Switzerland, 1839. Emigrated to the United States in Mar. 1855. P. O., Menomenee, Wisconsin.

DESCENDANTS OF CONRAD WISMER* OF AERZEN, GERMANY.

I. Conrad Wismer, bn. at Aerzen, Germany. Mrd. —. Farmer and miller. Aerzen is located about ten miles from the city of Hanover, Germany. Children: Conrad, Auguste, Elizabeth, Daughter, Johan.

II. Conrad Wismer, bn. at Aerzen, Germany, about 1790; died about 1853, in Scharzfeld, Germany. Mrd. —. Miller, owned the homestead mill at Aerzen, and also a mill at Scharzfeld. Children: Ferdinand and a daughter.

III. Ferdinand Wismer, bn. in 1830. Mrd. —. Miller, inherited his father's property. Had issue.

III. The daughter mrd. —, resided at Hildersheim, Germany.

II. Auguste Wismer, bn. about 1792; died —. Mrd. —— Piepenbrink, —. One child: **(III.)** Conrad Piepenbrink, bn. —. Probably never married.

II. Elizabeth Wismer, bn. —; died —. Mrd. —. Had a large family. Farmer near Hameln, Germany.

II. Daughter Wismer (name not known), bn. —; died —. Mrd. —. Farmer near Hameln, Germany. Had a large family, now supposed to be somewhere in the United States.

---

* A descendant of Peter Wismer, Wurtembergian counselor, born August 4, 1419.

II. John Henry Conrad Wismer, bn. at Aerzen,
Germany, Apr. 4, 1800; died Dec. 13, 1853. Mrd.
Elizabeth Dora Straup, in 1830. She was born in
Landsberg an der Warthe, Feb. 21, 1797; died Mar.
21, 1891, aged 94 years and 1 month. Mr. Wismer
went to Berlin, Germany, when quite young, where
he remained until he died. His occupation was that
of merchant tailor. Children: Auguste, Ferdinand,
Anna, Rudolph, Marie, Francis.

III. Auguste Wismer, bn. in Berlin, Germany, Dec.
16, 1831. Mrd. August Schrœder, —. Res. Berlin,
Germany. Machinist. No issue.

III. Ferdinand Henry Wismer, bn. in Berlin, Germany, July 27, 1833. Mrd. —. Mr. Wismer em-
barked for the United States on the 9th of Feb. 1852,
and landed March 31st of the same year at New
York. In Dec. 1852 he went to Newark, N. J., and
settled there permanently, and engaged very extensively in the manufacture of clothing, from which
business he retired several years ago.

Mr. Wismer has been, and is now connected
with a number of public and private enterprises.
He was elected and served three terms (nine years)
as water commissioner of the city of Newark, and
took a prominent part in securing for the city, under
the most favorable conditions for the same, the much
needed new Water Supply from the Pequannock
River. In 1887 he was appointed a member of the
State Board of Assessors of New Jersey, and is the
President of that Board. He is also President of
German Building and Loan Association, and of the
Finley Rubber Varnish Co., both very successful
corporations. Children: Francis, Ferdinand, Elizabeth, Dora, Auguste.

IV. Francis William Wismer, bn. in Newark, N. J.,
July 26, 1862. Mrd. Katie Schafer, May 5, 1886.
She was bn. in Newark, N. J. Res. Newark, N. J.
No issue.

IV. Ferdinand Henry Wismer, bn. in Newark, N. J., Dec. 10, 1864. Res. Newark, N. J. Carpenter. Served seven years in the 5th Regt. National Guards; four years as First Sergeant and received an honorable discharge June 1892. S.

IV. Dora Wismer, bn. in Newark, N. J.

IV. Auguste Isabella Wismer, bn. in Newark, N. J.

III. Anna Wismer, bn. in Berlin, Germany, May 15, 1835. Mrd. —— Heinrich, —. Res. Berlin, Germany.

III. Rudolph Wismer, bn. in Berlin, Germany, May 31, 1837. Mrd. —. Res. Berlin, Germany. Children: **(IV.)** Ottilie Wismer, bn. in Berlin, Germ. **(IV.)** Anna Wismer, bn. in Berlin, Germ. **(IV.)** Ferdinand R. Wismer, bn. in Berlin, Germ. Res. Newark, N. J. **(IV.)** Rosalie Wismer, bn. in Berlin, Germ. **(IV.)** Marie Wismer, bn. in Berlin, Germ. **(IV.)** Otto Wismer, bn. in Berlin, Germ. **(IV.)** Herman Wismer, bn. in Berlin, Germ. **(IV.)** Clara Wismer, bn. in Berlin, Germ. **(IV.)** Emma Wismer, bn. in Berlin, Germ.

III. Marie Wismer, bn. in Berlin, Germany, Apr. 24, 1839. She came to New York about 1865. Mrd. —— Fluegge, —. He died in 1876. No issue.

III. Francis Wismer, bn. in Berlin, Germany, June 6, 1842. Mrd. —. Res. Newark, N. J. Mr. Wismer came to the United States in 1863. Children all born in Newark, N. J. **(IV.)** Ida M. Wismer. **(IV.)** Anna C. Wismer. **(IV.)** Mamie Wismer. **(IV.)** Melinda Wismer. **(IV.)** Francis Wismer. **(IV.)** Rudolph Wismer.

OMISSIONS.

The following records should have been inserted on page 19, after Sarah Leatherman.

VI. John Leatherman, bn. Oct. 8, 1828. Mrd. Mary Moyer. Farmer. P. O., West Carlisle, Kent Co., Mich. Menn's. Children: Sarah, Susanna, Christian, Aaron, Abraham, Elizabeth, John, Amos, Mary, Nelson.

VII. Sarah Leatherman, bn. July 30, 1850. Mrd. Henry Garber. P. O., Bliss, Emmet Co., Mich. Farmer. Menn's. Children: Salina, Delia, Olin, Maude, Donald, Ellis.

VIII. Salina Garber, mrd. Charles Keyser. Farmer. P. O., Bliss, Mich. Children: (IX.) Lottie. (IX.) Elsie. (IX.) Infant.

VIII. Delia Garber.

VIII. Olin Garber.

VIII. Maude Garber.

VIII. Donald Garber.

VIII. Ellis Garber.

VII. Susanna Leatherman, bn. July 17, 1852; died July 31, 1852.

VII. Christian Leatherman, bn. Aug. 30, 1853; died June 11, 1884. Mrd. Malinda Nogle. Policeman. Res. Grand Rapids, Mich. Children: (VIII.) Alvin. (VIII.) Oliver (dec'd). (VIII.) Revilo (dec'd).

VII. Aaron Leatherman, bn. Aug. 27, 1856. Mrd. Caroline Benawa. Farmer. P. O., West Carlisle, Kent Co., Mich. Children: (VIII.) Otto. (VIII.) Gilbert (dec'd). (VIII.) Forrest.

VII. Abraham Leatherman, bn. Apr. 17, 1859. Mrd. Lydia Beery. Creamery business. Res. Muskegon, Mich. One child: (VIII.) Orr.

VII. Elizabeth Leatherman, bn. June 9, 1861; died May 4, 1863.

VII. John Leatherman, bn. Oct. 15, 1863. Mrd. Sarah Mervau. Creamery business. Muskegon, Mich. Children: (VIII.) Audie. (VIII.) Bert.

VII. Amos Leatherman, bn. Aug. 14, 1867. Mrd. Carrie Wells. Farmer. P. O., West Carlisle, Mich. Children: (VIII.) Rosamond. (VIII.) Clarence. (VIII.) Melburn H.

VII. Mary Leatherman, bn. Apr. 16, 1870. Mrd. Albert M. Brubacher, Dec. 16, 1891. U. B. Manufacturer of tablets, with Garden City Stationery Co., Elkhart, Indiana.

VII. Nelson Leatherman, bn. Sept. 21, 1873.

The following should have been inserted immediately after the descendents of **III** Daniel Wismer, on page 318.

III. Barbara Wismer, bn. —; died —. Mrd. Emanuel Gordon, —. Descendants not found.

III. Elizabeth Wismer, bn. —; died —. Mrd. an Everett, of New Jersey. Descendants not found.

III. Anna Wismer, bn. —; died —. Mrd. Jacob Angeny, —· Children: John, Abraham, Henry, Stophel, Catharine, David, Barbara.—Anna mrd. second husband, John Loux, —. One child: Moses.
IV. John Angeny, bn. —. Mrd. —. Children: (V.) Jacob, Henry, Bettsy, David, Kate.
IV. Abraham Angeny, bn. —. Never married.
IV. Henry Angeny, bn. —. Not married.
IV. Stophel Angeny, bn. —. Mrd. — Berger, —. Children: (V.) Elizabeth Angeny, bn. —; died in 1892. Mrd. Emanuel Wismer. (See Index of References No. 85.) (V.) Daughter, name not known.
IV. Catharine Angeny, bn. —. Not married.
IV. David Angeny, bn. —. Mrd. —. Lived in Canada.
IV. Barbara Angeny, bn. —; died —. Mrd. Dr. Henry Wismer. (See Index of References No. 86.)
IV. Moses Loux, bn. —.

CORRECTIONS AND OMISSIONS.

Page 16 read Maggie *Link* instead of Maggie Sink.
" 16 " *Maude* Leatherman instead of Mandie.
" 19 " **VII.** Albert Waterman instead of **VI.**
" 28 " Hazel Shively bn. *June* 29, instead of Feb. 29.
" 29 " *Ida* L. Eby instead of Ada.
" 30 The family of Christian Myers and V. Magdalena Overholt should appear in the following order: (**VI.**) Mary. (**VI.**) Salome. (**VI.**) Eliza. (**VI.**) Elias. (**VI.**) Sarah Ann. (**VI.**) Susanna. (**VI.**) Alfred. (**VI**) Sarah. (**VI.**) Emeline.
 VI. Elias Myers was bn. Dec. 1, 1824; died Aug. 3, 1850.
 VI Sarah Ann Myers was bn. Mar. 5, 1827; died Feb. 12, 1829.
 VI. Alfred Myers, bn. Jan. 5, 1834; died July 25, 1848.

Page 30 read Salome Kratz bn. *Aug.* 30, instead of July 30.
" 32 " **VII.** Sarah Ann Kreider mrd. George Beery.
Children: Lillian Grace, and Martha.
" 65 " **VI.** Hiram Moyer, mrd. Fannie Reinhart.
Have issue.
" 65 " **VI.** Mary Moyer, mrd. Antony Trudo. Son:
(**VII.**) Harry.
" 65 " **VI.** Hannah Moyer, mrd. Martin Grubb.
No issue.
" 65 " **VI.** Susan Moyer, mrd. Allen R. Hendricks,
(an omission). Children: (**VII.**) Olive G. (**VII.**)
Leon S.
" 65 " **VI.** Amanda Moyer, mrd. Warren Roath.
" 65 " **VI.** Lizzie Moyer, mrd. John Reitz. Children:
(**VII**) Arthur W. (**VII**) Mary E. (**VII.**) Walter
L. (**VII.**) Ada E. (**VII.**) Clayton E.
" 65 " **VI.** Samuel Moyer, mrd. Lorenza Hamblin.
Children: (**VII.**) Harry Martin. (**VII.**) Guy
LeRoy.
" 65 " **VI.** John Moyer, mrd. Gertie Lyle. No issue.
" 89 " **IV** Mark Fretz, mrd. Julia Ann Bissey. Children: Silas, Margaret, Mary —Mark mrd.
second wife Mary Magdalena Scheetz. Children: Wilson, Julia, Nelson, Jonas, Justus,
Clarissa, Sarah.

" 120 **III.** Joseph Wismer, bn. in Bucks Co., Pa.,
July 23, 1753; died in Chester Co., Pa., Aug.
30, 1820, aged 67 yrs., 1 m., 7 d. Married
Barbara Wismer, daughter of Henry Wismer.
" 128 **IV.** Henry Wismer, bn. in Bucks Co., Pa.,
Mar. 10, 1794; died in Waterloo Co., Ont.,
June 11, 1876, aged 82 yrs., 3 m., 1 d. Mrd.
Mary Cressman. She was bn. in Montg. Co.,
Pa., Aug., 17, 1792; died in Waterloo Co.,
Ont., July 12, 1872, aged 79 yrs., 10 m., 26 d.
Mr. Wismer went to Canada in 1815 and Mrs.
W. in 1806. Farmer. Mennonites. Children:
Barbara, Abraham, Daniel, Jacob, Elizabeth,
Esther, Mary, Henry.
" 129 **V.** Barbara Wismer, bn. Oct. 25, 1816; died
Aug 28, 1889. Mrd. David Baer, &c.
V. Abraham Wismer, bn. Sept. 2, 1818; died
Sept. 7, 1823.
V. Rev. Daniel Wismer, bn. in Waterloo Co.,
Ont., July 29, 1820. Mrd. Sallie Erb. She was
born in Waterloo Co., Ont., April 4, 1823; died
in Marion Co, Kan., Oct. 17, 1885. Farmer.
Minister in Mennonite ch. Children: Noah,
Moses, Isaac, Esther, Henry, Lydia, Daniel.
VI. Noah E. Wismer, bn. Dec. 29, 1844; died
April 9, 1867.

TABULATED STATEMENT OF THE DESCENDANTS OF
JACOB WISMER FROM 1723 TO 1893 AS FAR
AS RECEIVED.

Generation.	Children born bearing the name Wismer.	Died.	Living.	Total of Descendants born.	Died.	Living.
I.	1	1	0	1	1	0
II.	11	11	0	11	11	0
III.	37	37	0	43	43	0
IV.	106	93	13	202	176	26
V.	302	122	180	918	339	579
VI.	405	73	332	2334	478	1856
VII.	199	34	165	2313	347	1966
VIII.	4	0	4	366	33	333
IX.				4	1	3
	1065	371	694	6192	1429	4763

The total number of descendants reported is
6,192. Complete returns of all born bearing the name
Wismer, would probably bring the number up to
about 1,200, and the total number of descendants to
about 6,800 more or less.

DESCENDANTS OF JACOB WISMER, SON OF JACOB,
THE PIONEER, AS FAR AS RECEIVED.

Generation.	Children born bearing the name Wismer.	Died.	Living.	Total of Descendants born.	Died.	Living.
II.	1	1	0	1	1	0
III.	10	10	0	10	10	0
IV.	5	5	0	31	30	1
V.	0	0	0	177	68	109
VI.	0	0	0	477	111	366
VII.	0	0	0	780	125	655
VIII.	0	0	0	280	29	251
IX.	0	0	0	4	1	3
	16	16	0	1760	375	1385

DESCENDANTS OF ELIZABETH ANGENY, DAUGHTER
OF JACOB WISMER, AS FAR AS RECEIVED.

Generation.	Children born bearing the name Wismer.	Died.	Living.	Total of Descendants born.	Died.	Living
II.	0	0	0	1	1	0
III.	0	0	0	4	4	0
IV.	0	0	0	24	17	7
V.	0	0	0	96	29	67
VI.	0	0	0	260	54	206
VII.	0	0	0	119	8	111
				504	113	391

DESCENDANTS OF JOSEPH WISMER, SON OF JACOB
WISMER, AS FAR AS RECEIVED.

Generation.	Children born bearing the name Wismer.	Died	Living.	Total of Descendants born.	Died.	Living.
II.	1	1	0	1	1	0
III.	2	2	0	2	2	0
IV.	14	14	0	14	14	0
V.	18	9	9	72	35	37
VI.	4	0	4	180	32	148
VII.	0	0	0	246	34	212
VIII.	0	0	0	13	2	11
	39	26	13	528	120	408

DESCENDANTS OF HENRY WISMER, SON OF JACOB
WISMER, AS FAR AS RECEIVED.

Generation.	Children born bearing the name Wismer.	Died.	Living.	Total of Descendants born.	Died.	Living.
II.	1	1	0	1	1	0
III.	12	12	0	12	12	0
IV.	52	46	6	80	71	9
V.	143	62	81	371	137	234
VI.	236	53	183	1067	215	852
VII.	160	31	129	994	163	831
VIII.	4	0	4	70	1	69
	608	205	403	2595	600	1995

DESCENDANTS OF MARK WISMER, SON OF JACOB WISMER, AS FAR AS RECEIVED.

Generation.	Children born bearing the name Wismer.	Died.	Living.	Total of Descendants born.	Died.	Living.
II.	1	1	0	1	1	0
III.	9	9	0	9	9	0
IV.	34	27	7	43	36	7
V.	136	50	86	183	69	114
VI.	154	16	138	323	61	262
VII.	39	3	36	168	17	151
VIII.	0	0	0	3	1	2
	373	106	267	730	194	536

DESCENDANTS OF ABRAHAM WISMER, SON OF JACOB WISMER, AS FAR AS RECEIVED.

Generation.	Children born bearing the name Wismer	Died.	Living.	Total of Descendants born.	Died.	Living.
II.	1	1	0	1	1	0
III.	4	4	0	4	4	0
IV.	1	1	0	3	2	1
V.	5	1	4	7	1	6
VI.	11	4	7	18	4	14
VII.	0	0	0	4	0	4
	22	11	11	37	12	25

INDEX OF REFERENCES.

INDEX OF BRANCHES.

— 341 —

23

GENERAL INDEX.

In the following index, where there are more than two persons bearing the same family name, the family name is given only with the first name on the list. The first column of figures gives the generation, the last column the page on which the name is found.

6	Clark Hannah M	312	7	Cressman Samuel	126
6	John B	268	7	Selina	126
6	Susanna B	312	6	Susanna	128
6	William H	312	6	Crouthamel Elvey	228
6	Clemens Abraham	186	6	Emma	228
6	Hannah	185	6	Irwin	228
6	Henry	185	6	John T	228
6	Lydia	186	7	Culbert Evylena	298
6	Mary	186	7	Howard N	298
6	Noah	186	7	John H	298
7	Olive M	186	6	Culp Anna	273
8	Rachel	186	6	David H	272
6	Clymer Elmira	225	6	Dudley J	272
6	Emma E	225	6	Ella A	272
6	Jacob	225	6	Elizabeth S E	272
6	Mary	225	6	Emma E	266
6	Sallie	225	6	Evelyn L	272
7	Comfort Agnes A	245	6	Israel J	266
7	Comfort John H	245	6	Joshua F	272
7	Compton Anna Belle	69	6	James H	266
6	Coleman Arnetta J	305	6	Lettie B	266
6	Coleman Mary E	305	6	Mary U	272
5	Couse Anna	262	6	Martha C	272
5	Barbara	261	6	Matilda A	266
5	Catharine	262	6	Rosabella	273
5	Elizabeth	261	6	Silas W	272
5	Margaret	262	6	William D	273
5	Mary	262	6	Darrah Charles W	308
6	Craven Emma J	308	6	Darrah William T H	308
6	Cressman Abraham	126	6	Derstine John	104
6	Aaron	127	6	Mary	104
5	Anna W	124	6	Samuel	104
6	Anna	126	6	Detweiler Abraham L	177
5	Barbara	125	6	Abia J	74
7	Elma	126	7	Alice J	162
6	Enos	126	6	Anna	101
6	Esther	126	6	Anna W	162
5	Henry	128	7	Barbara	162
6	Henry	126	6	Catharine	177
6	Israel	127	6	Christian	162
6	John	127	6	Clayton S	74
5	John	125	6	Edwin S	74
5	Joseph	124	7	Elsie E	162
6	Joseph	124	6	Emma	138
7	Laura	126	7	Emma	101
6	Louisa	128	6	Enoch	162
6	Lucinda	128	7	George W	162
6	Mary	127	7	Harry	74
6	Menno	127	6	Hannah	74
6	Moses	124	6	Harvey J	74
6	Phillis	128	6	Henrietta	138
6	Samuel	126	7	Ira G	74

7	Myers S Allen	49	5	Nash William	49
6	Tobias N	48	6	Nells Anna E	272
7	Ulysses S G	48	6	Barbara M	272
7	William H	31	6	David H	272
6	William	66	6	Ella A	272
4	Nash Abraham	36	6	Emerson W	272
6	Abraham	41	6	James E	272
5	Abraham	44	6	Rowland C	272
6	Amanda	47	6	Newcomer Annie	69
7	Anderson	46	5	Barbara	67
6	Ann	45	6	Barbara	69
6	Anna	41	5	David	69
5	Anna	45, 50	5	Eliza	71
6	Daniel W	44	5	Jacob	71
6	Debbie A	47	5	Lavina	71
5	Elizabeth	36, 49	6	Mathias	69
6	Elizabeth	38, 47	5	Mary	69
4	Elizabeth	51	5	Nancy	67
5	Eli	50	5	Susan	71
6	Frances D	45	6	Nickerson Alice E	231
5	Hannah	51	6	John F	231
5	Henry	49, 50	6	Lillie C	231
4	Henry	50	6	Mary E	231
6	Huldah J	46	6	Nobbs Lillian M	286
6	Jacob	41, 45	6	Noble Abraham H	299
5	Jacob	45	6	Alfaretta	298
4	Jacob	45	6	Alzinah	298
7	John M	46	6	Lydia A	298
5	Rev Joseph	38	6	Nancy	298
5	Joseph	49	6	Thomas H	298
5	Julia A	50	7	Noggle Ellen A	197
6	Levi W	46	7	Rose E	197
5	Levi	50	4	Oberholtzer Anna	102
6	Marietta	47	4	Barbara	100
4	Mary	30	4	Maria	102
5	Mary	36, 50	6	Oldham Alexander	262
6	Mary	39, 44	6	James	262
7	Mary E	46	6	Jennie	262
5	Rebecca	42	6	Jesse	262
6	Rebecca	39	6	John	262
6	Reuben W	46	6	O'Neil Carrie	85
7	Reed	46	6	Margarette	85
6	Salome	41	6	Thomas R	85
6	Samuel S	41	6	Samuel H	85
5	Samuel	45, 50	7	Overholt Aaron	14
7	Samuel N	46	5	Abraham	10
6	Sophia	45	6	Abraham G	11
6	Susanna	44	7	Abraham	14
6	Susan W	45	6	Abraham	20
5	Susan	48	7	Albert	21
5	Tobias	50	8	Alice	13
6	William	45	8	Alpha V	14